New Life for Archaeological Collections

Society for Historical Archaeology Series in Material Culture

SERIES EDITORS

Annalies Corbin, PAST Foundation
Rebecca Allen, United Auburn Indian Community

New Life *for* Archaeological Collections

Edited by

REBECCA ALLEN AND BEN FORD

SOCIETY *for*
HISTORICAL
ARCHAEOLOGY

University of Nebraska Press and the Society for Historical Archaeology
Lincoln

Library of Congress Cataloging-in-Publication Data
Names: Allen, Rebecca, 1964– editor. | Ford, Ben, editor.
Title: New life for archaeological collections / edited
by Rebecca Allen and Ben Ford.
Description: Lincoln: University of Nebraska Press,
[2019] | Series: Society for Historical Archaeology
series in material culture | Includes bibliographical
references and index.
Identifiers: LCCN 2018047780
ISBN 9781496212955 (cloth: alk. paper)
ISBN 9781496213747 (epub)
ISBN 9781496213754 (mobi)
ISBN 9781496213761 (pdf)
Subjects: LCSH: Archaeological museums and
collections—United States—Management. |
Museums—Curatorship—United States. | United
States—Antiquities—Collection and preservation.
Classification: LCC CC55 .N49 2019 |
DDC 069/.068—dc23 LC record available at
https://lccn.loc.gov/2018047780

Set in Minion Pro by E. Cuddy.

[CONTENTS]

[FIGURES]

[MAPS]

[TABLES]

[INTRODUCTION]

Reclaiming the Research Potential of Archaeological Collections

REBECCA ALLEN, BEN FORD, AND J. RYAN KENNEDY

> Working with archaeological collections that have been in storage for years presents special challenges as well as promise. . . . Reports are sometimes incomplete and inadequate; the principal investigators may be dead or inaccessible; and field records and catalogs are confusing. The collections themselves are sometimes incomplete, due to substandard storage conditions. Preparation to conduct research often involves lengthy inventory and analysis of the records and collections, in effect doing "archaeology on the archaeology." . . . For researchers, this is an excellent opportunity to hone identification, interpretive, and archaeological skills.
>
> —Larry Felton (Felton et al. 2013:22)

Archaeological collections are physical representations of past research. Studying these collections is as simple and as complex as that statement. The acts of inventory, accessioning, cataloging, conserving, and curation are all oriented toward assisting future researchers to use, understand, and reclaim the importance of a particular archaeological collection. There are important parallels between archaeological collections and document archives. Both are the result of record gathering, containing primary sources of information that have accumulated over the course of a region's past. Approaching an archaeological collection, like archival research, takes training, practice, and a curious mind willing to ask new questions and explore new avenues of research.

One of the strengths of archaeology has always been to ask new questions of the documentary record and past histories and integrate those queries with archaeological findings. Our discipline now has many tools to ask new questions of existing archaeological collections, applying new methodological and theoretical approaches. This realization is driving a need for more access to collections, often by taking advantage of new technological platforms. Latent data within older collections are prompting inventive analytical methods, comparative research, and efforts that bring new sources of material to new studies (Zubrow 2011; Voss 2012:149).

For more than 30 years (Marquardt et al. 1982), archaeologists have acknowledged a "curation crisis" within our field, that is, too much stuff with too little interpretation and analysis. This crisis derives from the often unstable conditions in which some archaeological collections are stored, inadequate funding to address curation concerns, lack of proper collection and/or preservation of field documentation and contextual information, and insufficient space to store archaeological materials continually generated by fieldwork (Bawaya 2007). Why do archaeologists curate as part of their archaeological inquiries? Why do museums and repositories keep orphan and legacy collections? Where are the materials for archaeologists who want to study collections? We intend this volume to highlight our colleagues' active research with existing archaeological collections. We also want to tell the story of archaeologists taking steps (large and small) toward not only solving the dilemma of storage but recognizing the value of these collections. Curation, accessioning, inventorying, cataloging, rehousing, and artifact conservation have made more researchers aware of the research potential of archaeological collections.

Defining Legacy and Orphan Collections

Essays in this volume use several terms to describe archaeological collections. Not all collections are equal, and materials are curated for a variety of reasons. To simplify, we use two terms to describe archaeologically curated materials: legacy collections and orphan collections.

Legacy collections can be described as previously curated collections that are the result of planned and research-sponsored archaeological activities, whether originating from university, government agency, or cultural resource management activities. Following fieldwork, archaeologists initially study artifacts in a laboratory setting, then process and store them in an organized fashion that is acceptable at the time of curation. Documents such as field notes, maps, photographs, and detailed reports (and ideally publications) generally accompany these collections. Legacy collections are often larger assemblages, and many come from more well-known sites. These collections often represent iconic site types, such as an eminent residence from a particular time and place, a battlefield, or a large commercial or industrial locale. Archaeological inquiry also frequently focuses on smaller sites, and excavation results from these smaller or lesser-known sites similarly fill curation facilities. One of the end goals of anthropological inquiry is comparative research to better understand patterns of human behavior. When the sum of knowledge from these small sites is combined to meet comparative research goals, they too become legacy collections. Legacy collections may or may not meet modern curation standards.

Orphan collections are ones that were collected and curated in some fashion but were never analyzed or reported upon. These are the remnants of archaeologists excavating a site with the intent to study the artifacts at some future time that never materialized. These collections are produced by a variety of sources, such as "salvage" archaeology that rapidly collected materials before a site was destroyed; avocational archaeologists or local archaeological societies with good intentions but no follow-through; academic archaeologists who excavated with research plans that somehow did not come to fruition; and cultural resource managers excavating a site without the proper funding in place to study the materials in the laboratory or complete the final report. Orphan collections may or may not be accompanied by documents that detail the purpose and rationale for their excavation. More frequently than not, orphan collections are in haphazard condition at best.

Archaeological Resources Ethics and Law

Maximizing the research value of collections to their fullest extent is an ethical archaeological mandate. It is not just a matter of convenience or an optional task. Our review of international codes of archaeological ethics demonstrates this nearly universal directive (Table 1). Archaeologists have long argued that we must keep artifacts, notes, and samples so that future researchers can check our results and ask different questions as analytical techniques and theoretical perspectives advance. Ethical principles from leading archaeological societies contain phrases such as "long-term preservation," "archaeological collections," "conservation," "accessioning," "storage," "curation," "study of previously excavated material," and "transmission to future generations." Review of the ethical principles found in Table 1 establishes that the act of curation is at the heart of the discipline of archaeology. So too is the idea that collections are curated for the benefit of future archaeological studies, and thereby the benefit of future public audiences. Several of the international ethics principles also invoke terms such as "heritage" and "dissemination of results," implying a public as well as an archaeological audience.

Table 1. Ethics principles regarding curation from leading archaeological societies

Organization	Relevant Section	Organization Statement	Reference
Society for Historical Archaeology	Ethics Principle 2	Historical archaeologists have a duty to encourage and support the long-term preservation and effective management of archaeological sites and collections, from both terrestrial and underwater contexts, for the benefit of humanity.	https://sha.org/about-us/ethics-statement/
	Ethics Principle 4	Historical archaeologists have a duty to collect data accurately during investigations so that reliable data sets and site documentation are produced, and to see that these materials are appropriately curated for future generations.	https://sha.org/about-us/ethics-statement/
Society for American Archaeology	Principle of Archaeological Ethics 7	Records and Preservation: Archaeologists should work actively for the preservation of, and long term access to, archaeological collections, records, and reports. To this end, they should encourage colleagues, students, and others to make responsible use of collections, records, and reports in their research as one means of preserving the in situ archaeological record, and of increasing the care and attention given to that portion of the archaeological record which has been removed and incorporated into archaeological collections, records, and reports.	http://saa.org/AbouttheSociety/PrinciplesofArchaeologicalEthics/tabid/203/Default.aspx

Register of Professional Archaeologists			
	Code of Conduct 1.1	An archaeologist shall: actively support conservation of the archaeological resource base.	http://rpanet.org/?page=CodesandStandards
	Standards of Research Performance 1.3	The archaeologist has a responsibility to prepare adequately for any research project, whether or not in the field. The archaeologist must: develop a scientific plan of research which specifies the objectives of the project, takes into account previous relevant research, employs a suitable methodology, and provides for economical use of the resource base (whether such base consists of an excavation site or of specimens) consistent with the objectives of the project.	http://rpanet.org/?page=CodesandStandards
	Standards of Research Performance 4	During accessioning, analysis, and storage of specimens and records in the laboratory, the archaeologist must take precautions to ensure that correlations between the specimens and the field records are maintained, so that provenience contextual relationships and the like are not confused or obscured.	http://rpanet.org/?page=CodesandStandards
	Standards of Research Performance 5	Specimens and research records resulting from a project must be deposited at an institution with permanent curatorial facilities, unless otherwise required by law.	http://rpanet.org/?page=CodesandStandards

Organization	Code	Description	URL
Archaeological Institute of America	Code of Professional Standards 1.1	The purposes and consequences of all archaeological research should be carefully considered before the beginning of work. Approaches and methods should be chosen that require a minimum of damage to the archaeological record. Although excavation is sometimes the appropriate means of research, archaeological survey, study of previously excavated material, and other means should be considered before resort is made to excavation.	https://www.archaeological.org/pdfs/AIA_Code_of_Professional_StandardsA5S.pdf
American Cultural Resources Association	The ACRA Member's Responsibilities to the Public	Strive to actively support conservation of the cultural resource base.	http://www.acra-crm.org/code-of-ethics
International Council on Monuments and Sites	Ethical Principle 2a	ICOMOS members advocate and promote the conservation of cultural heritage and its transmission to future generations in accordance with the aims of ICOMOS.	https://www.icomos.org/images/DOCUMENTS/Secretariat/2015/GA_2014_results/20150114-ethics-asadopted-languagecheck-finalcirc.pdf
European Association of Archaeologists	Code of Practice, Archaeologists and Society	It is the duty of every archaeologist to ensure the preservation of the archaeological heritage by every legal means.	https://www.e-a-a.org/EAA/About/EAA_Codes/EAA/Navigation_About/EAA_Codes.aspx?hkey=714e8747-495c-4298-ad5d-4c60c2bcbda9#practice

Organization	Section	Text	URL
Australian Archaeological Association	Code of Ethics 2.1	Consonant with their obligations arising from government and international agreements, legislation and regulations, members will advocate the conservation, curation and preservation of archaeological sites, assemblages, collections and archival records.	https://www.australianarchaeologicalassociation.com.au/about/code-of-ethics/
Canadian Archaeological Association	Principles of Ethical Conduct, Stewardship	Conservation is a preferred option; Excavations should be no more invasive/destructive than determined by mitigation circumstances or comprehensive research goals.	https://canadianarchaeology.com/caa/about/ethics/principles-ethical-conduct
Chartered Institute for Archaeologists	Code of Conduct 2.1	A member shall strive to conserve archaeological sites and material as a resource for study and enjoyment now and in the future and shall encourage others to do the same. Where such conservation is not possible he/she shall seek to ensure the creation and maintenance of an adequate record through appropriate forms of research, recording, archiving of records and other relevant material, and dissemination of results.	http://www.archaeologists.net/codes/cifa
International Council of Museums	Code of Ethics Principle 3	Museums hold primary evidence for establishing and furthering knowledge. Museums have particular responsibilities to all for the care, accessibility and interpretation of primary evidence collected and held in their collections.	http://icom.museum/professional-standards/code-of-ethics/

| The Foundation of the American Institute for Conservation of Historic and Artistic Work | Core Values, Preservation of Cultural Heritage | FAIC promotes the preservation of cultural heritage as a means toward a deeper understanding of our shared humanity—the need to express ourselves through creative achievement in the arts, humanities, and sciences. We honor the history and integrity of these achievements through the preservation of cultural materials for future generations. | http://www.conservation-us.org/our-organizations/foundation-(faic)#.Wx7NYYpKiM9 |

Laws governing the curation of archaeological materials reflect the ethics of when they were conceived. Within the United States, cultural resource protection laws initially written for archaeological sites focused on the excavation of heritage-worthy sites, but not necessarily the long-term preservation of excavated collections. The National Historic Preservation Act of 1966, for example, was intended to preserve and protect archaeological and historical sites, created the National Register of Historic Places, encompassed the National Historic Landmark program, established State Historic Preservation Offices and the Advisory Council on Historic Preservation, and fashioned the Section 106 review process. Complementary regulations governing the curation of federally owned and administered archaeological collections (36 CFR 79) were not issued until 1990. The Archaeological Resources Protection Act of 1979 specifically addressed curation as an integral part of the planning and implementing of archaeological projects. Early on, researchers looking at collections of the National Park Service championed the research potential of curated archaeological resources (Brown 1981).

At the state level, many regulations were silent on the curation issue. As an example, the California Environmental Quality Act (CEQA) of 1970 did not address the issue of curation in its archaeological stipulations. Curation issues were often left to the discretion of the lead agency responsible for CEQA compliance. The California State Historical Resources Commission recognized this shortcoming and issued "Guidelines for the Curation of Archaeological Collections" in 1993. More recently "Archaeological White Paper: Curation," adopted by the Commission (2010), addressed the ongoing need for thoughtful curation conduct.

As a result of directions that are not always clear, national and state archaeological societies have stepped into the curation breach. In the U.S., the Society for Historical Archaeology (SHA), the Society for American Archaeology (SAA), and the American Cultural Resources Association (ACRA) include curation in their ethics statements, recognize the value of existing collections as a source for new research, and have formed curation committees to address growing curation needs. The SHA's Collections and Curation Committee issued "The Society for Historical Archaeology Standards and Guidelines for the Curation of Archaeological Collections" in 1993. Those standards noted that the purpose of long-term preservation was to maintain the "research and public education values" of archaeological materials. In 2006 the SHA's website published "Conservation FAQs and Facts" as a guide for not only how to preserve artifacts but how to conduct research and analysis on artifacts while maintaining their preservation (Brady et al. 2006; Williams and Ridgway, this volume). More recently the online blog of SHA Social published an article promoting collections-based research, especially as a comparative method (King 2014). The SAA Task Force on Curation made some recommendations in 1993, and in 2003 issued what they called a plan for the "archaeological curation crisis," noting that the accessibility of collections for their "education and research" value was endangered (SAA 2003). The SAA plan advocates "undergraduate and graduate-level training" in curation and creating an "annual award for collections-based research." Many state and regional archaeological societies have followed suit with ethical statements on the creation and research value of archaeological collections, often with nods to the national organizations.

Considerations for Adopting an Archaeological Collection

While archaeologists have discussed various solutions to the curation crisis, the resulting conversations often divorce curated collections from a central aspect of archaeological practice: research. One of the primary purposes of this volume is to encourage and entice others to adopt a collection for archaeological research, or several collections for comparative studies. Making use of archaeological collections takes foresight and understanding of the potential research value. It requires that researchers understand the kind of collection they are working with, as well as the purpose of conducting new research with collections. Voss (2012) argues that curation can be a powerful driver of archaeological research. Citing examples from the Market Street Chinatown Archaeological Project at

Stanford University, Voss demonstrates how research-driven curation of an orphan collection can produce valuable material culture and specialist analyses, reexaminations of field interpretations, targeted exploration of new research themes, and engagements for public outreach (Voss et al. 2013). Other archaeologists have similarly highlighted the potential for collections to contribute to broader archaeological discourse (Bailey and Warner 2016), including many of the articles in this volume. In these and other cases, researchers studying collections may encounter problems such as missing contextual information and disconnects between past field methods and present-day research questions. Despite these challenges, the value inherent in using archaeological collections for new research is such that some researchers pursue this work particularly because of the unique strengths that such collections offer.

One of the advantages of working with legacy and orphan collections is the ability to assess collection content and identify gaps in field records or collection procedures prior to analysis. This process is especially critical for archaeologists undertaking specialist analyses. The sheer quantity of artifacts that some legacy collections offer can be both a challenge and a windfall. Perhaps the greatest advantage of working with collections is selecting samples before beginning a project. This ability takes the guess work out of archaeology, allowing researchers to choose assemblages appropriate for their research questions rather than relying on unknown excavation results. Sample selection may be less important for generalists examining wide ranges of material classes, when selection criteria may center on artifact preservation, level of disturbance at a site, and adequate contextual documentation accompanying artifacts. For specialists (such as zooarchaeologists and ethnobotanists), the opportunity to select assemblages with adequate amounts of a particular material class or sample type gives considerable control over constructing a viable project.

The analysis of collections also presents challenges, many of which relate to difficulties in correlating archaeological materials with their corresponding contextual information or reconciling past field methods with modern research questions. The former may require significant amounts of work to overcome, depending on the state of curation and preservation of both archaeological collections and their corresponding field and laboratory records. Valuable information can be assembled from this process, provided that records have been preserved during curation (Kane 2011). Any researcher who adopts an orphan or legacy collection should take the time to reconstruct the assemblage's curation past: Were there materials discarded in the field or laboratory? What were the storage conditions for artifacts once they were stored? Have the collections and their accompanying documentation been moved, and what are the implications of those changes? Field records are perhaps one of the most valuable aspects of archaeological site collections. If field records are missing or partially lost, the value of the artifacts for research uses is diminished.

Understanding past archaeological field techniques requires researchers to remain flexible throughout project design and implementation. Just as with new excavations, archaeologists must situate their research questions at the intersection of field methods and the historical context in which they are working. With research on existing collections, archaeologists cannot modify past field strategies to suit their needs. It is important to understand the conditions under which the archaeological excavation occurred and artifacts were collected. Was it a field school? Salvage operation? Part of a longer-term series of academic-based excavations? If curated collections lack particular samples or field methods did not recover desired material types (e.g., small fish bones), then researchers will need to either modify their research questions or find alternative collections with which to work. The researcher should also be aware that when appropriate curated collections do not exist for a particular research topic, new excavation may be necessary, or alternatively the research topic can be adapted to the strengths of the collection. Archaeologists can and should engage in anthropological research and theoretical discussions while simultaneously contributing to efforts in addressing archaeology's continuously growing curation backlog.

There are other aspects of working with existing collections that bear consideration, particularly those that relate to funding for future archaeological projects. All of the authors in this volume have planned research with existing collections, in part out of a desire to help address archaeology's curation crisis, but also out of concerns about successfully funding a multiyear field project (Allen 1991, 1998; Ford, this volume; Kennedy 2016, this volume). Perhaps the best-case scenario is to have agency or university support, in collaboration with a group of researchers all interested in revitalizing older collections. Allen worked closely with state archaeologists from the California Department of Parks and Recreation (Farris, this volume), who had excavated at Mission Santa Cruz, written reports on archaeological excavations for the architectural restoration, but had not yet the time to write up the artifacts that Allen adopted for her dissertation. Ford (this volume) adopted a legacy collection from Pennsylvania that he and his students have adopted as a multiyear research project. Kennedy chose to work with the Market Street Chinatown collection adopted by the Stanford Archaeology Center (Voss 2012). He was fortunate to receive project funding from the Wenner-Gren Foundation, including monies dedicated to supplementary botanical analyses by other researchers, in addition to funding his own faunal analysis via equipment purchases, shipping costs, and travel expenses from Indiana University to Stanford University for pre-analysis examination of the collection and collaborative meetings. Research using existing collections is sometimes a less-expensive alternative to new fieldwork and offers extremely high payoff for the amount of money spent. It also has the potential to accelerate project completion times. The total cost of a project studying a collection can also be significantly lower when working with locally available collections that do not require shipping or associated travel.

Economical, high-quality archaeological projects may be a boon in an uncertain future funding climate. The recent 2016 U.S. presidential election has placed the future of traditional archaeological funding sources in doubt. The White House's Fiscal Year 2018 budget called for the elimination of the National Endowment for the Humanities (NEH) and the Institute for Museum and Library Sciences (ILMS), the two major federal funders of work on legacy collections. This is the first time since the creation of these organizations 50 years ago that they have been completely removed from a White House budget. Significant cuts to the National Science Foundation were also proposed. Lawmakers and governmental advisors have already attacked archaeological projects sponsored by the National Science Foundation (NSF; Lankford 2016:12). Regardless of the ultimate result of the political battles surrounding funding for the NEH, IMLS, and NSF, these events highlight the decidedly political nature of federal budgets and the precarious position of some of archaeology's most important funding sources.

With the security of federal funding for archaeological projects unlikely to improve in the near future, it seems prudent to consider an increased emphasis on more cost-effective projects using collections, especially ones conducted in a collaborative setting. This approach allows potentially shrinking research funds to be stretched across more projects and has the added benefit of disarming critiques of the expense of archaeological work relative to its benefit to taxpayers. This last point is as much about research as it is about public relations, and it suggests that archaeologists need to focus on making our research and the continued curation of existing collections relevant to nonarchaeologists.

Recognizing this need, some state agencies and archaeological societies are offering stipends for researchers to work with legacy and orphan collections. As examples, the Society for California Archaeology has an Orphaned Archaeological Collection Grant, and the Maryland Archaeological Conservation Laboratory offers the Gloria S. King Research Fellowship in Archaeology for research projects that use the lab's collections. Many other such grants exist for collections-based research, and they are a boon to any archaeological researcher under time or budgetary constraints.

The Veterans Curation Program (VCP; https://veteranscuration-program.org) is one of the more innovative government-based programs on archaeological collections. It was created to process collections that belong to the U.S. Army Corps of Engineers, many collections of which are considered "at risk," requiring new housing, cataloging, and photography. There are VCP labs across the U.S. that hire veterans for five months, training any interested veteran in archaeological processing, teaching them skills such as records processing, digital photography, and database entry. The program benefits from veterans' skills such as attention to detail and teamwork.

Given the uncertain future of archaeological funding, it is time for more archaeologists to consider turning to existing collections for future projects, not just for the archaeological community but for the general public. Just as archaeologists can give new life to older collections, older collections may be the key to giving new life to archaeology.

Volume Contents

This volume is an effort to capture the momentum that was a running theme of the 50th SHA anniversary. The editors invited many who had given papers at the 2016 SHA conference and also solicited essays from colleagues whose research we admired. The volume's common theme is that archaeological materials exhibit the infinite research and outreach possibilities inherent in all archaeological collections. There is innate research value in the act of storing, preserving, cataloging, and curating archaeological materials. Study of curated materials is itself an act of preserving the past. Research on curated archaeological collections holds promise for the future and sustainability of archaeology and provides a rich resource for public outreach efforts. To highlight these themes, we have divided the volume into three parts: new accessibility, new research, and new futures for legacy and orphan collections.

Part 1: New Accessibility for Archaeological Collections

Part 1 focuses on how to make archaeological collections more accessible and how to sustain them once they exist. Rebecca Morehouse details the journey of the Maryland Archaeological Conservation Laboratory to make their archaeological collections accessible while maintaining their preservation and long-term security. Lab staff assessed their more than 8 million artifacts, then created and enacted a plan to survey the collective knowledge of state archaeologists. The end result of this collaborative effort was the organization, rehousing, creation of finding aids, cataloging artifacts, targeted conservation efforts, and digitization of associated documents and photographs and the creation of Archaeological Collections in Maryland artifact web pages on the Jefferson Patterson Park and Museum website. University undergraduate and graduate students, local cultural resource management firms, other archaeological institutions, and the general public interested in archaeology are the beneficiaries of the Maryland lab staff's creative approach to this multidisciplinary effort.

On the other side of the country, Glenn Farris details efforts made by California State Parks to create a curation facility to house archaeological collections recovered from excavations within the parks. Farris acknowledges the decades-long struggle in California to justify the costs and need for long-term archaeological curation, systematically deciding which materials will be curated (and which will not) and the creation of a central statewide repository. As an experienced curator and archaeologist, he has useful insights into why and what gets curated, what gets studied, and how research questions change over time. In the late 1990s Farris and his colleagues began a concerted effort to entice students and professors to study the collections and offer some information online and instigated naming the curation facility the State Archaeological Collections Research Facility. This cooperative program of colleges, universities, individual researchers, and State Parks curation staff resulted in an impressive bibliography of theses, dissertations, and publications, training multiple generations of archaeologists and demonstrating the breadth and depth of possible new topics.

Ben Ford emphasizes the importance of hands-on learning and the availability of real collections and data for students to master archaeological skills. Legacy collections such as the one from Hanna's Town, one of the most important late-18th-century historic sites in Westmoreland County, Pennsylvania, offer students firsthand experience with curation, data analyses, and problem solving. Legacy collections such as this one also provide a ready resource of independent research for student papers, conference presentations, and theses. At the same time, the archaeological community benefits as this significant site and its nearly 1 million artifacts are being rehoused at the Westmoreland County Historical Society, making accessible newly generated information that offers insights into how the American Revolution shaped this frontier community.

Jillian Galle, Elizabeth Bollwerk, and Fraser Neiman recount the origin story and evolution of the Digital Archaeological Archive of Comparative Slavery (DAACS), the longest-running and one of the most research-fruitful digital archaeological archives to date. The Department of Archaeology at Thomas Jefferson's Monticello historic site embarked on this program to bring automated access to archaeological collections and their accompanying documentation to scholars everywhere. The intent was to advance the understanding of slave societies in, first, the Chesapeake area and, later, the British Atlantic World during the 17th to 19th centuries. DAACS grew from the underlying notion that the lack of accessible and open-access comparative data hobbles archaeological research and theoretical advances. DAACS serves as a model platform for the dissemination, preservation, and archaeological mastery of difficult and challenging historic topics and events. Digital access makes collections accessible and usable to more researchers, including archaeologists, historians, and other social scientists. All of these efforts give professionals the tools to make the past more relevant to everyone.

Barbara J. Heath, Mark A. Freeman, and Eric G. Schweickart offer practical approaches and solutions that form a how-to narrative for others beginning the process of reclaiming orphan collections, with the end goal of producing archaeological collections that are available for collaborative and comparative research. The authors discuss collections from Curles Neck, Virginia, a site occupied by prominent planters as well as enslaved and free laboring families and individuals from the 1640s to the early 1860s. More than 650 features were excavated, producing hundreds of thousands of artifacts, all waiting for future research efforts. Heath, Freeman, and Schweikart outline a two-year pilot project to make the collections accessible, highlighting digitization of documents, steps in translating coded data into searchable text, the addition of metadata, physical preservation of artifacts, and building a website. The authors make the critical point that preservation and access are interwoven actions.

Emily Williams and Katherine Ridgway highlight this last point and discuss the effect of analyzing and curating on the archaeological materials themselves. The acts of promoting, facilitating, managing, and accessing collections have to be balanced with preservation, which is one of the primary objectives of curation. This balance is a challenge requiring multidisciplinary expertise. The authors give informative examples of how to harmonize conservation with research, based on their experiences at Colonial Williamsburg and the Virginia Department of Historic Resources. Through curating stories, the authors discuss insect damage, Riker mounts, and other nightmares, as well as treatments and solutions taken to safely house the collections. They review past conservation successes and not-so-successful efforts. Importantly, dialogs and collaboration between conservators and archaeologists is a prominent thread, as are ways to make conservation practical and affordable.

Part 2: New Research with Archaeological Collections

Part 1 of this volume highlights how to make archaeological collections more accessible while preserving and curating them. Part 2 provides examples of new research that are emerging after collections are actively used and analyzed, and discussions of the benefits and challenges of using them. This section is intended to provide examples of and inspirations for varying kinds of research that can emerge. Data and histories gathered from legacy and orphan collections consistently address and analyze broader research themes. Part 2 also introduces new technologies that make existing collections more accessible.

D. Brad Hatch and Lauren K. McMillan benefited from the ongoing collaborative efforts to digitize and reclaim older collections described by Heath et al. in part 1. With a comparative framework in place, Hatch and McMillan build upon the past 40 years of archaeological knowledge, diving into excavated but never analyzed collections from the heart of the Chesapeake region. They summarize the depth of historical context known about two archaeological sites and their occupants and show how a reexamination of the archeological collections links the material culture to the Appamattucks community. New analysis at one site led to an earlier date and established ties to the locally well-known Ingle's Rebellion. New analysis of both sites, coupled with archival research, led to the discovery of community connections and strategies for survival.

Stefanie Smith picks up the thread of Hanna's Town in Pennsylvania introduced in part 1 (Ford, this volume). Her chapter focuses on the faunal remains excavated from the site as an illustration of information reclaimed from these collections. Smith's particular goal is to use food practices to illuminate the everyday lives of colonial inhabitants that were on the edge of the frontier during the late 18th century. Research on the subsistence of Hanna's Town inhabitants had not been previously published, despite a large collection assembled over several decades, and the documentary record was notably absent on this topic. Smith uses the data she gathered from three disparate faunal assemblages within Hanna's Town to confirm and challenge previous descriptions of site use and occupancy.

J. Ryan Kennedy's perspective stems from his experience analyzing faunal remains from several collections, including from the Market Street Chinatown, a challenging orphan collection from a late 19th-century site in San Jose, California. As noted earlier, he conducted his dissertation research as part of the collaborative effort known as the Market Street Chinatown Archaeological Project at Stanford University. Kennedy documents his journey of working with older, curated collections, as well as working with a larger collaborative group effort of academics, cultural resource managers, and the descendant community. He highlights the advantages of sampling a large existing faunal collection to hone his research into the foodways of a Chinese American community and expand his ability to conduct comparative research.

Introducing an old technology used for new purposes, Kerry S.

González and Michelle Salvato discuss the available and affordable use of x-radiography to further identify metal objects from archaeological contexts. While x-rays have long been used for maritime collections, they are rarely used on general historical archaeological collections. Instead catalogs new and old frequently mention "indeterminate metal." The authors present several case studies to demonstrate the usefulness of x-rays to reclaim new information. They extrapolate their findings from recently excavated material to older collections and note that x-ray techniques are a useful tool for identifying materials and for determining what cannot likely be identified. This in turn can affect long-term decisions on curation and lead to new site interpretations.

Jonathan Crise, Ben Ford, and George Schwarz show how to get more information from a single artifact, albeit a very large one. The American Continental Army's schooner *Royal Savage* had been moved multiple times since parts of it were hauled on shore and saved for posterity, beginning as early as 1868. The team oversaw a program of light detection and ranging (LiDAR) and digital photogrammetry on disarticulated timbers that had much of their provenience within the ship's form lost over time. Using traditional recordation methods and reconstruction made possible by new digitizing techniques, the authors describe their journey through technology and ultimate success in creating a three-dimensional model. Their example of a visual reproduction of this iconic ship holds promise for the future interpretation of archaeological finds and long-term public outreach and display.

Kelsey Noack Myers encountered challenges in using materials from a legacy site in Indiana known as the "Old Poste" or "Post Ouiatonon," identified by avocational historians and excavated by university affiliates. The site was first home to an Indiana University–Bloomington archaeological field school in 1968 and 1969; was excavated from 1974 to 1979 through the Museum at Michigan State University, providing topics for multiple dissertations; and was then again the site of a University of Southern Indiana field school in 2013. Although the 1969 excavation led to the site's being successfully nominated to the National Register of Historic Places, none of the earliest researchers fully analyzed or published data sets from the site. At the request of the local historical association in the interest of maintaining research at the site, multiple excavations by avocational teams also took place over the years. As a result, the sum of the various archaeological collections lacked standardization of cataloging, collection and curation methods, and spatial controls that would establish provenience. Noack Myers undertook a large effort to address spatial metadata issues. Her chapter presents a model for translating disparate sets of spatial data (maps, field notes, publications, etc.) into a usable format, linking information across field seasons and research institutions, and readying this part-legacy, part-orphan collection for future studies.

Part 3: New Futures for Archaeological Collections

Part 3 addresses the possibilities for reclaimed legacy and orphan collections beyond curation and traditional research. If one of the goals of archaeology is to highlight the past to inform the future, accessible and easily researched collections are critical to public outreach efforts. Archaeological collections have an important role in helping to interpret historic places and events. Definitions of "public" vary but include professionals of other disciplines, those generally interested in history and archaeology, and, perhaps most important, members of descendant communities. The public's thirst for archaeology is strong. As the chapters in this last section demonstrate, our profession needs creative ways to meet that desire.

Candace Ehringer and Rebecca Allen began their research and excavation program at a legacy site with the challenge of integrating older collections and field documents into a new program of archaeology and public outreach at the Cooper-Molera Adobe Complex in Monterey, California. Their chapter reviews the history of this important Californio site, as well as the series of excavations that occurred as the site became an active heritage site and tourist destination that highlights archaeological collections. As they delved into field documents and maps and closely worked with one of the previous excavators and site maintenance staff, Ehringer and Allen learned many lessons about what they would ideally like to leave behind for future researchers of legacy sites, as well as capturing the site's potential for continued public interpretation.

Alicia Paresi, Jessica Costello, Nicole Estey, and Jennifer McCann remind readers that one of the mission goals of the National Park Service is to preserve historic resources for the benefit of the people of the United States. After an intensive effort to rehouse old collections, NPS created the Archaeology Program at the Northeast Museum Services Center in 2003. Despite perennial funding issues, the center has continued to process new and old collections. While having exhibits at the center itself is not possible, NPS staff have resourcefully used public outreach platforms such as traditional exhibits at national parks, presentations, house tours, and living history programs to bring archaeologists and artifacts to the attention of the public as well as researchers. The authors also recount their creative efforts of using new social media sites such as WordPress, Facebook, and Instagram. The effect of reaching a community with elements of their past (good and bad) can have profound implications, especially for minority populations that generally do not dominate the historic limelight.

Sara Rivers Cofield and Caitlin Shaffer describe one of the benefits of making the archaeological collections from the Maryland Archaeological Conservation Laboratory accessible (Morehouse, this volume). Rivers Cofield and Shaffer note that while researchers and school groups now make regular use of the lab's collections, the general public does not. In response to this challenge, the authors created a particularly innovative way of bringing the artifacts to the public. Staff created *Artifacts of Outlander,* using the springboard of the popular novel and television series *Outlander* to promote and interpret Maryland's archaeological collections. The result was a very successful exhibit that uses pop culture and artifacts to highlight aspects of 18th-century domestic life, including cooking, entertaining, and consumption of goods. The chapter details the lab's response to a strong and sustained public demand.

Continuing the theme of successes at the Maryland Archaeological Conservation Laboratory, Patricia Samford and Rachelle M. Green relate their efforts at bringing archaeology to the school rooms of Huntingtown High School. Using an orphan collection from a mid-19th-century site in Baltimore, archaeologists and students discover and reconsider Baltimore's past with artifacts in hand. The actions of investigating history, considering archaeological contexts, and cataloging and analyzing artifacts teach the students valuable lessons in research, writing, creative design through exhibits, and public speaking via conferences and community-based lectures. The authors give well-researched advice on how to re-create the success of this program in schools within every archaeologist's community. Both the future of education and archaeology as well as the collections will benefit.

C. Riley Augé, Michael Black Wolf, Emerson Bull Chief, Kelly J. Dixon, Virgil Edwards, Gerald Gray, Conrad Fisher, Teanna Limpy, Katie McDonald, Ira Matt, John Murray, Raymond "Abby" Ogle, Sadie Peone, Alvin Windy Boy, and Darrell "Curley" Youpee wrap up the volume with a very strong message: the fate and use of archaeological collections matter to descendant communities. Collaboratively working with representatives from Montana's Native American communities, staff and researchers at the University of Montana's Anthropological Curation Facility developed policies and procedures for handling objects that aligned with indigenous ways of treating, storing, and using objects in the museum's collections. The result is a thoughtful and thought-filled process of learning to bridge the divide between anthropologists, museum staff, and researchers with tribal communities. Together the authors identify the common goal of seeking to protect and understand tribal heritage through the existence and study of material culture. The goal is to avoid harm to objects and their handlers due to cultural misunderstandings and in the process to bring new information, light, and renewed life to existing collections. The future will benefit from such efforts.

Acknowledgments

The editors approach this volume's topic from a personal interest in existing orphan and legacy collections. Rebecca Allen began her archaeological career working in museums and archaeological repositories. As a result of being intrigued and surrounded by old and odd collections, she based her master's and doctoral research and subsequent publications on existing collections, and was also one of the drivers (and now happily a passenger) for the Market Street Chinatown Archaeological Project. For the past five years Ben Ford has led students and faculty at the Indiana University of Pennsylvania in reanalyzing collections from the southwestern Pennsylvania colonial site of Hanna's Town (see Ford, this volume). This has deepened his appreciation for existing collections as a new data source as well as an ideal tool for teaching the next generation of archaeologists.

As volume editors, we have enjoyed working with each and every author in this volume. They have stretched our own understanding of the past and our aspiration to make archaeological collections more relevant to the present and the future. Special thanks go to Ryan Kennedy for sharing his point of view that further honed the purpose of the introductory chapter and the volume as a whole, and to Barbara Heath and Glenn Farris for advising us on how to more clearly convey our thoughts. Matt Bokovoy, Heather Stauffer, Joeth Zucco, Judith Hoover, and others at the University of Nebraska Press have supported this volume from the outset. UNP's solicitation of external reviews by Julia King and Lee Panich made for a stronger volume. As always, Annalies Corbin provides the lifeblood of the co-publications program of the Society of Historical Archaeology. She is in fact the Goddess of Global Learning, as her title at the PAST Foundation proclaims.

References

Allen, Rebecca

1991 Historical Archaeology in Pennsylvania during the Depression. *Pennsylvania Archaeologist* 61(2):18–30.

1998 *Native Americans at Mission Santa Cruz, 1791–1834: Interpreting the Archaeological Record.* Perspectives in California Archaeology, vol. 5, Institute of Archaeology, University of California, Los Angeles.

Bailey, Ralph and Mark S. Warner

2016 Successful Collections Management: Using Existing Collections for Research, Education, Public Outreach, and Innovation. Paper presented at the 49th Annual Conference of the Society for Historical Archaeology, Washington DC.

Bawaya, Michael

2007 Curation in Crisis. *Science* 317(5841):1025–1026.

Brady, Colleen, Molly Gleeson, Melba Myers, Claire Peachey, Betty Seifert, Howard Wellman, Emily Williams, and Lisa Young

2006 Conservation faqs and Facts. Online module hosted by Society for Historical Archaeology at https://sha.org/conservation-facts/. Accessed 28 April 2017.

Brown, James A.

1981 The Potential of Systematic Collections for Archaeological Research. In *The Research Potential of Anthropological Museum Collections*, Anne-Marie Cantwell, James Griffin, and Nan Rothschild, editors, pp. 65–77. New York Academy of Sciences, New York.

California State Historical Resources Commission

2010 Archaeological White Paper: Curation. Issued 30 July. http://ohp.parks.ca .gov/?page_id=26522. Accessed 11 June 2018.

Felton, David L., Glenn J. Farris, and Rebecca Allen

2013 Ceramic Assemblages: California State Parks Archaeological Collections Research Facility. In *Ceramic Identification in Historical Archaeology: The View from California, 1822–1940*, Rebecca Allen, Julia E. Huddleson, Kimberly J. Wooten, and Glenn J. Farris, editors, pp. 17–24. Society for Historical Archaeology, Special Publication Series No. 11. Germantown MD.

Kane, Megan S.

2011 Reconstructing Historical and Archaeological Context of an Orphaned Collection: Report on Archival Research and Feature Summaries for the Market Street Chinatown Archaeology Project. Market Street Chinatown Archaeology Project Technical Report No. 1. Stanford University, Stanford CA.

Kennedy, Jonathan Ryan

2016 *Fan and Tsai: Food, Identity, and Connections in the Market Street Chinatown*. Doctoral Dissertation, Department of Anthropology, Indiana University, Bloomington.

King, Julia A.

2014 Collections-Based vs. Field-Based Research: A Need for Dialogue. sha Social posting, December 22. https://sha.org/blog/2014/12/collections-based-vs -field-based-research-a-need-for-dialogue/. Accessed 28 April 2017.

Lankford, James

2016 Federal Fumbles: 100 Ways the Government Dropped the Ball, Vol. 2. https://www.lankford.senate.gov/imo/media/doc/Federal_Fumbles_2016 .pdf. Accessed 17 February 2017.

Marquardt, William H., Anta Montet-White, and Sandra C. Scholtz

1982 Solving the Crisis in Archaeological Collections Curation. *American Antiquity* 47(2):409–418.

Society for American Archaeology (SAA)

2003 The Archaeological Curation Crisis: An Integrated Action Plan for the saa and Its Partners. Submitted by the saa Advisory Committee on Curation. https://sha.org/resources/collections-management/. Accessed 11 June 2018.

Society for Historical Archaeology (SHA)

1993 The Society for Historical Archaeology Standards and Guidelines for the Curation of Archaeological Collections. Society for Historical Archaeology Newsletter 26(4). https://sha.org/resources/curation-standards-guidelines/. Accessed 28 April 2017.

State of California

1993 Guidelines for the Curation of Archaeological Collections. Issued by State Historical Resources Commission, Department of Parks and Recreation, 7 May.

Voss, Barbara L.

2012 Curation as Research: A Case Study in Orphaned and Underreported Archaeological Collections. *Archaeological Dialogues* 19(2):145–169.

Voss, Barbara L., Anita Wong Kwock, Connie Young Yu, Lillian Gong-Guy, Alida Bray, Megan S. Kane, and Rebecca Allen

2013 Ten Years of Community-Based, Collaborative Research on San Jose's Historic Chinese Community. *Chinese American History & Perspectives*. Chinese Historical Society of America, San Francisco CA.

Zubrow, Ezra B.W.

2011 Why Excavate? Triaging the Excavation of Archaeological Sites. *Archaeological Dialogues* 18(1):46–48.

PART 1

New Accessibility for Archaeological Collections

[ONE]

Yes! You Can Have Access to That!

Increasing and Promoting the Accessibility of Maryland's Archaeological Collections

REBECCA J. MOREHOUSE

In 1998 Maryland's archaeological collections were moved to the newly completed Maryland Archaeological Conservation Laboratory (MAC Lab) at Jefferson Patterson Park and Museum (JPPM) in St. Leonard. The MAC Lab is a 38,000-square-foot archaeological research, conservation, and curation facility, which is the designated clearinghouse for collections from terrestrial and underwater projects conducted throughout the state of Maryland (Figure 1, *top*). The MAC Lab's collections storage consists of two floors of compactible shelving, with a capacity of over 10,500 boxes of artifacts, as well as more than 50 artifact cabinets for study collections of diagnostic artifacts (Figure 1, *bottom right*) and an open area with stationary shelving for over 6,000 cubic feet of oversize objects (Figure 1, *bottom left*). The collection move ensured that after decades of storage in substandard facilities, the state's archaeological collections would finally be curated in a location conducive to long-term preservation, although there is more to curation than a state-of-the-art facility. Good curation practice requires more than just improving the storage and environmental conditions. Collections need to be well-organized, documented, and stored in such a way as to promote preservation and security, while also making collections accessible for research and educational purposes.

For years archaeologists, scholars, students, and the general public had expressed frustration at their inability to easily access Maryland's archaeological collections. Understaffed curation facilities

FIGURE 1. *Top*, Maryland Archaeological Conservation Laboratory; *bottom left*, oversize objects in the MAC Lab's Collections Storage; *bottom right*, study collection of diagnostic artifacts. (Photos: MAC Lab.)

and collections in desperate need of upgrading and organization contributed to this frustration. In the first few years that followed the collections' move, the MAC Lab made improving accessibility to collections its primary mission. This meant dedicating time and resources to upgrading and organizing collections, as well as finding new and innovative ways to get information about the collections out into the public sphere.

The state of Maryland has been collecting archaeological materials for over four decades. An estimated 8 million artifacts have been recovered from more than 2,000 archaeological sites throughout the state, excavated by both amateur and professional archaeologists, from state, private, and federally owned land, and representing 13,000 years of human history. Preserving and creating access to archaeological collections of this size, including the associated records, was an enormous challenge that did not have one obvious and simple answer. Rather than being overwhelmed by trying to focus on all 8 million artifacts, staff chose to first direct their attention to some of the most significant sites in the state, both temporally and regionally, that may be the most useful for research, education, and exhibition. After thoughtful consideration and consultation with archaeologists throughout Maryland, 34 archaeological sites were chosen. These sites ranged from the Paleo Indian Period (ca. 9,000 B.C.) to the early 20th century, and from western Maryland to the state's Eastern Shore.

In 2001 the MAC Lab secured funding from the National Endowment for the Humanities (NEH) through a series of grants to assist with the accessibility efforts. These grants paid for the development of an artifact catalog database and the digitization of all associated field records and photographic documentation from the 34 chosen sites. Finding aids, including detailed site and excavation descriptions, were created for each collection and, along with all digitized data, were made available on JPPM's Archaeological Collections in Maryland web page (http://www.jefpat.org/NEHWeb/). This made it possible to access information about some of Maryland's most important collections via the internet.

In preparation for the work completed by the NEH grants, the MAC Lab curation staff spent several months organizing and rehousing the collections. This involved replacing all acidic tags, bags, and boxes with archival equivalents. MAC Lab conservation staff then conducted assessments and conserved a selection of the diagnostic artifacts. These curatorial and conservation efforts improved the condition of the artifacts and helped to increase the efficiency of the NEH project to catalog artifacts and scan documents. At the conclusion of the grant projects, a large portion of the state's collections still required attention to make them more accessible. The NEH projects were a good start, but full accessibility required additional efforts from the MAC Lab staff.

Most of the collections that were part of the NEH-funded projects were well known and easy to locate within the large MAC Lab collection. Staff expected that other sites within the collection, yet to be identified, may be just as significant. In order to locate these sites, a full physical inventory of the MAC Lab's holdings was needed. The inventory required an examination of every collection, box by box, and verification that all items were properly identified, accessioned, and entered into a collections management database. Both the paper accession file and the database noted the accession number, project, site information, artifact box contents, and storage locations, as well as information on the associated records. It took curation staff seven years to inventory over 7,000 boxes, representing 4,300 sites from over 1,800 projects. Based on previous consultations with the archaeological community in choosing sites with the most research potential, MAC Lab curation and research staff were able to prioritize the rehousing of these remaining collections based on their research, education, and exhibit value. Artifacts were then chosen for conservation treatment and study collections were created for the diagnostic artifacts most likely to be requested by researchers. Placing these study collections in artifact cabinets separate from the boxed collection allowed for much easier access, while accession numbers and storage locations in the collections management database maintain a collection's integrity. The curation staff was not able to create a digital archive for these collections as grant-funded staff had been able to, but their efforts went a long way toward making these collections more accessible for on-site research. At of the end of 2017, the rehousing of the state's collections was ongoing.

As more and more of the collections became better organized and brought up to current curation standards, MAC Lab staff strategized ways to actively promote their availability for research, education, and exhibit. One of the most obvious and easiest ways to do this was through the JPPM Diagnostic Artifacts in Maryland web page (http://www.jefpat.org/diagnostic/index.htm). Created in 2002 with funding from the National Center for Preservation Technology and Training, the web page was designed as a reference for the types of artifacts most often found on archaeological sites in Maryland. Its initial focus was prehistoric and colonial ceramics, but since 2008 the web page has expanded to include several additional categories, such as several types of postcolonial ceramics, projectile points, and a variety of small finds. "Small finds" is a broad term encompassing a group of artifact types usually found in small quantities on an archaeological site but that still have the potential to provide good dating information. The web page consists of detailed descriptions of the artifact types, as well as photographs of individual examples of those types. The small finds added to the Diagnostic Artifacts web page in recent years include horse-related artifacts (such as leather ornaments, bridle bosses, and spurs), bodkins, sleeve buttons, smoker's companions, religious artifacts, bottle seals, marbles, and toothbrushes. All artifacts on the Diagnostic Artifacts web page are curated in type collection cabinets at the MAC Lab for easy access.

MAC Lab staff also made artifact information accessible through the monthly Curator's Choice series, which highlights an unusual or significant artifact from the MAC Lab's collections. At the beginning of each month a new Curator's Choice is posted to the JPPM web page, and the previous month's is moved to the Curator's Choice Archive. As of the end of 2017 there were over 120 articles on individual artifacts or artifact types in the archive which can be used as a reference tool very similar to the Diagnostic Artifacts webpage.

From 2009 to 2013, of the approximately 1 million visits to the JPPM website, over 500,000 were to the Diagnostic Artifacts web page and over 20,000 were to the Curator's Choice Archives, while the Archaeological Collections in Maryland web page, which provides broader and more in-depth site and collection data, received only just over 4,000 visits. This was an indicator that visitors were using the JPPM website more for artifact-specific information to assist them with artifact identification and less for site- and collection-specific information. As of 2017, this trend has continued. The JPPM website received 600,000 visits in 2017 with just over 425,000 to the Diagnostic Artifacts web page and 6,000 to the Curator's Choice Archives.

With the realization that the majority of the web-based access was more for artifact identification and less for site-specific research, MAC Lab research staff thought the best approach would be to make broader site and contextual information available via the JPPM website. This could help inform interested individuals about the collections available at the MAC Lab for in-person access. In 2013 the MAC Lab received grant funds from the Maryland Department of Transportation's Transportation Enhancement Program (TEP) to create a database of feature contexts across archaeological sites with collections generated from Phase II and Phase III projects. The TEP database provides detailed contextual information from more than 250 archaeological sites currently curated at the MAC Lab. This database, along with site summaries, has been made available on the JPPM web page (http://jefpat.org/mdunearth/) and provides the type of information necessary to assist researchers, students, and the general public in determining whether or not the MAC Lab curates collections that would meet their research, exhibit, or educational needs.

In an effort to encourage this type of on-site research, the MAC Lab offers the Gloria S. King Fellowship each year. Dr. Julia King established the fellowship in memory of her late mother. The fellowship is specifically for artifact-based research using Maryland's archaeological collections. Open to students, academics, and professionals, the fellowship has supported research in a wide variety of areas, such as the study of Native American copper and shell artifacts in relation to trade in the mid-Atlantic; faunal remains of draught animals and how they inform understanding of the transition from tobacco to mixed-grain agriculture; how the presence of Native American pottery on 17th-century sites informs women's roles and influence during the contact period; post-1750 ceramic assemblages and international trade; and earth-fast structures on Maryland's colonial frontier.

The King Fellowship has raised awareness of the collections available for research at the MAC Lab, although these fellows make up only a fraction of the approximately 35 unfunded individuals who visit the MAC Lab in an average year to access collections. Most access requests are associated with undergraduate and graduate student

research requests from universities throughout the country, archaeological consulting firms conducting additional excavations on sites
with existing collections, and institutions that wish to borrow artifacts for use in future exhibits.

As knowledge of the MAC Lab's collections has grown, so has the
number of requests to borrow artifacts for research, education, and
exhibit. The MAC Lab has loan agreements with over 50 different
institutions throughout the mid-Atlantic region and up and down
the East Coast. In recent years the MAC Lab has provided collections
for exhibits at institutions ranging from the Smithsonian to small
county historical societies and libraries. The MAC Lab has also loaned
artifacts for research purposes to students and professors at universities throughout the mid-Atlantic region and to various universities
and museums for hands-on activities, including student training.

The MAC Lab has also made its collections accessible by creating
its own exhibits. MAC Lab and JPPM staff worked together to create
the FAQ Archaeology exhibit at the JPPM Visitor Center. This exhibit
addresses the many questions that the public asks about archaeology, such as: How do archaeologists know where to dig? How deep
do you dig? Do you get to keep what you find? What is the coolest
thing you've ever found? It also includes a wall of drawers that contain artifacts from each county in Maryland, a section on the importance of conservation and curation with interactive displays, and a
series of site-specific case studies that illustrate how archaeology is
used to help understand past peoples and environments.

Realizing that the MAC Lab's remote location can present a challenge to many visitors, and in an attempt to dispel the myth that once
collections enter the MAC Lab for curation they never leave, MAC
Lab staff teamed up with Maryland Historical Trust staff to send
collections back to their counties of origin. With funding from the
National Park Service's Preserve America grant program, the MAC
Lab undertook a project to create traveling exhibits in two Maryland
counties: St. Mary's in the south and Washington in the west. In St.
Mary's County, the lab partnered with the St. Mary's County Public
Library, and in Washington County, partners included the Wash-

ington County Historical Society and the Hagerstown-Washington County Convention and Visitor's Bureau. The exhibits included artifacts from three archaeological sites in each county, representing a range of time periods. The exhibits were displayed in libraries, visitor centers, and small museums. One exhibit is still on display at Fort Frederick State Park in Washington County. The effort resulted in a more public discussion of the importance of archaeology both locally and statewide, not just through the exhibits themselves but through the public programming that accompanied them. JPPM education staff created a program for children on Native American lifeways. The children had the opportunity to learn how to make fire, cordage, and pottery and also learned about Native American agriculture and hunting. In Washington County, MAC Lab staff provided a presentation on archaeological research, conservation, and curation, including an opportunity for the public to examine and handle several additional artifacts from archaeological sites around Washington County.

The MAC Lab's most popular exhibit initiative by far has been *The Artifacts of Outlander* exhibit (Rivers-Cofield and Shaffer, this volume). Since much of the popular *Outlander* book series by Diana Gabaldon is set in the 18th century and many of the most impressive artifact collections at the MAC Lab date from the same period, curation and conservation staff proposed creating an *Outlander* exhibit using the MAC Lab's collections. Artifacts such as drinking and serving vessels, stemware, utensils, buttons, buckles, leather ornaments, and flintlocks and gunflints were included. These items help make the everyday life of the *Outlander* characters more tangible for the general public.

The MAC Lab and JPPM also offer many educational opportunities that use the state's archaeological collections. The JPPM Education Department uses archaeological artifacts for hands-on activities in its fourth and sixth grade programs. The fourth grade program includes a visit to a postbellum African American cabin site, where students learn about the lives of the African American sharecroppers who lived there by examining artifacts from the site. The sixth grade program provides students with an opportunity to analyze a group of prehistoric artifacts and to come up with a story about the people who may have used them. The students then present their story as a movie plot and must pitch their movie trailer title and storyline to the group. This program also includes a scavenger hunt through the FAQ Archaeology exhibit in the JPPM Visitor's Center, where students learn to identify key steps in the process of archaeology from site discovery to curation and conservation.

MAC Lab and JPPM education staff works with high school as well as elementary and middle school students. Collaboration with a local high school provided an opportunity for staff to offer hands-on experience processing artifacts and conducting analysis on an old and underanalyzed archaeological collection. Baltimore City's Federal Reserve Bank site was excavated in the 1980s but had never been properly processed or analyzed. This relationship afforded the MAC Lab an opportunity to have an old collection brought to current curation standards, while providing an educational opportunity to high school students with an interest in archaeology. For more on this relationship see Samford and Green in this volume.

MAC Lab and JPPM staff also make artifacts available through a variety of public events, lectures, and tours. Throughout the year staff provides artifact displays for local history events, fairs, and festivals at JPPM, as well as at venues throughout the state. Staff gives lectures at JPPM and at local historical and archaeological societies. The MAC Lab is open several times a month for free behind-the-scene tours.

When the MAC Lab opened its doors in 1998, its staff made a commitment to increasing collections access through online resources, loans to various institutions, participation in public events, and on-site research. Access has not been at the expense of good and responsible collections care; indeed, quite the contrary. Collections that are organized, well cared for, and easily accessed on a regular basis are much more likely to have issues such as failing artifact bags or conservation needs discovered and addressed. Also, making collections accessible through public exhibits and educational programming is essential to teaching not just the public but also those who make funding decisions that affect collections care about the important role archaeological collections can play in telling the stories of the past. With this in mind, MAC Lab and JPPM staff will continue to strive to make the state of Maryland's archaeological collections more accessible and to support those who wish to use those collections in new and innovative ways.

TWO

The History and Revitalization of the California State Parks Archaeological Collections

GLENN J. FARRIS

California State Parks was the first among the various Californina state landholding agencies to establish its own collections facilities, starting with the State Indian Museum in downtown Sacramento. State Parks hired the first California government agency archaeologists in the mid-1960s, beginning with Francis "Fritz" Riddell and William Olsen. Starting in that same decade, major state water projects throughout the Central Valley along with the construction of Interstate 5 that cut through the old part of Sacramento resulted in large collections of prehistoric and historic artifacts (Schulz, Hastings, and Felton 1980). The Old Sacramento projects continued through the 1970s under the impetus to reconstruct the Gold Rush "49er Scene." Although there were several colleges and universities involved in work in various parts of the state, most of the collections ended up housed at the park in which the dig took place or at the State Indian Museum.

Following disastrous flooding in Old Sacramento that badly affected the collections housed in the basements of several old structures, in 1976 the artifacts were moved to a rented warehouse in West Sacramento that was simply called the "Archaeology Lab." This location was particularly intended for collections that were still being analyzed and written up (including collections from Old Sacramento, Fort Ross State Historic Park, Yreka Chinatown, and more). Archaeologists were assigned to the facility to work up information on old projects as well as to be available for assignment to new archaeological projects related to survey and construction in various state parks. This was particularly true in the last few years of the 1970s, when Parks was awarded funding through a Title Two grant of the Public Works Employment Act of 1976 (see comments by David L. Felton in Blount 2014:57).

The archaeological staff in West Sacramento sought to upgrade the collections facility over time. At first they scrounged for supplies for storage, putting to use cigar boxes, baby food jars, and other containers. Dumpster diving was just part of life in those days. We reclaimed wooden trays to store artifacts from the University of California, Berkeley, at a time when the Anthropology Department was upgrading its own facilities. (The joke at the time was that the trays had been constructed by Ishi when he worked for the old UC archaeological museum.) After several decades and years of funding requests, in the early 2000s we were at last able to graduate to metal compactor shelving and create major improvements in climate and vermin control.

Another site chosen for warehousing State Parks collections was a tunnel that had been constructed at the San Luis Reservoir for loading construction material. This facility was intended as a storage area with no associated staff and no control of temperature, moisture, or vermin. Many artifacts had been packed into 55-gallon steel drums, a number of which rusted, allowing pests to enter and eat away at the paper bags holding the artifacts. Years later, when a team of archaeologists went to the site to recover these artifacts to bring them to the West Sacramento Archaeology Lab, the full extent of the damage was realized. There is a certain thrill in opening a "sealed" container only to have a rather sizable snake come popping out.

For several decades State Parks was the only California state agency to employ archaeologists and for a while made their archaeological staff available to work on projects of other state and federal agencies. Both the California Department of Water Resources and the California Department of Transportation used Parks archaeologists to undertake excavation projects that resulted in collections. Neither of these organizations maintained its own collections facilities, so the artifacts generally were housed in various repositories throughout the state, although some ended up in the West Sacramento Archaeology Lab.

Expanding the State Archaeological Collections
Research Facility

Over the span of some 35 years that the state archaeological collections facility was housed in West Sacramento the space available filled up. Despite employing the compactor storage systems, the quantity of collections was so voluminous that it became necessary to turn down other agencies that had also accumulated collections. Although a movement for decentralization has a certain amount of appeal, an argument in favor of having the centralized facility was its value to researchers looking to sample a variety of collections from different areas, but with a common theme. One obvious example is in California Mission-era research. Having collections from multiple mission sites throughout the state at the West Sacramento Archaeology Lab proved to be useful to researchers interested in comparing and contrasting such sites, an activity that would be made more complex by having to travel to multiple facilities. Ultimately the stumbling block to decentralization of State Parks collections was the cost of creating new collections facilities. One notable example of a success is the Begole Archaeological Research Center collections facility, built in 2006 at the Anza-Borrego Desert State Park to house the extensive collections generated from excavations in that area.

Recently State Parks overcame the lack of sufficient centralized space in 2013 with the creation of a large, joint museum facility built in the decommissioned air force base known as McClellan Park in North Sacramento (California State Parks 2013; Figure 2). The new building is vast (270,000 square feet), so the concern over lack of space has been mitigated. It was constructed with very thick walls, which help to insulate from the weather extremes common in Sacramento. State archaeological collections joined the State Parks museum collections, document archives, photo collections, and library. This makes for better access to other resources for archaeological researchers, especially the remarkable number of antique, complete objects with which fragmentary finds may be compared. In addition, there are more opportunities for curators involved in setting up exhibits that would benefit from archaeological finds to work more closely with archaeologists.

FIGURE 2. Scenes from California State Archaeological Collections Research
Facilities. (Photos: Glenn J. Farris and Rebecca Allen.)

Creating an Environment for Collections Research

The interaction of collections managers and archaeological researchers often is less than smooth. The curators take their job as caretakers and protectors of the collections under their management very
seriously: to preserve these artifacts in perpetuity. The archaeologists
largely accept this mandate but recognize that there are a number of
artifacts that only an archaeologist could appreciate and that in some
cases might have to be sacrificed in order to elicit their information
potential. Fragments of bone and obsidian, for instance, are excellent
candidates to provide data pertinent to chronological studies, DNA,
or sourcing. All too often, once an item has been accessioned into
a museum collection, it reaches a holy status of an item to be PRE-
SERVED, and thus any thought of destructive testing is anathema.
I must admit that I have had qualms about the unsightly cuts made
into beautiful projectile points for the sake of obsidian hydration, but

in many other cases of fragmentary objects that would be rejected by most exhibit designers, the choice to realize their potential value even if it meant destruction of the item was not difficult to make.

Another aspect of the situation was that several members of upper management, right up to the level of director of State Parks, had on occasion announced that the department was "not in the business of doing research." Even as management of the collections was of paramount importance, efforts to answer the questions leveled by parks management as to why we needed to devote park resources to the expenses necessary to retain and protect artifacts they saw as just so much refuse were constantly on the horizon. Somehow they had the notion that the job of archaeologists was simply to do excavations to clear the way for the development project at hand and store away the goodies we found, with no further time to be spent by staff on follow-up research and report writing. The Native American community raised similar questions, ultimately framed in the Native American Graves Protection and Repatriation Act (NAGPRA). Fortunately, subsequent management came to accept the contributions provided by the archaeologists, historians, curators, and the collections themselves, and the archaeological staff followed their professional ethics to persevere in hopes of better developments. This did mean that many project studies and reports were inevitably cut short as funding for the postexcavation analysis was prematurely terminated. For the archaeological staff, simply to say that these collections would someday be important to future research rang hollow. What was really needed was a proactive program to introduce bright young scholars to the collections and their research potential, and find new ways to make the collections accessible as an online resource.

Student Involvement

The number of reports on file with the State Parks repository that are termed "Draft" or "Preliminary" with no "Final" report accomplished is embarrassingly large, and the term "skeletons in the closet" goes far beyond sites with human remains (Blount 2014:91). Yet, in some sense, claiming to have truly finalized a site report is misleading as there are always new discoveries and updated methods that would lead to a revision of the original findings or, more likely, an expansion on these findings with new perspectives or research directions. The chief argument for permanent curation beyond the point at which a final report had been written has much to do with the potential of these collections to be reanalyzed and thus yield even more information on the site. And if one considers archaeology a scientific endeavor, the question of replicability of the findings becomes a notable factor. If a curation facility is successful, it must create mechanisms for continuing research on the collections.

The academic study of archaeological collections taken from California State Parks was initially an occasional occurrence. Perhaps one of the crew members on a particular project would go on to seek a graduate degree and utilize data from a given collection that he or she was familiar with from personal participation in the fieldwork. One example is the master's degree study of historic architecture in Old Sacramento (Schulz 1981; see Theses, Dissertations, and Articles Using Collections from California State Parks in the references). Another is the case of the ceramic finds from Fort Ross; Maureen O'Connor (1984) was working in the State Parks Archaeology Lab in West Sacramento when she encountered these artifacts and chose to study them in greater depth for her thesis work.

An important event for me was in responding to a request from my colleague Dr. Robert Schuyler of the American Studies Department at the University of Pennsylvania in Philadelphia. Bob explained that he had a graduate student named Rebecca Allen who was interested in taking an archaeological collection from a mission-era site and analyzing it for her doctoral dissertation. After puzzling over various possibilities, I proposed she take on the collection from the excavations at the Santa Cruz Mission Adobe. In this regard, I enlisted the help of the principal investigator on the project, David L. "Larry" Felton. In due course, Rebecca packed up her worldly belongings and resettled in Sacramento to begin a several-year period of close study of the artifacts and documents associated with this site, an extant example of a building used for the housing of the mission

Indian families in California. Rebecca completed her dissertation (see Theses, Dissertations, and Articles Using Collections from California State Parks in the references) and went on to a highly successful career in California archaeology.

One of my early and longtime research interests was at Fort Ross State Historic Park in Sonoma County, where I first excavated a site in 1981. Later in the 1980s I had the pleasure of meeting a new, young professor at the University of California, Berkeley, named Kent Lightfoot who was seeking a site for research, especially with the idea of running field schools. Kent had been raised in Santa Rosa, not too far from Fort Ross, so the idea of working in this area had an additional appeal. As he and his students undertook more and more archaeological survey and excavation projects at Fort Ross, it was natural that some of these students, both undergraduate and graduate, would consider topics relating to this exotic historic site that had been home to Kashaya Pomo, Russians, and Alaska natives. I very much enjoyed meeting and interacting with Kent and his students and discussing their finds in light of my own archaeological work and study of historical documents relative to the area and its history.

In the year 2000, following these successful collaborations, I found myself put in the position of supervisor of the State Parks Archaeology Lab. Because my own interests tended toward research, I suggested a change in name of the facility, to the State Archaeological Collections Research Facility. My intention was to emulate the example of the Archaeological Research Facility of the University of California, Berkeley, making it clear that it was more than just a warehouse or repository but was also an ongoing facility for systematic research of the collections housed there. A key part of the rationale was that if the collections were simply seen as objects to be stored away at great expense with no clear use being made of them, it was a mere step away from questioning why they should be retained at all. This was an especially touchy point when certain of our State Parks colleagues would pointedly refer to the collections as trash and junk, questioning our decision to keep them at all. They might understand why we would retain a whole bottle or ceramic bowl or projectile point, but they did not afford the broken stuff any value.

At any rate, in the course of renaming the facility and embarking on a more open policy of use of the collections, a great deal of support was received from our new division chief, Steade Craigo, who had transferred over from the Office of Historic Preservation. Because State Parks staff did not have much, if any, discretionary time to work on research with the collections, I began working with Lightfoot and other university professors to identify students who were in need of a thesis or dissertation topic. These studies included senior theses, master's theses, and doctoral dissertations. In addition, some collections were excavated at State Parks by graduate students who then used their own finds to write their thesis or dissertation. Others studied collections still housed at individual state parks (see Theses, Dissertations, and Articles Using Collections from California State Parks in the references). When students and other researchers came in with a desire to formulate a project, staff would work with them to determine the amount of time they had available and their particular interests, and then suggest one or more collections that they might take on to analyze and write up. The advantage field archaeologists brought to this situation, which could not be duplicated by our collections manager, was that in many cases they had worked on the excavation projects that produced the collections, or at least had useful background knowledge of the excavation project to help guide the student. It is not simply the artifacts that factor into the study; one must also have an understanding of the field notes, maps, photographs, and drawings as well as the historic documents associated with a site. These were facets that the archaeological staff brought to the table to help the students get through their own academic projects. We were also in a position to review and comment on their findings before they received the imprimatur of the student academic committees, and in some cases we served on those committees.

Over the years I learned that creating a program wedding students with collections like this is unlikely to succeed by simply providing access to the collections and turning the individual loose, although in certain cases of focused research on a specific type of artifact, the researcher may be able to work without much help. Having a person (or several people) with a working knowledge of the myriad collections available to each student will maximize the final benefits. To keep most individuals on track, a certain amount of encouragement combined with solid background knowledge is required.

A Good Outcome for All!

The cooperative program between colleges and the archaeological collections facility at California State Parks proved to be good for both the students and State Parks. Students obtained access to some really interesting collections, many drawn from iconic historic locations throughout California. At the same time, collections that were in a state of limbo were given the attention they deserved, and the information developed in the preparation of theses based on the site excavation records and associated collections benefited the interpretive mission of California State Parks. Application of this model has great potential value for many state and federal agencies that hold extensive archaeological collections, many of which may have had limited study, thus minimizing the great information potential that is the raison d'être of archaeological finds. At the same time, it provides students with a chance to work with collections and site records that are already extant prior to tackling their own site fieldwork. The opportunity to work through a project that has already been done permits the students to think critically about the positive and negative qualities of the work entailed in the creation of the collections. I know that from my own experience, the action of creating a report on the archaeological excavation is the moment of truth, when you either appreciate the value of thorough and painstaking recordation or agonize over what is missing in the account that should have been there to fill in the gaps in the analyses and interpretations of the findings. For a student to have the chance to learn some of these lessons prior to being turned loose on an undisturbed site is undoubtedly a valuable experience—good for the student and good for the resource.

Extending Online Access

State Parks archaeologists also have been wrestling with how to catalog artifacts and extend knowledge of those catalogs to the general public as well as other archaeologists. According to Larry Felton (Blount 2014:70), efforts had been made to develop archaeological collections databases in the early 1980s, but it was not until about 1986 that a system known as ARGUS, developed by the archaeologist Steven LeBlanc, was first employed. One downside of the ARGUS system was that it was all text-based with no capacity to include images. This was rectified by the adoption of a later system called TMS (The Museum System), which is still used today (Blount 2014:57). One nice aspect of the catalog is that it incorporates both archaeological collections and the extensive museum collections of historic and ethnographic artifacts held by California (David L. Felton, 2017, pers. comm.). This collections management system included a number of modules, one of which was a public outreach access site (California State Parks 2010) through which people outside of California State Parks can view the collections, although it is by no means a way of access to all the collections records on the department's full TMS database.

Remaining Challenges to Overcome

As the momentum for accessing the collections increased, a new difficulty arose: staffing. Beginning in 2008 with the downturn in the U.S. economy, State Parks was also hit by greatly curtailed funding and a period of increased attrition of staff. Several of the longtime archaeologists who had been closely associated with the collections retired within a few years and were generally not replaced. This placed a heavy burden on the few remaining individuals, who valiantly soldiered on. During the physical transition of collections from West Sacramento to the new facility, along with staff transition, another element was lost: the all-important institutional memory associated with the collections and the projects that had generated them. New sources of funding are beginning to revitalize the collections and their accessibility, but staffing challenges remain.

Ironically the intent of creating the name State Archaeological Collections Research Facility with no specification that it was limited to State Parks was that a cooperative, interagency facility might come into being. This would benefit a number of other state agencies, particularly Caltrans, and would create a source of expanded funding and even staffing. This plan, although enthusiastically greeted at staff level, has not been realized, but I sincerely hope that the concept of a true interagency archaeological collections facility will be revisited at some point in the future. Ideally this would be one in which State Parks can join with other state agencies, as well as federal agencies operating in California, to develop a vibrant collections facility with an incomparable range of site collections and excavation records combined with a staff to help it realize its enormous research potential. The list Theses, Dissertations, and Articles Using Collections from California State Parks in the references highlights the research that has been done. The references demonstrate the wide range of topics possible, and as examples of how to select and refine a topic for curation research. Research on State Parks Collections has generated many publications, and I believe that the future holds more.

Theses, Dissertations, and Articles Using Collections from California State Parks

The majority of research efforts resulted from collaborations with students from the following universities:

Boston University
California State University, East Bay
California State University, Monterey Bay
California State University, Sacramento
California State University, San Francisco
California State University, Sonoma
University of California, Berkeley
University of California, Davis
University of California, Santa Barbara
University of California, Santa Cruz
University of Delaware
University of Nevada, Reno

University of Oregon

University of Pennsylvania

Allan, James M.

2001   *Forge and Falseworks: An Archaeological Investigation of the Russian Amer-ican Company's Industrial Complex at Colony Ross*. Doctoral dissertation, Department of Anthropology, University of California, Berkeley. University Microfilms International, Ann Arbor MI.

Allen, Rebecca

1992   The Use of Shellfish and Shell Beads at Mission Santa Cruz. *Pacific Coast Archaeological Society Quarterly* 28(2):18–34.

1995   *An Archaeological Study of Neophyte Cultural Adaptation and Modification at Mission Santa Cruz, California*. Doctoral dissertation, Department of American Civilization, University of Pennsylvania. University Microfilms International, Ann Arbor MI.

1998   *Native Americans at Mission Santa Cruz, 1791–1834: Interpreting the Archaeological Record*. Perspectives in California Archaeology, vol. 5, Institute of Archaeology, University of California, Los Angeles.

2010a Alta California Missions and the pre-1849 Transformation of Coastal Lands. *Historical Archaeology* 44(3):69–80.

2010b Rethinking Mission Land Use and the Archaeological Record in California: An Example from Santa Clara. *Historical Archaeology* 44 (2):72–96.

Allen, Rebecca, Glenn J. Farris, David L. Felton, Edna E. Kimbro, and Karen Hildebrand

2003   Restoration Research at Santa Cruz Mission State Historic Park: A Retrospective. In *Proceedings of the 20th Annual Conference of the California Mission Studies Association*, Rose Marie Beebe, editor, pp. 1–20. California Mission Studies Association, Santa Barbara.

Allen, Rebecca, David L. Felton, and Christopher Corey

2013   Ceramic Trends and Timeline from a California Perspective. In *Ceramic Identification in Historical Archaeology: The View from California, 1822–1940*, Rebecca Allen, Julia E. Huddleson, Kimberly J. Wooten, and Glenn J. Farris, editors, pp. 25–51. Society for Historical Archaeology, Special Publication Series No. 11. Germantown MD.

Allen, Rebecca A., Julia E. Huddleson, Kimberly J. Wooten, and Glenn J. Farris (editors)

2013   *Ceramic Identification in Historical Archaeology: The View from California, 1822–1940*. Society for Historical Archaeology Special Publication Series No. 11. Germantown MD.

Armstrong, Jane R., and Peter D. Schulz

1980   Pontil Scars and Snap Cases as Dating Tools for Nineteenth Century Glass:
        New Light from Old Sacramento. In *Papers on Old Sacramento Archeol-
        ogy*, Peter D. Schulz and Betty Rivers, editors, pp. 45–48. California Arche-
        ological Reports No. 19, California Department of Parks and Recreation.
        Sacramento.

Ballard, Hannah S.

1995   Searching for Metini: Synthesis and Analysis of Unreported Archaeologi-
        cal Collections from Fort Ross State Historic Park, California. Senior hon-
        ors thesis, Department of Anthropology, University of California, Berkeley.

Barter, Eloise Richards

2003   The French Potter of Monterey: Archeological Investigation of a 1860s Kiln
        in Monterey, CA. California Department of Parks and Recreation, Cultural
        Resources Division. Sacramento.

Bingham, Jeffrey C.

1978   *Archeological Test Excavations within Border Field State Park, San Diego
        County*. California Archaeological Reports No. 16, California Department
        of Parks and Recreation. Sacramento.

Blount, Clinton (interviewer)

2014   *Conversations with John Foster, David L. Felton and Glenn Farris: Thirty
        Years of Cultural Stewardship at California's State Parks*. Publications in
        Cultural Heritage, No. 31. California Department of Parks and Recreation,
        Cultural Resources Division. Sacramento.

California State Parks

2010   Museum Collections. http://www.museumcollections.parks.ca.gov/code
        /emuseum.asp. Accessed 21 June 2018.

2013   State Parks Cultural Archives' New Home. *News & Views,* Summer issue,
        pg. 12. California State Parks. Sacramento.

Cannon, Renée

2000   Mission San Juan Bautista: A Study of Acculturation through the Material
        Remains of the Neophyte Population. Senior honors thesis, Department of
        Anthropology, California State University, Monterey Bay.

2003   Beneath the Plaza Hotel: In Search of the San Juan Bautista Mission Escolta.
        Master's thesis, Department of Anthropology, California State University,
        Hayward (now California State University, East Bay).

Cohen, Allison

1992   Using Window Glass to Interpret Archaeological Context. Senior honors
        thesis, Department of Anthropology, University of California, Berkeley.

Costello, Julia Garvin

1990   *Variability and Economic Change in the California Missions: An Historical
        and Archaeological Study*. Doctoral dissertation, Department of Anthropol-

ogy, University of California, Santa Barbara. University Microfilms International, Ann Arbor MI.

Curtis, Freddie

1964 *Arroyo Sequit, Archeological Investigation in Leo Carrillo State Park, Los Angeles County, California.* California Archeological Reports No. 9, California Department of Parks and Recreation. Sacramento.

Deetz, James F.

1978 Archaeological Investigations at La Purísima Mission. In *Historical Archaeology: A Guide to Substantive and Theoretical Contributions*, Robert L. Schuyler, editor, pp. 160–190. Baywood, Farmingdale NY.

Dowdall, Katherine M.

1995 Temporal Contrasts in Archaeological Site Usage on the Northern Sonoma Coast. Master's thesis, Department of Anthropology, Sonoma State University.

Dunwoody, Karin P.

2003 A Morphometric Database for Cattle (*Bos taurus*) from Spanish Colonial California (ca. 1769–1830). Master's thesis, Department of Anthropology, Boston University.

Farris, Glenn J.

1979 "Cash" as Currency: Coins and Tokens from Yreka Chinatown. *Historical Archaeology* 13:48–52.

1980 Coins and Tokens of Old Sacramento. In *Papers on Old Sacramento Archeology*, Peter D. Schulz and Betty Rivers, editors, pp. 23–44. California Archeological Reports No. 19, California Department of Parks and Recreation. Sacramento.

1990 Fort Ross, California: Archaeology of the Old *Magazin*. In *Russia in North America: Proceedings of the 2nd International Conference on Russian America, Sitka, Alaska, August 19–22, 1987*, Richard A. Pierce, editor, pp. 475–505. Limestone Press, Fairbanks AK.

1997 Archeological Excavation of the "Old Warehouse" and Granary at La Purísima Mission SHP. *Pacific Coast Archaeological Society Quarterly* 33 (Fall 1997):1–28.

2008 The "Filtre Chamberland": A Late 19th Century Device to Guard against Typhoid in Drinking Water. In *Ceramics in America*, Robert Hunter, editor, pp. 322–325. Chipstone Press, Milwaukee WI.

2011 A Vision of a Technological Wonder in 1830s California. In *Ceramics in America 2011*, Robert Hunter, editor, pp. 173–174. Chipstone Press, Milwaukee, WI.

2013 Mexican Period Ceramics in California. In *Ceramic Identification in Historical Archaeology: The View from California 1822–1940*, Rebecca Allen, Julia E. Huddleson, Kimberly J. Wooten, and Glenn J. Farris, editors, pp. 105–124. Society for Historical Archaeology Special Publication Series No. 11. Germantown MD.

Felton, David L.

1978   *The Central Pacific Railroad Passenger Station, Sacramento: Historic Sites Archeology at the Site of the Western Terminus of the Transcontinental Railroad.* California Archeological Reports No. 15. California Department of Parks and Recreation. Sacramento.

Felton, David L. (editor)

1984   *The Chinese Laundry on Second Street: Papers on Archeology at the Woodland Opera House Site.* California Archeological Reports No. 24. California Department of Parks and Recreation. Sacramento.

Felton, David L., Glenn J. Farris, and Rebecca Allen

2013   Ceramic Assemblages: California State Parks Archaeological Collections Research Facility. In *Ceramic Identification in Historical Archaeology: The View from California, 1822–1940*, Rebecca Allen, Julia E. Huddleson, Kimberly J. Wooten, and Glenn J. Farris, editors, pp. 17–24. Society for Historical Archaeology, Special Publication Series No. 11. Germantown MD.

Felton, David L., Glenn J. Farris, and Eloise Richards Barter

2014   Native American Ceramics Found at Old Town San Diego: Trade or Local Manufacture? In *Ceramic Production in Early Hispanic California: Craft, Economy and Trade on the Frontier of New Spain*, Russell Skowronek, M. James Blackman, and Ronald L. Bishop, editors, pp. 218–241. University Press of Florida, Gainesville.

Felton, David L., and Peter D. Schulz

1983   *The Diaz Collections: Material Culture and Social Change in Mid-Nineteenth Century Monterey.* California Archeological Reports No. 23. California Department of Parks and Recreation. Sacramento.

Fenner, Morgan

2003   An Analysis of the Occupants of CA-SON-670/H at Fort Ross State Historic Park. Senior honors thesis, Department of Anthropology, University of California, Berkeley.

Furnis, C. Lynn

1999   From Canton Ticino to County of Sacramento: An Historical Ethnography of a Migrant Italian-Swiss Population. Master's thesis, Department of Anthropology, University of Nevada, Reno.

Ginn, Sarah (Peelo)

2009   *Creating Community in Spanish California: An Investigation of California Plainwares.* Doctoral dissertation, Department of Anthropology, University of California, Santa Cruz. University Microfilms International, Ann Arbor MI.

Gobalet, Kenneth

1997   Fish Remains from the Early 19th Century Native Alaskan Habitation at Fort Ross. In *The Archaeology and Ethnohistory of Fort Ross, California, Vol.*

2, *The Native Alaskan Neighborhood: A Multiethnic Community at Colony Ross*, Kent G. Lightfoot, Ann M. Schiff, and Thomas A. Wake, editors, pp. 319–327. University of California Press, Berkeley.

Goetter, Karin

2005 Lime Light: The Lime Manufacturing Industry in 19th Century Oroville, Butte County, CA. Master's thesis. Department of Anthropology, Sonoma State University.

Hartzell, Leslie L.

1992 *Hunter-Gatherer Adaptive Strategies and Lacustrine Environments in the Buena Vista Lake Basin, Kern County, California.* Doctoral dissertation, Department of Anthropology, University of California, Davis. University Microfilms International, Ann Arbor MI.

Humphrey, Richard V.

1965 The La Purisima Mission Cemetery. *University of California, Los Angeles, Archaeological Survey Annual Report*, Vol. 7, pp. 183–192.

1969 Clay Pipes from Old Sacramento. *Historical Archaeology* 3:12–33.

Jewell, Donald P.

1964 Archeology of the Oroville Dam Spillway. *California Archeological Reports*, No. 10, pp. 1–39. California Department of Parks and Recreation. Sacramento.

Kennedy, Michael Anthony

2005 *An Investigation of Hunter-Gatherer Shellfish Foraging Practices: Archaeological and Geochemical Evidence from Bodega Bay, California.* Doctoral dissertation, Department of Anthropology, University of California, Davis. University Microfilms International, Ann Arbor MI.

Kennedy, Michael A., Ann D. Russell, and Tom P. Guilderson

2004 Seasonal Shellfish Foraging Strategies from Bodega Bay, California. In *Proceedings of the 37th Annual Meeting of the Society for California Archaeology*, Vol. 17, Gregory G. White, Rosemary K. White, Donna Day, Sharon Waechter, and Katy Coulter, editors, pp. 141–150. Society for California Archaeology, Sacramento.

Leavitt, Robert C.

2004 Taking the Waters: Stoneware Jugs and the Taste of Home They Contained. Master's thesis, Department of Anthropology, University of Nevada, Reno.

2013 The Westerwald Jugs. In *Ceramic Identification in Historical Archaeology: The View from California 1822–1940*, Rebecca Allen, Julia E. Huddleson, Kimberly J. Wooten, and Glenn J. Farris, editors, pp. 323–335. Society for Historical Archaeology Special Publication Series No. 11. Germantown MD.

Liu, Danny

2006 The Archaeological Collection of Yreka Chinatown. Master's thesis, Department of Anthropology, San Francisco State University.

Mills, Peter R.

1997   Slate Artifacts and Ethnicity at Fort Ross. In *The Archaeology and Eth-nohistory of Fort Ross, California, Vol. 2, The Native Alaskan Neighbor-hood: A Multiethnic Community at Colony* Ross, Kent G. Lightfoot, Ann M. Schiff, and Thomas A. Wake, editors, pp. 238–247. University of California Press, Berkeley.

Motz, Lee, and Peter D. Schulz

1979   European "Trade" Beads from Old Sacramento. In *Papers on Old Sacramento Archeology*, Peter D. Schulz and Betty Rivers, editors, pp. 49–68. California Archeological Reports No. 19. California Department of Parks and Recreation. Sacramento.

Newquist, Ingrid

2002   Kashaya in Post-Russian Times: Analysis of Archaeological Materials from a Multi-Occupation Site at Fort Ross, California. Senior honors thesis, Department of Anthropology, University of California, Berkeley.

O'Connor, Denise Maureen

1984   Trade and Tableware: A Historical and Distributional Analysis of the Ceramics from Fort Ross, California. Master's thesis, Department of Anthropology, California State University, Sacramento.

Olsen, William H.

1961   *Archeological Investigations at Sutter's Fort State Historical Monument.* California Archeological Reports No. 1, California Department of Parks and Recreation. Sacramento.

Olsen, William H., and Louis A. Payen

1968   *Archeology of the Little Panoche Reservoir, Fresno County, California.* California Archeological Reports No. 11, California Department of Parks and Recreation. Sacramento.

Olsen, William H., and Francis A. Riddell

1962   *The Archeology of the Western Pacific Railroad Relocation, Oroville Project, Butte County, California.* California Archeological Reports No. 7, California Department of Parks and Recreation. Sacramento.

Osborn, Sannie K.

1997   *Death in the Daily Life of the Ross Colony: Mortuary Behavior in Frontier Russian America.* Doctoral dissertation, Department of Anthropology, University of Wisconsin, Milwaukee. University Microfilms International, Ann Arbor MI.

Payen, Louis A.

1961   *Excavations at Sutter's Fort, 1960.* California Archaeological Reports No. 3, California Department of Parks and Recreation. Sacramento.

Praetzellis, Mary, Betty Rivers, and Jeanette Schulz

1983   *Ceramic Marks from Old Sacramento*. California Archeological Reports No. 22, California Department of Parks and Recreation. Sacramento.

Pritchard, William E.

1970   *Archeology of the Menjoulet Site, Merced County, California*. California Archeological Reports No. 13, California Department of Parks and Recreation. Sacramento.

Reinoehl, Gary L.

1998   Terrible Conflagration: Disaster or Opportunity. Master's thesis, Department of Anthropology, Sonoma State University.

Ross, Lester A.

1997   Glass and Ceramic Trade Beads from the Native Alaskan Neighborhood. In *The Archaeology and Ethnohistory of Fort Ross, California, Vol. 2, The Native Alaskan Neighborhood: A Multiethnic Community at Colony Ross*, Kent G. Lightfoot, Ann M. Schiff, and Thomas A. Wake, editors, pp. 179–212. University of California Press, Berkeley.

Schiff, Ann M.

1997a Lithic Assemblage at the Fort Ross Beach and Native Alaskan Village Sites. In *The Archaeology and Ethnohistory of Fort Ross, California, Vol. 2, The Native Alaskan Neighborhood: A Multiethnic Community at Colony Ross*, Kent G. Lightfoot, Ann M. Schiff, and Thomas A. Wake, editors, pp. 213–237. University of California Press, Berkeley.

1997b Shellfish Remains at the Fort Ross Beach and Native Alaskan Village Sites. In *The Archaeology and Ethnohistory of Fort Ross, California, Vol. 2, The Native Alaskan Neighborhood: A Multiethnic Community at Colony Ross*, Kent G. Lightfoot, Ann M. Schiff, and Thomas A. Wake, editors, pp. 328–336. University of California Press, Berkeley.

Schulz, Jeanette K.

1981   Salvaging the Salvage: Stratigraphic Reconstruction and Assemblage Assessment at the Hotel de France Site, Old Sacramento. Master's thesis, Department of Anthropology, University of California, Davis.

Schulz, Peter D.

1982   Sacramento: Urbanism in the Pacific West. *North American Archaeologist* 3(3):243–257.

Schulz, Peter D., Rebecca Allen, Bill Lindsey, and Jeanette K. Schulz (editors)

2016   *Baffle Marks and Pontil Scars: A Reader on Historic Bottle Identification*. Society for Historical Archaeology, Special Publication Series No. 12. Germantown MD.

Schulz, Peter D., and Sherri M. Gust

1983   Faunal Remains and Social Status in 19th Century Sacramento. *Historical Archaeology* 17 (1):44–53.

Schulz, Peter D., Richard B. Hastings, and David L. Felton

1980   A Survey of Historical Archeology in Sacramento. In *Papers on Old Sacramento Archeology, California Archeological Reports*, No. 19, pp.1–22. California Department of Parks and Recreation. Sacramento.

Schulz, Peter D., and Frank Lortie

1985   Archaeological Notes on a California Chinese Shrimp Boiler. *Historical Archaeology* 19(1):86–95.

Schulz, Peter D., Betty J. Rivers, Mark M. Hales, Charles A. Litzinger, and Elizabeth A. McKee

1980   *The Bottles of Old Sacramento: A Study of Nineteenth Century Glass and Ceramic Retail Containers, Part I.* California Archeological Reports, No. 20, California Department of Parks and Recreation. Sacramento.

Schwaderer, Rae

1992   Archaeological Test Excavation at the Duncan's Point Cave, CA-SON-348/H. In *Essays on the Prehistory of Maritime California*, Terry Jones, editor, pp. 55–71. Center for Archaeological Research at Davis, Publication Number 10. University of California, Davis.

Silliman, Stephen W.

1997   European Origins and Native Destinations: Historical Artifacts from the Native Alaskan Village and Fort Ross Beach Sites. In *The Archaeology and Ethnohistory of Fort Ross, California, Vol. 2, The Native Alaskan Neighborhood: A Multiethnic Community at Colony Ross*, Kent G. Lightfoot, Ann M. Schiff, and Thomas A. Wake, editors, pp. 136–178. University of California Press, Berkeley.

2000   *Colonial Worlds, Indigenous Practices: The Archaeology of Labor on a 19th Century California Rancho.* Doctoral dissertation, Department of Anthropology, University of California, Berkeley. University Microfilms International, Ann Arbor MI.

2004   *Lost Laborers in Colonial California: Native Americans and the Archaeology of Rancho Petaluma.* University of Arizona Press, Tucson.

Skowronek, Russell K., M. James Blackman, and Ronald L. Bishop (editors)

2014   *Ceramic Production in Early Hispanic California: Craft, Economy and Trade on the Frontier of New Spain.* University Press of Florida, Gainesville.

Tushingham, Shannon

2009   *The Development of Intensive Foraging Systems in Northwestern California.* Doctoral dissertation, Department of Anthropology, University of California, Davis. University Microfilms International, Ann Arbor MI.

Wake, Thomas A.

1995   *Mammal Remains from Fort Ross: A Study in Ethnicity and Culture Change.* Doctoral dissertation, Department of Anthropology, University of California, Berkeley. University Microfilms International, Ann Arbor MI.

1997a Bone Artifacts and Tool Production in the Native Alaskan Neighborhood. In *The Archaeology and Ethnohistory of Fort Ross, California, Vol. 2, The Native Alaskan Neighborhood: A Multiethnic Community at Colony Ross*, Kent G. Lightfoot, Ann M. Schiff, and Thomas A. Wake, editors, pp. 248–278. University of California Press, Berkeley.

1997b Mammal Remains from the Native Alaskan Neighborhood. In *The Archaeology and Ethnohistory of Fort Ross, California, Vol. 2, The Native Alaskan Neighborhood: A Multiethnic Community at Colony Ross*, Kent G. Lightfoot, Ann M. Schiff, and Thomas A. Wake, editors, pp. 279–309. University of California Press, Berkeley.

1999 Trans Holocene Subsistence Strategies and Topographic Change on the Northern California Coast: The Fauna from Duncan's Point Cave. *Journal of California and Great Basin Anthropology* 22(2):295–320.

Walker, Phillip L.

1995 Problems of Preservation and Sexism in Sexing: Some Lessons from Historical Collections for Palaeodemographers. In *Grave Reflections: Portraying the Past through Cemetery Studies*, Shelley R. Saunders and Ann Herring, editors, pp. 31–47. Canadian Scholars' Press, Toronto.

Walker, Phillip L., and John R. Johnson

1994 The Decline of the Chumash Indian Population. In *In the Wake of Contact: Biological Responses to Conquest*, C. S. Larsen and G. R. Milner, editors, pp. 109–120. Wiley-Liss, New York.

Walker, Phillip L., John R. Johnson, and Patricia M. Lambert

1988 Age and Sex Biases in the Preservation of Human Skeletal Remains. *American Journal of Physical Anthropology* 76:183–188.

Walth, Cherie K.

1990 Analysis of Faunal Material from the Santa Cruz Mission Adobe State Historic Park. Study done for class in osteology, Department of Anthropology, University of California, Santa Cruz.

Watson, Margaret Hambly

1993 The Graham Affair: The Role of Artifacts in the Definition of Culture: Monterey, California, 1840. Master's thesis, Department of Early American Culture, University of Delaware.

West, G. James

1979 *The Archeology of Ven-100*. California Archaeological Reports No. 17. California Department of Parks and Recreation. Sacramento.

Whitaker, Adrian Robert

2008 *The Role of Human Predation in the Structuring of Prehistoric Prey Populations in Northwestern California*. Doctoral dissertation, Department of

Anthropology, University of California, Davis. University Microfilms International, Ann Arbor MI.

White, John R.

1977   Aboriginal Artifacts on Non-Traditional Material: Six Specimens from Fort Ross, California. *Northwest Anthropological Research Notes* 11(2):240–247.

Wilson, Richa L.

1998   The Rotchev House, Fort Ross California: A Historic Structure Report. Master's thesis, Department of Historic Preservation, University of Oregon.

THREE

A Million Ways to Teach Archaeology

The Hanna's Town Collection

BEN FORD

Research experience is widely recognized as a high-impact educational practice that improves undergraduate engagement, retention, and learning. Active and early student involvement in the excitement of answering real questions with real data helps undergraduates appreciate what they learn in classes and makes them more likely to persist in a program of study (Kuh 2008). Research experience is doubly valuable in archaeology, where much of the data are qualitative. Hands-on learning is a necessary component of mastering archaeological skills, as is active experience with learning how varying methods affect what research questions can be answered. Providing these experiences raises issues of scale and intensity for instructors. The experiences need to be deployable at a scale that meets the university's minimum class size requirement so that all students are exposed to research and allows interested students to continue research beyond the classroom. While a guided research experience may be sufficient to solidify basic concepts in the mind of the average student, few things are more effective at deadening the interest of a motivated student than withdrawing access to research once he or she has been hooked.

At the graduate level, research is obviously mandatory but comes with its own set of challenges for the instructor or thesis committee chair. In programs such as the one at Indiana University of Pennsylvania (IUP) that offers an Applied Archaeology master's degree, students are required to develop their own research topic and carry the project from proposal to completion, rather than complete one component of a larger, faculty-determined research agenda. This experience is invaluable for students who will lead projects in applied archaeology fields such as cultural resources management. The requirement for independent research, combined with a large number of students who begin graduate study with research interests narrowed only to "archaeology," can require a significant amount of work and creativity on the part of faculty to mentor a student toward an appropriate thesis project.

Legacy collections in general, and the Hanna's Town collection in particular, offer an efficient way to address many of the challenges of high-impact undergraduate education and graduate research. Consisting of nearly 1 million artifacts from nearly a half century of excavation, the Hanna's Town artifact collection offers almost endless opportunities to engage students in archaeological research at various levels. Between 2011 and 2016 approximately 110 IUP-affiliated students conducted research at the Hanna's Town site or used its collection, ranging from field schools to independent research. The historical significance of the site and the uniqueness of the collection, which includes such evocative objects as reconstructed polychrome white salt-glazed stoneware tea ware, make it compelling for students recently introduced to archaeology. The size and diversity of the collection is excellent for teaching about material culture and curation, data analysis, and many other useful skills. The challenges of notes and collections generated by multiple generations of excavators allow IUP faculty to teach problem-solving skills and discuss best practices. All of these skills and experiences are becoming progressively valued and marketable as 21st-century archaeology increasingly recognizes the benefits of working with existing collections (Drennan and Mora 2001:7; Voss 2012).

Using legacy collections for teaching and student research, while also respecting the collection as important evidence of past human lives and answering research questions that matter to someone beyond the students involved, brings its own challenges. The following discussion of how IUP faculty and students have explored and learned from the Hanna's Town artifact collection highlights these challenges and how IUP has attempted to overcome them.

The History and Archaeology of Hanna's Town

On 16 May 1775 the inhabitants of Westmoreland County, Pennsylvania, declared "to the world," that "animated with the love of liberty . . . it is our duty to maintain and defend our just rights and transmit them entire to our posterity." They went on to resolve "to arm and protect themselves" against the loss of liberty. Their full list of complaints against the "wicked British Ministry and corrupt Parliament," and the community's planned actions, were called the Hanna's Town Resolves after the town where the meeting occurred (Steeley 2000:4). Seven years later, on 13 July 1782, a combined Seneca and British raiding party razed Hanna's Town (Richardson 2010, 2011). Between the Resolves and the raid, and in the years leading up to the American Revolution, Hanna's Town was an important social, legal, and economic center on the Pennsylvania frontier. Nearly all residents of western Pennsylvania periodically visited Hanna's Town, the first British county seat west of the Allegheny Mountains, to settle court cases and register property. Because of its position along Forbes Road, the main east-west Pennsylvania thoroughfare, the town grew quickly. In 1775 it contained 30 houses and three taverns, one of which hosted the court, a fort, and various craftspeople catering to farmers of the surrounding communities and travelers pressing farther west. After the 1782 raid, Hanna's Town never recovered; the state road and county seat soon moved to Greensburg, and Hanna's Town became a farm field (Richardson and Wilson 1976; Carlisle 2005). One hundred eighty-seven years later archaeology began at Hanna's Town, and after nearly five decades of primarily avocational excavation (Grimm 1972) Indiana University of Pennsylvania adopted the site as a field classroom with the goal of interpreting life on the Pennsylvania frontier. Hanna's Town is arguably the most important historical site in Westmoreland County. As a toehold for Anglo-American western expansion and the home of the Hanna's Town Resolves, it played important judicial, economic, social, military, and cultural roles in the formation of western Pennsylvania.

Hanna's Town owed its existence to two seminal events in American history: the Treaty of Fort Stanwix and the opening of Forbes Road. Sent to remove the French from Fort Duquesne (now Pittsburgh) in 1758, Gen. John Forbes ordered a road built from Carlisle, Pennsylvania, to Fort Duquesne. Forbes was successful, and with the end of the French and Indian War, his road became one of the main routes west, providing an artery for a flood of Pennsylvanians and other easterners to enter the Ohio Country. These settlers were briefly held in check by the Royal Proclamation of 1763, which forbade settlement west of the Appalachian Mountains, but with the Treaty of Fort Stanwix (1768) the dam was broken. The treaty, negotiated between the British and the Iroquois, extended the settlement line southwest across Pennsylvania and Kentucky, into the lands of the Shawnee and Lenape, and allowed British colonists to legally settle in western Pennsylvania.

Straddling the Forbes Road at the head of a branch of Crabtree Creek, and nearly equidistant from Fort Pitt and Fort Ligonier, Jacob Miers first owned the land that became Hanna's Town, obtaining it through a military permit. Miers built a waystation to profit from express riders on the road but soon transferred the property to Lt. Col. John Wilkins of Fort Pitt before Robert Hanna purchased it in 1769 (Hahn 2008). Within a year of the Treaty of Stanwix, Hanna had established a tavern beside Forbes Road to serve travelers.

As the population of western Pennsylvania grew, settlers west of the mountains began to complain about the arduous journey to register property and settle court cases in Bedford, Pennsylvania. In response, Westmoreland County was separated from Bedford County in 1773 and, after some political wrangling, Hanna's tavern became Westmoreland's county seat (Hahn 2008; Steeley 2009). Hanna also began selling lots in the town that year, and Hanna's Town quickly took shape. As county seat, Hanna's Town was the site of the county's first courts, making it at least an occasional destination for settlers in southwestern Pennsylvania (Carlisle 2005:1). Due to the necessity of visiting the court for criminal proceedings or land transactions, as well as the settlement's position along one of the major overland routes to the Ohio Country, Hanna's Town developed into a thriving community of nearly 100 buildings, including approximately 30 homes, protected by a stockade fort and supporting multiple craftspeople along four streets. Several taverns were established in the town to provide lodging for travelers. The houses were a minimum of 18 feet on a side, while the taverns, which also served as homes for their proprietors, were somewhat larger (Richardson 1998:14; Richardson 2010:15; Hahn 2008:19).

A month after the battles of Lexington and Concord, the inhabitants of Westmoreland County adopted the Hanna's Town Resolves on 16 May 1775. Signed at Hanna's Town, this document declared that the citizens were "resolved" to resist the tyranny of Britain, which local residents perceived in the Boston Port Bill, Massachusetts Government Act, Administration of Justice Act, Quartering Act, and Quebec Act, often referred to together as the Intolerable Acts. Robert Hanna and James Cavet represented Westmoreland County at a Committee of Correspondence assembly held in Philadelphia in July 1774 and remained active in the community organizing that led to the American Revolution. The local Committee of Correspondence was likely responsible for much of the wording of the Hanna's Town Resolves, as similar language was used in many other parallel resolves passed in the year prior to the Declaration of Independence. The Hanna's Town Resolves were an early, local response to the Intolerable Acts, one of many that formed the broader national movement toward rebellion (Steeley 2000).

The resolve of Hanna's Town citizens continued throughout the war, with local men joining militias and participating in battles throughout the Northwest Territory. In response to these battles, as well as American attacks on Native settlements, including the egregious massacre at Gnadenhutten, Hanna's Town became the target of one of the final acts of aggression in the American Revolution. On 13 July 1782 a raiding party of 250 to 300 primarily Seneca and British soldiers led by Sayenqueraght attacked the town, burning its buildings and slaughtering livestock. The residents of Hanna's Town were able to shelter in the fort and weather the attack with only two casualties, but the town was nearly destroyed—only two homes and the fort were not razed. The raiding party also attacked a wedding at Miller's Station and a local farm and killed approximately three people and took six captive (Warren 2001; Richardson 2010, 2011).

Hanna's Town never fully recovered from this attack and was subsequently abandoned as the state road and county seat shifted to nearby Greensburg by 1786. Residents slowly drifted away from the town, and the lands were converted to fields, so that by 1800 only a few houses remained and those were gone within approximately a decade. The archaeological site of Hanna's Town thus presents a vignette of frontier life during a crucial moment in U.S. history and westward expansion. The lots of the village were eventually aggregated into the Steel family farm, which included two houses, a barn, and several outbuildings north of Forbes Road. The Steels continued to farm the property until it was purchased by Westmoreland County in 1969. At the same time that Westmoreland County acquired the 286 acres containing the site of Hanna's Town, it also entered into an agreement with the Westmoreland County Historical Society (wchs) to administer and interpret the site. Westmoreland County and wchs have erected two reconstructed log buildings, rebuilt the fort on its original footprint, transported two additional 19th-century log buildings to the site, and built various park facilities, including pit toilets and a pavilion (Steeley 2007).

Because of its historical significance, the Hanna's Town site was placed on the National Register of Historic Places in 1970. Recognizing the historical significance and archaeological potential of the site, avocational archaeologists began excavations within months of the purchase and have continued intermittently since. Initially led by Jacob Grimm, the early excavations were remarkably successful; during the first season of fieldwork at Hanna's Town, excavators uncovered a structure they believed to be Robert Hanna's tavern. Two years later they discovered the site of the fort where the townspeople took refuge during the 1782 raid (Grimm 1972; Smith

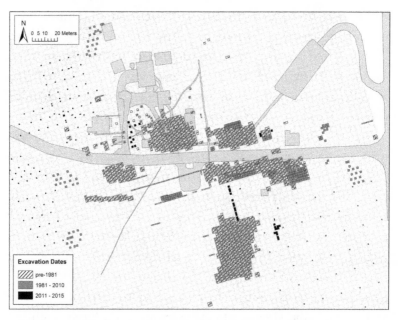

MAP 1. Map of excavated areas, Hanna's Town, Westmoreland County, Pennsylvania. (Map: Ben Ford)

1980). During these early years, a University of Pittsburgh field school directed by James Richardson also excavated two trash pits associated with Foreman's tavern (Richardson and Wilson 1976; Richardson 1998). In the subsequent decades others, including Peggy Fields, Ann Warren, Verna Cowin (1984), Thomas Baker (1998, 2006), Christine Davis (Davis and Biondich 2000), Robert Fryman, John Eddins (Fryman and Eddins 1985), and Al Auffart led professional and volunteer fieldwork at Hanna's Town almost yearly until 2006 (Map 1). As a result of these excavations, portions of the village were found in the undisturbed areas between farm buildings north of Forbes Road, often as a result of intensive excavations preceding re-created buildings; many features were recorded beneath the plow zone south of the road. These excavations have also produced nearly 1 million artifacts and tens of linear feet of documentation, but precious few publications. Many of the previous excavators were avocational archaeologists who were more interested in discovery than publication. As a result, this nationally important site is not well known or understood.

Using Hanna's Town and Its Collection to Teach Archaeology

IUP entered into an agreement with WCHS in 2011 to provide IUP students and faculty with access to the Hanna's Town site and associated artifact collections while providing WCHS with new archaeological interpretations and ways to increase awareness of the site's significance. This is an ongoing relationship with many facets, ranging from the creation of a digital artifact catalog and map to consultation regarding ground-disturbing maintenance at the park. The most important aspect of IUP's involvement with Hanna's Town has been hands-on student education through field schools, class projects, theses, and work experience. These endeavors have the overarching goal of supporting the WCHS mission by generating new knowledge about Hanna's Town and presenting that knowledge to the public, while also giving students experience with archaeological research utilizing existing collections to support the goals of archaeological stewardship (Society for American Archaeology [1996] Principle of Archaeological Ethics 1; Society for Historical Archaeology [2015] Ethics Principle 2). The Hanna's Town collection provides an excellent venue to train students in how to use existing collections to generate more knowledge about the past while digging less.

Students also learn skills specific to working with legacy collections. Because the Hanna's Town collection was assembled over four decades under the direction of several different investigators with varying research questions and types of training, the curation and cataloging of the collection is uneven. Most investigators used a consistent horizontal provenience system based on units, blocks, and baulks, but the minimum unit size ranged from 5 x 5 ft. to 50 x 50 ft., and sometimes larger. Stratigraphy was often recorded using bespoke terms such as "Hanna's Town Brown" to describe a layer often associated with colonial artifacts rather than absolute measurements, and the level of detail fluctuated from campaign to campaign. The data recorded for artifacts also vary significantly, with different terms used to describe similar artifacts. The collection and records contain a wealth of information; they just require a bit of effort to tease out that information. Students learn not only to decipher questionable handwriting but to apply their anthropological training to understand the goals and demands of various excavation campaigns in order to make informed inferences when the records are vague. Similarly the benefits of consistency in data recording and the reasons for being conservative when interpreting unclear data are driven home with each new catalog sheet or bag of artifacts. The size of the collection also allows students to experiment with relational databases and statistics, in many cases providing a first chance to understand the real power of a large data set. All of these data are hard-won and far more challenging, but also more rewarding, to analyze than a clean, canned data set. While the specifics of these difficulties are idiosyncratic to the Hanna's Town data, similar problems are common in legacy collections so that the lessons students learn can be applied to other legacy collections and archival collections more broadly. They also develop valuable critical thinking skills while deciphering the data and begin to populate the list of mistakes not to make in their own work.

Initial efforts with the collection focused on stability and accessibility. When IUP became involved, the collection was housed in three different locations, and artifacts were stored in a variety of lunch bags (both brown paper and lightweight, clear "sandwich" varieties) within various reused cardboard boxes, many of which were deteriorating. The artifacts were generally grouped by material type within site loci, but there were also boxes of general artifacts from across the site, unprovenienced artifacts, and "special" items that were stored separately and grouped by function. The records were organized by provenience and material, except the "specials," which were cataloged separately. While the artifact records were generally consistent, they lacked specificity. For example, a pilot study using the records for 65,345 ceramic sherds found that only 157 were identified to the component level (base, handle, etc.). IUP faculty and students began by centralizing the collection at one location and reboxing the least stable artifacts. We also conducted a visual assessment of the collection and attempted to organize it in such a way that specific boxes could be found and that there was separation between boxes that we had reanalyzed and those that were still largely unknown. We then began the necessary and ongoing task of digitizing the data into a relational database and geographic information system (GIS).

Graduate students designed the ArcMAP GIS and Microsoft Access database infrastructure, which provided them with employment and required them to creatively use the skills they learned in previous courses (Carn 2016). The digital catalog is a custom Access database designed to accommodate the unique provenience system developed by the site's original excavators as well as the wide range of material culture recovered from the site (Figure 3). Provenience information is entered in a string of fields that divide the alphanumeric unit, block, and baulk system into individual components that parallel the fields of an excavation grid layer in the GIS so that the two can eventually be merged. Since the GIS and database have not yet been merged, the similarity in format currently helps students working with subsets of the collection to situate their artifacts within the site. The database also includes a data entry page with drop-down menus to limit identification variability. These fields were adapted and expanded from the Sonoma Historic Artifact Research Database (SHARD) in order to accommodate the 18th- and 19th-centruy materials not included in SHARD (Praetzellis 2009). As cataloging progresses, it is occasionally necessary to add new terms to the menus to account for previously unrecorded material. Each addition is checked against the existing terms to ensure consistency. The GIS contains information on recorded features, excavations at the site, and disturbances since the early 19th century and will eventually be linked to the artifact database. Together the database and GIS make intelligible the several linear feet of paper documents created by previous excavators. As the GIS and database are completed, it will be possible to separate specific artifact classes, explore decoration types on ceramics, study the distribution of artifacts and features across the site, and construct complex queries that take into account time, space, and human agency. Student employees and volunteers have

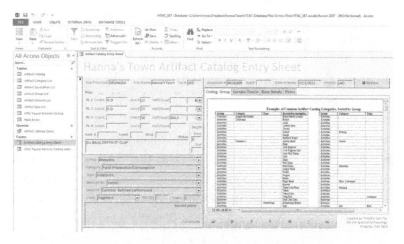

FIGURE 3. Hanna's Town artifact catalog data entry form.
(Form created by Timothy Carn)

been working on the digitization steadily since 2011 with approximately 50,000 records entered, representing nearly 260,000 individual artifacts; the project will likely be completed in 2019.

Students have also been engaged in re-identifying artifacts. As part of a regularly taught historic artifact analysis course, teams of students identify and catalog a selection of artifacts. Undergraduate students then perform basic analyses of their individual assemblages, and the graduate students aggregate the class-generated data and perform more nuanced analyses. This is a form of research-based high-impact educational practice that allows up to 25 students at a time to engage in real-world learning by doing. The breadth of material included in the Hanna's Town collection allows the students to gather experience with a variety of material types. For the graduate students, combining their classmates' data and attempting to analyze it serves as an object lesson on data standardization. These activities have the added benefit of expanding the artifact catalog because the structure of the digital database forces even the least motivated student to include more information about the artifacts than was captured by the paper record sheets. Additionally the students bag the artifacts in closable polyethylene bags.

As the collection becomes more organized in physical space and easier to understand through digital records, students are increasingly able to use it for independent research. Since generating an interesting and answerable question is an important part of research, students are given significant latitude in selecting a topic. One advantage of a large, diverse, and poorly understood collection is that it can accommodate a wide variety of topics, although some questions require more preparatory work than others. More nuanced questions will be possible once fundamental questions of distribution and variety are answered. The provenience data will eventually, however, impose a limit on question specificity. The majority (approximately 90%) of the artifacts retains their original provenience information, but this information is never more precise than a 1-x-5-ft. baulk and is often limited to a 50-x-50-ft. block. The stratigraphy was similarly recorded as visually defined layers with no smaller arbitrary levels. Questions requiring precise context and associations will likely never be answered. And there are lingering concerns about the sampling of small artifacts. Water screening was used during only one excavation campaign, and screen size is not specified in the notes of the other campaigns. Yet the substantial number of small items, such as straight pins and eggshell, and the copious amount of mundane material, such as the daub used to chink cabin walls, suggest that the excavators were careful to collect all the cultural material they saw.

Hanna's Town has thus far been the subject of seven graduate theses and three undergraduate theses, ranging in topics from buttons to geophysics. These projects illustrate the diversity of questions that can be answered with a legacy collection, as well as the accommodations necessitated by shortcomings in the original records. Similar to the class projects, these thesis projects also allow for a reanalysis of portions of the collection and act as a check on the original catalogs.

Stefanie Smith (2014) examined animal bones from three loci within the site to explore variations in diet among the townspeople. She limited her analysis to specific areas associated with domestic structures and limited her conclusions to the household level. Her chapter in this volume discusses her results. In summary, she showed that most people were eating a mixture of domestic and wild animals but that the inhabitants of one locus ate significantly more domestic animals than their neighbors. These results, combined with ceramics data gleaned from the digital catalog, showing a predominance of pearlware in this portion of the site, suggest that this locus was inhabited later than other buildings at the site and was likely reinhabited after the 1782 attack. Smith's research also revealed a substantial number of gray squirrel bones in trash deposits associated with the Foreman Tavern (Richardson and Wilson 1976), suggesting that squirrel stew may have been served in respectable creamware bowls at the tavern. Renate Beyer (2016) also focused on the Foreman Tavern, specifically reanalyzing the glass and ceramics from two well-recorded features and comparing them to a tavern closer to Philadelphia. She found that the Foremans were adopting new fashions almost as quickly as their eastern counterparts and that new types of ceramics first appeared in showier pieces such as tea services. It seems that the upper echelon of Hanna's Town society was well connected to the tastes and trade networks of the more established regions of the colony.

To further understand the flow of ceramics to Hanna's Town and the distribution of wealth within the settlement, James Miller (2017) analyzed the approximately 3,000 pieces of white salt-glazed stoneware previously recovered from the site for his undergraduate honors thesis. By studying the decorations on these sherds and where they were found within the site, he found that Hanna's Town lagged about five years behind in the adoption of new styles and that white salt-glazed stoneware was evenly distributed across the domestic structures. While undergraduates are not required to complete a thesis, doing so gives them an advantage in applying for jobs and graduate programs because it shows that they can take a research project from plan to completion.

Miller also developed a clever way to deal with the variety of provenience information. His collection included artifacts recovered from the plow zone that were recorded to 50-x-50-ft. blocks, as well as artifacts from features below the plow zone that were recorded to

5-x-5-ft. units so that the horizontal precision changed with depth for artifacts recovered from the same area. To solve this problem, Miller created a GIS layer containing artifact counts for the minimal spatial units in each area and depth. He then generated centroids for each area and linked them to the artifact counts. Many areas had multiple centroids as the excavation progressed from plow zone stripping in a 50-x-50-ft. block, to more careful excavation in a 10-x-10-ft. area, and finally excavating features within a 5-x-5-ft. unit. By then creating a density map interpolated from all of the centroids, Miller was able to determine the density of various types of white salt-glazed stoneware across the site, despite varying levels of horizontal record keeping.

Jay Taylor (2016) analyzed the metal artifacts in the Hanna's Town collection to better understand what occupations were practiced in the town. In his summary of the history of Hanna's Town, Ronald Carlisle (2005:47) posited that the town likely included the "necessities of frontier life [such] as a blacksmith and/or farrier's shop, perhaps a shoemaker and/or tanner, some means of grinding grain, a sawmill, and perhaps a distillery." Little direct evidence for these crafts has been archaeologically identified at the site. Taylor endeavored to identify the types and locations of various craftspeople within the town by studying the previously recovered tools, which helped him understand what sort of services Hanna's Town offered to settlers in the surrounding region and to travelers on Forbes Road.

Cheryl Frankum (2016) also investigated local industry by determining sources of the redware found at Hanna's Town. Utilizing a portable X-ray florescence instrument, Frankum tested a sample of redware from Hanna's Town and compared it to samples from other 18th-century sites in the region to better understand if redware was produced locally or imported from elsewhere. This is the first research on the Hanna's Town redware, which dominates the site's ceramic assemblage. Both Taylor and Frankum asked questions that apply to the site as a whole and can be answered by investigating all of the relevant artifacts, in Taylor's case, or an appropriate sample of the much larger collection, in Frankum's case.

Other collections-based theses are studying the buttons and pre-contact artifacts from the site. Nichole Keener (2015) studied the 962 buttons and 181 cufflinks in the collection to reconstruct the clothing of Hanna's Town residents. While some of the buttons postdate the period of Hanna's Town and likely relate to the farm that operated on the site in the 19th and 20th centuries, Keener hoped to shed some light on the fashions of Hanna's Town. Eden VanTries (2017), an undergraduate, studied the people who lived at Hanna's Town before Hanna and his predecessor Jacob Miers. In the course of previous excavations, approximately 1,200 precontact artifacts, including flaked and ground stone tools and debitage, were recovered. VanTries found that the site was occupied during the Middle Archaic period and then reoccupied, possibly less intensively, during the Late Woodland period.

Three additional students provided context for the artifacts and site. Undergraduate Kelsey Schneehagen used GIS to study Hanna's Town in relation to other European and Native American settlements and roads within western Pennsylvania to better place the site in its regional context. Graduate student David Breitkreutz (2016) built on the work of a previous IUP archaeological geophysics class and research by a former undergraduate, Chloé Stevens (2014), to better understand the site's layout (Beyer et al. 2011). The historical record is clear that the town lots were 60 x 240 ft., but in the absence of a contemporaneous map or thorough property descriptions there has long been uncertainty about how the lots aligned with the archaeologically recorded structures (Fryman and Eddins 1985). Using an IDS Stream X multisensor ground-penetrating radar recently acquired by IUP, Breitkreutz surveyed approximately 3.25 acres south of Forbes Trail Road in the heart of the site. It is hoped that evidence of houses burned during the 1782 attack will be evident in these data. Ashley Taylor (2016) used ground-penetrating radar, magnetometry, and electrical resistance geophysical techniques to investigate the Hanna's Town cemetery. The cemetery is of particular importance because it is the last aboveground physical link with the original town. By finding grave shafts outside of the cemetery fence Taylor showed that the cemetery was once larger than the current boundary.

IUP has also hosted biennial basic and advanced field schools at Hanna's Town since 2011. The primary goal of the field schools has been to teach proper excavation and recording techniques, with the secondary goals of testing previously uninvestigated portions of the site and better understanding the post–Hanna's Town formation of the site. These field schools were successful in identifying the western edge of the town and have indicated that previous investigators excavated much of the core of the site. This realization further reinforces the importance of the Hanna's Town legacy collection because any new information about the site is more likely to come from the collection than from additional excavation.

Conclusion

Together the various organizational, teaching, and research activities are beginning to bring the rich Hanna's Town archaeological collection into focus. The transitions from a frontier depot to a county seat to a regional center to a smoldering ruin can be traced in the daily lives of the inhabitants. At this point we have only an inkling of these lives, including their tastes in ceramics and meats, but each new study adds a pixel to the picture. Each individual project answers its own questions and contributes to the larger digital database of features and artifacts. Ultimately the individual student projects and theses will be combined with the completed database and GIS to look at the site as a whole. The student projects also suggest important avenues for future research. This project benefits from having many bright young minds thinking about it and providing suggestions for how the data might be best analyzed. By balancing data standardization with a student-centered approach to research questions the Hanna's Town project is slowly building toward a cohesive but broad investigation of the entire town. The result will be one of the few comprehensive studies of a frontier settlement during the American Revolution that draws extensively on both archaeological and historical evidence.

The Hanna's Town site represents a single occupation extending from circa 1769 to 1787. As such it offers unparalleled archaeological focus, allowing the material culture and lives of the inhabitants to be investigated with little confusion from later occupations. Combined with the historical record, the Hanna's Town archaeological site is an excellent window into how the American Revolution affected people on the U.S. frontier. Once completed, all of the student theses, as well as the digital data, will be available through the Westmoreland County Historical Society so that other researchers can access it and integrate Hanna's Town into further studies of the 18th-century frontier, and so that other students of history and archaeology can continue to make productive use of the collection.

Acknowledgments

Without the original excavators and the hard work of IUP students, none of the archaeology at Hanna's Town would be possible. Lisa Hays, Joanna Moyar, Joe Wightman, and the staffs at Westmoreland County Historical Society and Westmoreland County Parks and Recreation have been the most gracious and helpful partners imaginable. The Pennsylvania Historical and Museum Commission supported this research through a Keystone Historic Preservation Grant, and IUP provided funding through the College of Humanities and Social Sciences Special Project Fund and the University Senate Research Committee Small Grant Program. This chapter substantively benefited from the helpful commentary of Barbara Heath, Mark Freeman, and Rebecca Allen.

References

Baker, Thomas R.

1998 An Archaeological Investigation of a Proposed Parking Lot at Hanna's Town (36WM203), Hempfield Township, Westmoreland County, Pennsylvania. Report prepared for the Westmoreland County Historical Society. Greensburg PA.

2006 Archaeological Investigations Conducted at the Site of a Proposed Heritage Education Center at Historic Hanna's Town (36WM203), Hempfield Township, Westmoreland County, Pennsylvania. Report prepared for the Westmoreland County Historical Society. Greensburg PA.

Beyer, Renate

2016   Foreman's Tavern: A Glimpse into a Pennsylvania Frontier Tavern. Master's thesis, Department of Anthropology, Indiana University of Pennsylvania.

Beyer, Renate, Randy Kuhlman, Eric Ptak, and Sara Rubino

2011   Geophysical Investigations at Hanna's Town, 36WM203: Examination of Proposed Lot Boundaries and Evidence of the Historic Town. Report prepared for the Westmoreland County Historical Society. Greensburg PA.

Breitkreutz, David

2016   Spatial Analysis of Hanna's Town: Settlement and Geophysical Frontiers. Paper presented at the 49th Annual Conference on Historical and Underwater Archaeology. Washington DC.

Carlisle, Ronald C.

2005   An Overview of Prior Historical Research on Hanna's Town, the First County Seat of Westmoreland County, Pennsylvania. Report prepared for the Westmoreland County Historical Society. Greensburg PA.

Carn, Timothy A.

2016   Database Creation for the Legacy Collection of Hannastown. Paper presented at the 49th Annual Conference on Historical and Underwater Archaeology. Washington DC.

Cowin, Verna

1984   Archaeology and History: Hanna's Town Field Report. Westmoreland Archaeological Institute and Westmoreland County Community College Continuing Education Division. Report prepared for the Westmoreland County Historical Society. Greensburg PA.

Davis, Christine E., and Curtis L. Biondich

2000   Master Plan, Hanna's Town Archaeological Site, Westmoreland County, Pennsylvania. Christine Davis Consultants, Inc. Report prepared for the Westmoreland County Historical Society. Greensburg PA.

Drennan, Robert D., and Santiago Mora

2001   Archaeological Research and Heritage Preservation. In *Archaeological Research and Heritage Preservation in the Americas*, Robert Drennan and Santiago Mora, editors, pp. 3–9. Society for American Archaeology. Washington DC.

Frankum, Cheryl

2016   How Non-Destructive is XRF: Testing Sample Preparation Techniques for Redware. Poster presented at 81st Annual Meeting of the Society for American Archaeology. Orland FL.

Fryman, Robert J., and John T. Eddins

1985   1984 Archaeological Testing Project, Settlement Boundaries and Lot Place-
        ment at Old Hanna's Town. Report prepared for Westmoreland County His-
        torical Society. Greensburg PA.

Grimm, Jacob L.

1972   Hanna's Town. *Carnegie Magazine* June:225–235.

Hahn, Edward H.

2008   Hanna's Town: The Founding of a Village on the Pennsylvania Frontier.
        Westmoreland History Fall:16–19.

Keener, Nichole

2015   Hanna's Town Unbuttoned: An Archaeological Study of Clothing Adorn-
        ment and Fasteners. Poster presented at 80th Annual Meeting of the Soci-
        ety for American Archaeology. San Francisco.

Kuh, George D.

2008   *High Impact Educational Practices: What They Are, Who Has Access to Them,
        and Why They Matter.* Association of American Colleges and Universities.
        Washington DC.

Miller, James

2017   Distribution of White Salt Glazed Stoneware, Hanna's Town, Westmore-
        land County. Undergraduate honors thesis, Department of Anthropology,
        Indiana University of Pennsylvania.

Praetzellis, Adrian

2009   Sonoma Historic Artifact Research Database. Sonoma State University,
        Anthropological Studies Center. http://www.sonoma.edu/asc/shard/. Accessed
        14 April 2017.

Richardson, James B., III

1998   The Excavation of Foreman's Tavern: A Lesson in Frustration and Interpre-
        tation. *Westmoreland History* Summer:14–18.

2010   The Destruction of Hanna's Town, Part 1. *Westmoreland History* Winter:13–22.

2011   Who Were Those Guys? The Destruction of Hanna's Town, Part II. *West-
        moreland History* Spring:18–26.

Richardson, James B., III, and Kirke C. Wilson

1976   Hannas Town and Charles Foreman: The Historical and Archaeological
        Record, 1770–1806. *Western Pennsylvania Historical Magazine* 59:52–83.

Smith, Helene

1980   *Getting Down to Earth: The Story of the Hanna's Town Dig.* Westmoreland
        County Historical Society. Greensburg PA.

Smith, Stefanie

2014   Foodways in Colonial Western Pennsylvania: An Analysis of Faunal Remains
        from Hanna's Town (36WM203). Master's thesis, Department of Anthropol-
        ogy, Indiana University of Pennsylvania.

Society for American Archaeology

1996 Principles of Archaeological Ethics. http://www.saa.org/AbouttheSociety /PrinciplesofArchaeologicalEthics/tabid/203/Default.aspx. Accessed 5 June 2018.

Society for Historical Archaeology

2015 SHA Ethics Principles. https://sha.org/about-us/ethics-statement/. Accessed 5 June 2018.

Steeley, James V.

2000 The Hanna's Town Resolves: A "Declaration of Independence" in Historical Perspective. *Westmoreland History* Spring:4–11.

2007 Old Hanna's Town Remembered. *Westmoreland History* Spring:16–19.

2009 Old Hanna's Town and the Westward Movement, 1768–1787. *Westmoreland History* Spring:20–26.

Stevens, Chloé

2014 Geophysics at Historic Hanna's Town. Poster presented at IUP Undergraduate Scholars Forum. Indiana PA.

Taylor, Ashley

2016 Geophysics at Hanna's Town Cemetery, Westmoreland County, Pennsylvania. Paper presented at the 49th Annual Conference on Historical and Underwater Archaeology. Washington DC.

Taylor, Jay

2016 Taking History to Task: An Investigation of Metal Artifacts from Historic Hanna's Town. Poster presented at 81st Annual Meeting of the Society for American Archaeology. Orland FL.

VanTries, Eden

2017 Historic Hanna's Town: Prehistory? Undergraduate honors thesis, Department of Anthropology, Indiana University of Pennsylvania.

Voss, Barbara

2012 Curation as Research: A Case Study in Orphaned and Underreported Archaeological Collections. *Archaeological Dialogues* 19(2):145–169.

Warren, Anna L.

2001 The Burning of Hanna's Town, Part I. *Westmoreland History* Summer:31–46.

[FOUR]

The Digital Archaeological Archive
of Comparative Slavery

A Case Study in Open Data and Collaboration
in the Field of Archaeology

JILLIAN E. GALLE, ELIZABETH BOLLWERK, AND FRASER D. NEIMAN

In January 2000 Monticello's Department of Archaeology embarked on an ambitious four-year initiative to use digital technologies to foster new kinds of information sharing and collaboration among scholars and to advance our understanding of the evolution of slavery in the Chesapeake Region during the 17th, 18th, and early 19th centuries. Nineteen years later, thanks to funding from the Andrew W. Mellon Foundation, the National Endowment for the Humanities, and numerous donors, the Digital Archaeological Archive of Comparative Slavery (DAACS, http://www.daacs.org) is the longest running, and continuously expanding, digital archaeological archive to date. The success of the Archive rests on three critical pillars that were inherent in its initial design: (1) the Archive would provide free and open access to fine-grained data on all artifacts and their archaeological contexts, including complete archaeological data sets; (2) all data in the Archive would be created using the same set of explicitly defined and completely documented classification and measurement protocols and hierarchical data structures developed by archaeologists working in the field and instantiated in a Structured Query Language (SQL) database; and (3) the Archive would focus on a specific culture-historical context: slave societies of the British Atlantic world.

At the time DAACS was conceived by Fraser Neiman (1999), archaeologists had excavated scores of sites and hundreds of thousands of artifacts associated with slavery across North America and the Caribbean. The majority of this fieldwork was accomplished by the research arms of history museums in pursuit of concrete details to add to the sketchy picture of slave life derived from documents (e.g., Monticello, Stratford Hall, St. Mary's City, Colonial Williamsburg, Mount Vernon, Poplar Forest, The Hermitage) and by cultural resource managers intent on salvaging archaeological data from destruction by the modern development of well-known sites. Information from these early decades of fieldwork and research was put to good use in educational venues, where it has served to enlarge historical memory to include slave life (Kelso 1997) and to guide accurate museum reconstructions of the vanished physical environments in which slaves lived and worked (Chappell 1989, 1999; Armstrong 2011). Successful scholarly applications were more limited. Despite demand for synthetic analysis from archaeologists and especially social historians (Walsh 1997; Morgan 1998), the best work in the late 1990s was still limited to site-specific treatments of archaeological data, accompanied by speculations about relationships with larger regional trends outlined by social historians using the documentary record (Franklin 1997).

Although the causes of this situation were complex, one of the biggest hurdles was the difficulty researchers faced in gaining access to archaeological data in a form that made quantitative comparisons possible. Most of the detailed evidence required to build convincing syntheses was buried in field notes, finds lists, and artifact storage boxes. Moreover these important metadata were scattered in archaeology labs around the region. The only apparent exception to data sets with this problem also proved the rule. Synthetic analyses of archaeological evidence derived from systematic comparisons among multiple sites that did exist were based on architectural evidence (Samford 1996, 2000; Neiman 2008). Unlike the complex and multidimensional information associated with a ceramic or faunal assemblage, a house plan was easily distilled on a single, measured drawing.

The lack of readily accessible comparative data hobbles archaeological research, not only on issues of slavery in the early modern

Atlantic world but also across time and space. A key problem is the use of incommensurate classification and measurement protocols by different investigators or by the same investigator at different times. One of the most difficult parts of integrating data produced by multiple sources as identified by multiple archaeological studies is the use of nonstandardized terms, measurements, and methods of recording information by different researchers (Kintigh 2006; Watrall 2011:171–172; Kansa et al. 2014; Kintigh et al. 2014:879; Freeman 2015; Kansa 2015:226–227). This lack of standardization means that researchers who want to compare data created from different projects spend many hours tracking down analysis codes or trying to understand how data were collected and recorded instead of analyzing it (Atici et al. 2013; Faniel et al. 2013; Kansa et al. 2014; Kansa 2015:226–227). In addition, once a researcher has worked out the idiosyncrasies of a data set the additional information that puts the data in context is not necessarily passed on for future use. The larger problem caused by the lack of standards in the terms and categories used for data collection, however, is that it prevents researchers from performing comparative quantitative analyses across sites. Determining the meaning of data codes cannot facilitate comparative research if the terminology used to describe data varies from project to project. Creating data that are consistent only within one project or a few projects limits their usability. There is also the threat of losing digital legacy data stored in unsupported formats (Ross and Gow 1999).

Without access to comparable digital data, the long-term, multigenerational trends that the archaeological record is uniquely good at revealing remain inaccessible. The unavoidable focus on single sites makes regional variation invisible. These issues were pervasive at the start of the DAACS project and remains relatively unresolved in the discipline of archaeology as a whole. Making progress requires simultaneous exploration of diverse approaches (King 2009; Kintigh 2009; Spielmann and Kintigh 2011; Galle 2012). The Digital Archaeological Archive of Comparative Slavery forges one such approach.

Structuring Goals and Historical Issues

The fundamental purpose of DAACS is to convert archaeological artifacts and data into evidence that can be brought to bear on important questions in the cultural, social, and economic history of British North America and the Caribbean. Slavery powerfully shaped nearly all aspects of life in these regions. The archaeological record, a physical remnant of dynamic strategic relationships among slave owners and slaves, offers uniquely systematic evidence about change over time in the conflicting strategies enslaved and enslaver used to further their own and their families' interests. Strategic outcomes were affected by a variety of circumstances. Three factors were key: slave origins in Africa, demography in the plantation setting, and the niche that plantations occupied in the Atlantic economy and consequent variation in slave work routines required for economic success (Ortiz 1947; Berlin 1998; Morgan 1998). Note that recent scholarship has explored the role of Native American slaves in Virginia and the broader British Atlantic (Gallay 2003; Hatfield 2008; Everett 2009; Gallay 2009; Shefveland 2016). The sites of enslavement in DAACS were likely home to both enslaved Natives and Africans, but without detailed historical demographic research it is difficult to tease apart the ethnicity of individual enslaved persons or communities.

From its inception, DAACS (2017g) targeted sites from places and times that would strengthen our ability to assess how variation in these factors affected the trajectory of historical change in each region. The regions represented in DAACS received different proportions of enslaved Africans from different areas within West Africa. For example, roughly 60% of Africans imported into the lower Chesapeake in the early 18th century came from the Bight of Biafra. In contrast, the majority of slaves imported into the upper Chesapeake, including Maryland, came from Senegambia (Walsh 2001). The majority of Africans brought to Jamaica were from the Gold Coast and adjacent Bight of Benin (Morgan 2006). On the other hand, people enslaved and brought from Angola were the majority group in early South Carolina (Morgan 1998).

The demographic experience of enslaved Africans imported into each of the DAACS regions was also highly variable. Slave populations in the Chesapeake experienced demographic stability early (Kulikoff 1986), largely due to a more benign disease environment. The more deadly environments of South Carolina and Jamaica meant higher death rates, with heavy African importation required to meet labor demands. As a result, the relative frequency of newly imported Africans in the population was lower, sex ratios more balanced, and rates of family formation higher in the Chesapeake than in any of the other regions (Morgan 1998).

The archaeological sites in DAACS were also chosen to deliver sharper insights into the effects of variable labor regimes on the dynamics of slave societies. The labor requirements of tobacco and later small-grain agriculture typical of the Chesapeake differ. So do the requirements of Caribbean sugar cultivation, which differ from the rice and indigo regimes of South Carolina. Different work routines select for different labor management strategies, which in turn potentiate different strategies of slave resistance (Morgan 1998). The archaeological record can uniquely inform these differences, provided that scholars have access to systematically collected data with associated contextual information from spatially and temporarily diverse sites.

Research Foci

Four aspects of everyday life in the early modern Atlantic world were initially singled out as likely foci for research based on Archive data, and we (Neiman and Galle) kept them in mind when selecting sites for DAACS. The first set of issues related to the arrangement and use of domestic architectural space. Of particular interest were patterns of change and variation in the amount of influence enslaved individuals had over their living conditions. How much control did they have over the size and composition of their residential groups? How did African slaves manage to establish and nurture families and, later, multigenerational kin networks? As task differentiation increased, did task-based residential groupings emerge?

A second cluster of historical issues revolved around consumer goods and the extent of slave participation in a burgeoning "consumer revolution" that swept the Atlantic world in the late 17th and 18th centuries (Carson 1994). How variable was access to costly ceramic and glass vessels or fashionable clothing accoutrements like buttons, buckles, and beads? What were the payoffs to enslaved individuals for such access, and did they change over time? To what extent did the trajectories of change in preferred styles and uses of consumer goods diverge among slaves living in different regions and subject to different labor demands and labor management strategies?

A third set of key questions revolved around subsistence (Bowen 1996). What were the determinants of variation in the quality of food from domestic mammals and fish with which the enslaved were provisioned by owners? What caused variation in slave mobility across the landscape, as measured by the habitat preferences of wild species that they foraged? How did the extent to which reliance upon wild resources vary with the quality of the provisioned diet and the amount of geographical mobility they enjoyed? What were the ecological and social determinants of species preferences among slave foragers?

Archaeologists and historians have also been intrigued by the possibility of identifying African cultural and religious influences in material remains of the period (Sobel 1987; Ferguson 1992; Franklin 1997). It has been suggested that nearly all categories of material culture excavated from sites associated with enslaved populations belong to arenas of traditional African practice, from patterning in the processing of animal bones (Bowen 1996) and the unusual contextual associations of artifacts (Samford 1996; Russell 1997) to techniques used in the construction of locally made ceramics (Deetz 1988; Ferguson 1992:1–32; Deetz 1999:78–90; Mouer et al. 1999). Those important and tantalizing issues had been addressed only in a largely anecdotal fashion at the time of the Archive's inception. Data in DAACS now make it possible to document shared similarities among sites that might betray common African traditions or the later emergence of African American social identities in each region. They can also reveal the extent of regional variation in similarities that might be correlated with the origins of enslaved Africans within Africa.

These four historical issues remain central to the structure of DAACS and the research that is produced by DAACS staff. While they guide DAACS research and eligibility criteria for inclusion in the Archive, the archaeological data in DAACS can be used to address any research question a scholar brings to the data. The manner in which DAACS data are collected and structured allow these and numerous other historical questions to be addressed in a systematic way for the first time.

Designing DAACS

The ability to address these questions and meet our goals relied on making systematic and complete archaeological data, analyzed using the same set of classification and measurement protocols, publicly accessible. The general approach that DAACS adopted has been to use the internet to facilitate communication and community building among researchers, based on shared engagement with large amounts of fine-grained data, conforming to explicit protocols that researchers themselves helped devise. Hence the initial step for the DAACS project in 2000, when the founding grant was awarded from the Andrew W. Mellon Foundation, was to engage leading archaeologists and historians working on slave societies to help us identify the major research issues and the kinds of data required to address them. These scholars were brought to Monticello for a series of meetings to discuss everything from the overarching research questions bedeviling the field to the minutiae of which specific data attributes should be recorded for material culture such as beads, buttons, and tobacco pipes. These scholars make up the DAACS Steering Committee, an advisory committee that has grown over the past 18 years as the archive has expanded and which continues to help shape the archive's direction (DAACS 2017b).

By 2001 DAACS staff and collaborators had delineated data structures for both artifacts and the excavation contexts in which the artifacts were found, along with explicit classification and measurement protocols and data structures for both artifacts and contexts. It was clear from the outset that existing collections management software packages with archaeological components were not sufficiently robust to contain the hierarchical relational data that DAACS aimed to collect and deliver to users. As a result we undertook the development of the DAACS database, initially a Structured Query Language database (MSSQL Server) backend with an accompanying Visual Basic data-entry client. SQL is a programming language designed to manage and modify (e.g., query, insert, delete) data held in a relational database management system. At its inception, the DAACS SQL Server backend contained roughly 200 related tables, including authority tables. It resided on a single server at Monticello.

The database has grown, and today its data structures and cataloging protocols are rigorously defined and documented on the DAACS (2017c, 2017d) website. The database has since moved to a PostgresQL (an open-source system) platform. A Ruby-on-Rails interface (Rails combines the Ruby programming language with HTML, CSS, and Javascript to build complex websites and applications) delivers data to the website via queries and facilitates a new internet-accessible data-entry interface for accredited DAACS collaborators. This significant programming development is discussed in greater detail below.

Once programming for the DAACS client-server application was completed in 2001, artifacts and field records from sites across the Chesapeake were brought to the DAACS lab at Monticello for analysis. Twenty archaeological sites from across Virginia were carefully chosen for initial analysis to provide representative temporal and geographical coverage. Site occupations spanned the late 17th century into the early 19th century, making it possible to study African American experience in the Chesapeake over a century-long time scale, a span represented by no single site. Equally important, the sample included sites from both the Coastal Plain and Piedmont provinces, making it possible for the first time to study systematically regional variation. Finally, the site's principal investigators, and the institutions that housed the collections, were eager to share their data publicly, which was not the case for all eligible sites.

The sites in the initial sample fell into two groups. Group 1 comprised sites with no digital record or with an incomplete and inconsistent digital record. They included five sites from Mulberry Row at Monticello, dating from the late 18th and early 19th centuries; two important early 18th-century sites in James City County (44JC298 and 44JC546); one site from Stratford Hall (ST116); and the Pope Site, a mid-18th-century site in Southampton County. For these sites, all components of the digital archive were created from the ground up, from the identification and cataloging of every single artifact in these assemblages to the digitization of the original paper field records, the creation of digital site maps from individual paper context maps, and the digitization of slides and photographs. The artifacts and archival records for each site were brought to the DAACS lab at Monticello, where DAACS archaeological analysts, trained in the minutiae of DAACS cataloging protocols, identified and digitized the materials and entered those data into the DAACS database.

The second group of sites had relatively complete and consistent digital artifact catalogs. They included sites from Colonial Williamsburg (Richneck Quarter and Palace Lands Quarter), Poplar Forest (North Hill and Quarter site), Monticello (Sites 7 and 8), Mount Vernon (House for Families and South Grove), and Utopia (Quarter Sites 2, 3, and 4, excavated by the James River Institute for Archaeology). For these sites, all beads, buckles, buttons, ceramic and glass vessel sherds, tobacco pipes, and utensils were individually cataloged by DAACS analysts using the protocols and standards established with the help of the DAACS Steering Committee. For all "general artifacts," nails, window glass, brick and mortar, charcoal, toys, tools— any artifact not falling into the previously listed "special artifact classes"—we digitally mapped the existing digital artifact catalog entries onto the DAACS data fields and corresponding artifact lexicon. We then transferred the newly DAACS-standardized data into the DAACS database. Context records, site plans, and photographs were digitized from the original paper and film records. For all sites, the faunal remains were analyzed by Joanne Bowen and Steve Atkins at Colonial Williamsburg's Zooarchaeological Laboratory, and their data were entered into the faunal module of the DAACS database.

As the first sites were being analyzed and entered into the database, we developed the DAACS website from which the data being collected would be served to the public. DAACS Steering Committee members, as well as students and nonaffiliated archaeologists, were enlisted to test the interface and help refine its design. Using a simple point-and-click interface, written in Hypertext Preprocessor, website users were able to run sophisticated SQL queries that return data from multiple sites. All of the data returned on both contexts and artifacts conform to the same set of measurement protocols, and the complex hierarchical relationships among them are encoded in the same relational database schema. The use of standardized protocols and a single schema enabled the systematic quantitative comparison of hundreds of thousands of artifacts from 10 sites in multiple regions excavated by different archaeologists over many decades for the first time. That number has grown to over 2 million artifacts from 85 site and growing. No other digital archive of archaeological information delivers such detailed, standardized data presented for seamless statistical comparison of assemblage content within and among sites and regions and across decades of excavation.

While all the artifact and context data were entered using standardized terminologies, DAACS also provides users with a suite of eight different web pages dedicated to each archaeological site in DAACS. The *Site Home* page provides a site map and brief facts at a glance. The *Site Background* page provides a detailed summary of site excavations and describes field and laboratory methods used for data collection and curation. It describes the excavations conducted over all field seasons and summarizes any documentary evidence of prior occupations of the site. It also discusses any previous research or analysis that has been done on artifacts or the site's occupational history. Web links to citations for site reports and associated gray literature are included if researchers want more detailed information.

One of the ways DAACS documents the variation between sites is with the *Before You Begin* page on the website. Each site has a *Before You Begin* page that outlines key pieces of information or variation in the data set that may impact analysis. Some of the *Before You Begin* pages are very straightforward and list only a few bullets that outline basic

information on measurement and screening techniques (https://www
.daacs.org/sites/ashcombs-quarter/#before). Other sites require a page
that provides a detailed documentation of decisions DAACS staff made
during data entry to help the data set conform to DAACS protocols,
including how analysts handled missing artifacts and contextual information (https://www.daacs.org/sites/house-14/#before). Most important,
this page documents any major differences in the way the artifact data
were generated so researchers know how the data have been entered.

Another considerable challenge in comparing artifacts between
different sites lies in understanding the chronology of the site and
how it relates to other sites on a temporal scale. To address this challenge, each site in the archive has a *Chronology* page and a *Harris
Matrix* page. DAACS staff use a multivariate statistical technique
called correspondence analysis (CA) to analyze ceramic data from
each site to create occupational phases for each site, and they calculate
terminus post quem and mean ceramics dates for these CA-derived
phases. The *Chronology* page describes the CA method used and presents the resulting occupational phases and dates. These phases are
applied to the detailed Harris Matrix for each site, which are created
by DAACS staff using the stratigraphic relational information contained in the site's context information. Finally, a *Site Images and
Maps* page provides users with access to download images and site
maps in pdf, dxf, and dgn formats.

When the DAACS website launched in 2004, it contained data
from nine of the sites in the initial grant proposal: Monticello's five
Mulberry Row sites, Colonial Williamsburg's Richneck Quarter,
Mount Vernon's House for Families, and Stratford Hall's ST116 and
44JC298. Development of the database and cataloging protocols took
an entire year, substantially longer than anticipated in the initial
grant proposal to the Mellon Foundation. Perhaps more significant, assemblage sizes were vastly underestimated in the initial proposal, in some cases with collections two or three times larger than
initial assessments. By the end of 2005 analysis and data entry for
all 20 sites from the initial grant was completed and the sites were
launched on the DAACS website.

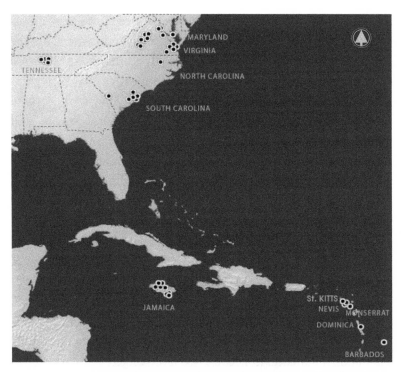

MAP 2. Archaeological sites currently in the Digital Archaeological Archive of Comparative Slavery (www.daacs.org)

DAACS Expansion

As of early 2019 the DAACS website serves complete archaeological data from more than 85 sites of slavery excavated in Maryland, Virginia, North and South Carolina, Tennessee, Mississippi, Jamaica, Nevis, Barbados, Dominica, Montserrat, St. Croix, and St. Kitts (Map 2). These data include millions of records on artifacts and their archaeological contexts. To ensure data accuracy and reliability archaeologists and zooarchaeologists trained and certified by DAACS are the sole creators of these data. The process is time-consuming but ensures that Archive users have easy access to detailed, comparable data that conform to a single standard.

Since the online launch of the archive in 2004, DAACS has developed its content and audience by establishing collaborative relationships with archaeologists and students working throughout the

Atlantic world. Much of this expansion has been funded by grants from the Mellon Foundation, the National Endowment for the Humanities (NEH), and Save America's Treasures. In other cases, the DAACS endowment, established in 2001 with a challenge grant from NEH and matches from several generous donors, has covered the cost of adding new sites. Some principal investigators who want to include their sites in DAACS have provided funding.

Expansion outside of the Chesapeake began in 2004, when a second grant from the Mellon Foundation allowed DAACS to broaden its geographical scope to include sites related to slavery in the Carolinas and the Caribbean. Between 2004 and 2008 we focused on including sites from Jamaica, Maryland, South Carolina, and Virginia. Among the significant sites added during this grant were assemblages from Leland Ferguson's (1992) excavation at Middleburg Plantation in South Carolina, from Barry Higman's (1998) groundbreaking excavations at Montpelier Planation in Jamaica in the 1970s, and from Douglas Armstrong's (2011) work at Seville Plantation in Jamaica. Collections from the United States traveled to the DAACS lab at Monticello, while DAACS staff relocated to Kingston, Jamaica, for five months in 2006 to catalog the Jamaica collections curated by the University of the West Indies, Mona, and the Jamaica National Heritage Trust.

A number of long-term collaborations emerged from the second Mellon grant that contributed to the Archive's continued growth. In 2008 Monticello's Department of Archaeology received funding from NEH to contribute nine additional sites from Monticello's Mulberry Row over a period of three years. DAACS's relationship with the South Carolina Institute of Archaeology and Anthropology, forged during our work on the Middleburg assemblage, led to a collaboration funded by Save America's Treasures that allowed the Institute to rehouse and inventory the Yaughan and Curriboo Collections, the first major excavations of slavery-related contexts in the South Carolina Low Country (Wheaton et al. 1983; Wheaton and Garrow 1985). After one year of collections work, the Yaughan and Curriboo assemblages traveled to the DAACS lab at Monticello, where they were cataloged and digitized into DAACS. The sites went live on the DAACS website in 2014.

DAACS's work with Armstrong's assemblage from Seville, Jamaica, branched into two separate longer-term collaborations: one working with Armstrong and his students on new sites in Barbados and Jamaica, and another with the University of West Indies and the Jamaica National Heritage Trust on new excavations and collections from Jamaica. Our collaborations in the Caribbean have led to the DAACS Caribbean Initiative (DCI), a long-term research project devoted to collaborative field research on plantations and associated slave villages on the islands of Jamaica, Nevis, and St. Kitts. The DCI has grown to focus on fieldwork in Jamaica and serves as a model for uploading recently excavated material online within months of excavation. In addition to DCI-sponsored excavations, Douglas Armstrong, Hayden Bassett, and Sean Devlin are working with DAACS to publish their field data within months of excavation (Figure 4).

The DCI received a major boost when DAACS was awarded a NEH-JISC Transatlantic Digitization Collaboration Grant, which funded a partnership with the International Slavery Museum, Liverpool, and the University of Southampton to conduct archaeological surveys on 18th-century village sites inhabited by enslaved populations on Nevis and St. Kitts. The resulting data from five village sites on Nevis and St. Kitts were launched on the DAACS website in 2010, only 18 months after fieldwork. In 2012 the International Slavery Museum launched a detailed, publicly oriented website dedicated to the project (National Museums Liverpool and International Slavery Museum 2017).

DAACS Satellite Laboratories

Throughout all of the preceding collections work, the emphasis remained on replicating DAACS cataloging standards. This goal was relatively easy to achieve as analysis was conducted by DAACS and Monticello staff at Monticello or by DAACS staff working remotely in the Caribbean, all using a single instance of the DAACS SQL

FIGURE 4. *Clockwise from lower left*: A DAACS Research Consortium training workshop on Monticello; Leslie Cooper, senior DAACS archaeological analyst, cataloging artifacts at DAACS Lab at Monticello; Hayden Bassett, cataloging artifacts into the DAACS database in Falmouth, Jamaica; the DAACS/UWI, Mona, Archaeological Field School, Jamaica, 2011. (Photos: Jillian E. Galle, Fraser D. Neiman, and Madeleine Bassett)

server database housed on a server at Monticello. As early as 2007 archaeology programs excavating sites of slavery expressed interest in using DAACS as their main archaeological database. In 2008 Kevin Bartoy, then director of archaeology at The Hermitage, the home of Andrew Jackson, located outside of Nashville, Tennessee, approached DAACS about establishing a satellite DAACS lab there. He wished to analyze previously excavated assemblages from domestic sites of slavery at The Hermitage and make them available to the public via the DAACS website. A successful Institute of Museum and Library Services grant in 2007 allowed Bartoy to establish a DAACS Satellite Lab at The Hermitage. An instance of the DAACS database was installed at The Hermitage, and four Hermitage archaeologists received three weeks of cataloging and protocol training at the DAACS lab at Monticello. These archaeologists then returned to The Hermitage, where they began cataloging into the Hermitage's DAACS database. The plan was to digitally transfer their data into Monticello's DAACS database when the project was completed. A subsequent NEH grant to The Hermitage in 2008 facilitated the start of a major effort to catalog into DAACS the complete archaeological assemblages from 12 domestic sites of slavery at The Hermitage. The closure of The Hermitage's Archaeology Department in 2009 led to the transfer of the NEH grant to DAACS. A second NEH grant, this time awarded directly to DAACS in 2014, is allowing for the completion of The Hermitage project by June 2019.

At the same time The Hermitage was setting up a DAACS satellite laboratory in Tennessee, other museums and universities began to use the DAACS database as their primary method for managing their archaeological collections. The archaeology departments at Washington and Lee University, Mount Vernon, and Drayton Hall chose DAACS as their primary cataloging system. Staff from each department spent at least four weeks in the DAACS lab learning DAACS cataloging protocols and standards. The DAACS SQL server database was installed on dedicated servers at each institution. In spring 2013 Eleanor Breen and Mount Vernon launched the Mount Vernon Midden website (http://www.mountvernonmidden.org/), which contains archaeological data delivered from the DAACS database. Numerous graduate students, after training at DAACS, also installed the DAACS SQL server database on their laptops for use at their own sites. Other museums, organizations, and individuals approached DAACS about adopting the DAACS database but were daunted by the technical skills required to install and manage their own version of the database.

While the expansion of the DAACS program outside of Monticello confirmed that the database was fulfilling the professional needs of historical archaeologists, it grew increasingly difficult to keep the satellite DAACS database synchronized with the home DAACS database at Monticello. By the early 2010s the importance of making DAACS a cloud-based resource, in which users could enter data into a single instance of the DAACS database via an internet-based browser, was clear.

DAACS Research Consortium

In March 2013 DAACS was given the chance to develop such a cloud-based resource through a third major Mellon grant for a project called the DAACS Research Consortium (DRC). The DRC is an innovative attempt to create for the discipline of archaeology the promise of what has been called "contributed cataloging," devising ways for many scholars to contribute to a larger project, while providing them with novel venues in which to publish their work and their data (Waters 2009). This project is the critical first step in creating a network of collaborating scholars linked by DAACS software, protocols, and analytical skill, and interacting at levels that have hitherto been possible only within a single campus.

Over the course of two years DAACS, in collaboration with the University of Virginia's Institute for Advanced Technology in the Humanities (http://www.iath.virginia.edu), Convoy, Inc. (http://www.weareconvoy.com/), and DRC partners, developed a new open-source software infrastructure that allows geographically dispersed DRC members to digitize, analyze, and share their data with one another and eventually with the wider archaeological community and the public via the DAACS website. The old DAACS MS-SQL server database at Monticello was migrated to a new PostgresQL database. Prior to the migration, DAACS staff fine-tuned the backend data structures and authority terms, using input from our DRC partners. DAACS staff also translated copies of the remote instances of the DAACS database running in the archaeology departments at Mount Vernon and Drayton Hall and with several graduate students, into the Monticello SQL server backend. This process was arduous due to minor, nonshared variations in table structure and authority terms that had crept into each backend database since its creation. It affirmed the decision to move the new DRC database architecture and its single, shared PostgresQL backend.

Programmers at the Institute for Advanced Technology in the Humanities developed an internet-accessible frontend data-entry application, written in Ruby-on-Rails code, that incorporated HTML/

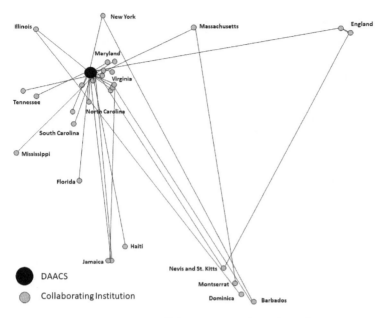

FIGURE 5. DAACS collaborator network as of March 2017.
(Graphic: Jillian E. Galle, Fraser D. Neiman, and Elizabeth Bollwerk)

CSS and Javascript frontend components. The DRC Application, available to DRC partners with a log-in, is an easy-to-use database with a robust query module (www.daacsrc.org) that allows data entry into a single DAACS database, ensuring comparability and ease of launching data on the DAACS website. Funding in 2017 from the NEH's Office of Digital Humanities provided for an expansion of the database user interface offered to DRC partners. The expansion helped forge new scholarly collaborations with government organizations, museums, and CRM firms seeking to make their data publicly accessible. The Expanding DRC grant also allowed DAACS to provide free in-depth training programs in DAACS database use and cataloging protocols, which is making new kinds of scholarly collaboration and data sharing possible.

Our partners in the DRC include faculty and their students at leading graduate programs focusing on the archaeological study of early modern Atlantic slave societies (Figure 5; DAACS 2017e). The consortium also includes scholars from research institutions that hold major archaeological collections from those societies. All DRC partners entering data into DAACS are required to undertake significant training at the DAACS lab at Monticello. Trainees take material culture assessments, or quizzes, throughout their time at Monticello and must pass a thorough material culture examination before they are certified to enter data into DAACS for presentation to the public. These material culture assessments are critical to ensuring the accurate identifications and quality of data in DAACS.

The ongoing DRC project aims to contribute to a larger effort to explore and perfect ways to use the internet to advance scholarly collaboration and knowledge of the past in the discipline of archaeology. Its design brings together recent threads in humanistic and scientific scholarship. The first is the concept of "contributing cataloging" (Waters 2009). DRC explores how archaeologists at scattered institutions might contribute comparable and accurate data to an integrated database and share the results with colleagues and the public. The second thread originates in the sciences, where many fields have benefited from the establishment of "core facilities" that house costly informatics, analytical infrastructure, and expertise that can be shared (Farber and Weiss 2011). The third thread is the growing recognition in the sciences, social sciences, and humanities that researchers have ethical obligations to make the entire research process more open to colleagues, other stakeholders, and the general public (Miguel et al. 2014). Openness is an ethical issue because it impacts the legitimacy and credibility of all archaeological inquiry and the well-being of all who participate in it (Lupia and Elman 2014; Marwick 2016). At DAACS we strive for transparency in all aspects of the process of creating and publishing the data. The *About the Database* section of the DAACS (2017a) website provides dozens of documents and manuals outlining how DAACS data are created.

Data Dissemination, Preservation, and Literacy

The data generated through these processes—whether sites are cataloged by DAACS archaeologists in the DAACS lab or digitized by DAACS Research Consortium members at their home institutions or field sites—are made available through the DAACS website to anyone, anywhere in the world. There are two primary ways of navigating the website: a series of dropdown menus and a map of sites created with a Google Maps interface. The context and artifact data are made available in point-and-click data queries. These queries are tied to SQL code that retrieves the data from the database. Context and artifact queries enable researchers to subset artifact queries by context or chronological phase. These queries can be easily run with data from multiple sites in the archive. The aggregated data sets are available as html tables and downloadable as .csv files that can be analyzed in any statistical program. In addition, DAACS also makes digital map files in CAD formats from each site accessible for those who want to do their own spatial analyses.

Providing aggregated data sets of artifact and contextual data that have been cataloged and recorded in a database using a single, standardized set of protocols from over 85 archaeological sites is a unique offering of DAACS. There are other projects, including the Chaco Research Archive (www.chacoarchive.org), that provide access to standardized, aggregated data that have been reanalyzed using a standard set of protocols. A variety of other digital archaeological projects also provide access to various types of archaeological data, including collection finding aids that have not been analyzed using standardized protocols (Pylos Regional Archaeological Project, http://classics.uc.edu/prap/; Archaeological Data Service), individual object records, general information on archaeological sites, but not necessarily artifacts (Digital Archaeological Atlas of the Holy Land, https://daahl.ucsd.edu/DAAHL/), or aggregated data sets from different sites that are downloadable but are not immediately interoperable (the Digital Archaeological Record, https://www.tdar.org/; A Comparative Archaeological Study of Colonial Culture, http://www.chesapeakearchaeology.org/; Open Context, https://opencontext.org/). The Digital Index of North America Archaeology, made available through Open Context, provides a web-based index of data pertaining to over 450,000 archaeological sites in North America. While all of these projects are valuable, when determining which archive or repository to use it is important for archaeologists to consider how the different goals and methods impact the types of data offered.

Besides making archaeological data available, DAACS is committed to maintaining the long-term health and sustainability of the database. This concern was one of the driving forces behind the move to PostgresQL. Long-term sustainability and access to archaeological data is a major issue noted by multiple researchers (Kintigh and Altschul 2010; Kansa and Kansa 2011; Watrall 2011). DAACS's endowment guarantees minimal DAACS staffing and the maintenance of the DAACS website and ensures that data are migrated, programs upgraded, and servers replaced on a regular basis. DAACS then draws on grant funds to tackle larger projects that the endowment cannot support.

Another necessary step to making data useful is ensuring users know how to interact with and analyze them. Part of the DRC workshops entailed short courses on data querying using Navicat, a SQL code-writing tool and data analysis using the statistical software program R. We choose R because it is widely used among statisticians, data miners, and (increasingly) archaeologists, is open source, and has an active and welcoming online community of users. In addition to university faculty members using DAACS to teach graduate and undergraduate courses (Agbe-Davies et al. 2013; our more detailed discussion of this below), DAACS staff members also teach data analysis workshops to students and archaeological professionals. These courses and workshops have revealed what we consider to be two major challenges for historical archaeology and the archaeological discipline as a whole. First, there is a lack of training in formulating research questions and methods for evaluating them (i.e., using statistical analysis). This is an issue regardless of whether the data are from new excavations or legacy collections, although archaeologists seem to struggle more with formulating research questions using legacy collections or digital archives. As highlighted by other recent collaborations (Arbuckle et al. 2014; Kansa et al. 2014), users need to go through the process of managing, integrating, and analyzing data before they can be considered "data literate" and understand what aspects and operations of data collection and preservation are necessary to make it comparable and usable on a larger level. Increasing data literacy enables researchers to better understand the processes that are necessary for data collection and management because they are more aware of what is needed to evaluate hypotheses and draw conclusions from data.

Second, there is a lack of training on how to use specific software applications like Excel, Tableau, and R to analyze data to answer proposed research questions. This problem can be categorized as a lack of digital literacy or "the ability to use information and communication technologies to find, evaluate, create, and communicate information" (Visser 2012). While working to become more data literate is vital, providing training in the use of specific digital tools is equally important because the proper use of software tools is an integral part of the research process. Moreover improving digital literacy among archaeologists enables well-documented, transparent, and reproducible data analysis workflows, which are critical if archaeology is to be a part of the Open Science movement (Marwick 2016).

Outcomes: Scholarly and Educational Impacts

Over the past 19 years DAACS has grown into the largest and longest-lived archive of downloadable, commensurate archaeological data for any specific region or time period. Evidence for the success of the DAACS project can be found in several different domains. The first is the history of positive endorsement by the scholars who sit on peer-review committees for the four grant-giving institutions, in addition to Mellon, from which DAACS continues to receive significant financial support: NEH, JISC, SAT, and IMLS.

DAACS has also been influential in the field of digital archaeology. It was the inspiration for the highly successful Chaco Research Archive (CRA) project, founded by Stephen Plog and based at the University of Virginia. Together DAACS and CRA have helped clarify the overlapping but complementary niches occupied by "research archives" and "preservation archives" in the discipline of archaeology (Plog 2010; Galle 2012). The former, like DAACS and CRA, aim to catalyze collaboration among scholars studying particular cultural and historical periods. The latter, like the Digital Archaeological Record in the U.S. (http://www.tdar.org/) and the Archaeological Data Service in the U.K. (http://archaeologydataservice.ac.uk/), aim to preserve digital data for the long term from any and all cultural and historical contexts (Richards 2008).

Besides CRA, DAACS has also inspired scholarly partners to carry on our mission to make historical archaeology data accessible from other regions of the United States. In 2016 DAACS began a two-year NEH-funded partnership with Charles Cobb and colleagues at the Florida Museum of Natural History. The Digitizing Franciscan Missions from La Florida project adapts and expands DAACS's database fields and protocols to encompass the physical variability in material culture from 16th- and 17th-century Spanish Mission sites in Florida. The data from these sites will be entered directly into the DAACS PostgreSQL database by our trained collaborators at the Florida Museum of Natural History and served out through a dedicated Comparative Missions Archaeology Portal (CMAP) website. This project has served as a valuable testing ground for DAACS to expand beyond the British Atlantic.

Research takes time, and although digital resources are often perceived as producing instant results, research using digital sources takes as long as scholarly work derived from nondigital sources. DAACS's influence on archaeological scholarship is evident in an accelerating stream of journal articles, monographs, and theses that make use of the data that the DAACS website offers. DAACS data figure importantly in recent comparative work on change and variation in the architecture of houses and quartering areas for enslaved people (Samford 2007; Neiman 2008) and assemblage content (Heath and Breen 2009) in the Chesapeake. Scholars have used DAACS data to chart for the first time variation in the means and motives of enslaved people to participate in the wider consumer economy in the Chesapeake (Galle 2006, 2010; Bloch and Agbe-Davies 2017) and to discover and explain striking contrasts in patterns of consumption on domestic slaves sites in North America and Jamaica (Galle 2011, 2017).

Archaeologists have begun to use DAACS measurement protocols and data to provide a wider context necessary for understanding the uniqueness of archaeological patterns in their own data at the regional or site level. Examples include studies of domestic sites occupied by enslaved Gullah peoples on the South Carolina Coast (Barnes and Steen 2012), enslaved agricultural laborers at Thomas Jefferson's Poplar Forest Plantation in Virginia (Heath 2012), enslaved industrial workers at Monticello (McVey 2011), middling tobacco planters in Virginia (Zevorich 2006), free townspeople in North Carolina (Gabriel 2012) and enslaved laborers on sugar plantations in Antigua (Rebovich 2011). Archaeological sites featured in DAACS have yielded insights into the social and economic dynamics behind the spatial organization of sugar plantations in Jamaica (Bates 2007, 2014, 2015, 2016, 2017; Armstrong 2011) and the effects of plantation location and crops on market access for enslaved people (Reeves 2011). DAACS data have also yielded new insights into the economic and social determinants of variation among both enslaved and free households in the use of particular classes of material culture, for example English clay tobacco pipes (Barca 2012) and locally produced and marketed, wheel-thrown coarse earthenwares in the Chesapeake (Bloch 2011, 2015, 2016). Furthermore, each year since 2006 a new crop of masters and doctoral students have contributed data to DAACS and engaged directly with DAACS data for their theses and dissertations (Fashing 2005; Galle 2006; Bloch 2011; McVey 2011; Rebovich 2011; Barca 2012; Breen 2013; Brown 2014; Bates 2015; Bloch 2015; Freeman 2015; Hacker 2016; Joy 2016; Bassett 2017; Beier 2017; Smith 2017; Harris 2019; dissertations in preparation by Joy; Platt; Stroud-Clarke).

Some of the most innovative and compelling uses of DAACS data have come from historians, not archaeologists. Historians have used DAACS data to document surprisingly frequent access to firearms by enslaved people in North America (Morgan and O'Shaughnessy 2006). They have also mined DAACS for systematic evidence of literacy among enslaved populations in the form of writing slates and slate pencils (Bly 2008). DAACS also figures importantly in historians' reflections on the ways archaeological data might advance their understanding of changing slave lifeways (Morgan 2006, 2011). Thus open-source data archives, like DAACS, offer some of the best opportunities for building interdisciplinary research opportunities for data analysis and dissemination.

Recent authoritative reviews by archaeologists have highlighted DAACS's role in advancing the cause of digital data sharing and collaboration in archaeology (Richards 2008; Arkush 2011). They have also pointed to the potential of DAACS data to advance the study of the experience of Africans and their descendants, both in the Americas (Fennell 2011) and in the larger African diaspora (Singleton 2010), as well as DAACS's potential to enhance public understanding of history and archaeology (Little 2007; Gonzalez-Tennant 2011). DAACS's Caribbean research has been featured in several popular publications, including *Jamaica Journal* (Francis-Brown 2009) and a cover story in *American Archaeology* (Bawaya 2010). DAACS data and research have also driven numerous exhibits, both online and in museums.

Archaeologists at universities across the country are using DAACS for teaching. Colleagues at Syracuse University, Northwestern University, the University of North Carolina, DePaul University, the University of Virginia, the University of California at Santa Cruz, and the University of the West Indies have developed courses that feature student projects built around the analysis of DAACS data. These courses range from general introductions to archaeology to graduate-level seminars focusing on the archaeology of slave societies. They vary widely in the extent to which they emphasize anthropological and archaeological theory, analytical methods, and historical issues, although they share the common and widely validated premise that learning outcomes benefit from serious engagement with complex archaeological data. Agbe-Davies et al. (2013) make this case and provide details, while the DAACS (2017f) website provides access to syllabi from several undergraduate and graduate courses that use DAACS data.

Conclusions

Nineteen years after its inception DAACS's structuring goals have largely been met. We have discovered that there is still much work to be done when it comes to making legacy collections accessible and usable. In addition to continuing to make legacy collections publicly accessible through the Archive, in the coming decade DAACS's efforts will focus on three critical, underserved areas in historical archaeology: (1) making data management and analysis a more accessible and familiar practice for students and archaeological professionals, (2) providing material culture resources and training that emphasizes the importance of standardized identification and measurements, and (3) helping interested archaeologists access and use the DAACS database for their own curatorial and analytical needs. Archaeologists have an ethical obligation to ensure that the data they produce through excavations or collections reassessments are transparent and accessible to the public. If the field of archaeology wants to be taken seriously in the Open Science/Open Source movement, practitioners must embrace preparing data not only for curation but also for sharing and reuse (Faniel et al. 2013; Freeman 2015; Kansa et al. 2014; Marwick 2015, 2016). DAACS is well-poised and eager to help historical archaeologists, and the archaeological discipline, meet these goals and obligations to our professional colleagues and the general public.

Acknowledgments

We thank Ben Ford and Rebecca Allen for inviting us to contribute to this volume and for their time, effort, and editorial skills. Lynsey Bates and Leslie Cooper provided constructive comments on a draft. Monticello's Department of Archaeology is home to DAACS. Its staff provides invaluable support. Over the past 18 years Leslie Cooper, Jesse Sawyer, Lynsey Bates, Elizabeth Bollwerk, Beatrix Arendt, Lindsay Bloch, and Katelyn Coughlin have been the primary archaeological analysts for DAACS and have generated the tremendous amount of high-quality data available through the Archive.

DAACS is funded through generous grants from the Andrew W. Mellon Foundation, the National Endowment for the Humanities, Save America's Treasures, the Reed Foundation, and generous private donations. Finally, we express our deep gratitude and appreciation to the archaeologists who have generously shared their data and collaborated with DAACS since its inception. Without their contributions, large-scale comparative archaeological studies of slavery would not be possible.

References

Doctoral dissertations in preparation that were referenced in this chapter include the following: Brandy Joy, University of South Carolina, Columbia; Sarah E. Platt, Syracuse University; Sarah Stroud-Clarke, Syracuse University.

Agbe-Davies, Anna, Jillian Galle, Mark Hauser, and Fraser Neiman

2013   Teaching with Digital Archaeological Data: A Research Archive in the University Classroom. *Journal of Archaeological Method and Theory*. DOI 10.1007/s10816-013-9178-3.

Arkush, Elizabeth

2011   Explaining the Past in 2010 (The Year in Review). *American Anthropologist* 113(2):200–212.

Armstrong, Douglas V.

2011   Rediscovering the African Jamaican Settlements at Seville Plantation, St. Ann's Bay. In *Out of Many, One People: The Historical Archaeology of Colonial Jamaica*, James Delle, Mark A. Hauser, and Douglas V. Armstrong, editors, pp. 77–101. University of Alabama Press. Tuscaloosa.

Arbuckle, Benjamin S., Sarah Whitcher Kansa, Eric Kansa, David Orton, Canan Çakırlar, Lionel Gourichon, Levent Atici, Alfred Galik, Arkadiusz Marciniak, Jacqui Mulville, Hijlke Buitenhuis, Denise Carruthers, Bea De Cupere, Arzu Demirergi, Sheelagh Frame, Daniel Helmer, Louise Martin, Joris Peters, Nadja Pöllath, Kamilla Pawłowska, Nerissa Russell, Katheryn Twiss, and Doris Würtenberge

2014   Data Sharing Reveals Complexity in the Westward Spread of Domestic Animals across Neolithic Turkey. *PLOS ONE* 9(6):e99845. https://doi:10.1371/journal.pone.0099845.

Atici, Levent, Sarah Kansa, Justin Lev-tov, and Eric Kansa

2013   Other People's Data: A Demonstration of the Imperative of Publishing Primary Data. *Journal of Archaeological Method and Theory* 1(3): 1–19.

Barca, Kathryn

2012 "The Best Kind of Long Ones": Tobacco Smoking at George Washington's Mount Vernon. Master's thesis, Department of Anthropology, George Washington University. Washington DC.

Barnes, Jodi, and Carl Steen

2012 Archaeology of the Gullah Past. *South Carolina Antiquities* 44:86–95.

Bassett, Hayden

2017 *The Archaeology of Enslavement in Plantation Jamaica: A Study of Community Dynamics among the Enslaved People of Good Hope Estate, 1775–1838.* Doctoral dissertation, College of William and Mary. ProQuest, Ann Arbor MI.

Bates, Lynsey A.

2007 *Surveillance and Production on Stewart Castle Estate: A GIS-Base Analysis of Models of Plantation Spatial Organization.* B.A. Honors Thesis with Highest Distinction, Department of Anthropology, University of Virginia, Charlottesville.

2014 "The Landscape Cannot Be Said to Be Really Perfect": A Comparative Investigation of Plantation Spatial Organization on Two British Colonial Sugar Estates. In *The Archaeology of Slavery: A Comparative Approach to Captivity and Coercion*, Lydia W. Marshall, editor, pp. 116–142. SIU Occasional Paper No. 41. Center for Archaeological Investigations. Carbondale IL.

2015 *Surplus and Access: Provisioning and Market Participation by Enslaved Laborers on Jamaican Sugar Estates.* Doctoral dissertation, University of Pennsylvania. ProQuest, Ann Arbor MI.

2016 Provisioning and Marketing: Surplus and Access on Jamaican Sugar Estates. In *Archaeologies of Slavery and Freedom in the Caribbean: Exploring the Spaces in Between*, Lynsey A. Bates, John M. Chenoweth, and James A. Delle, editors, pp. 79–110. University Press of Florida. Gainesville.

2017 Exploring Enslaved Laborers' Ceramic Investment and Market Access in Jamaica. In *Material Worlds: Archaeology, Consumption, and the Road to Modernity.* Barbara J. Heath, Eleanor E. Breen, and Lori A. Lee, editors, pp. 192–213. Routledge. London.

Bawaya, Michael

2010 An Examination of Slavery: Archaeologists Are Studying Changes in Slaves' Lives in the Caribbean and the United States. *American Archaeology* 14(2):12–18.

Beier, Zachary

2017 *All the King's Men: Slavery and Soldiering at the Cabrits Garrison, Dominica (1763–1854).* Doctoral dissertation, Syracuse University. ProQuest, Ann Arbor MI.

Bloch, Lindsay

2011   *An Archaeological Study of Common Coarse Earthenware in the Eighteenth-Century.* Master's thesis, Department of Anthropology, University of North Carolina at Chapel Hill. ProQuest, Ann Arbor MI.

2015   *Made in America? Ceramics, Credit, and Exchange on Chesapeake Plantations.* Doctoral dissertation, University of North Carolina at Chapel Hill. ProQuest, Ann Arbor MI.

2016   An Elemental Approach to the Distribution of Lead-Glazed Coarse Earthenware in the Eighteenth-Century Chesapeake. *American Antiquity* 81(2):231–252.

Bloch, Lindsay, and Anna Agbe-Davies

2017   "With Sundry Other Sorts of Small Ware Too Tedious to Mention": Petty Consumerism on U.S. Plantations. In *Material Worlds: Archaeology, Consumption, and the Road to Modernity*, Barbara J. Heath, Eleanor E. Breen, and Lori A. Lee, editors, pp. 119–140. Routledge. London.

Berlin, Ira

1998   *Many Thousands Gone: The First Two Centuries of Slavery in North America.* Harvard University Press. Cambridge MA.

Bly, Antonio T.

2008   "Pretends He Can Read": Runaways and Literacy in Colonial America, 1730–1776. *Early American Studies: An Interdisciplinary Journal* 6(2):261–294.

Bowen, Joanne

1996   Foodways in the 18th-Century Chesapeake. In *The Archaeology of 18th-Century Virginia*, T. R. Reinhart, editor, pp. 87–130. Special Publication no. 35, Archaeological Society of Virginia. Richmond.

Breen, Eleanor E.

2013   The Revolution before the Revolution? A Material Culture Approach to Consumerism at George Washington's Mount Vernon VA. Doctoral dissertation, University of Tennessee, Knoxville. ProQuest, Ann Arbor MI.

Brown, David A.

2014   *An Enslaved Landscape: The Virginia Plantation at the End of the Seventeenth Century.* Doctoral dissertation, College of William and Mary. ProQuest, Ann Arbor MI.

Carson, Cary

1994   The Consumer Revolution in Colonial British America: Why Demand? In *Of Consuming Interests: The Style of Life in the 18th Century*, Cary Carson, Ronald Hoffman, and Peter J. Albert, editors, pp. 483–700. University Press of Virginia. Charlottesville.

Chappell, Edward

1989   Social Responsibility and the American History Museum. *Winterthur Portfolio* 24:247–265.

1999 Museums and American Slavery. In *I, Too, Am America: Archaeological Studies of African-American Life*, Theresa A. Singleton, editor, pp. 240–260. University Press of Virginia. Charlottesville.

Digital Archaeological Archive of Comparative Slavery (DAACS)

2017a About the DAACS Database. http://www.daacs.org/about-the-database/. Accessed 2 March 2017.

2017b Collaborating Scholars. http://www.daacs.org/aboutdaacs/acknowledgements /collaborating-scholars/. Accessed 2 March 2017.

2017c DAACS Cataloging Manuals. https://www.daacs.org/about-the-database/daacs -cataloging-manual/. Accessed 2 March 2017.

2017d DAACS Database Structure. https://www.daacs.org/about-the-database /database-structure/. Accessed 2 March 2017.

2017e DAACS Research Consortium Members. https://www.daacs.org/aboutdaacs /acknowledgements/daacs-research-consortium-members/. Accessed 2 March 2017.

2017f Doing Research and Teaching with DAACS Workshop Materials. https:// www.daacs.org/research/workshops/. Accessed 2 March 2017.

2017g Project List: Archaeological Sites Currently in DAACS. http://www.daacs.org /about-the-database/project-list/. Accessed 2 March 2017.

Deetz, James

1988 American Historical Archaeology: Methods and Results. *Science* 239:362–367.

1999 Archaeology at Flowerdew Hundred. In *"I, Too, Am America": Archaeological Studies of African-American Life*, Theresa A. Singleton, editor, pp. 39–46. University Press of Virginia. Charlottesville.

Everett, C. S.

2009 "They Shalbe Slaves for Their Lives": Indian Slavery in Colonial Virginia. In *Indian Slavery in Colonial America*, Alan Gallay, editor, pp. 67–109. University of Nebraska Press. Lincoln.

Faniel, Ixchel, Eric Kansa, Sarah Whitcher Kansa, Julianna Barrera-Gomez, and Elizabeth Yakel

2013 "The Challenges of Digging Data: A Study of Context in Archaeological Data Reuse." In JCDL 2013 *Proceedings of the 13th ACM/IEEE CS Joint Conference on Digital Libraries*, 295–304. ACM. New York. http://dx.doi.org/10.1145/2467696.2467712.

Farber, Gregory K., and Linda Weiss

2011 Core Facilities: Maximizing the Return on Investment. *Science Translational Medicine* 3(95):95cm21.

Fashing, Maria. T.

2005 Recognizing Variability in Eighteenth-Century Plantation Diet through Pattern Analysis. B.A. honors thesis, Department of Anthropology, College of William and Mary, Williamsburg VA.

Ferguson, Leland

1992 *Uncommon Ground: Archaeology and Early African America, 1650–1800.* Smithsonian Institution. Washington DC.

Fennell, Christopher C.

2011 Early African America: Archaeological Studies of Significance and Diversity. *Journal of Archaeological Research* 19(1):1–49.

Francis-Brown, Suzanne

2009 Disinterring History at Papine. *Jamaica Journal* 32(1/2): 66–80.

Franklin, Maria

1997 *Out of Site, Out of Mind: The Archaeology of an Enslaved Virginian Household, ca. 1740–1778.* Doctoral dissertation, University of California, Berkeley. ProQuest, Ann Arbor MI.

Freeman, Mark A.

2015 "Not for Casual Readers": An Evaluation of Digital Data from Virginia Archaeological Websites. Master's thesis. University of Tennessee, Knoxville.

Gabriel, Jennifer L.

2012 *New Data, Old Methods: A Functional Analysis of Colonial Era Structures on the "Wooten Marnan Lot" at Brunswick Town, North Carolina.* M.A. thesis, Department of Anthropology, East Carolina University, Greenville NC. ProQuest, Ann Arbor MI.

Gallay, Alan

2003 *The Indian Slave Trade: The Rise of the English Empire in the American South, 1670–1717.* Yale University Press. New Haven CT.

Gallay, Alan (editor)

2009 *Indian Slavery in Colonial America.* University of Nebraska Press. Lincoln.

Galle, Jillian E.

2006 *Strategic Consumption: Archaeological Evidence for Costly Signaling among Enslaved Men and Women in the 18th-Century Chesapeake.* Doctoral dissertation, University of Virginia, Charlottesville. ProQuest, Ann Arbor MI.

2010 Costly Signaling and Gendered Social Strategies among Slaves in the 18th-Century Chesapeake. *American Antiquity* 75(1):19–43.

2011 Assessing the Impacts of Time, Agricultural Cycles and Demography on the Consumer Activities of Enslaved Men and Women in 18th-Century Jamaica and Virginia. In *Out of Many, One People: The Historical Archaeology of Colonial Jamaica*, James Delle, Mark Hauser, and Douglas Armstrong, editors, pp. 211–242. University of Alabama Press. Tuscaloosa.

2012 Will Today's Graduate Training in Historical Archaeology Predict the Future of Digital Research Archives? Society for Historical Archaeology Blog. http://www.sha.org/blog/?p=1684. Accessed 2 March 2017.

2017   The Abundance Index: Measuring Variation in Consumer Behavior in the Early Modern Atlantic World. In *Material Worlds: Archaeology, Consumption, and the Road to Modernity*, Barbara J. Heath, Eleanor E. Breen, and Lori A. Lee, editors, pp. 162–191. Routledge. London.

Gonzalez-Tennant, Edward

2011   *Archaeological Research and Public Knowledge: New Media Methods for Public Archaeology in Rosewood, Florida*. Doctoral dissertation, University of Florida, Gainesville. ProQuest, Ann Arbor MI.

Hacker, Stephanie N.

2016   Slave Subsistence Strategies at Thomas Jefferson's Monticello Plantation: Paleoethnobotanical Analysis and Interpretation of the Site 8 (44AB442) Macrobotanical Assemblage. Master's thesis, Department of Anthropology, University of Tennessee, Knoxville.

Harris, Khadene

2019   A Hard Kind of Freedom: Land Labor and Material Culture in Postemancipation Dominica. Doctoral dissertation, Northwestern University.

Hatfield, April L.

2008   *Atlantic Virginia: Intercolonial Relations in the Seventeenth Century*. University of Pennsylvania Press. Philadelphia.

Heath, Barbara J.

2012   Slave Housing, Household Formation and Community Dynamics at Poplar Forest, 1760s–1810s. In *Jefferson's Poplar Forest: Unearthing a Virginia Plantation*, Barbara J. Heath and Jack Gary, editors, pp. 105–128. University Press of Florida. Gainesville.

Heath, Barbara, and Eleanor Breen

2009   Assessing Variability among Quartering Sites in Virginia. *Northeast Historical Archaeology* 38(1):1–28.

Higman, B. W.

1998   *Montpelier, Jamaica: A Plantation Community in Slavery and Freedom, 1739–1912*. University of the West Indies Press. Mona, Jamaica.

Joy, Brandy

2016   *A Study of the Material Diversity in the Carolina Colony: Silver Bluff, Yaughan, Curriboo, and Middleburg Plantations*. Master's thesis, Department of Anthropology, University of South Carolina, Columbia. ProQuest, Ann Arbor MI.

Kansa, Eric, and Sarah Whitcher Kansa

2011   Toward a Do-It-Yourself Cyberinfrastructure: Open Data, Incentives, and Reducing Costs and Complexities of Data Sharing. In *Archaeology 2.0: New Approaches to Communication and Collaboration*, Eric Kansa, Sarah Whitcher Kansa, and Ethan Waltrall, editors, pp. 57–92. Cotsen Institute of Archaeology Press. Los Angeles.

Kansa, Eric, Sarah Whitcher Kansa, and Benjamin Arbuckle

2014 Publishing and Pushing: Mixing Models for Communication Research Data in Archaeology. *International Journal of Digital Curation* 9(1):57–70.

Kansa, Sarah Witcher

2015 Using Linked Open Data to Improve Data Reuse in Zooarchaeology. *Ethnobiology Letters* 6(2):224–231.

Kelso, William M.

1997 *Archaeology at Monticello.* Monticello Monograph Series. Thomas Jefferson Memorial Foundation. Charlottesville VA.

King, Julia A.

2009 The Challenges of Dissemination: Accessing Archaeological Data and Interpretations. In *Archaeology and Cultural Resource Management: Visions for the Future,* Lynne Sebastian and William D. Lipe, editors, pp. 141–167. School for Advanced Research. Santa Fe NM.

Kintigh, Keith W.

2006 The Promise and Challenge of Archaeological Data Integration. *American Antiquity* 71(3):567–578.

2009 The Challenge of Archaeological Data Integration. In *Technology and Methodology for Archaeological Practice: Practical Applications for the Past Reconstruction.* BAR *International Series S, 2029,* pp. 81–86, Archaeopress, Oxford.

Kintigh, Keith W., and Jeffrey H. Altschul

2010 Sustaining the Digital Archaeological Record. *Heritage Management* 3(2):264–274.

Kintigh, Keith W., Jeffrey H. Altschul, Mary C. Beaudry, Robert D. Drennan, Ann P. Kinzig, and Timothy Kohler

2014 Grand Challenges for Archaeology. *Proceedings of the National Academy of Sciences of the United States of America* 111(3):879–880. doi:10.1073/pnas.1324000111. http://www.pnas.org/content/111/3/879.short.

Kulikoff, Allan

1986 *Tobacco and Slaves: The Development of Southern Cultures in the Chesapeake, 1680–1800.* University of North Carolina Press. Chapel Hill.

Little, Barbara. J.

2007 What Are We Learning? Who Are We Serving? Publicly Funded Historical Archaeology and Public Scholarship. *Historical Archaeology* 41(2):72–79.

Lupia, Arthur, and Colin Elman

2014 Openness in Political Science: Data Access and Research Transparency. PS: *Political Science & Politics* 47(1):19–42.

Marwick, Ben

2015   How Computers Broke Science—And What We Can Do to Fix it. *The Conversation*. https://theconversation.com/how-computers-broke-science-and-what-we-can-do-to-fix-it-49938. 9 November.

2016   Computational Reproducibility in Archaeological Research: Basic Principles and a Case Study of Their Implementation. *Journal of Archaeological Method and Theory* 24(2):1–27.

McVey, Shannon L.

2011   A House but Not a Home? Measuring "Householdness" in the Daily Lives of Monticello's "Nail Boys." Master's thesis, Department of Anthropology, University of South Florida, Tampa.

Miguel, E., C. Camerer, K. Casey, J. Cohen, K. M. Esterling, A. Gerber, R. Glennerster, D. P. Green, M. Humphreys, G. Imbens, D. Laitin, T. Madon, L. Nelson, B. A. Nosek, M. Petersen, R. Sedlmayr, J. P. Simmons, U. Simonsohn, and M. Van der Laan

2014   Promoting Transparency in Social Science Research. *Science* 343(6166): 30.

Morgan, Philip D.

1998   *Slave Counterpoint: Black Culture in the Eighteenth-Century Chesapeake and Lowcountry*. Published for the Omohundro Institute of Early American History and Culture, Williamsburg, Virginia. University of North Carolina Press. Chapel Hill.

2006   Archaeology and History in the Study of African-Americans. *African Re-Genesis: Confronting Social Issues in the Diaspora*, Jay B. Haviser and Kevin C. MacDonald, editors, pp. 53–61. Left Coast Press. Walnut Creek CA.

2011   The Future of Chesapeake Studies. In *Early Modern Virginia*, Douglas Bradburn and John C. Coombs, editors, pp. 300–333. University of Virginia Press. Charlottesville.

Morgan, Philip. D., and Andrew. J. O'Shaughnessy

2006   Arming Slaves in the American Revolution. In *Arming Slaves: From Classical Times to the Modern Age*, Christopher Leslie Brown and Philip D. Morgan, editors, pp. 180–208. Yale University Press. New Haven CT.

Mouer, Daniel L., Mary Ellen N. Hodges, Stephen R. Potter, Susan L. Henry Renaud, Ivor Noel Hume, Dennis J. Pogue, Martha W. McCartney, and Thomas E. Davidson

1999   Colonoware Pottery, Chesapeake Pipes and "Uncritical Assumptions." In *I, Too, Am America: Archaeological Studies of African American Life*, Theresa Singleton, editor, pp. 47–82. University Press of Virginia. Charlottesville.

Neiman, Fraser D.

1999 The Digital Archaeological Archive of Slavery in the Chesapeake. Grant proposal to the Andrew W. Mellon Foundation. Manuscript, Thomas Jefferson Foundation, Department of Archaeology, Charlottesville VA.

2008 The Lost World of Monticello in Evolutionary Perspective. *Journal of Anthropological Research* 64:161–193.

National Museums Liverpool and International Slavery Museum

2017 The Archaeology of Slavery. http://www.liverpoolmuseums.org.uk/ism /slavery/archaeology/index.aspx. Accessed 5 March 2017.

Ortiz, Fernando

1947 *Cuban Counterpoint*. Knopf. New York.

Plog, Stephen

2010 Sustaining Digital Scholarship in Archaeology. In *Online Humanities Scholarship: The Shape of Things to Come*. Jerome McGann, editor, pp. 273–279. Rice University Press. Houston TX.

Rebovich, Samantha A.

2011 *Landscape, Labor, and Practice: Slavery and Freedom at Green Castle Estate, Antigua*. Doctoral dissertation, Department of Anthropology, Syracuse University. ProQuest, Ann Arbor MI.

Reeves, Matthew

2011 Household Market Activities among Early Nineteenth-Century Jamaican Slaves: An Archaeological Cast Study from Two Slave Settlements. In *Out of Many, One People: The Historical Archaeology of Colonial Jamaica*, James A. Delle, Mark W. Hauser, and Douglas V. Armstrong, editors, pp. 183–210. University of Alabama Press. Tuscaloosa.

Richards, Julian D.

2008 Internet, Archaeology on. In *The Encyclopedia of Archaeology*, pp. 1526–1529. Academic Press. New York.

Ross, Seamus, and Ann Gow

1999 Digital Archaeology: Rescuing Neglected and Damaged Data Resources. A JISC/NPO Study within the Electronic Libraries (eLib) Programme on the preservation of electronic materials. Project Report. Library Information Technology Centre, South Bank University. London. http://eprints.gla.ac .uk/100304/1/100304.pdf. Accessed 12 June 2018.

Russell, Aaron E.

1997 Material Culture and African American Spirituality at The Hermitage. *Historical Archaeology* 31(2):63–80.

Samford, Patricia

1996 The Archaeology of African-American Slavery and Material Culture. *William and Mary Quarterly*, 3rd series, 53:87–114.

2000   *Power Runs in Many Channels: Subfloor Pits and West African–Based Spiritual Traditions in Colonial Virginia.* Doctoral dissertation, University of North Carolina, Chapel Hill. ProQuest, Ann Arbor MI.

2007   *Subfloor Pits, and the Archaeology of Slavery in Colonial Virginia.* University of Alabama Press. Tuscaloosa.

Shefveland, Kristalyn

2016   *Anglo-Native Virginia: Trade, Conversion and Indian Slavery in the Old Dominion, 1646–1722.* University of Georgia Press. Athens.

Singleton, Theresa A.

2010   African Diaspora in Archaeology. In *The African Diaspora and the Disciplines,* Tejumola Olaniyan and James H. Sweet, editors, pp. 119–141. Indiana University Press. Bloomington.

Smith, Hope

2017   Adorned Identities: An Archaeological Perspective on Race and Self-Preservation in 18th-Century Virginia. Doctoral dissertation, Department of Anthropology, University of Tennessee, Knoxville.

Spielmann, Katherine A., and Keith W. Kintigh

2011   The Digital Archaeological Record: The Potentials of Archaeozoological Data Integration through tDAR. *SAA Archaeological Record* 11(1): 22–25.

Sobel, Michel

1987   *The World They Made Together: Black and White Values in 18th-Century Virginia.* Princeton University Press. Princeton NJ.

Visser, Marijke

2012   Digital Literacy Definition. American Library Association. http://connect.ala.org/node/181197. 14 September.

Walsh, Lorena

1997   *From Calibar to Carter's Grove.* University Press of Virginia. Charlottesville.

2001   The Chesapeake Slave Trade: Regional Patterns, African Origins, and Some Implications. *William and Mary Quarterly,* 3rd series, 58(1):139–170.

Waters, Donald J.

2009   Archives, Edition-Making, and the Future of Scholarly Communication. https://mellon.org/media/filer_public/30/9d/309de9a1-94fa-40fb-bb1f-f087333e8658/djw-archives-edition-making-2009.pdf. Accessed 12 June 2015.

Watrall, Ethan

2011   iAKS: A Web 2.0 Archaeological Knowledge Management System. In *Archaeology 2.0: New Approaches to Communication and Collaboration,* Eric Kansa, Sarah Whitcher Kansa, and Ethan Waltrall, editors, pp. 171–184. Cotsen Institute of Archaeology Press. Los Angeles.

Wheaton, Thomas, Jr., and Patrick Garrow

1985   Acculturation and the Archaeological Record in the Carolina Lowcountry. In *The Archaeology of Slavery and Plantation Life,* Theresa A. Singleton, editor, pp. 239–269. Academic Press. Orlando FL.

Wheaton, Thomas, Jr., Patrick Garrow, and Amy Friedlander
1983   *Yaughan and Curriboo Plantations: Studies in Afro-American Archaeology.*
        Report to National Park Service, Southeastern Regional Office, Atlanta,
        from Soil Systems, Inc., Marietta GA.
Zevorich, L. M.
2006   Ceramic Analysis of a Middling European American Planter Site in Vir-
        ginia Using the Digital Archaeological Archive of Comparative Slavery.
        Journal of Middle Atlantic Archaeology 22:91–102.

[FIVE]

Integration and Accessibility

A Case Study of the Curles Neck (44HE388) Legacy Data

BARBARA J. HEATH, MARK A. FREEMAN, AND ERIC G. SCHWEICKART

For the past decade, faculty and graduate students in the histori-cal archaeology program at the University of Tennessee, Knoxville, have undertaken collections reassessments of significant plantation sites excavated from the 1960s to the 1990s in Virginia. These sites include Newman's Neck (44NB180) in Northumberland County and the Hallowes Site (44WM06) and Nomini (44WM12) in Westmore-land County (Heath et al. 2009; Hatch et al. 2013, 2014; Hatch 2015; McMillan 2015; McMillan et al. 2015; Heath 2016). With support from the Virginia Department of Historic Resources (VDHR) through the Threatened Sites Program, the authors are currently conducting a multiyear reassessment project to increase access to and better pre-serve collections relating to archaeological research conducted at Curles Neck (primarily 44HE388 but also 44HE636 and 44HE677). The site was excavated from 1985 to 1997 under the direction of L. Dan-iel Mouer, formerly of Virginia Commonwealth University (VCU). Located along the James River east of Richmond, Curles Neck was occupied by some of Virginia's most prominent planters—the Har-rises, Bacons, and Randolphs—as well as enslaved and free labor-ing families and individuals. Excavations there produced a wealth of information about an important place that was continuously occu-pied from the frontier era of the 1640s to the outbreak of the Civil War (Mouer 1988, 1991, 1997, 1998).

The Curles Neck project ran for 12 field seasons. Researchers were able to target areas of the site with the most archaeological potential for excavation, and recovered hundreds of thousands of artifacts from over 650 individual features. The artifacts and architectural data could provide the raw material for any number of theses, dissertations, and scholarly publications about the history and development of the property itself and contribute comparative data to address a wide range of research questions, including the development of and regional variation between 17th- through 19th-century landscapes and architecture; local, regional, and international trade and exchange; material conditions of and responses to enslavement; foodways; and consumer behavior. Prior to the reassessment, the collections had been largely inaccessible since the project ended in the late 1990s, and most scholars inside and outside of Virginia are unaware of their potential.

Archaeological research is increasingly rooted in multisited comparative analyses that address continuities and changes over time and across space. Beginning in the early 21st century, collaborating groups of archaeologists working in the Chesapeake region have created and digitally published multisited data sets designed to facilitate research on topics such as slavery in North America, the rise of consumerism, the development of plantations, and the materiality of colonial encounters (A Comparative Archaeological Study of Colonial Chesapeake Culture 2009; Colonial Encounters 2016; Digital Archaeological Archive of Comparative Slavery [DAACS] 2016). Recent endeavors have also begun to harness the power of crowdsourced data for understanding the distribution of specific types of artifacts (Council of Virginia Archaeologists 2012a, 2012b, 2012c).

Each of these projects is dependent on the availability of existing collections and their related documentation to populate their data sets, and each has grappled with the problem of transforming data, created through disparate methods of recovery and standards of recording, to provide a degree of uniformity that allows them to be productively compared. Approaches have varied from hands-on recataloging of major portions of the collections by a highly trained, long-term staff (DAACS) to normalizing existing data and limiting recataloging to a few specific classes of data (Colonial Encounters) and restricting the focus of the data set to a specific type of artifact with a limited number of attributes and allowing contributors to supply their own data (Council of Virginia Archaeologists). To varying extents, the crowdsourcing approach separates specific artifacts from the broader contexts of the sites in which they were found, while the availability of well-cataloged or well-documented collections constrains the number of sites included in the integrated, multisited data sets. This latter limitation has led, unintentionally, to the creation of a research bias that promotes the sites included in the data sets at the cost of others whose data are less easily accessed.

As a new generation of digitally savvy scholars replaces practitioners more accustomed to working with physical collections, this research bias will only increase. Despite the promise of digitization, without progress toward more widespread accessibility of older collections and better training addressing their use and value, archaeologists run the risk of excluding vast amounts of legacy (currently nondigital) data from future research. Such exclusion will not only affect the quality of research but may undermine efforts to preserve these collections as their research value goes unrealized. Curles Neck is one such site. This chapter outlines the steps taken during a two-year pilot project at the University of Tennessee to make the collections accessible for research through physical preservation techniques, digitization of materials, the addition of metadata, and building a project website.

Collections Access and Preservation

After the sudden conclusion to the Curles Neck project in 1997, the physical collection was moved to a noncuratorial facility with no systematic consolidation or organization of associated records or digital data. It was not alone; the physical condition and accessibility of archaeological collections in Virginia has long been an area of concern to the professional archaeological community. In an effort to understand the extent and condition of curated resources, members of the curation committee of the Council of Virginia Archaeologists conducted an assessment of archaeological collections in depositories throughout Virginia in 2012 (White et al. 2012). As part of that study, they sampled digital site forms (n=321) curated by the VDHR in their cultural resource information system. They found that nearly half of the forms—many from sites recorded prior to 1990—had no information about where the collections were housed (White et al. 2012:25). Of those collections that were recorded, over a third indicated that they were held at the cultural resource management company that excavated the archaeological site. These findings are problematic given that some of these firms are no longer in business and that they were not intended to permanently curate the collections they hold. Furthermore, 61% of forms did not record the depository of field notes and 71% did not record photographs, both of which provide vital contextual data (White et al. 2012:27–28). These collections are difficult to access on any level.

Freeman's (2015:49) study of the institutional websites of the same depositories found that almost 75% included no information of any type about archaeology, while only 18% included archaeological data. He concluded that a large number of collections can only be discovered by visits to depositories by researchers already aware of the material's existence. These problems stymie the growing emphasis in archaeology on collaboration, data sharing, and the use of existing collections, as well as the broader goal of digital preservation. Kintigh et al. (2015:879) have called for "far more comprehensive online access to thoroughly documented research data and to unpublished reports detailing the contextual information essential for the comparative analyses." Currently the state of physical and digital collections in Virginia underscores that need.

Preservation and access are intertwined concepts. Physical and digital archaeological materials and data need to be preserved for future study, but they also need to be discoverable. Digital preservation "combines policies, strategies and actions that ensure access to digital content over time" (Association for Library Collections and Technical Services 2009:para. "Short Definition"). Archaeologists create digital surrogates for physical materials through artifact catalogs, digital photographs, 3D scans, and a wealth of analytical data based on the physical collections. Digital content is fragile, needs management, and has to be supported by discovery tools and robust metadata.

The development of the Digital Archaeological Record (tDAR)—an archival depository for archaeological data—and its promotion and publication of metadata standards have answered some of the problems of preservation and access (McManamon et al. 2010). But tDAR contains only a relatively small number of sites, and the amount of archaeology done in the United States over the past 50 years in response to changing legislation, coupled with the ever-increasing volume of digital data collected by archaeologists, suggest that the problems of access and preservation may be worsening. In fact, in part because of digitization, Harley et al. (2010:87) predicted in 2010 that 80% to 90% of archaeological data is in danger of being lost. Before turning to the complexities of digital preservation and access to the Curles Neck data, we review recent efforts to preserve the physical collections from that site.

Assessing the Curles Neck Collection

Before our project began, we were given an unofficial estimate of the size of the Curles Neck artifact collections of 90 to 100 boxes. This estimate formed the basis for the initial reassessment proposal. In fact the collections are far more extensive, consisting of 314 boxes of artifacts, environmental samples, and architectural fragments for site 44HE388—the main domestic complex for the succession of landowners—and 15 boxes for sites 44HE636 and 44HE677, slave quarters associated with the plantation. Additional boxes of records, reports, notes, photographs, negatives, slides, and small artifacts, as well as paper maps, are housed at the VDHR.

The principal artifact collection is currently stored at EnTrust Records Management in Richmond; it was stored with nonarchaeological materials at the VCU Re-Use Warehouse. Prior to our work in the spring of 2016, access to the collection was confounded by a number of factors, some of which have been resolved and some of which remain. First, artifacts from Curles Neck were stored with other materials excavated by archaeologists at VCU in the 1980s and 1990s. Within the past decade the Curles Neck collections had been rebagged and reboxed to meet current curation standards, but at some point in the past few years the warehouse staff consolidated materials to save shelf space. In the process, they mingled collections from various sites across multiple rows of shelving units. During the first phase of the project, we reorganized the shelves to place all of the Curles Neck boxes together, and then renumbered them sequentially. Finally, we created a box inventory tied to the new numbering system that is available on the project website discussed below. It includes box number, year, excavation unit, box label text, types of artifacts stored, and brief comments. The inventory serves as a finding aid for visitors to the physical collections.

The internal organization of the collections continues to create problems of access. Some artifacts are stored by excavation unit. VCU archaeologists had pulled others for study and reboxed them by material type. Objects that were placed on exhibit during the course of the project are now stored with other exhibited artifacts rather than by context or material type, and yet others were removed from the collections and are curated at the VDHR. This lack of uniformity in storage makes locating portions of the collection, or specific artifacts, extremely difficult. An examination of the artifact bags within the boxes indicated that many are in very poor shape. Some are brittle and tear with handling; others fall apart when opened. The unstable condition of the bags threatens to separate specific artifacts from their excavation contexts, particularly those made of iron for which the only context information is written on the storage bag. The loss of context, which would further complicate attempts to make the collection useful for research, is being addressed through a rebagging effort that has, to date, covered 5% of the collection to ensure its preservation into the future. Additional phases of the project are necessary to complete the rebagging initiative.

Digital Collections: Converting Physical and Legacy Digital Data to Current Digital Formats

Most of the efforts of the reassessment project have been directed at converting existing legacy data—paper records and old digital files—

into digitally accessible formats. At this stage of the project we have not prioritized recataloging or other steps that will generate new data.

Paper Records

Paper records include synthetic site histories, conference papers, maps, and artifact and context summaries as well as data sheets recording specific artifacts and individual archaeological contexts. Four boxes of documents associated with the Curles Neck excavations were brought from the VDHR to the Charles Faulkner Archaeology Laboratory at the University of Tennessee, Knoxville, for digitization. An initial inventory determined the types of documents in the collection and their priority for digitization. When multiple copies existed, only one was scanned. Some documents relating to public events at the site or field school administration were judged to have little archaeological value or to contain private information and were not digitized.

Documents determined to be the highest priority for digitization were scanned as PDF files. Documents that were originally typed were converted into text-searchable files using the optical character recognition (OCR) function in Adobe Acrobat Pro DC. A paper inventory sheet was prepared for each preexisting folder of documents that lists the type of record digitized, the name of each record, the initials of the person who scanned it, and the date it was scanned. Maps too large to fit on the scanner were photographed and stored as .jpg files. Acid-free replacements were substituted for the acidic folders and dividers that previously were in place in order to meet curation standards that promote the long-term preservation of the documents.

While field paperwork from all of the excavation seasons was contained in the four boxes of documents, artifact inventories from several field seasons were missing. We do not know if any individual excavation unit or feature records are also missing. Since all of these documents are handwritten, and therefore cannot be converted into machine-readable text, an analyst will have to review them one by one to determine if there are any gaps in the data. The handwritten nature of the field documentation also presents challenges to researchers seeking to use the data.

Currently most of the digital records of each data type are placed together in a single PDF file by field season, and while these files are available online, anyone seeking information on any particular excavation unit will have to manually search through the entire document to find the record of interest. Thus, while the reassessment project has made it possible for an interested researcher to quickly determine the type of data that is available in the Curles Neck collections, accessing and analyzing the spatial aspects of the site is still a difficult process. Reorganizing the digitized forms and linking them to the geodatabase for Curles Neck will do much to increase access to, and therefore interest in, this significant and well-excavated site.

Legacy Digital Records

As part of the reassessment project, more than 100 digital .doc files (Microsoft Word), dating from the mid- to late 1990s, were opened, renamed, and saved in Word 2010, simple text, and as PDF files. When the original format was unknown, the files were opened in Notepad++. These files were cleaned of special characters and reformatted. The naming convention for digital files was "project" "year" "topic"_"subtopic"_dig. All of the original digital files were kept in an archive file. A spreadsheet of digital data files with a summary statement showing metadata for all converted digital files was created.

Artifact Catalog

Comprehensive artifact data existed in two formats: a partial catalog recorded on encoded data sheets and a set of finds lists from four paper documents providing data from three years (1993, 1994, and 1995). Using the finds lists, we built a minimum artifact catalog database (Table 1) that could serve as an initial guide to the collections, provide simple comparative data, and integrate the interrelated excavation unit and feature data. Even these relatively limited goals were challenged by the lack of a cataloging standard for historical archaeology to guide us in parsing the data and the limits of the typed finds lists.

Table 2. Artifact database fields, Curles Neck project

Element	Description
Site	Virginia trinomial site number for project
EU	Excavation Unit (see features data)
Art_ID	Batch Artifact ID (1995 data only)
Count	Number of fragments or objects
Year	Excavation year
Class	General material (created from original description), example: Ceramic, Faunal, Glass, Metal, Organic, Stone, Synthetic
Form	Object form (created from original description)
Element	Portion of object extant (created from original description), example: rim, base
Material	Specific material of which the object is made (created from original description)
Ware	Ceramic ware type (created from original description), example: creamware
Origin	Place where object originated (created from original description)
Manf_tech	How object was made (created from original description), example: turned, wrought
Body_dec	Surface treatment (created from original description), example: molded
Surface_dec	Decoration (created from original description), example: hand painted
Color	Primary color (created from original description)
Dimensions	Dimensions (created from original description)
Bore_diam	Bore diameter for tobacco pipes in 64ths of an inch
Description	Original text from Finds List
Recat_by	Person who converted Finds List
Recat_date	Date Finds List converted

The lack of cataloging standards provides three challenges for data interoperability. The first is one of nomenclature; there is no agreed-upon authority of terminology. The museum field provides some standardized terms through sources such as Nomenclature 4.0 (Bourcier and Dunn 2015) and the Getty's Art and Architecture

Thesaurus (Getty Research Institute 2016), but these do not cover the breadth of archaeological material. One solution effectively employed by DAACS was the creation of cataloging manuals that standardize language and provide explicit instructions about appropriate terms to use when describing a variety of artifact attributes. Comparative digital collections such as those provided by the Diagnostic Artifacts in Maryland website (Maryland Archaeological Conservation Lab 2002) can also serve as online references. Such resources could potentially be developed with permanent virtual locations (Uniform Resource Identifiers) to support Linked Open Data, providing a consistent reference for some artifact types. The Getty's Art and Architecture Thesaurus is currently being made available as Linked Open Data. The second challenge lies in combining data that have been generated using different protocols for parsing information into discrete fields. Currently data sets from different sites have to be matched, or cross-walked, to find comparable data. For example, different institutions either batch similar artifacts from a single context or record them individually. While it is necessary to consider how a new database will be used to answer a project's specific research questions, every variation in structure should be balanced against the potential future problems of data interoperability. The third challenge arises from the lack of a standard for artifact attributes that must be universally captured so that the data achieve a minimum level of comparability. Agreeing on a core set of fields, with the possibility of including additional optional fields, seems a reasonable starting point. At least in the Chesapeake, the Colonial Encounters (2016) fields developed by Julia King and her colleagues provide a de facto standard that can be used for future projects.

Colonial Encounters incorporates 34 individual sites, including individual databases generated by contributors and "comprehensive" data built from the "least common denominator" (King 2010), which we understand as commonly shared fields that provide a minimum cataloging standard. King and her colleagues addressed the challenge of combining data from many different legacy collections, and the common fields they adopted served as a good baseline for our own structuring of the Curles Neck data. Since Colonial Encounters provides important comparative data for the Curles Neck collection, using their data structures makes good sense from the perspective of research as well as access. The artifact table from Colonial Encounters, with sub-tables for certain artifact types, is still more comprehensive than the limited information that the Curles Neck finds lists could support, but it does provide a basis for comparison.

The next step was to build the database for Curles Neck. The following process was used for conversion:

- The paper finds lists were scanned and converted into readable text through the OCR process in Adobe Acrobat.

- Tabula (http://tabula.technology/), an open-source program, was used to convert the tables from the PDF files into columnar data. The resulting output was saved as a .csv file.

- .csv data were imported into Excel. This was not an entirely clean process and required some manual adjustments. Columns were created for the site ID, year, and Excavation Unit values and added manually. In addition, cataloger and update fields were added and populated, and each artifact row was given a unique value.

- The "Text to columns" function in Excel was used to split the data into Artifact ID, Count, and Description.

- Filters were used on the Description field to parse the data. From the resulting subsets of data, the following fields were populated: class, form, element, material, ware, origin, manufacture technique, body decoration, surface decoration, color, dimensions, and bore diameter. The unparsed description field was also included to show the original source data (Archaeology Digital Data 2016).

While we attempted to document and be consistent in the filter and parsing phase, it was not a scripted process. We used some simple nomenclature to complete the class and material fields. For example, creamware found in the description field was used to complete the "ware" field. In this case, ware type also implied "material: earthenware" and "class: ceramic." Of considerable help in this process was the fact that the original finds lists showed a high degree of consistency in terminology. When the filter and parsing phase was complete, the resulting table was subject to data normalization to identify and address outlying values and misspellings. The final output was saved as an open-format .csv file and posted to the project website, along with a metadata file that described the fields.

Artifact data from some of the years for which finds lists are not available were recorded by hand on paper code sheets. These sheets provided a challenge for data conversion since they were not readable from a scan using OCR, nor could they be easily and accurately transcribed. After experimentation we determined that using voice recognition software provided the fewest transcription errors, and the codes were read into Microsoft Word, then parsed into spreadsheet data. The final stage involved writing a script that used the VCU-ARC Inventory Codebook to translate the spreadsheet table back to text, and then mapping the resulting output to the converted finds lists to ensure consistency across all of the artifact data.

Feature and Excavation Unit Data

During excavations, each context at the Curles Neck site was assigned an EU (Excavation Unit) number. After each field season, a summary of every EU that was excavated that year was compiled and saved as a text document. Similarly, every feature uncovered during the excavation was given a unique feature number, and a summary of every assigned feature number was entered into a text document. During the reassessment project, printed versions of the final EU and feature summaries were scanned and integrated into a database using the same methods that were used for the artifact data. EU descriptions were captured as entered with some cleanup for OCR errors. The original data for EUs were much less homogeneous and more descriptive than the artifact data, but we were able to create a table describing 1,159 unique excavation contexts that could be related to the artifact data, with six fields (Table 2).

Loading these data into the web-based database meant that relationships between the artifact and field records could be discoverable online. Searching for artifacts (through any number of fields) presents the related EU number as a link that populates a section on the page, giving immediate context. Additionally, many EU summaries that refer to feature contexts also contain the unique number of their associated feature in the description field.

After processing the feature summary document, 665 records were extracted and divided into six fields (Table 3). Using these results, researchers can search for particular types of features or quickly look up a description of features that interest them. Both the EU and Feature summaries are available on the project website in open .csv format, which can be easily imported into a database or spreadsheet. While the data contained in these summaries match the handwritten field forms fairly well, the field forms and summaries both have an unknown number of discrepancies, some of which were identified during the creation of the spatial geodatabase.

Table 3. Excavation Unit database fields, Curles Neck project

Element	Description
EU	Excavation Unit
Description	Unit description
N	Northing
E	Easting
Type	Type of context: plow zone, feature, trench (from original description)
Date	Excavation date

Table 4. Feature database fields, Curles Neck project

Element	Description
Site	Virginia trinomial site number for project
ER	Feature number
Description	Feature description
Notes	Notes made by digitizer
Cat. By	Name of digitizer
Cat. Date	Date digitized

The spatial extent of and relationships between archaeological contexts, whether arbitrarily imposed grid squares or inductively defined architectural and sedimentary features, form an essential part of many archaeological analyses (Kvamme 1999). In order to provide researchers with access to this information, we developed a geodatabase describing the spatial extent of and relationship between each surface collection area, square of excavated plow zone, trench, and feature. Spatial information extracted from digitized data, including the EU summary table, scanned field notes, photographed large-scale site maps, and scanned individual feature maps, was uploaded into ESRI ArcGIS (version 10.2.2). These data were used to create a unique polygon for each discrete context associated with the main Curles Neck site (44HE388). Each of these elements is projected onto an arbitrary grid matching the northings and eastings used by the excavators.

Arbitrary contexts, including surface collection grids, plow zone squares, and most trenches, were placed in space according to the recorded location of their southwest corners and their size, whereas features and judgmentally placed trenches were traced from georeferenced site maps and individual feature maps. The EU numbers and feature numbers (if applicable) related to each contextual unit were added to each data set under the "Associated_EUs" and "Associated_Features" columns. The description field from the feature summary .csv document was embedded in each archaeological feature polygon under the "Feature_Description" column. (If a context had multiple feature numbers, the most descriptive one was selected.) While most of the excavated contexts are represented in this geodatabase, an unknown amount of information is missing. A systematic examination of the handwritten field records is required to make a complete list of archaeological contexts lacking spatial information.

Other Digital Data

Other digital data from the project include a number of site and artifact images that had been printed and placed in storage with the field records. These were scanned and posted to the project website. Unfortunately, most were not labeled and have very limited information. We were able to extract the image metadata, which can provide a wealth of technical information but sadly does not describe the content of the photograph. The majority of the photo archive is in storage at the VDHR and should be mined for additional data as part of a future phase of the reassessment project.

In addition to images, paper files included site reports, conference papers, and a compilation of documents transcribed by a member of the VCU team during the original project. These have all been converted to PDF files with citation information. We were able to gather a number of emails and other correspondence but do not plan to make them part of the public archive due to privacy concerns.

Website

The Archaeology Digital Data website (add.utk.edu) was developed as a place for data storage and data sharing. Hosted by the University of Tennessee, it benefits from the university's infrastructure, which provides some support through backups and a degree of permanence and allows a virtual space in which all the Curles Neck digital material can be placed and researched (add.utk.edu /Curles/curles.html).

Underpinning the website is a relational database that promotes the discoverability of these resources and maintains context through a hierarchical structure. Site files are at the top of this digital tree, and all resources contain the unique site number. A table includes reference to specific features, and excavation records and unique IDs provide context for the artifacts. Technically the website is built with a MySQL database, supported through PHP scripts and JavaScript. The downloadable .csv files include metadata that allow the relationships between tables to be recreated through Foreign key definitions (W3C 2015), but for active research on the collections it is important that the relationships between these data are explicit. On the website, feature and site information is displayed within the artifact pages, with links to the original source data (PDFs). Understanding context is a central tenet of the discipline of archaeology, and maintaining and presenting that context should be equally central in data presentation.

Copies of the final digital materials will also reside at the VDHR. Consideration is being given to making some of the material—that part relating to the 17th and early 18th centuries—available on the Colonial Encounters website. For final archival purposes, some files have been deposited with tDAR following the simple principle of LOCKSS (lots of copies keep stuff safe).

Metadata

"Best practices" for digital data have emerged from the Archaeology Data Service (ADS) and tDAR (Archaeology Data Service & Center for Digital Antiquity 2013). In addition, the W3C (2015) tabular metadata standard, specifically designed to describe tabular data, has been used to describe the columns and values in artifact and feature record spreadsheet data. The W3C standard allows for the recognition that the tables are linked, supporting the archaeological information infrastructure. This means that artifact records are explicitly linked to excavation units and site records, and these relationships can be re-created from the individual downloaded tables. The recommendations for suggested metadata, supported file format standards, and preservation practices provided guidance for metadata standards for Curles Neck. The final project files included:

- Project information and project metadata (based on tDAR and ADS best practices)
- Site and feature summaries and GIS maps
- Excavation information
- The box inventory at VCU Re-use Warehouse
- EU open data (.csv format)
- Feature open data (.csv format)
- Artifact open data (.csv format), 1993–1995

- Features forms, EU forms, trench forms, and hand-drawn maps by year (PDF format)
- Field and artifact images JPG format
- Transcribed documents (PDF format)

One of the challenges of orphaned collections is reconstructing data provenance. Provenance can explain how results were derived from input data, as well as the scientific workflow and the process by which data sets were created (Kintigh et al. 2015:7). For the reassessment project, data provenance tracks the steps taken to get from the paper finds lists to the digital catalog. Additionally, as archaeologists are well aware, site excavations and laboratory techniques vary between projects, driven by external factors such as the nature of the excavation and differences in training and practice among project staff. An understanding of the data has to be contextualized by both knowledge of the excavation methodology and of cataloging procedures in the archaeology laboratory, including protocols for the batching of artifacts, terminology used in classification, and methods of cross-mending or determining minimum vessel counts. Providing at least a description of these processes supports the interoperability of data, and we are looking at further developing metadata to document these processes.

Recording data provenance also acknowledges supporting data sets. Borgman (2010:193, 189) observed that the incentives for creating digital data sets are more in data use than in data sharing, noting that "those whose data collections and analysis were the least automated and most labor intensive were most likely to guard their data." Kratz and Strasser (2015:6) found strong support among researchers for formal data citation being the correct approach to receiving credit for data sets. If we want to build larger sets of comparable data and encourage future data sharing, we need to find a way to acknowledge the efforts of those who created the data. The Archaeology Digital Data website, where the Curles Neck data are currently housed, provides a suggested citation for these data, following the advice of Mooney and Newton (2012:14) that while "conciseness is an important principle of citation . . . comprehensive information should be of greater value."

The website also makes licensing of the data explicit. Despite the easy availability of Creative Commons licenses, clear statements about how data can be reused are still uncommon (Freeman 2015:56). Data interoperability needs to be matched with legal interoperability (Kansa and Kansa 2011:12). Explicit licensing statements on use and reuse provide clarity and avoid problems if researchers assume that restricted data are free to use.

Promotion

Information about the Curles Neck reassessment project has been presented nationally at the Society for Historical Archaeology's annual conference and regionally at the Middle Atlantic Archaeological Conference (Freeman 2016; Freeman and Heath 2017). In addition to forming the focus of this chapter, the collection will also be promoted through archaeology newsletters and regional social media outlets. While data citation is an emerging topic in historical archaeology, it is hoped that, like article citation, the importance and use of these collections will grow through an expanding body of work. Making the data available through multiple outlets and creating machine-readable metadata formats for the data will hopefully support their discovery.

Conclusions

The archaeological remains associated with Curles Neck provide a unique set of data that directly speak to a host of cultural processes relevant to contemporary concerns within historical archaeology, from colonial expansion and the rise of capitalism to the construction and maintenance of the racial and class-based hierarchies that have come to shape contemporary American culture. Beyond the historical significance of the site's inhabitants, the quantity and preservation of the material associated with the Curles Neck site is extraordinary. The initial results of the reassessment project have helped to preserve these data and provide a solid basis for future efforts aimed at restructuring them for ease of use for popular and scholarly interpretations of Virginia's past.

The Curles Neck project highlights the multiple technical, preservation, and interpretive problems associated with orphaned collections, many of which arise from excavations conducted within the academy or by private organizations whose work often falls outside of the federal regulatory system. Though the particulars may vary, there are some issues of archaeological practice and some broader structural issues that contribute to the continued neglect of many archaeological collections. Digital data need to be actively managed to remain accessible. Changes in practice should include an explicit policy for the frequent archiving and migration of data so that records are not lost; the adoption of metadata standards that are applied consistently to data sets so that outside researchers can understand the specific processes through which the data were created and catalogued; and the development of a curation plan at the outset of every project so that the disposition of the collection, broadly conceived to include artifacts, images, and paper and digital documentation, is clear and its long-term care is ensured. We advocate for continuing the practice of creating paper field records, including maps, in addition to digital surrogates, both as a form of redundancy that will help ensure the preservation of data and because of their value in interpreting the archaeological record through the process of manually recording it. Existing structural issues that remain to be solved include a lack of recognition and reward for the time-consuming production of high-quality digital data resulting from field research; limited institutional awareness of the importance of collections, which generally results in a shortage of long-term, sustained resources for curation (both physical and digital) once field projects are complete; and as yet unresolved challenges in promoting awareness of and making data accessible to scholars who are interested in working with these collections.

One encouraging trend is the emergence of the Open Data concept, supported by the federal government. The Office of Science and Technology Policy asks that "digitally formatted scientific data should be stored and publicly accessible to search, retrieve, and analyze" (White House 2013). This policy is effectively implemented through data management plans, seen in the requirements for the National Science Foundation (2013) and the National Endowment for the Humanities (2016). Archaeologists working on projects funded by federal grants must now create a plan that addresses how they will manage, preserve, and provide access to their data, with allowance for the norms in their discipline. Despite these important advances, there is a backlog of archaeological material, complicated by a period of "digital dark ages" with differing file formats and limited metadata, which will contribute to the many challenges that lie ahead.

Legacy archaeological data will be lost or continue to be inaccessible unless funding is found for care of existing collections. We suggest that the low-cost solution presented here, using existing data and some simple tools to convert it to digital formats and to describe it via accompanying metadata, provides a minimum threshold of accessibility and could be widely applied. While our work may ultimately result in a more detailed reanalysis and more robust data sets, it is our hope that the current improvement in access to this important collection will contribute to its long-term preservation and promote its relevance to the broad and varied communities interested in Virginia's past.

References

Archaeology Data Service & Center for Digital Antiquity
2013   *Caring for Digital Data in Archaeology: A Guide to Good Practice.* Oxbow Books. Oxford.
Archaeology Digital Data
2016   Data Explorer. http://add.utk.edu/Curles/Scripts/curles-explore.html. Accessed 10 December 2016.
Association for Library Collections and Technical Services
2009   Definitions of Digital Preservation. http://www.ala.org/alcts/resources/preserv/2009def. Accessed 10 December 2016.
Borgman, Christine L.
2010   *Scholarship in the Digital Age: Information, Infrastructure, and the Internet.* MIT Press. Cambridge MA.

Bourcier, Paul, and Heather Dunn (editors)

2015   *Nomenclature 4.0 for Museum Cataloging: Robert G. Chenhall's System for Classifying Cultural Objects.* Rowman & Littlefield. Lanham MD.

Childs, S. Terry, and Seth Kagan

2008   *A Decade of Study into Repository Fees for Archeological Curation.* U.S. National Park Service Publications and Papers, Paper 98. Washington DC.

Colonial Encounters

2016   Technical Overview. http://colonialencounters.org/Technical/TechnicalData .aspx. Accessed 4 December 2016.

A Comparative Archaeological Study of Colonial Chesapeake Culture

2009   A New Look at Early Chesapeake Sites. http://www.chesapeakearchaeology .org/. Accessed 22 December 2016.

Council of Virginia Archaeologists

2012a Culture Embossed. http://www.cova-inc.org/wineseals/. Accessed 22 December 2016.

2012b Culture Impressed. http://www.cova-inc.org/pipes/. Accessed 22 December 2016.

2012c Culture in Stone. http://www.cova-inc.org/points/. Accessed 22 December 2016.

Digital Archaeological Archive of Comparative Slavery (DAACS)

2016   http://www.daacs.org. Accessed 4 December 2016.

Freeman, Mark A.

2015   "Not for Casual Readers": An Evaluation of Digital Data from Virginia Archaeological Websites. Master's thesis, School of Information Science, University of Tennessee, Knoxville. http://trace.tennessee.edu/utk_gradthes/3476/.

2016   Digital Archaeological Data: Interoperability, Access, and Data Provenance. Paper presented at the Middle Atlantic Archaeology Conference, Ocean City MD.

Freeman, Mark, and Barbara J. Heath

2017   Curles Neck: A Collections Reassessment. Paper presented at the 50th Annual Meeting for the Society of Historic Archaeology, Fort Worth TX.

Getty Research Institute

2016   Getty Vocabularies as Linked Open Data. http://www.getty.edu/research /tools/vocabularies/lod/index.html. Accessed 31 January 2017.

Harley, Diane, Sophia Krzys Acord, Sarah Earl-Novell, Shannon Lawrence, and C. Judson King

2010   *Assessing the Future Landscape of Scholarly Communication: An Exploration of Faculty Values and Needs in Seven Disciplines.* Center for Studies in Higher Education. University of California Press. Berkeley.

Hatch, D. Brad

2015   *An Historical Archaeology of Early Modern Manhood in the Potomac River Valley of Virginia, 1645–1730.* Doctoral dissertation, Department of Anthropology, University of Tennessee, Knoxville. University Microfilms International, Ann Arbor MI.

Hatch, D. Brad, Barbara J. Heath, and Lauren K. McMillan
2014 Reassessing the Hallowes Site: Conflict and Settlement in the 17th-Century Potomac Valley. *Historical Archaeology* 48(4):46–75.

Hatch, D. Brad, Lauren K. McMillan, and Barbara J. Heath
2013 Archaeological Reassessment of the Hallowes Site (44WM6). Report submitted to the Virginia Department of Historic Resources by the Department of Anthropology, University of Tennessee, Knoxville.

Heath, Barbara J.
2016 Dynamic Landscapes: The Emergence of Formal Spaces in Colonial Virginia. *Historical Archaeology* 50(1):27–44.

Heath, Barbara J., Eleanor E. Breen, Dustin S. Lawson, and Daniel W. H. Brock, with contributions by Jonathan Baker and Kandace Hollenbach
2009 Archaeological Reassessment of Newman's Neck (44NB180). Report submitted to the Virginia Department of Historic Resources by the Department of Anthropology, University of Tennessee, Knoxville.

Kansa, Sarah, and Eric Kansa
2011 Enhancing Humanities Research Productivity in a Collaborative Data Sharing Environment. *White Paper NEH Division of Preservation and Access.* https://alexandriaarchive.org/wp-content/uploads/2011/09/white_paper_PK _50072.pdf. Accessed 22 December 2016.

King, Julia A.
2010 The Challenges of Dissemination: Accessing Archaeological Data and Interpretations. In *Archaeology and Cultural Resource Management: Visions for the Future,* Lynne Sebastian and William D. Lipe, editors, pp. 141–167. School for Advanced Research. Santa Fe NM.

Kintigh, Keith W., Jeffrey H. Altschul, Ann P. Kinzig, W. Fredrick Limp, William K. Michener, Jeremy A. Sabloff, Edward J. Hackett, Timothy A. Kohler, Bertram Ludäscher, and Clifford A. Lynch
2015 Cultural Dynamics, Deep Time, and Data Planning Cyberinfrastructure Investments for Archaeology. *Advances in Archaeological Practice* 3(1):1–15.

Kratz, John Ernest, and Carly Strasser
2015 Researcher Perspectives on Publication and Peer Review of Data. *PLOS One* 10(2).

Kvamme, Kenneth
1999 Recent Developments and Directions in Geographic Information Systems. *Journal of Archaeological Research* 7(2):153–201.

MacFarland, Kathryn, and Arthur W. Vokes
2016 Dusting Off the Data, Curating and Rehabilitating Archaeological Legacy and Orphaned Collections. *Advances in Archaeological Practice* 4(2):161–175.

Marquardt, William H., Anta Montet-White, and Sandra C. Scholtz

1982 Resolving the Crisis in Archaeological Collections Curation. *American Antiquity* 47(2):409–418.

Maryland Archaeological Conservation Lab

2002 Diagnostic Artifacts in Maryland. https://www.jefpat.org/diagnostic/index .htm. Accessed 23 December 2016.

McManamon, Francis P., Keith W. Kintigh, and Adam Brin

2010 Digital Antiquity and the Digital Archaeological Record (tDAR): Broadening Access and Ensuring Long-term Preservation for Digital Archaeological Data. *CSA Newsletter* 23(2). http://csanet.org/newsletter/fall10/nlf1002 .html. Accessed 22 May 2018.

McMillan, Lauren K.

2015 *Community Formation and the Development of a British Atlantic Identity in the Chesapeake: An Archaeological and Historical Study of the Tobacco Pipe Trade in the Potomac River Valley ca. 1630–1730*. Doctoral dissertation, Department of Anthropology, University of Tennessee, Knoxville. University Microfilms International, Ann Arbor MI.

McMillan, Lauren K., D. Brad Hatch, and Barbara J. Heath

2015 Dating and Chronology at the John Hallowes Site (44WM6), Westmoreland County, Virginia. *Northeast Historical Archaeology* 43:18–36.

Mooney, Hailey, and Mark P. Newton

2012 The Anatomy of a Data Citation: Discovery, Reuse, and Credit. *Journal of Librarianship and Scholarly Communication* 1(1):1.

Mouer, L. Daniel

1988 In the Realm of "The Rebel": Archaeology of Nathaniel Bacon's Brick House at Curles Plantation. *Henrico County Historical Society Magazine* 12:3–20.

1991 Digging a Rebel's Homestead. *Archaeology* 44(4): 54–57.

1997 The "Mansions" of Curles Plantation, ca. 1630–1860. *Henrico County Historical Society Magazine* 21:46–77.

1998 Thomas Harris, Gent., as Related by His Second Sonne. *Historical Archaeology* 32(1):4–14.

National Endowment for the Humanities

2016 Data Management Plans for NEH Office of Digital Humanities Proposals and Awards. https://www.neh.gov/files/grants/data_management_plans _2018.pdf. Accessed 22 December 2016.

National Science Foundation

2013 Chapter II: Proposal Preparation Instructions. http://www.nsf.gov/pubs /policydocs/pappguide/nsf13001/gpg_2.jsp#iic2j. Accessed 22 December 2016.

Sullivan, Lynne, and S. Terry Childs

2003 *Curating Archaeological Collections: From the Field to the Repository.* Altamira Press. Walnut Creek CA.

W3C

2015 Metadata Vocabulary for Tabular Data. W3C Recommendations. https://www.w3.org/tr/2015/rec-tabular-metadata-20151217/. Accessed 12 December 2016.

White, Esther C., Eleanor Breen, Amelia Chisolm, Dee DeRoche, Lori Lee, Bernard Means, and Elizabeth Moore

2012 A Survey of Archaeological Repositories in Virginia. http://cova-inc.org/resources/COVAcollectionsSurvey.pdf. Accessed 6 December 2016.

White House

2013 Increasing Access to the Results of Federally Funded Scientific Research. https://obamawhitehouse.archives.gov/sites/default/files/microsites/ostp/ostp_public_access_memo_2013.pdf. Accessed 3 April 2017.

SIX

Balancing Access, Research, and Preservation

Conservation Concerns for Old Collections

EMILY WILLIAMS AND KATHERINE RIDGWAY

"Old," "orphan," and "archived" are all terms used for collections that were built up in a somewhat undefined but distant past. These terms imply different levels of care and/or research potential. Although in the field of archaeology the term "old" has a certain cachet (think of the many times artifacts and sites are referred to as "the oldest example of x"), when heritage professionals think of old collections we frequently think of collections that were excavated using antiquated methodology, where the documentation may be poor or even absent and the materials used to house the collection may not be up to modern standards. The term "orphan" or "orphaned" may connote a lack of intellectual guidance. Although the collection may once have been cared for, it no longer enjoys the protection and intellectual engagement of its creator. In short, the terms "old" and "orphaned" summon up images of the last scene in *Raiders of the Lost Ark*: countless rows of boxes, of all types and sizes, silently stored in a forgotten warehouse no longer accessible and no longer actively contributing to archaeological research.

Similarly, the term "repository" (often used to describe large archaeological storage facilities that house these older collections), with its roots in the word "repose," has an equally passive quality. The collections in them slumber, no longer actively engaging with the field that labored to create them. In the United Kingdom the term "archive" is more frequently used than "repository" (Swain 2010). "Archived" collections sound a little more positive. We think of libraries and of paper collections, and the connotation is one of organization, acid-free storage, controlled lighting, and well-organized materials either already actively contributing to scholarly pursuits or waiting in anticipation of the new research questions they can answer. The question for older assemblages, then, is how to move them from their status as "old" and/or "orphaned" collections to the status of "archived" collections.

The process consists of achieving a delicate balance between preserving the materials in the collection, facilitating research on them and on the sites from which they came, and promoting and managing access to the materials. It is an undertaking that involves many individuals with varied expertise, from archaeologists and collections managers to scientists, and it is one to which conservators can make significant contributions as well.

Older collections have many of the same preservation issues as freshly excavated materials; soluble salts and active corrosion may threaten the stability and/or the morphology of individual materials, necessitating intervention. Similarly, archival housing materials are needed to ensure that artifacts are contained, supported, and stabilized. Older collections also present unusual opportunities to bring new analytical techniques to bear and to assess the historic preservation methods employed. What is unique about them is the chance they afford to pause, plan, collaborate, and consider the process of collection building, and to think about information retrieval in ways that are sometimes difficult to achieve and maintain in the dynamic and rapidly changing environment of an ongoing excavation. The following examples highlight some of the interesting conservation challenges and conundrums the authors have faced working with older collections.

Packaging, Pests, and Preservation: The Accessioning of the Hatch Site

Each "old" collection presents its own unique challenges, informed by the way it was excavated, the quirks of its excavator, and its past treatment. Packaging issues are generally common to all collections excavated prior to the 1990s (as well as some excavated since then). Addressing these issues is sometimes as simple as rebagging an artifact, but occasionally the challenges are more complex and require different approaches.

Leverette "Lefty" Gregory, Jr., a longtime Virginia archaeologist, passed away in July 2015. His death left several "orphaned" collections, including the materials from the Hatch site (44PG0051), located near Hopewell, Virginia. Fieldwork at this important Woodland period site was carried out during the 1970s and 1980s. The artifacts from the collection, both prehistoric and historic, fill over 550 Hollinger boxes and consist of a wide variety of materials. Following excavation, the collection was stored in three well-maintained sheds on Gregory's property. Realizing the importance of the collection, his widow, Eve, was anxious to ensure that the collection would be kept together and that it would go to a repository that could properly care for it and provide continual access for future research and exhibits. She offered to donate it to the Virginia Department of Historic Resources (VDHR).

VDHR, like many archaeological archives, has limited storage space; however, it was widely felt that this substantial collection was too important not to accept. The first step in the acquisition process was for a team from VDHR, consisting of the state archaeologist, the senior curator, and the conservator, to visit the property, assess the collection, and begin to formulate plans for the move. The preliminary visit was carried out in mid-April 2016. The sheds and artifacts appeared to be in good condition. The primary concern was the condition of the packaging and storage materials. Archival boxes had been used mainly, but they had become heavily infested by a number of pests over the decades of storage. Silverfish had damaged many of the paper labels as well as the exteriors of many of the boxes. There was also evidence of carpet beetles and spiders. Wasps and mice had built nests in the boxes. Boxes had become weakened and the labeling was compromised. One box had been almost entirely consumed. The level of infestation and the deterioration to the packaging materials posed a risk to the safe movement of the collections (Figure 6), but

FIGURE 6. Bag from Hatch site near Hopewell, Virginia. Note the pest damage
to the labels. Damage to the plastic bag as a result of pests caused the bag
to fall apart when lifted. (Photo: Katherine Ridgway)

it also threatened the safety of collections already stored at VDHR,
as well as to the collections of the Virginia Museum of History and
Culture (VMHC), with which VDHR shares a building.

Some of these pests, such as spiders and wasps, do not eat collections, but others pose a direct threat. Silverfish thrive in warm,
moist environments (the sort common in sheds all along the mid-
Atlantic during the summer). They are partial to starch-based adhesives and will often feed on labels made with these materials, leading
to the loss of crucial information about collections. Carpet beetles
are especially fond of materials containing animal proteins (such as
horn, wool, and silk). While these materials are underrepresented
in most archaeological collections, they are very common in decorative arts collections, such as those housed at VMHC. Since carpet beetles also feed on the carcasses of dead animals and insects,
their presence, like that of the spiders, also indicated the extent of
the infestation. Not only were there live pests, but they were dying in
significant enough numbers to attract and support secondary pests.
The threat posed by the mice lay both in their nesting habits and in
their urine. Mice need only a few minutes to chew through a large
number of materials in search of an ideal nesting spot. They will tear

up paper, cardboard, and polyethylene bags in order to create nesting materials, and their urine can act as an attractant to other pests, such as carpet beetles, which will often eat urine-soaked cellulosic materials. In all these cases, it is the potential loss of vital information about the sites and the contexts from which the artifacts were recovered that poses the greatest threat for archaeological assemblages. It is this information that gives archaeological collections their greatest value.

Clearly it was important to avoid moving these pests to VDHR, thus importing and spreading the infestation. Three options presented themselves as a means for mitigating the threat: quarantine, fumigation, and repackaging.

Quarantining or fumigating a collection is an expensive proposition, especially if both must be employed. Quarantining a single object (a step that many museums undertake when they suspect that an object might be infested) can be successfully carried out by wrapping the object in a thick polyethylene bag and carefully securing the opening. After several weeks, if the object is infested, frass and/or other materials should be visible in the bottom of the bag. Then a decision can be made about how to address the infestation. This form of quarantine is rarely an option for a large collection. Quarantining a collection requires holding it in an interim space that does not share any ducting or air exchange with the main collection space. Unless such a space was deliberately created when a repository was built, it is more feasible to use an off-site area. However, there are likely to be costs associated with this.

Once an infestation has been confirmed and isolated, removing the pests is the next step. Fumigation is one option. Few fumigants can safely be used on all materials. Some fumigants pose risks to collection materials, whereas others pose risks to both humans and the environment (Makos and Hawks 2014). In order to safely fumigate a collection, one must know what is in it, which may mean sorting through it or processing it first. This cannot be done in the main storage space because of the risk that any pests will seek new sources of food and the infestation will spread. Other techniques for eradicating pests, such as freezing and anoxia, are difficult to scale up to the size required for a large archaeological collection.

Given the extent of the infestation, it was clear that the boxes could not be brought into the building as is, but VDHR also faced constraints in terms of the time available for the move and the finances that could be devoted to it. It was important to develop a plan that safeguarded the collections and the vulnerable and crucial field notes and site reports that accompanied them. The plan also needed to be efficient and cost-effective and not place existing collections, either at VDHR or the VMHC, at increased risk of infestation.

VDHR staff had three days to move the collection. As the pests were primarily feeding on the housing materials rather than the artifacts themselves, the conservator decided that all the boxes should be replaced with new Hollinger boxes before they were moved, since insects can easily hide in the corrugations of archival boxes and eggs could be present on or in the old boxes. All paper items, such as field notes and paper bags, stored in the infested boxes were put into resealable polyethylene bags as a quarantine measure. The infested boxes were disposed of at a recycling center near the Gregorys' property, and the newly rehoused collections were moved to VDHR. Every possible effort was made to avoid cross-contaminating the new boxes at the site. Once the new boxes were placed on the shelves at VDHR, pest traps were placed around them to catch "escapees" and to alert staff to any continuing pest problems. This pseudo-quarantine approach may not be sufficient in all circumstances, and it is important to determine which pests are present, what their life cycle is, and what they may be feeding on in order to ensure success. In this instance, the approach worked well. Regular monitoring over six months did not reveal any evidence of new or increased pest activity. VDHR staff and volunteers can now take their time to properly rehouse this important collection, making it available for new research, exhibition, and conservation.

One other aspect of the packaging in the Hatch site collections is worthy of comment. In the 1970s and 1980s Riker mounts were commonly used to display artifacts. They are flat, glass-fronted cases filled with a soft polyester batting. The artifacts are typically held in place in the box using pressure. Material from the Hatch site was placed in these boxes to illustrate the types of materials found at the site and to illustrate its importance to Virginia history. The displays frequently mixed artifacts from several proveniences in one container. To further complicate matters, the numbered artifacts from the site had been glued to the batting, in many cases on the side bearing the artifact number. Although typed cards, featuring artifact descriptions and context numbers, had been added to the case, they included generic descriptions such as "three La Croix points from context 114, four Savannah points from context 120 and two Savannah points from context 125."

Removing the objects from the batting and reuniting them with their original context presented both a curatorial and a conservation challenge that could be solved only through interdisciplinary teamwork and collaboration. Although conservators can become very skilled in detecting the subtleties of object types they see frequently, in this case it was important for the archaeologist to distinguish between the types of objects and to help reidentify objects that may have been incorrectly identified in the first place. Similarly, where naming conventions had changed over the years, it was incumbent on the archaeologist to determine not only what the object was now identified as but what it might have been called at the time the Hatch site was excavated. For the conservator, the task was to minimize the loss of any labeling during the process of separating the artifact from the batting. Working under a microscope, using different lighting and recording techniques, and employing a range of solvents and mechanical techniques all aided this process. The project highlighted the sort of cross-disciplinary collaboration and detective work that is often needed to reunite older objects with their contexts and to preserve as much information about a site as possible.

Aging Gracefully? The Value of Historic Conservation Treatments

Like many older collections, the Hatch material contained some interesting examples of historical approaches to conservation. Some of these treatments, such as the stripped and overcleaned metals found on many mid-Atlantic sites, were products of their time and reflect as much about the history of historical archaeology as they do about conservation. They date to a period when archaeologists were focused on building typologies and reflect their need to see the morphology of the piece unencumbered by any overlying corrosion. Approaches to the treatment of metals changed in the late 1980s and 1990s as conservators realized that the original form of the piece was often preserved in its corrosion layers. Important information, such as the presence of secondary metal coatings or mineral-preserved organics, was frequently removed with the corrosion layers in those well-intentioned early conservation efforts. Today treated archaeological metal looks substantially different from its earlier counterparts. This is not the only reason that historical treatments may be of interest.

Conservation methods are predicated on the knowledge that all materials age and deteriorate. To be successful in their treatments, conservators rely on a detailed understanding of how the materials from which an object is made deteriorate and how the materials we add to it fare over time. This understanding is informed by observation, analysis, and experimentation. Before any treatment material is adopted by the field, it is tested. Frequently these tests include accelerated aging experiments, which provide indicators as to how the material will perform over time. Accelerating aging tests cannot substitute for observing actual aging over a range of environmental conditions.

At Colonial Williamsburg we are lucky to have nearly 90 years of archaeological conservation treatments represented in our collections. The ability to study and evaluate these treatments guides our storage decisions and our retreatment efforts, and it also informs our current conservation efforts, helping us to recommend more effective treatments for our collections and those at other sites. Two recent projects highlight the ways we have reevaluated past treatments. The first project centers around the reassessment of surface coatings used on archaeological iron. The second project involves an international study to reassess alum-treated waterlogged wood. Both projects evolved from a series of collection-wide condition surveys conducted on Williamsburg's archaeological collection.

One of the ways conservators assess the well-being of collections is through condition surveys. Surveys act a little like audits; they help to identify work to be done (for example, which pieces need stabilization) and help to identify areas where we are succeeding. Surveys can be material-specific or may be conducted across all the materials in a collection. They can be written to target very specific issues that a conservator is seeking additional information about, or they can be designed to give the broadest possible overview of the collection. For larger collections it may be necessary to sample the collection. In such a case it is important to establish a strategy that is both representative and statistically valid.

Between 1998 and 2005 a series of material-specific surveys were conducted at Colonial Williamsburg. These surveys were specifically designed to assess the performance of past treatments. Condition was evaluated and linked to the manner in which the object had been treated. The goal was to identify trouble spots and to help better target retreatment efforts. For example, when the surveys identified a particular treatment regimen as routinely less stable than another method, retreatment of the materials in the first group was considered. If large quantities of objects were impacted, it was necessary to nuance the approach to allow for economies of effort and scale.

Among the many interesting findings from the survey, one discovery in particular influenced our current treatment practices. When conserving archaeological iron, it is customary to apply a surface coating near the end of the treatment. Such coatings are designed to slow down interactions between any exposed metal and environmental factors, but they also help to protect the material during handling. (Note: Although it is always preferable to wear gloves when handling archaeological metals to avoid transferring salts and other contaminants from one's skin to the metal surface, coatings may help to protect the metal from accidental contact.) A variety of materials have been used as surface coatings, but perhaps the two most popular ones involve wax (typically microcrystalline wax mixtures) and lacquer coatings (typically acrylic resins, such as Acryloid B-72). Both types of coating were used at Williamsburg between 1960 and 2000.

Interestingly the survey revealed that when all other factors were equal, the choice of surface coating had a significant impact on the long-term stability of the object. Iron coated with a lacquer coating was four times more stable than iron that was treated by identical methods and coated with microcrystalline wax. One reason for this may be the thickness and consequent weight of the wax coating, which leads to cracking of the coating, exposing the iron to the atmosphere. Even small openings in the coating lead to accelerated corrosion by concentrating oxygen and moisture at the opening and creating a concentration cell. This concentration results in pitting, stimulating the concentration cell and exacerbating the cycle. Also, wax is not as efficient a water vapor barrier as lacquers are (Horie 1987); therefore, over time moisture penetrates the coating, leading to renewed corrosion. Finally, it was noted that wax coatings are trickier to remove than lacquer coatings; the process is time-consuming and is never fully successful. As a result, it appeared that there may have been a slight retreatment bias; since the lacquer-coated items were easier to retreat, they may have been tackled more readily, especially when time was limited. This bias was not significant enough to account for the disparity in performance between the two coatings, but it did highlight how human factors can play a role in treatment decisions. The survey report recommended that an acrylic resin be used for all future surface coatings of archaeological iron. Although slightly glossy in comparison to wax, matting agents can be added to acrylic coatings; the coating has the added advantage of being easy to remove should the object require retreatment.

The recommendations from the iron survey resulted in a quick fix that could be easily implemented; this was not the case with the alum-treated wood. In the 1950s Colonial Williamsburg's conservator, John van Ness Dunton, began using the alum treatment to conserve waterlogged wood. Alum is soluble in water and, in solution, can penetrate the wood, replacing free and bound water and reinforcing the wood structure through the formation of alum crystals. Alum treatments were pioneered in Scandinavia as an attempt to bulk up the wood and prevent it from shrinking and collapsing during drying. This approach was popular in Norway, Sweden, and Denmark between the 1850s and 1960s but fell out of favor with the introduction of polyethylene glycol treatments in the 1960s. Alum-treated wood is problematic because the alum did not always penetrate the full thickness of the wood, leaving untreated areas in the core. Also, as the alum decomposes it releases acids, which can have a detrimental effect on the wood. In the past decade major research projects have been launched in Sweden and Norway to fully understand the deterioration processes and to develop new treatments (Braovac and Kutzke 2012; Häggström and Sandström 2013).

The material at Colonial Williamsburg represents one of the few pockets of alum-treated material outside Scandinavia. (A second one, also treated by Dunton, is located at Fortress Louisbourg in Canada.) Visually the Williamsburg wood is in better condition than many of the Scandinavian pieces, which raises many questions: Does the wood from Williamsburg simply look better because it was treated more recently than many of the Scandinavian samples? Does wood species influence preservation? Does the degree of deterioration prior to treatment impact the later condition of the wood? Initially it was thought that alum treatments were best suited to highly degraded wood, but wood from historic contexts in Williamsburg rarely falls into this category. Did Dunton alter the treatment in some manner that is not recorded in the treatment notes that he kept? What role does the posttreatment storage environment play in accelerating or slowing the degradation processes? The wood stored in Williamsburg has been kept in a fairly stable environment, while the Scandinavian wood was likely subject to greater fluctuations in relative humidity over its life.

We do not have answers to all these questions yet. The project is an ongoing one that illustrates the importance of considering not only a pocket of material treated by a particular technique but also relating it to other, similarly treated materials. Work at Colonial Williamsburg has focused on augmenting the information captured by the survey and establishing baseline condition reports for all our alum-treated wood. It is important that these reports list the same criteria as work done elsewhere to ensure that the results are comparable. We have also been collecting all the environmental data available from the storage area and working with European colleagues to analyze some of our samples using techniques that can be compared directly with the analyses they are undertaking. Some of the results to date have been surprising. Preliminary analyses carried out by scientists at the University of Pisa suggest that Dunton altered the treatment method from what he recorded. Although his treatment reports suggest that only alum was used, the analyzed samples contained both linseed oil and glycerol in addition to the alum, and the deterioration of the wood was markedly different from that found on comparable Scandinavian wood samples (Lucejko and Tamburini 2016). As a result of this project, we are learning more about the materials used to treat artifacts at Colonial Williamsburg and the transmission and adaptation of treatment methods.

Access, Diplomacy, and Conservation Education: The Conner's Midden Ceramic Collection

Studying every older treatment or treatment method does not always lead to changes in our approach to the conservation of archaeological materials. If that were the case, it would be nearly impossible to address the needs of recently excavated materials. Previously conserved materials may be able to teach in other ways. The ongoing retreatment of ceramics from the Conner's Midden site at VDHR is an excellent example of this.

Ceramics in older collections were often rinsed and then mended. Extraneous surface material, such as dirt, insoluble salts, and iron concretions, was rarely removed from historic ceramics. If these materials were present on the edges of sherds (as opposed to the face), they held the sherds apart and impeded the formation of a good bond between the fragments. Most ceramics were mended with whichever adhesive could be purchased near the site, including Duco cement and Elmer's glue. Duco cement is a cellulose nitrate–

based adhesive that initially has favorable properties but ages poorly. Over time it shrinks, yellows, and becomes brittle. Elmer's glue, a polyvinyl acetate–based adhesive, also yellows and loses strength as it ages. Not only does the yellowing impact the aesthetic qualities of the reconstructed vessel, but even handling becomes difficult as both adhesives age. Sherds have been known to drop off ceramics in storage, and ceramics mended with Duco cement in particular may come apart when handled.

The ceramics from Conner's Midden (44HA0011), a prehistoric site located in Halifax County, Virginia, were excavated during the 1950s. Thousands of pottery sherds eventually made their way to VDHR. The ceramics from the site represent particularly fine examples of prehistoric pottery that reflect a number of different functions, sizes, and shapes and clearly illustrate how various decorative techniques were used to enliven the surface. Many of the ceramics were mended by an archaeologist in the 1960s as part of a three-month-long project. He used Duco cement to mend the ceramics. He also used plaster as a fill material for two of the more notable objects, a very large prehistoric storage vessel and a small funerary urn. Due to the limited duration of the project, many of the mends were done quickly. Large amounts of adhesive were used, which sometimes led to poor alignment of the sherds, and a lot of adhesive was smeared on the surface. Recently there has been renewed interest in the ceramics from Conner's Midden, and the state archaeologist requested that the ceramics be reassessed and remended. In particular, he felt that the yellowing and failing Duco cement, as well as the presence of plaster fills on some, made them aesthetically unpleasant and was distracting both to the public who might see the ceramics on exhibit and to scholarly researchers (Figure 7).

Collections similar to the Conner's Midden ceramics exist in every archaeological archive. They represent hours of retreatment time. Without a stimulus, such as the state archaeologist's request, they may be fit into a conservator's schedule only as time permits. Realistically this means that a few pieces may be completed each year and the total rehabilitation of the site may stretch over the course

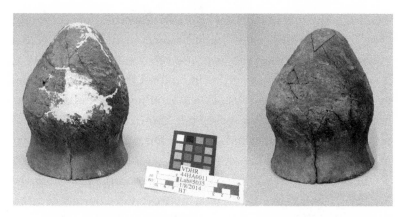

FIGURE 7. Ceramic from Connor's Midden. Image on left shows condition before retreatment; after-retreatment image on right. (Photo: Katherine Ridgway)

of the conservator's career. Moving a site like this to the front of the treatment queue inevitably means that other projects drop farther back. In a desire to avoid that, the retreatment of the Conner's Midden ceramics was approached as a teaching opportunity.

Staff at VDHR frequently partner with students at local universities as part of an internship program. Although these internships focus on many areas, some time is usually spent in the conservation lab. Conservators and archaeologists share a common interest in material culture but approach the material from different vantage points. Although the situation is different in Europe, in the United States few archaeological conservators train with archaeologists. This can contribute to miscommunication that is often compounded by the fact that few archaeological curricula even introduce conservation. For archaeology students, the opportunity to work with a conservator can serve as an introduction to the field.

The Conner's Midden ceramic project proved to be a particularly valuable tool for introducing students, at the beginnings of their careers, to the field of conservation. One of the perceptions that archaeologists often have about conservation is that conservators are inordinately slow and persnickety. The opportunity to undo past treatment decisions powerfully reinforced the reasons why it was important to choose the right adhesive, to align the joints well, and to allow time for mends to cure before adding additional weight to them. Although these steps may seem tedious or time-consuming, there are long-term payoffs. One element that was stressed during the student training was the necessity to reserve judgment on past treatments. Time may not have served certain treatments well, but it is important to understand that they were done with good intentions. Like the present generation, the one before was also interested in the preservation of the objects. They too wanted to learn from the artifacts and make them accessible to others. Remembering that those who interact with collections are motivated to do good helps to dispel another perception about conservation: that conservators exist solely to say no to archaeologists. Finding shared ground helps to build a foundation on which more successful solutions can be built.

Many interns have taken on a piece or two of the Conner's Midden collection as part of a larger learning experience. It has proven an effective way to teach many of the basic tenets of conservation while providing a hands-on experience with real artifacts. One of the archaeology interns reported going to a site after her time in the lab and being asked to mend ceramics with Elmer's glue. She was able to discuss different approaches with the archaeologists and share new materials and techniques with them.

Another intern, who had worked with Virginia Commonwealth University's Virtual Curation Unit, turned the experience into an opportunity to explore the potential of three-dimensional scanning and printing for mending ceramics. She mended three sherds the old-fashioned way, by carefully reversing the previous adhesive, cleaning the edges, and remending the ceramic fragments. She also attempted to mend them virtually. She scanned each piece separately and attempted to stitch them together. The three pieces she chose had a gap in the center when mended together, a feature that can be difficult for a 3D printer to interpret. She also scanned the sherds once she had physically mended them together in order to compare how close to reality her virtual mends came. She compared the time taken for both approaches and developed a cost-benefit analysis of the two techniques.

The goal was to see whether virtual mending might be an option when real mending was not an option for one reason or another. Although there are instances where 3D scanning has been used successfully to mend (or unmend) very high-profile artifacts, such as the *Forma Urbis Romae*, a marble map of ancient Rome, and Michelangelo's Florentine Pietà sculpture, her experiment confirmed that for the everyday mending of archaeological ceramics, the traditional methods still work best. Although neither approach was particularly quick or painless, she found that there were still advantages to being able to feel the fragments lock into place and to be able to subtly alter the orientation of abraded edges to confirm whether a mend was real. There is also a time savings once one builds a familiarity with the mending process that cannot be matched by the scanning process.

Investments, Inventorying, and Investigation

Another misconception about conservation is that it is always expensive. Both Colonial Williamsburg and VDHR employ an archaeological conservator. At these institutions remedial work on older collections is seen as part of the basic job description. Conservators may at times initiate or spearhead efforts to reevaluate collections, and at other times they may be available as consultants and curators on projects driven by archaeologists, curators, or external researchers. Most institutions lack a staff conservator, and access to one may be limited. A project undertaken recently at VDHR serves as a model for a different form of engagement. In 2016 funding became available for VDHR to hire inventory staff for a large-scale project, the ultimate goal of which was to increase access to the collection by barcoding it. Several temporary staff members were hired. Their job was to look at every box with artifacts in the collection and identify its location and provenience information. This provided a unique opportunity to obtain a snapshot of the collection's condition, a project that the conservator had not been able to undertake due to the size of the collection and the demands of other projects. At the inception of the project, the conservator taught staff members to identify common conservation concerns, such as inadequate housing material, corroding metals, pest issues, and tape on the surface of artifacts. These issues were noted during the inventory, and the list was given to the conservator to double check.

The inventory identified many action items that could be prioritized and some that could be addressed at a later date. Some were very straightforward and consisted simply of rehousing items. Many artifacts packed with silica gel were identified and could be added to a rotation for artifacts that need a dry environment. Other artifacts had more complicated problems. For example, several artifacts remained in jars of water even after several decades in storage! This raised questions about stability, health, and safety factors and whether the object should be immediately removed for treatment.

Tying the process to an existing initiative reduced the conservator's involvement substantially. Armed with a list of known issues, the conservator could go straight to the artifacts in question and create a triage list of what to treat sooner rather than later and what could be delayed. Rather than having the conservator involved the whole time, she was involved for a minimal amount of time: a day of training at the start of the project and the equivalent of two days answering queries. Depending on the type of problems found, the conservator's involvement during the project could have been adapted to provide training about rehousing or small stabilization measures. Small upfront investments such as these can produce well-thought-out lists of conservation needs that can be effective for fundraising. In the late 1990s Alexandria Archaeology leveraged a similar project into an "Adopt an Artifact" program. Visitors were given the opportunity to fund small-scale conservation treatments. In acknowledgment of their support they were sent before- and after-treatment images of the object. Objects were displayed with a plaque acknowledging the funder's patronage. Similarly, the lists produced from projects like the inventory project often serve as supporting materials for successful grant applications.

Research, Analysis, Interpretation, and Integration:
The Anderson Armoury Tin Shop Project

Often new excavations provide opportunities to reexamine older collections and to integrate them into new conceptual frameworks. Materials analysis, a key component of conservation practice, often plays a role in this reinterpretation. This was true during recent excavations in Williamsburg at the Anderson Blacksmith site.

The blacksmith shop is one of the most popular trade shops in Colonial Williamsburg's Historic Area. It was first reconstructed in the 1980s when attention focused primarily on James Anderson's career as a smith. Subsequently years of research by archaeologists, architects, historians, and Colonial Williamsburg's master blacksmith, Ken Schwarz, have uncovered new and exciting information about the period when Anderson operated the Public Armoury for the newly independent Commonwealth of Virginia. Anderson's recently discovered daybook indicates that the Armoury engaged in a broad range of repair and production activities. These included the manufacture of iron items and, beginning in 1778, the creation of tinned vessels to help provision the troops during the American Revolution. In 1780, when Virginia's capital moved to Richmond, Anderson closed up shop and followed suit.

The site has been extensively excavated over the years; the forge area was excavated from 1975 to 1976, and the yard area was excavated in the 1980s and again in the early 1990s. In 2000 further excavations in the yard uncovered the southwest corner of a structure. Significant amounts of sheet iron recovered from this excavation had evidence of a secondary metal on the surface. The conservation lab was asked to test samples of the sheet metal to determine the composition of the secondary metal. Of the 24 samples tested, 14 were positive for tin. These results, in combination with some of the other archaeological evidence, led the project archaeologist, Katherine Schupp, to tentatively suggest that this structure might have been the location of a tin shop (henceforth referred to as the "2000 tin shop"). A subsequent discovery of a document referring to a tin shop on another part of the Anderson site (henceforth referred to as the "Stith tin shop") prompted a reevaluation of the archaeological evidence. In 2010 the archaeologists returned to the site to clarify which of the two areas served as the Public Armoury's tin shop.

Tinsmiths rely on a discrete set of tools. Compared to ironworking and the large footprints left by brick forges, they do not leave a substantial architectural footprint. In the absence of a clear, identifying architectural feature, the artifacts, particularly the sheet metal, appeared to hold the key to identifying the shop. The archaeological conservation lab was asked to consider ways of analyzing the tin from the site. Because there was tinned sheet metal at the site of the "2000 tin shop," it was important to determine whether a background level of tinned material might be present across the site. It was plausible that such material might not have been identified in the earliest excavations because the project archaeologists were focused on the iron production activities at the site and were not thinking about tin production.

Therefore we pulled all of the sheet metal from both the 2010 and 2000 tin shop excavations as well as from the excavations carried out in the yard areas in the 1980s and early 1990s. Each piece was visually examined, described, and weighed, and a Bruker Tracer III-V portable x-ray fluorescence spectrophotometer (pxRF) was used to analyze the surfaces of the pieces. The pxRF proved to be more sensitive than visual examination and helped to identify a number of tinned iron fragments where the secondary metal was not visible due to corrosion or surface dirt. Overall more than 14 kg of tin were analyzed over the course of several months!

As expected, there was clear evidence of tinned iron from the "2000 tin shop" area. Much greater quantities of tinned iron were located at the site of the "Stith tin shop." No tinned iron was identified in the yard area from the Public Armoury period. These results suggest that the tin-related activity evident in both areas is related to a discrete rather than diffuse set of activities; in other words, the activity was centered on the two structures and did not spill into the yard. Given the comparative amounts of tin between the two structures, we posited that the Stith shop was the area of primary activity, and the "2000 tin shop" served as a secondary or seasonal workspace.

Another question we were interested in answering was whether the waste from tinsmithing could reliably be separated from degrading tinplate objects, such as tin cans. If not, we risked solely proving the presence of tinplate rather than the manufacture of tinned items. Therefore all of the tinned samples were x-rayed. Examination of the x-radiographs showed that there is also a discernible difference in the way a tinned vessel deteriorates and the shapes of the waste fragments. Typically waste fragments retain harder edges, whereas the fragments of a disintegrating vessel, or tin can, are more amorphous due to the manner in which they tear or break away from the vessel. Additionally, and rather surprisingly, we found that vessels break up less readily than one might suppose. Frequently they are crushed, but often they retain their form. The presence of rolled edges also indicated a finished piece, such as a can.

Anderson's daybook recorded the production of a large number of camp kettles, plates, dishes, bowls, mugs, and coffeepots, as well as storage containers and miscellaneous camp equipment, such as lanterns (Kenneth Schwarz 2012, pers. comm.) However, the volume of tinned iron, less than a third of all the sheet iron analyzed, from each structure seemed low. To determine whether this was just a case of modern expectations being at odds with 18th-century production levels, we analyzed the tinned material from one additional site: Monticello's Building L. Building L was excavated between 1979 and 1981 and is the only other 18th-century American tin shop that has been excavated. It was the site of a short-lived tinsmithing experiment; like the Public Armoury, tin production at Building L took place for only a two-year period. The same methodology was applied to the Building L sheet metal as was used on the Anderson site sheet metal, allowing us not only to compare surviving materials but also to consider disposal patterns. The material from all three sites showed a high preponderance of rectangular snips and the triangular spandrels. A smaller proportion of the material had soldered edges, suggesting that manufacture rather than repair was the focus of the work at both sites. Also, the largest concentrations of tin fragments seemed to come from post holes or other holes. This led us to speculate that because tin scraps are quite sharp, perhaps they were collected and buried deliberately.

Integrating material from recent excavations as well as from past excavations, both at Colonial Williamsburg and Monticello, allowed us to look at tinplate, a fairly ubiquitous material on historic period sites, with fresh eyes. We were able to see patterns that had not been evident previously and develop new working protocols that will inform our approaches to other areas of the site and perhaps to other craft sites. The study reinforced the importance of retaining archaeological materials for future examination, and the shared discussions between archaeologists and conservators throughout the project led to more integrated and nuanced approaches to the excavation of the site and the study of artifacts coming from it.

Deaccessioning as a Means of Preservation?

Although important discoveries clearly still wait to be made in older collections, it is also important to consider the management of these collections. Many archaeologists still adhere to the concept of "preservation by record" (Swain 2010). This notion specifies that since archaeological excavation cannot be repeated, there is a duty to preserve everything from a site (i.e., the record of the site) so that it can be reexamined and studied by subsequent generations. A product of the early 20th century, when there were deeply rooted beliefs about the objectivity of archaeology, this notion and its corollary, that once in storage the objects must be kept safe from deterioration forevermore, have contributed to sustainability issues for archaeological collections (Swain 2010). Preserving ever-growing collections in perpetuity requires a considerable commitment of money and personnel. Staffing is needed to migrate and safeguard records, to facilitate access for researchers, to conserve materials, and to rehouse collections as storage materials reach their natural lifespans. Similarly, although advances in preventive conservation have improved our ability to stabilize large numbers of artifacts by maintaining the correct environmental parameters, resources are needed to maintain building envelopes, to replace obsolete or broken HVAC equipment, and to meet the energy costs associated with running such systems. The expectation that collections can grow unchecked also puts a strain on the physical spaces within which they are housed. It is unrealistic to expect that collections can move to ever larger repositories as they outgrow each space. As facilities reach their capacity or extend beyond them, overcrowding begins to have a detrimental effect on the collections and the volume of curated materials can inhibit access.

As collections grow, it may be necessary to look at targeted deaccessioning and/or alternative storage solutions as a way to address these issues. One solution may lie in reburial. Reburial is increasingly being carried out in Europe to safeguard marine sites as well as waterlogged terrestrial sites. The technique seeks to emulate the original depositional environment and thereby create a storage environment with preservation properties that meet or exceed a "normal" museum storage environment. Treatment and long-term maintenance costs are not incurred, which may be advantageous, but a disadvantage lies in the interconnectivity of sites and their environments. For example, research at Starr Carr, a Neolithic site in England and one of the pioneering sites of the reburial movement, has shown that drainage miles away has had a negative effect on site preservation (High 2014). Other disadvantages lie in the lengthy analyses needed to truly understand and re-create the predisturbance environment and the fact that optimal reburial methods are still being defined.

In 2007 Colonial Williamsburg's bulk archaeological collection was in the process of being moved from an aged and overcrowded facility to one that offered better environmental controls and adequate space for long-term growth. Near the end of the move, 50 pallets of architectural materials excavated from the Historic Area were transferred to the Department of Archaeological Research. Recovered prior to the use of stratigraphic excavation at Williamsburg, the material consisted largely of brick and stone fragments from building foundations. The material was not cataloged and was housed in pine crates that had clearly not been accessed in many years, judging by the mice nests, snakeskins, and other detritus in them. Many of the pine crates and the wooden pallets they rested on were disintegrating, the result of action by powderpost beetles. In total, the material represented over 5,000 cubic feet of storage, or approximately 45% of the budgeted long-term growth space. In considering the material and its information potential against that of the archaeological collection as a whole it became clear that there was an imbalance that posed a risk to the long-term preservation of the archaeological collection. The architectural material required huge amounts of curatorial time to catalog it and make it accessible for researchers and scholars. Furthermore scarce resources were needed to rehouse the material in archival packaging, a process that would create a larger footprint because of spacing and weight factors, and divert attention from other objects in more dire need of stabilization. Viewing the archaeological collection holistically it could be argued that the needs of the architectural collection were out of balance with the collection as a whole, particularly given its collection history and lack of true provenience. To address its needs meant prioritizing this material above objects generated by systematic stratified excavation and diverting resources from other projects. To ignore its needs imperiled other artifacts in the collection in both the short term, by putting them at risk of pest infestation, and in the longer term, due to overcrowding and the pressures that it exerts on a collection.

It was necessary to find a solution quickly. At the time, the archaeologists were excavating a site in the historic area with a large brick-lined cellar, and it was proposed that we sort through the material, select nondiagnostic pieces, and rebury them at the site. This course of action took advantage of the durability of the materials and recognized the fact that much of the material might be of little research value under current conditions, but retained the option that should circumstances change, the material could be excavated and studied. It is not an approach that we might have felt as comfortable adopting had the materials been more prone to deterioration during burial or had they been associated with tightly dated contexts.

The particulars of the reburial project have been published elsewhere (Williams 2011), so only a brief description is provided here. Items were chosen for reburial based on a number of criteria, including size, lack of diagnostic features, redundancy, and condition. Samples of even the most ordinary broken brick, stone, and mortar were retained for testing, comparison with other examples in the archaeological collection, and a general understanding of all materials represented in the different groupings. Whole brick, shaped brick, stone with any markings, attachments, finished edges, wear marks, or other use and construction evidence were all retained. Of the items selected for reburial, 91% were stone fragments less than 4 in. in dimension. The items to be reburied were placed in sound crates, grouped by site with spacing between them to aid future recovery, and covered with engineering sand prior to the backfill of the cellar site (Figure 8).

Although one of the disadvantages of reburial when compared to storage in an archive is the loss of access, in this case the limitations placed on accessibility were offset by the preservation gains made by the collection as a whole. In the 1930s, as the Foundation sought to restore Williamsburg's colonial heritage and appearance, the architectural materials provided a valuable link to the city's physical past. Over 80 years of subsequent archaeological excavations have generated an enormous research collection that provides insight into every aspect of the city's history and that can answer broader questions of how people lived and worked in Colonial Williamsburg. As new collections are generated, old collections must be reassessed to ensure that preservation goals, accessibility, storage limitations, and research potential are all considered and evaluated. The need to reassess collections on a periodic basis is a basic tenet of collections building within the museum community, but it is one that is often ignored by the archaeological community, where preservation by record has become the norm. Reburial of materials that currently hold no tangible research or scientific value offers a solution that balances the needs of the collections manager and facility with those of the archaeological community, preserving those materials for future investigation as technology advances. Conservators have traditionally shied away from making value judgments about artifacts or col-

FIGURE 8. Reburial site prior to backfilling.
(Photo: Colonial Williamsburg Foundation)

lections, although there is growing recognition that decisions about what to treat and how to treat it are based on just such judgments and may ultimately impact the artifact's worth, both financial and informational (Cane 2009). While archaeologists and curators have greater insight into the significance of individual finds or groups of finds (particularly as these change from site to site and era to era), conservators have unique perspectives to add about the condition of artifacts, their long-term stability, and their scientific potential.

While reburial offered a viable solution in this case, it may not be suitable in all situations. Like any treatment, there is a danger that actions taken to mitigate one risk may impose a new one. Reburial is not as final as deaccessioning, but it necessitates long-term involvement from both archaeologists and conservators in order to ensure its sustainability. Projects, such as the innovative Reburial and Analyses of Archaeological Remains project in Sweden (Bergstrand and Nyström-Godfrey 2007), which set out to look at the deterioration of reburied archaeological materials over a 50-year period, have experienced funding issues the further they moved away from the initial reburial. Similarly there is a danger that officials and policymakers can overlook a buried collection in future plans since it is "out of sight, out of mind." When this happens the reburial site may become nothing more than an artifact dump. There is also the perennial concern that reburial may create false sites that will confuse archaeologists in the future.

Conclusions

Perhaps the greatest advantage in working with an older collection is the opportunity it offers to slow the archaeological process and think as a team about how to approach and mine its full potential. During an active excavation the pace can be frenetic and the work of specialists may lag behind that of the excavators. Everyone works on a piece of the puzzle, but it can be hard for them to see the whole; it's a little like the story of the blind men and the elephant. With an older collection, a more unified approach can be taken. Research questions from a wide variety of areas can be discussed and brought to bear. In many ways the collaborative teamwork these collections engender enriches not only the project at hand but numerous others. As shared understandings are developed, new avenues of research are also identified that have the potential to inform not only the collection at hand but also future excavations.

Each of the older collections discussed in this chapter held surprises, inspiration, and a rich trove of information. The widely aired Capitol One commercial asks, "What's in your wallet?," but we think a better question is "What's in your (old) collection?"

Acknowledgments

We would like to thank the many archaeologists, conservators, and interns with whom we have partnered to explore the older collections at both our institutions. It truly does take a village.

References

Bergstrand, Thomas, and Inger Nyström-Godfrey (editors)
2007   *Reburial and Analyses of Archaeological Remains: Studies on the Effect of Reburial on Archaeological Materials Performed in Marstrand, Sweden 2002–2005.* Bohusläns Museum och Studio Vastsvensk Konservering. Uddevalla, Sweden.

Braovac, Susan, and Hartmut Kutzke

2012   Past Conservation Treatments and Their Consequences: The Oseberg Find as a Case Study. In *Proceedings of the 11th ICOM-CC Group on Wet Organic Archaeological Materials Conference, Greenville 2010*, Kristiane Straetkvern and Emily Williams, editors, pp. 481–496. ICOM-CC Wet Organics Archaeological Materials Group. Greenville NC.

Cane, Simon

2009   Why Do We Conserve? Developing Understanding of Conservation as a Cultural Construct. In *Conservation Principles, Dilemmas and Uncomfortable Truths*, Alison Richmond and Alison Bracker, editors, pp. 163–176. Butterworth Heinemann. London.

Häggström, Carola, and Tom Sandström (editors)

2013   *Alum-Treated Archaeological Wood: Characterization and Re-conservation.* Swedish National Heritage Board. Stockholm.

High, Kirsty

2014   Fading Star: Understanding Accelerated Decay of Organic Remains at Star Carr. Doctoral dissertation, Department of Chemistry, University of York, England.

Horie, Charles Velson

1987   *Materials for Conservation: Organic Consolidants, Adhesives and Coatings.* Butterworth Heinemann. London.

Lucejko, Jeannette, and Diego Tamburini

2016   Py(HMDS)-GC/MS Analysis of Wooden Samples Treated with Alum, Linseed Oil and Glycerol. Unpublished report on file in the Department of Conservation, Colonial Williamsburg Foundation VA.

Makos, Kathryn, and Catherine Hawks

2014   Collateral Damage: Unintended Consequences of Vapor-Phase Organic Pesticides, with Emphasis on p-dichlorobenzene and Naphthalene. Museums Pests. http://museumpests.net/wp-content/uploads/2014/05/4-1-Hawks -and-Makos-paper-formatted.pdf. Accessed 16 November 2016.

Swain, Hedley

2010   A Change in Philosophy for the Care of Archaeological Collections? In *The Conservation of Archaeological Materials: Current Trends and Future Directions*, Emily Williams and Claire Peachey, editors, pp 145–151. Archaeopress. Oxford.

Williams, Emily

2011   Deep Storage: Reburial as a Conservation Tool. *Objects Specialty Group Postprints* 18:25–31. American Institute for Conservation. http://resources .conservation-us.org/wp-content/uploads/sites/8/2015/02/osg018-03.pdf. Accessed 2 December 2016.

PART 2

New Research with Archaeological Collections

[SEVEN]

Reanalyzing, Reinterpreting, and Rediscovering the Appamattucks Community

D. BRAD HATCH AND LAUREN K. MCMILLAN

Communities in the 17th-century Chesapeake experienced a sex ratio of six men to every woman, an average age of death at 48 years, an average age of marriage in the mid- to late 20s, and a population dominated and reproducing through immigration rather than natural increase (Morgan 1975; Horn 1979; Walsh 1979; Menard 1988). Many historians have noted that these factors, among others, hindered the formation and reproduction of stable Chesapeake communities, causing a great deal of imbalance and upheaval during this time period (Morgan 1975; Carr and Walsh 1977; Horn 1994). Recent archaeological research in the Potomac Valley has challenged the notion that social, demographic, and political upheavals were hindrances to community cohesion (King 2011; Hatch 2015a; Heath 2017; McMillan 2015a). Rather people along the Potomac were quick to adapt to these new circumstances and used them to help form community bonds within and outside of the Chesapeake region. Reanalysis of old archaeological collections has allowed researchers to rediscover these communities and provide new interpretations of 17th-century Chesapeake society. Using one of these communities, the Appamattucks community, we show how the process of reanalyzing old collections has led to new insights about life along the Potomac in the 17th century. The Appamattucks community settled on the southern shore of the Potomac River in modern-day Westmoreland County, with boundaries that stretched from Mattox Creek to Nomini Bay. A group of English colonists formed the community; many came from Maryland around 1647 as a result of Ingle's Rebellion. These men and women arrived with, or quickly formed, strong social, political, and familial ties, seen in both the historical and the archaeological records.

Prior to 1990 professional and avocational archaeologists excavated several archaeological sites within the historic Appamattucks community, including the John Washington site (44W M204), the Henry Brooks site (44W M205), and Clifts Plantation (44W M33). The history and archaeology of two additional "orphan collections," the John Hallowes (44W M6) and Nomini Plantation (44W M12) sites, both within the heart of this community, serve as an example of how the people in the region adapted to the unique circumstances of the Chesapeake, forged connections, and passed down ideologies through multiple generations (Map 3). These two sites, whose analysis is the focus of this chapter, serve as excellent examples of the amount of rich data that can be gathered from previously excavated but never analyzed archaeological collections. Through the examination of the material remains left by the people who occupied these sites over 300 years ago, which were then excavated more than 40 years ago, combined with close readings of historical records, we learned how kinship, economic connections, and material culture played major roles in the ultimate success of the community at Appamattucks.

This chapter draws on the results of several larger collections-based research projects conducted in the Potomac River Valley, beginning in 2008. Barbara Heath at the University of Tennessee has spent nearly a decade actively revisiting collections from previously excavated 17th-century sites on the Northern Neck of Virginia in Westmoreland and Northumberland counties (Heath et al., this volume). These sites include the Newman's Neck site (44NB180), the John Hallowes site, and Coan Hall (44NB11), where she is actively excavating one of the oldest European sites on the Northern Neck (Heath et al. 2009; Hatch et al. 2013, 2014; McMillan et al. 2014; Heath 2016, 2017).

Research in this chapter was also conducted as part of a National Endowment for the Humanities funded research grant, *Colonial Encounters: The Lower Potomac River Valley at Contact, 1500–1720*

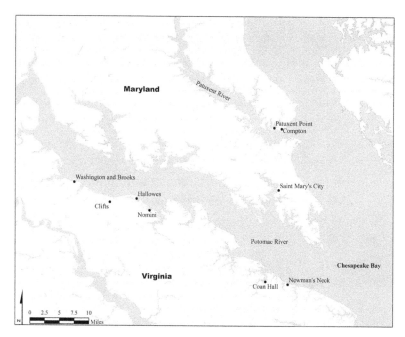

MAP 3. Archaeological sites in the Chesapeake region.
(Map: Lauren K. McMillan, adapted from a map by Andrew Wilkins)

AD (http://colonialencounters.org/index.aspx), under the direction of Julia King (2011) of St. Mary's College of Maryland. For this project, scholars from various institutions cataloged or recataloged data from 34 previously excavated Native American and European colonial sites on both the Maryland and the Virginia sides of the Potomac River.

Finally, both Hatch and McMillan have used data from previously excavated sites, several of which, although curated, had never been fully cataloged or analyzed, including the Nomini and Hallowes collections. Hatch (2015a) explored the creation and maintenance of manly identity and authority in the early modern Potomac River Valley, focusing on the material culture of foodways. McMillan (2015a) investigated community formation in the Potomac River Valley through an examination of imported colonial-made clay tobacco pipes, focusing on the impacts of politics and conflict on trade and exchange among European colonists in Virginia and Maryland.

Reanalysis of these collections provides an opportunity to apply modern analytical techniques and interpretive frameworks to older collections. While many of these collections reflect knowledge accumulated by 17th-century material culture scholars over the past 40 years, recataloging (or cataloging for the first time) leads to more accurate identification of artifacts and refinement of site dates. In some cases, these refined dates can drastically change the interpretations. Reexamination of these sites, individually and as a group, allows them to be situated in contemporary historic and interpretive frameworks that did not exist when the sites were first excavated. By examining the sites at multiple scales and crafting detailed historical contexts, we are able to relate artifacts, kinship networks, and site structures on a local level to broader regional and Atlantic concepts of politics and authority.

Data Sets

In the two larger projects on which this study is based (Hatch 2015a; McMillan 2015a), we drew on two separate but complementary sources of evidence: primary source historical records and archaeological materials. Within the category of archaeological materials, we focused on three subsets: ceramics and faunal remains (Hatch 2015a) and European and locally made clay tobacco pipes (McMillan 2015a). We chose these materials and the focus of these projects for a variety of reasons.

As graduate students at the University of Tennessee, Knoxville, studying under Barbara Heath, we worked in the Historical Archaeology Laboratory with and for Heath. She brought us into her larger project of reanalyzing old and forgotten collections from the Northern Neck of Virginia, all but abandoned in storage at the Virginia Department of Historic Resources. As part of this project, we assisted with the rehousing, cataloging, and analysis of the John Hallowes site (Hatch et al. 2013). As we discuss below, much of the materials recovered from the Hallowes site was unprovenienced or surface-collected, so we relied upon artifacts with firm *termini post quem* and short date ranges of manufacture, such as marked clay tobacco pipes and specific types of ceramics, in our analyses and crafted research questions that would not be heavily influenced by small degrees of temporal uncertainty, which involved using phases of occupation in certain analyses. Hatch focused on the ceramics and faunal remains, given his interest in foodways and plantation management practices. McMillan (2010, 2016a) focused on the clay tobacco pipes, given her previous research on pipe stem dating and her interest in trade networks.

As we delved deeper into the primary documents of the 17th-century Potomac River Valley in order to better contextualize our archaeological findings, we became intensely interested in the kinship and trade networks seen in the historical record. Specifically, in our research we noticed the same people interacting with one another in both Maryland and Virginia. We started to trace the personal histories of site occupants, which included their social and political networks, and we began to wonder if people who were socially and politically connected in the historical record would have consumed similar types of materials and structured their plantations in similar ways, providing tangible links between archaeological sites. Along these lines, we also wondered if people who were on opposing ends of political debates and ultimately violent uprisings would have been integrated into a completely different exchange network. We sought out archaeological sites (allied, opposing, and unknown/neutral) specifically to answer these questions.

Between us, we examined 17 archaeological collections (Table 5). All 17 of the archaeological sites used were excavated, or at least first identified, prior to 2000, most at the height of the "golden age" of Chesapeake historical archaeology during the 1970s and 1980s (Hudgins 1993:171–172). Some of the sites had not been fully analyzed until recently, and most have not been looked at since their initial investigation. Our research takes advantage of advances made in the late 20th and early 21st centuries concerning 17th-century material cultural analysis and identification, colonial Chesapeake social history, and the digitization of archaeological collections and archival materials to ask new questions of old collections.

Table 5. Archaeological collections used in authors' research

Site	Location	Date
Old Chapel Field (18sT233)	Maryland	1637–1660
St. John's (18sT1–23)	Maryland	1638–1715
Pope's Fort (18sT1–13)	Maryland	1645–1655
Hallowes (44wM6)	Virginia	1647–1681
Nomini (44wM12)	Virginia	1647–1722
Compton (18cV279)	Maryland	1651–1685
Patuxent Point (18cV271)	Maryland	1658–1690
Coan Hall (44NB11)	Virginia	1662–1727
Mattapany (18sT390)	Maryland	1663–1689
John Washington (44wM204)	Virginia	1664–1704
Smith's Ordinary (18sT1–13)	Maryland	1666–1678
Big Pit (18sT1–13)	Maryland	1669–1670
Clifts Plantation (44wM33)	Virginia	1670–1730
Newman's Neck (44NB180)	Virginia	1672–1747
King's Reach (18cV83)	Maryland	1690–1711
Henry Brooks (44wM205)	Virginia	1700–1725
Maurice Clark (44sT174)	Virginia	1694–1727

In addition to the Hallowes site, we also conducted an analysis of the Nomini Plantation site in the Historical Archaeology Laboratory at the University of Tennessee, Knoxville, using ceramics, pipes, and faunal remains; we are currently finishing the analysis, cataloging the metals, glass, and other small finds in the Department of Historic Preservation Archaeology Laboratory at the University of Mary Washington. For most of the remaining 15 sites, we relied primarily upon analysis by other archaeologists and examined only the artifact categories relevant to our projects. During the course of examining these artifacts, however, specifically the ceramics, the dates for the John Washington and Henry Brooks sites were reevaluated, improving the resolution for the occupations of both sites (Hatch 2015a:208, 240). These analyses required us to travel all over the coast of Virginia and Maryland, visiting several different repositories, including the Virginia Department of Historic Resources, George Washington's

Ferry Farm, George Washington's Birthplace National Monument, the Maryland Archaeological Conservation Laboratory, and Historic St. Mary's City. Obviously a lot of time, travel, and money went into these trips, especially when you factor in the commute from Knoxville. Another major hurdle that we had to overcome was learning and ultimately having to intimately understand 17 different archaeological excavation processes and analyses. We had to become not only familiar with but gain an expertise in a variety of field methods, note taking, cataloging procedures, nomenclature, and analytical techniques spanning nearly 30 years. These obstacles do not even touch on the immense amount of primary source research we conducted to contextualize the finds at the sites and re-create social and political networks.

Ultimately, despite the difficulties of collections-based research, we decided that such analyses, focusing on previously excavated sites, allowed for a broader and deeper understanding of the 17th-century Potomac River Valley that could never be gleaned through one or two sites. Additionally, using these old collections was the most cost-effective, time-efficient, and logical way to test ideas about community formation from an archaeological perspective in the region. The wealth of data from the sites excavated in this region suggested to us that there was little reason to generate more data through excavation before we first understood what other sites contained and how they stacked up to one another when systematically compared (especially given that in the case of the Hallowes and Nomini collections, complete site analyses and reports had never been generated). By not excavating new sites for our projects, we were able to look at more materials relevant to our research without contributing to the curation crisis. Ultimately the reanalysis of these materials, although circumscribed by varied methodologies, provided us with a baseline for comparison and helped to craft new research questions that could eventually be tested with excavations.

Mid-17th-Century Politics in the Potomac River Valley

The story of the Appamattucks community began in Maryland and has roots in the political, economic, and religious struggles that occurred in Lord Baltimore's colony (Hatch 2015a; McMillan 2015a). Many of the struggles that occurred in 17th-century Maryland stemmed not only from tensions between Catholic governance and Protestant citizenry but from the manorial system instituted by Cecil Calvert, Lord Baltimore, that emphasized strict social hierarchy with rule by the landed elite and tenants tied to the land through rent payments and manorial courts (Stone 1982). Additionally, conflicts between Parliamentarians and Royalists in the metropole during the English Civil War first manifested in the Chesapeake in 1644. That year, at a court in St. Mary's City, Maryland, Giles Brent, a Catholic and distant cousin of Calvert, accused Richard Ingle, a Protestant and a merchant, of treason for a political disagreement that had occurred two years earlier concerning the contemporary upheavals in England, in which Ingle insulted the king and proclaimed his loyalty to Parliament (Riordan 2004). Ingle fled Maryland in the midst of the investigation, upset over the political leanings of the colony's Proprietary leaders.

In February 1645 Ingle returned to Maryland with men he had recruited from the Northern Neck of Virginia, most notably from Chicacoan, a neighborhood currently being explored by Heath (2017). Ingle and his mercenaries invaded and captured St. Mary's City in the name of Parliament. Throughout the next year the Protestant rebels looted much of the countryside until Proprietary forces could take back the colony in December 1646. Several former rebels fled across the Potomac River in 1647 and established a new settlement in the Appamattucks area. John Hallowes and Thomas Speke were two of these rebels.

The John Hallowes Site

The John Hallowes site is on Currioman Bay, at the juncture of Nomini Bay and the Potomac River in Westmoreland County, Virginia. In 1968, prior to the construction of a planned community along the bay, Virginia Sherman and William T. Buchanan, Jr. surveyed the area and discovered the Hallowes site (Buchanan and Heite 1971:38). From July 1968 to August 1969, Buchanan and Edward Heite (1971:40), along with a crew of volunteers, excavated on the weekends. The archaeological investigation of the site revealed a single earthfast dwelling with bastions located on two opposing corners of the house. Excavations followed standard practices of the time, including mechanical and manual stripping of the plow zone and no screening. The majority of the artifacts recovered from the site were designated "surface collected" and, based on the fact that most of these artifacts are rather large, appear to have been picked out of the stripped plow zone and collected as they eroded out of the stripped surface. A comprehensive report on the site was never written by the original excavation team due to the lack of funding for the excavation and subsequent analysis. The most detailed analysis and interpretation of the site, until recently, was an article by the site's excavators Buchanan and Heite (1971) in *Historical Archaeology* in which the authors dated the site from 1687 to 1716. Bastion fortifications related to the dwelling at the site were initially associated with Bacon's Rebellion and interpreted as protection against raids by Susquehannock Indians in 1676 (Neiman 1980:75; Carson et al. 1981:191; Hodges 1993:205–208; Hodges 2003:509; Carson 2013:96–97).

From 2010 to 2012 Heath and students from the Department of Anthropology at the University of Tennessee, Knoxville, initiated a reanalysis of the site (Hatch 2012, 2015a; Hatch et al. 2013, 2014; McMillan et al. 2014; McMillan 2015a, 2015b). By combining detailed historical documentation relating to site residents with the analysis and reanalysis of material culture from the excavations, new and significantly different interpretations of the site have emerged. Based upon this recent work, the Hallowes site is now interpreted to have been occupied from 1647 to 1681 and the fortifications built at the site related to Ingle's Rebellion, not Bacon's Rebellion.

The site derives its name from the original owner of the property, John Hallowes, who was born in Lancashire, England, and immigrated to Maryland in 1634 at the age of 19 as an indentured servant. Hallowes completed his term of indenture in 1639 and married his first wife, Restitute Tew, that same year. John and Restitute continued to live in Maryland for another eight years. During his time in

Maryland, Hallowes was described as a carpenter, mariner, planter, privateer, and trader (Browne 1885:67, 83, 186, 214, 259; Sherman 1969; Buchanan and Heite 1971:38–39).

Hallowes was no stranger to violence and fighting; he had participated in the Chesapeake Fur Wars; fought at Kent Island for his master, Thomas Cornwalyes, and Lord Baltimore (Browne 1887:22; Fausz 1988:71); and was a participant in Ingle's Rebellion. Hallowes likely participated in the failed uprising because of his position as a newly wealthy Protestant freeman who resented the limits placed on him by the manor lords and Proprietary government. After Baltimore quelled Ingle's Rebellion, Hallowes and other failed rebels were forced to take an oath of fealty to the governor of Maryland in 1647 (Browne 1885:174).

Shortly after he was forced to bow down to Baltimore and his Proprietary rule, Hallowes, and several other former rebels, fled Maryland to the southern shores of the Potomac River, forming the Appamattucks community in 1647. Hallowes lived at his plantation along Currioman Bay until his death in 1657. The property passed to his second wife, and then their daughter, until it was abandoned in 1681, ending the occupation of the site (Library of Virginia [LOV] 1653–1671:16; LOV 1675–1689:22; Nicklin 1938:440–444; Buchanan and Heite 1971:39).

Historical research conducted as part of the reanalysis allowed for the creation of a hypothesized date range of occupation of 1647 to 1681. This date range is bracketed on one end by Hallowes's arrival in Virginia, and on the other by the eviction of the tenants from the property by John Manley, Hallowes's son-in-law. The hypothesized date range yielded a mean occupation date of 1664 that is consistent with the dates arrived at through the analysis of the archaeological assemblage, including a *terminus post quem* of 1675, an adjusted mean ceramic date (South 1977) of 1667, a Binford (1962) pipe stem date of 1660, and a Hanson (1971) pipe stem date of 1665. For a detailed explanation of the dating methods used in the interpretation of this site, see Hatch et al. (2013) and McMillan et al. (2014).

The Hallowes site produced an assemblage of 4,581 artifacts and

3,675 faunal remains, excluding nine artifacts on loan to the West-moreland County Museum that were unavailable for study. These diagnostic pieces were previously reported (Buchanan and Heite 1971). Based upon their descriptions, the unavailability of these artifacts did not significantly impact the interpretations. Additionally eight boxes of brick were excluded from the reanalysis. Overall, historic ceramics and clay tobacco pipes constituted the majority of the artifact assemblage: 34% (n=1,599) and 22% (n=1,021), respectively.

The primary issues with analyzing the Hallowes collection stemmed from the fragmentary nature of the excavation records and the excavation methods that were used. Determining the excavation methods and provenience numbering at the site required examining hand-written notes, multiple site maps, site photographs, the journal article written by the excavators, and contemporary publications by other authors that used data from the site. In all cases the site notes were not standardized, and information such as context depth, soil color, and soil texture were not systematically recorded. Additionally, photographs existed for only a handful of contexts on the site, and no profile drawings survived. In the case of this collection, the hand-drawn maps, site photographs, and context numbering system were the most useful pieces of information that were used in reconstructing the methods for the excavation (Hatch et al. 2013:8–15). By combining evidence from each of these sources and cross-referencing them, a more complete understanding of the site was possible that revealed relatively good horizontal and vertical context for many of the artifacts.

As stated, much of the collection derived from plow zone contexts. While a grid had been superimposed on the site, there was no systematic collection of artifacts from plow zone units. Rather, based on the notes and general condition of the collection, it appeared that only "interesting" or large artifacts were collected during excavation. Although some of these objects were sometimes labeled with their grid provenience, many were simply lumped into a general surface collection provenience. Despite this, artifacts with provenience allowed for a cursory examination of spatial distributions at the site. The materials from general surface proveniences served to provide more data for dating the relatively short occupation of the site, with certain tightly dated artifacts that could be associated with specific households.

Nomini Plantation Site

Nomini Plantation is near the Hallowes site on the shores of Nomini Bay in Westmoreland County. Vivienne Mitchell of the Archeological Society of Virginia led a group of avocational archaeologists, excavating a large, stratified midden at the site from 1970 to 1982. Similar to the Hallowes site, no formal report was written on the excavations, although Mitchell (1975, 1976, 1983; Mitchell and Mitchell 1982) published several articles on the artifacts recovered from the site. Recently completed historical research and analysis of the 17th-century midden indicate that there were three distinct phases of use: 1647–1679, 1679–1700, and 1700–1722 (McMillan and Hatch 2013; Hatch 2015a; McMillan 2015a). This site, like the Hallowes site, was established by a former participant in Ingle's Rebellion who fled Maryland in 1647.

Thomas Speke (LOV 1643–1651:207) first patented the land that came to be known as Nomini Plantation in 1649. The site was likely occupied as early as 1647, when Speke and his wife Anne fled Maryland. Sometime around 1655 Anne died and Speke married Frances Gerrard, the daughter of Thomas Gerrard, who participated in Ingle's Rebellion in 1645 and in Fendall's Rebellion in 1660 (Browne 1885:174, 407; LOV 1653–1659:53). Upon Speke's death in 1659, the majority of his property passed to Frances, who was given a life interest in the plantation. Frances married four more times, to Valentine Peyton (1659), John Appleton (1676), John Washington (1676), and William Hardidge II (1679).

Frances and William Hardidge II lived at Nomini Plantation until their deaths in the late 17th century. It is unclear when Frances died, but it was likely sometime around 1691, as indicated by Hardidge's trip to England to purchase the property from the Speke family (Sherman and Mitchell 1983:107). Hardidge died in 1694 and the property passed to his and Frances's daughter, Elizabeth (LOV 1690–1698:129). Elizabeth lived at Nomini until her death in 1722, as did her husband, Henry Ashton, until his death in 1731 (LOV 1690–1698: 87, 197), ending the occupation of the site.

The stratified midden at the site represented three successive households that occupied the plantation from 1647 to 1722. We analyzed the ceramics and pipes and identified three distinct strata using profile drawings, field notes, and ceramic data, including cross mends, in addition to ceramic presence or absence, and abundance of certain diagnostic ceramic types (McMillan and Hatch 2013).

Phase I represents the occupation of Thomas Speke, Frances, and three of her husbands from circa 1647 to 1679. Phase II consists of the Hardidge occupation from circa 1679 to 1700. Phase III contains the refuse of Elizabeth Hardidge and her husband, Henry Ashton, from circa 1700 to 1722. The identification of these three distinct strata allows for the examination of the materiality of the Appamattucks community over time.

Like the Hallowes collection, Nomini Plantation posed a challenge for reanalysis. Prior to our examination of the midden collection, no significant effort had been made to understand the excavation or composition of this feature. Even Mitchell had given up hope in understanding the assemblage, as evidenced by a handwritten note among the paperwork for the site that read "all this trash deposit material would be best used as a study collection" (Figure 9). Rather than being discouraged by this note, as many previous researchers no doubt had, we viewed the collection as a challenge. There was such a diversity and so much exceptional 17th-century material in the collection that we felt the effort to reanalyze and make sense of this feature would pay great dividends. Ultimately we were correct, but making sense of the midden excavation was no small feat.

The primary hindrance to the reanalysis of Nomini Plantation was the fact that three different context numbering systems had been used during its excavation. Essentially, one group of volunteers excavated units in one half of the midden using their own system, while Mitchell excavated the other half using her system. To

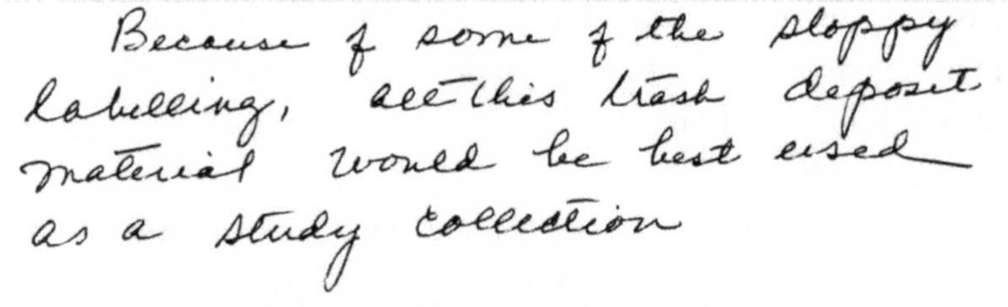

Because of some of the sloppy labelling, all this trash deposit material would be best used as a study collection

FIGURE 9. Vivienne Mitchell's handwritten note about the Nomini Plantation midden collection. (Courtesy of Virginia Department of Historic Resources)

complicate matters, Mitchell changed her numbering system midway through the project after a visit to the site by William Kelso. Field notes, and some profile drawings, for most of the units excavated within Mitchell's half of the feature survived. In general, the notes completed by Mitchell contain sufficient detail to understand much of the composition of the midden, but almost no notes for the other half of the midden were present. Fortunately, three pages of profile drawings for the other half of the midden did survive, which proved to be the Rosetta Stone for the site. Additionally, Mitchell had written eight pages of notes laying out some of the basics of the context numbering system used by her and Kelso. These notes, the profile drawings, and a detailed examination of artifacts allowed for strata within both halves of the midden to be correlated to one another, though not always in a one-to-one fashion (McMillan and Hatch 2013).

Marriage, Kinship, and the Role of Material Culture in Community Formation

Many Chesapeake historians have argued that multiple marriages due to high mortality rates greatly contributed to the instability of the region until early in the 18th century (Morgan 1975; Carr and Walsh 1977; Walsh 1979). Based on our reanalysis of these collections and the histories associated with them, we argue that this constant cycle of widowhood and remarriage in Appamattucks actually served to strengthen that community and caused local power and status to remain among the same group of rebels, and their descendants, for decades (Hatch 2015a). Examples from the historical research related to the reanalysis of the Hallowes and Nomini collections illustrate how kinship ties were created and community connections were reinforced for both immigrants and creole-born colonists during different stages of their lives and at different times for the Appamattucks community.

Prior to the outbreak of Ingle's Rebellion in 1645, a community of people with similar political leanings was already being created in Maryland through the bonds of marriage. John Hallowes's marriage to Restitute Tew in 1639 was among the first of these alliances cemented through matrimony (Browne 1887:52). Restitute provided John with numerous advantages in Maryland society that helped to influence his decision to rebel against Baltimore in 1645 and led to his success before and after his flight from Maryland.

Hallowes's marriage provided him with a claim to authority that many men in the early colonial Chesapeake would not have possessed due to a strongly imbalanced sex ratio. Because of a lack of marriage partners and a high rate of widowhood, marriage became an important factor in accumulating wealth and climbing the social ladder for men, who could marry widows and gain control over the holdings of their former husbands, and for women, who had the power to select the most advantageous partners available (Morgan 1975:165–168). His relationship to John Tew, another rebel and Restitute's father, also probably spurred him on to rebellion (Browne 1885:174). When John and Restitute moved to Virginia in 1647, John Tew moved as well, essentially helping to transplant the Maryland community of rebels, where kinship ties had already been formed, across the Potomac. When Restitute died in 1655, John Hallowes's second wife, Elizabeth Sturman, helped to reinforce both his status and authority within the Appamattucks community and his commitment to the political ideas central to the former rebels, since she was the widow of another former rebel within this network (Nicklin 1938:444; Riordan 2004:186). The fact that she and Hallowes married indicates that they likely shared similar political views and sought to strengthen these ideas within the community by seeking like-minded partners.

Frances Gerrard, who married Thomas Speke, was one of the major female figures that helped cement bonds within the Appamattucks community through marriage. She incorporated several men into this community, including John Washington, George's great-grandfather, who eventually became a powerful resident of Appamattucks despite his late arrival to the region. Frances's two other husbands prior to Washington (Valentine Peyton and John Appleton) had also been county commissioners, indicating that they too were well-respected within the Appamattucks community (LOV 1665–1677:127; LOV 1675–1689:90).

Later, the marriage of William Hardidge II to Frances Gerrard Speke Washington merged real and fictive kinship connections among no fewer than eight distinct families that were supporters of Ingle's Rebellion and the rebel ideology along the Potomac. This marriage, and the connections it fostered, illustrates how creole-born colonists were able to continue building kinship ties within the Appamattucks community and keep political power in the hands of people sympathetic to the ideology of the former Maryland rebels (Hatch 2015a:177–184).

While marriage and kinship ties were creating and maintaining community cohesion in the Appamattucks region, the trade in portable goods was also supporting this rebel ideology, well beyond the first generation of settlers. The potter Morgan Jones made coarse earthenware from 1661 to 1691. His wares illustrate the persistence of this community and share a deep history and connection with the inhabitants of Appamattucks (Kelso and Chappell 1974; Straube 1995). Jones's connections to the rebel community, centered on Appamattucks, influenced the distribution of his wares and the location of his kilns and helped to reinforce community bonds that had been forged twenty years earlier. Jones came to Charles County, Maryland, in 1661 as an indentured servant to Robert Slye (King and Breckenridge 1999). He likely started producing his wares soon after his arrival in Maryland, but by 1667 he had completed his term of indenture and was independently producing pottery. Importantly, Slye was the son-in-law of Thomas Gerrard, father to Frances Gerrard Speke and father-in-law to John Washington and William Hardidge II. The strong economic connections with this community in Virginia likely influenced Jones's decision to move to Westmoreland County in the late 1660s, so that he could be geographically closer to some of the major consumers of his wares (Hatch 2015b). Jones's construction in 1677 of a kiln at Glebe Harbor, only a few miles from Nomini Bay, helps to support the hypothesis that he was a significant supplier of ceramics within the former rebel community.

The presence and concentration of Jones's wares among those within the former rebel community is easily seen in the fact that sites with direct connections to that community have the largest proportions of this ware. The two sites with the highest proportions, Hallowes and Nomini, were both settled in 1647 by former rebels who had fled Maryland (Table 6).

While Jones's connections through the Gerrard family and Robert Slye likely introduced him to the economic networks of the former rebel community, people within that community probably consumed his wares to a greater degree because of his alliances with like-minded people in Maryland and Virginia. In this sense, the consumption of Morgan Jones ceramics helped to signal membership in the former rebel community in Westmoreland County and perpetuate an anti-Calvert ideology. People within the former rebel network clearly favored Jones's wares or had better access to them, or both.

Table 6. Morgan Jones ceramics by sherd and vessel counts at sites along the Potomac River

Site	Date Range	Morgan Jones Sherd Count	Total Ceramic Sherd Count	% of Morgan Jones Sherds	% of Morgan Jones Vessels
18CH621 (Westwood Manor)	1680–1715	11	1,978	1	
18CH805 (Fendall)	1675–1715	16	544	3	
18ST390 (Mattapany)	1665–1740	6	2,620	0	

18sT677 (Tudor Hall)	1660–1690	5	203	2	
44nb180 (Newman's Neck)	1672–1747	30	413	7	9
44sT130 (Brent)	1660–1725	27	1,169	2	
44wm6 (Hallowes)	1647–1681	955	1,600	60	55
44wm204* (John Washington)	1664–1704	47	2,083	2	18
44wm33 (Clifts)	1670–1735	937	14,211	7	7
44wm12 (Nomini Plantation)	1647–1722	724	3,368	21	23

* Counts for Morgan Jones sherds were not derived from the reanalysis of the John Washington site. Instead a minimum vessel count was performed on the site during the reanalysis. Based upon the comparison of sherd percentages to sherd counts for the other sites where this is available, it is likely that the sherd count at the John Washington site is low and is probably closer to the percentage of vessels.

Locally made clay tobacco pipes also materially illustrate the social networks formed and fostered through this rebel mindset along the southern shores of the Potomac River. These colonial-made pipes, specifically three pipe types, exchanged among members of the Appamattucks community illustrate shared economic interests among colonists settled on the southern shores of the Potomac River, as well as how material culture can help create and reproduce communities and ideologies.

Eleven belly-bowl pipes with a single band of rouletted decoration along the bowl-stem juncture at the back of the bowl and around the bowl rim were recovered from three sites: the Hallowes site (n=4) and Nomini Plantation (n=3) in Virginia, and Pope's Fort (18sT1–13) (n=4) in St. Mary's City, Maryland. The rouletting is located low on the juncture, closer to the stem than the bowl, and terminates on the side in the middle of the low elongated heel. This style of pipe has not been found on 46 other sites examined in the Potomac River Valley, nor in the James River Valley, based on evaluations of other studies (Miller 1991; Agbe-Davies 2010:73; Agbe-Davies 2015:99) and McMillan's (2016b) own research in that geographic area. McMillan has termed the pipe style from the three sites in the Potomac Valley the "Ingle's Rebellion" type, based on the association of all three sites' occupants with the failed uprising. Pope's Fort was the center of the rebellion, and both John Hallowes and Thomas Speke participated in the rebellion before fleeing to Virginia. These distinctly decorated pipes indicate that the occupants of the Hallowes, Pope's Fort, and Nomini Plantation sites were engaged in similar local trade networks that may have been influenced by their political alliances. Both Hallowes and Speke served in the Westmoreland County government after they fled to Virginia and hosted political gatherings at their homes. Its presence could have also indicated in-group membership to other people in the know.

Another particularly interesting motif that appeared on locally made pipes found at Nomini Plantation (n=2) and the John Hallowes site (n=1) is the Tudor Rose. Eleven other locally made pipes stamped with the Tudor Rose motif were found on other sites in the area, including at Pope's Fort, Compton (18CV279), and Patuxent Point (18CV271), all of which were occupied by men and women who were staunchly anti-Calvert and anti-Catholic. The Tudor Rose became synonymous in Europe with Protestant resistance to the Stuart monarchy and when placed on pipes by Dutch and exiled English makers symbolized the freedom and prosperity that they enjoyed under the Netherlands' liberal government (Duco 1981:397; Dallal 2004:212–214). Similar interpretations can be made of the locally made pipes marked with the Tudor Rose motif (Figure 10). In the Potomac River Valley, the Tudor Rose may have represented resistance to Calvert, Catholicism, and proprietary restrictions to civil liberties. The Tudor Rose symbolized their membership within the group of those opposed to Calvert.

Hallowes and Speke were interacting and trading with one another and with other members of the Appamattucks community. There

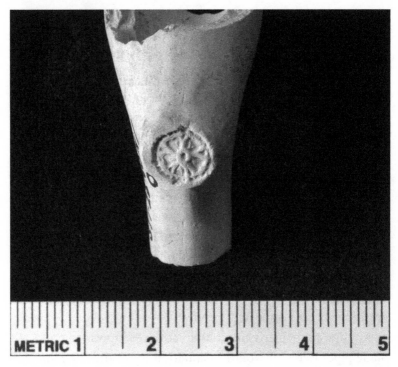

FIGURE 10. Locally made pipe with a Tudor Rose stamp on the heel. Pipe from Pope's Fort, site 18ST1-13. (Photo: McMillan, with permission of Historic St. Mary's City)

is both historical and archaeological evidence that ties Nomini to nearby plantations, including a pipe style McMillan has termed the Imitation-Bristol type (Figure 11). This type, represented by two handmade stems, one from Nomini Plantation and one from the John Washington site, was decorated with elaborate rouletting and white infill that looks very similar to pipes manufactured in Bristol, England, in the second half of the 17th century. There is not enough contextual information to determine when exactly these pipes were made and exchanged, but they were likely traded between these two sites due to the tight-knit nature of the Appamattucks community.

Locally made colonial pipes and ceramics, such as those produced by Morgan Jones, can be used to trace and reveal connections within the Appamattucks community. These connections follow

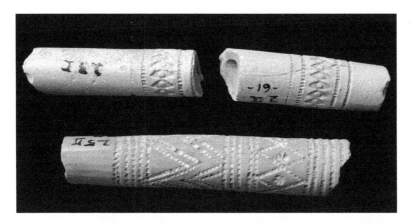

FIGURE 11. Two English pipes with Bristol Diamond rouletting decoration (*top*) and a locally made Imitation Bristol Diamond Type (*bottom*) from Nomini Plantation, site 44WM12. (Photo: McMillan, with permission of the Virginia Department of Historic Resources)

kinship ties and political alliances, both of which sat firmly on and supported economic connections among this group of colonists on the southern shores of the Potomac River. Some of these bonds were forged before the colonists settled on the Northern Neck, such as the relationship between Hallowes, Speke, and their descendants and illustrated by their shared exchange and use of locally made pipes and ceramics. Although pipes and locally made earthenware are quotidian objects, they were an extremely important part of the social lives of colonists. Everyone smoked and everyone ate and processed food, thus consuming both pipes and earthenware. The choices of which pipes or ceramics to purchase, barter, or exchange reflect larger choices and relationships made among members of the Appamattucks community.

Conclusions

All of the sites discussed in this chapter were excavated prior to the 1980s and, with the exception of Clifts Plantation (Neiman 1980), were never fully analyzed, and in some cases never completely cataloged. The Hallowes site was a salvage project conducted by avocational archaeologists; the original researchers did as much as they could with limited time and funds. The new research conducted on this site has benefited from over 40 years of research into Chesapeake colonial history and material culture, allowing for vastly new conclusions about the site's date and purpose. Specifically, new analysis suggests that its occupation had an earlier date and that fortifications at the site were likely related to Ingle's Rebellion (Hatch et al. 2014).

Excavations at Nomini Plantation were also conducted by avocational archaeologists, but over a longer period of time, and, like Hallowes, a full report was never completed. When the excavations of Nomini ended in the 1980s, the archaeologists who excavated the site felt that the interpretive value of the early midden feature was not great due to different artifact labeling methods employed over the years. Mitchell herself dismissed the utility of this collection, which all but sealed the fate of this extraordinary assemblage of mid- to late 17th-century material culture. Detailed reanalysis of the collection has shown that it is an untapped and rich resource that still has much to teach about life in the 17th-century Potomac River Valley.

Comparative analysis is at the heart of archaeological research, and through collections-based research we have been able to examine and explore a large amount of data without generating additional material that would then need to be processed and curated. As this chapter has shown, reanalysis of old collections can be a strongly effective way to generate new interpretations and evaluate long-standing beliefs about the history and society of a region. The brief examples discussed here of the ways the community at Appamattucks strengthened and reproduced itself are not unique to the John Hallowes and Nomini Plantation sites. These connections and community survival strategies in the face of an uncertain demographic environment can be seen, in one way or another, at all of the sites connected to the supporters of Ingle's Rebellion (Hatch 2015a; McMillan 2015a). Although Chesapeake society may have been demographically unstable in the mid-17th century, people were able to adapt and form meaningful and long-lasting community connections. The materiality of these community connections is readily visible, but only if deep contexts for sites, individuals, and artifacts are developed. Understanding the mundane items of 17th-century life such as coarse earthenware and pipes from this perspective allows us to trace the people, events, connections, and ideologies that would go on to influence generations of people living in the Potomac River Valley, ultimately providing a powerful interpretive framework for the archaeology and history of the region. These interpretations are possible only through the large-scale, synthetic studies currently being conducted in the Potomac River Valley. These studies necessarily heavily rely on collections-based research.

References

Agbe-Davies, Anna S.

2010   Social Aspects of the Tobacco Pipe Trade in Early Colonial Virginia. In *Social Archaeologies of Trade and Exchange: Exploring Relationships among People, Places, and Things*, Anna Agbe-Davies and Alexander A. Bauer, editors, pp. 69–98. Left Coast Press. Walnut Creek CA.

2015   *Tobacco, Pipes, and Race in Colonial Virginia: Little Tubes of Mighty Power.* Left Coast Press. Walnut Creek CA.

Binford, Lewis R.

1962   A New Method of Calculating Dates from Kaolin Pipe Stem Samples. *Southeastern Archaeological Conference Newsletter* 9(1):19–21.

Browne, William Hand (editor)

1885   *Proceedings of the Council of Maryland 1636–1667, Vol. 3, Archives of Maryland.* Maryland Historical Society. Baltimore. Archives of Maryland Online http://aomol.msa.maryland.gov/000001/000003/html/index.html. Accessed 10 February 2017.

1887   *Judicial and Testamentary Business of the Provincial Court 1637–1650, Vol. 4, Archives of Maryland.* Maryland Historical Society. Baltimore. Archives of Maryland Online http://aomol.msa.maryland.gov/000001/000004/html/index.html. Accessed 10 February 2017.

Buchanan, William T., Jr., and Edward F. Heite

1971   The Hallowes Site: A Seventeenth-Century Yeoman's Cottage in Virginia. *Historical Archaeology* 5:38–48.

Carr, Lois Green

2009   William Hardidge (1622–1668). Dr. Lois Green Carr's Biographical Files of 17th and 18th Century Marylanders. Maryland State Archives, Annapolis. http://msa.maryland.gov/megafile/msa/speccol/sc5000/sc5094/001800/html/sm1813.html. Accessed Fall 2016.

Carr, Lois Green, and Lorena S. Walsh

1977   The Planter's Wife: The Experience of White Women in Seventeenth-Century Maryland. *William and Mary Quarterly* 34(4):542–571.

Carson, Cary

2013   Plantation Housing: Seventeenth Century. In *The Chesapeake House: Architectural Investigation by Colonial Williamsburg*, Cary Carson and Carl R. Lounsbury, editors, pp. 86–115. University of North Carolina Press. Chapel Hill.

Carson, Cary, Norman F. Barka, William M. Kelso, Garry Wheeler Stone, and Dell Upton

1981   Impermanent Architecture in the Southern American Colonies. *Winterthur Portfolio* 16(2/3):135–196.

Dallal, Diane

2004   The Tudor Rose and the Fleurs-de-Lis: Women and Iconography in Seventeenth-Century Dutch Clay Pipes Found in New York City. In *Smoking and Culture: The Archaeology of Tobacco Pipes in Eastern North America*, Sean M. Rafferty and Rob Mann, editors, pp. 207–240. University of Tennessee Press. Knoxville.

Duco, Don H.

1981   The Clay Tobacco Pipe in Seventeenth Century Netherlands. In *The Archaeology of the Clay Tobacco Pipe: V Europe 2*, Peter Davey, editor, pp. 368–468. British Archaeological Reports International Series 106(ii). Oxford.

Fausz, J. Frederick

1988   Merging and Emerging Worlds: Anglo-Indian Interest Groups and the Development of the Seventeenth-Century Chesapeake. In *Colonial Chesapeake Society*, Lois Green Carr, Philip D. Morgan, and Jean B. Russo, editors, pp. 47–98. University of North Carolina Press. Chapel Hill.

Hanson, Lee, Jr.

1971   Kaolin Pipestems—Boring In on a Fallacy. *Conference on Historic Site Archaeology Papers 1969* 4(1):2–15.

Hatch, D. Brad

2012   Venison Trade and Interaction between English Colonists and Native Americans in Virginia's Potomac River Valley. *Northeast Historical Archaeology* 41:18–49.

2015a   An Historical Archaeology of Early Modern Manhood in the Potomac River Valley of Virginia, 1645–1730. Doctoral dissertation, Department of Anthropology, University of Tennessee, Knoxville.

2015b   Morgan Jones Pottery and the Maintenance of Community Relationships in the Early Modern Potomac Valley. Paper presented at the 45th Annual Middle Atlantic Archaeological Conference, Ocean City MD.

Hatch, D. Brad, Barbara J. Heath, and Lauren K. McMillan

2014 Reassessing the Hallowes Site: Conflict and Settlement in the 17th-Century Potomac Valley. *Historical Archaeology* 48(4):46–75.

Hatch, D. Brad, Lauren K. McMillan, and Barbara J. Heath

2013 Archaeological Reassessment of the Hallowes Site (44WM6). Manuscript, Virginia Department of Historic Resources, Richmond.

Heath, Barbara J.

2016 Dynamic Landscapes: The Emergence of Formal Spaces in Colonial Virginia. *Historical Archaeology* 50(1):27–44.

2017 Life on the Borderlands of the Colonial Potomac: Exploring Chicacoan. Paper presented at the 50th annual conference of the Society for Historical Archaeology, Fort Worth TX.

Heath, Barbara J., Eleanor E. Breen, Dustin S. Lawson, and Daniel W. H. Brock

2009 Archaeological Reassessment of Newman's Neck (44NB180). Manuscript, Virginia Department of Historic Resources, Richmond.

Hening, William Waller

1823a *The Statutes at Large; Being a Collection of All the Laws of Virginia from the First Session of the Legislature in the Year 1619.* Vol. 1. R. & W. & G. Bartow. New York.

1823b *The Statutes at Large; Being a Collection of All the Laws of Virginia from the First Session of the Legislature in the Year 1619.* Vol. 2. R. & W. & G. Bartow. New York.

Hodges, Charles T.

1993 Private Fortifications in 17th-Century Virginia: A Study of Six Representative Works. In *The Archaeology of 17th-Century Virginia*, Theodore R. Reinhart and Dennis J. Pogue, editors, pp. 183–221. Dietz Press. Richmond VA.

2003 Forts of the Chieftains: A Study of Vernacular, Classical and Renaissance Influence on Defensible Town and Villa Plans in 17th-Century Virginia. Master's thesis, Department of Anthropology, College of William and Mary, Williamsburg VA.

Horn, James

1979 Servant Emigration to the Chesapeake in the Seventeenth Century. In *The Chesapeake in the Seventeenth-Century: Essays on Anglo-American Society*, Thad W. Tate and David L. Ammerman, editors, pp. 51–95. University of North Carolina Press. Chapel Hill.

1994 *Adapting to a New World: English Society in the Seventeenth-Century Chesapeake.* University of North Carolina Press. Chapel Hill.

Hudgins, Carter L.

1993 Seventeenth-Century Virginia and Its 20th-Century Archaeologists. In *The Archaeology of 17th-Century Virginia*, Theodore R. Reinhart and Dennis J. Pogue, editors, pp.167–182. Dietz Press, Richmond VA.

Kelso, William M., and Edward A. Chappell

1974   Excavation of a Seventeenth Century Pottery Kiln at Glebe Harbor, West-moreland County, Virginia. *Historical Archaeology* 8:53–63.

King, Julia A.

2011   Colonial Encounters: The Lower Potomac River Valley at Contact, 1500–1700 AD. Proposal submitted to the National Endowment for the Humanities.

King, Julia A., and Curt Breckenridge

1999   Morgan Jones(es) Timeline. Manuscript, Maryland Archaeological Conservation Lab, Jefferson Patterson Park and Museum, St. Leonard MD.

Library of Virginia (LOV)

1643–1651 Virginia Land Office Patents no. 2, microfilm reel 2. Library of Virginia, Richmond.

1653–1659 Westmoreland County Deeds, Wills, and Patents, microfilm reel 1. Library of Virginia, Richmond.

1653–1671 Westmoreland County Deeds and Wills, No. 1, microfilm reel 2. Library of Virginia, Richmond.

1665–1677 Westmoreland County Deeds, Patents, Etc., microfilm reel 1. Library of Virginia, Richmond.

1675–1689 Westmoreland County Order Book, microfilm reel 51. Library of Virginia, Richmond.

1690–1698 Westmoreland County Order Book, microfilm reel 52. Library of Virginia, Richmond.

McMillan, Lauren K.

2010   Put This in Your Pipe and Smoke It: An Evaluation of Tobacco Pipe Stem Dating Methods. M.A. thesis, Department of Anthropology, East Carolina University, Greenville NC.

2015a Community Formation and the Development of a British-Atlantic Identity in the Chesapeake: An Archaeological and Historical Study of the Tobacco Pipe Trade in the Potomac River Valley ca. 1630–1730. Doctoral dissertation, Department of Anthropology, University of Tennessee, Knoxville.

2015b The Multiple Interaction Spheres of Tobacco Pipes at the John Hallowes Site, Westmoreland County, Virginia. *Journal of Middle Atlantic Archaeology* 31:1–22.

2016a An Evaluation of Tobacco Pipe Stem Dating Methods. *Northeast Historical Archaeology* 45:18–42.

2016b Imported and Locally-Made Tobacco Pipes in the 17th-Century Chesapeake: Analysis and Trade Network Implications. Fellowship presentation, Omohundro Institute for Early American History and Culture and Jamestown Rediscovery, Jamestown VA.

McMillan, Lauren, and D. Brad Hatch

2013 Reanalyzing Nomini Plantation (44w m12): Preliminary Results. Paper presented at the 73rd Annual Meeting of the Archeology Society of Virginia, October 25–27, Virginia Beach.

McMillan, Lauren K., D. Brad Hatch, and Barbara J. Heath

2014 Dating Methods and Techniques at the John Hallowes Site (44w m6): A Seventeenth-Century Example. *Northeast Historical Archaeology* 43:18–36.

Menard, Russell R.

1988 British Migration to the Chesapeake Colonies in the Seventeenth Century. In *Colonial Chesapeake Society*, Lois Green Carr, Philip D. Morgan, and Jean B. Russo, editors, pp. 99–132. University of North Carolina Press. Chapel Hill.

Miller, Henry

1991 Tobacco Pipes from Pope's Fort, St. Mary's City, Maryland: An English Civil War Site on the American Frontier. In *The Archaeology of the Clay Tobacco Pipe XII, Chesapeake Bay*, Peter Davey and Dennis J. Pogue, editors, pp. 73–88. British Archaeological Reports International Series 56. Oxford.

Mitchell, Vivienne

1975 Glass Wine Bottle Seals Found at Nominy Plantation. *Quarterly Bulletin of the Archeological Society of Virginia* 29(4):203–208.

1976 Decorated Brown Clay Pipes from Nominy Plantation: Progress Report. *Quarterly Bulletin of the Archeological Society of Virginia* 31(2):83–92.

1983 The History of Nominy Plantation with Emphasis on the Clay Tobacco Pipes. In *Historic Clay Tobacco Pipes Studies*, Vol. 2, Byron Sudbury, editor, pp. 1–38. N.p.

Mitchell, Vivienne, and Sherwood Mitchell

1982 Clay Tobacco Pipes from Nominy Plantation. *Northern Neck of Virginia Historical Magazine* 32(1):3707–3714.

Morgan, Edmund S.

1975 *American Slavery, American Freedom: The Ordeal of Colonial Virginia*. Norton. New York.

Neiman, Fraser D.

1980 Field Archaeology of the Clifts Plantation Site, Westmoreland County, Virginia. Manuscript, Robert E. Lee Memorial Association, Inc. Stratford va.

Nicklin, John Bailey Calvert

1938 Immigration between Virginia and Maryland in the Seventeenth Century. *William and Mary Quarterly* 18(4):440–446.

Riordan, Timothy B.

2004 *The Plundering Time: Maryland and the English Civil War 1645-1646*. Maryland Historical Society. Baltimore.

Sherman, Virginia W.

1969   Major John Hallowes (1615–1657). Manuscript, Virginia Department of Historic Resources, Richmond.

Sherman, Virginia W., and Vivienne Mitchell

1983   Nominy Plantation. In *Westmoreland County, Virginia: 1653–1983*, Walter Briscoe Norris, Jr., editor, pp. 105–110. Westmoreland County Board of Supervisors. Montross VA.

South, Stanley

1977   *Method and Theory in Historical Archaeology*. Academic Press. New York.

Stone, Garry Wheeler

1982   *Society, Housing, and Architecture in Early Maryland: John Lewger's St. John's*. Doctoral dissertation, Department of American Civilization, University of Pennsylvania. ProQuest, Ann Arbor MI.

Straube, Beverly

1995   The Colonial Potters of Tidewater Virginia. *Journal of Early Southern Decorative Arts* 21(2):1–39.

Toner, Joseph M.

1891   Wills of the American Ancestors of General George Washington. *New England Historical and Genealogical Register* 45:199–215.

Walsh, Lorena S.

1979   "Till Death Us Do Part": Marriage and Family in Seventeenth-Century Maryland. In *The Chesapeake in the Seventeenth-Century: Essays on Anglo-American Society*, Thad W. Tate and David L. Ammerman, editors, pp. 126–152. University of North Carolina Press. Chapel Hill.

[EIGHT]

Dust and Bones

A Modern Analysis of Hanna's Town Fauna

STEFANIE M. SMITH

In the early to mid-18th century the portion of modern-day Pennsylvania that lies west of the Allegheny Mountains was considered a part of the unsettled American frontier: "On no map showing the country before 1700 is the section that we know today as Western Pennsylvania definitely outlined" (Wright and Corbett 1940:12). As populations in the eastern portion of the state grew and the battles of the French and Indian War ended, more settlers began to make their way west in search of unsettled land on which to make their homes. Sometime between 1759 and 1773 a man named Robert Hanna and a group of his compatriots settled along the Forbes Military Road in Westmoreland County, ultimately naming their settlement Hanna's Town. Established as an official county in 1773, Westmoreland County quickly became the center of westward expansion in Pennsylvania. Hanna's Town survived the threats of the frontier for approximately 13 years as the first English court and county seat west of the Allegheny Mountains.

Archaeological excavations of Hanna's Town (36WM203) began in 1969 after Westmoreland County obtained ownership of the property (Carlisle 2005). In the five decades since, numerous archaeological excavations and surveys have been conducted on the site in order to further define the boundaries of the settlement and the lots within, as well as to determine where particular buildings and structures were originally located (Grimm 1972; Richardson and Wilson 1976; Fryman and Eddins 1985). During these excavations an estimated 1 million artifacts have been recovered and foundations of several buildings have been found. The artifacts recovered from Hanna's Town include a variety of cultural material, such as ceramics, architectural materials, personal items, and approximately 20,000 faunal specimens. Today historic Hanna's Town serves as a living history museum and interpretive site. To date, two of the original Hanna's Town structures have been reconstructed on site, and many of the original artifacts are on display in the small museum space. Those artifacts not on display are currently stored in buildings on the Hanna's Town property. Some limited cataloging and curation of artifacts has taken place over the years. Currently Ben Ford and Indiana University of Pennsylvania are working with the Westmoreland County Historical Society to produce a cohesive and descriptive catalog of the Hanna's Town artifacts (Ford, this volume). As part of this initiative, all artifacts currently stored at Hanna's Town are being sorted, identified, and properly curated.

Throughout the nearly 50 years of excavations that have been conducted at Hanna's Town, a variety of artifact collection and curation methods have been employed. These methodologies have had varying effects on the survival and preservation level of the recovered artifacts. Legacy faunal collections like that of Hanna's Town contain excellent material for case studies on the effects of second-order taphonomic changes, as defined by Reitz and Wing (2008). Legacy faunal collections contain an enormous amount of data, not only pertaining to the archaeological sites from which they originate but also on the evolution of archaeology and curation as fields of professional and academic inquiry. When we apply modern methods of analysis to legacy collections, it is imperative to consider what role second-order changes may have played in the current state of these collections. These types of changes include those that are directly influenced by the choices of the archaeologist or zooarchaeologist and may relate to excavation method, laboratory processing procedure, and curation and storage technique.

Excavation method is most likely to affect an assemblage by creating bias in the types of remains that are recovered. The use of smaller screen size may ensure a higher rate of recovery for smaller elements, while the use of flotation increases the likelihood that even the smallest remains are also recovered. When only larger screen sizes are used, the probability that smaller, more fragile remains will be recovered drops significantly. The Hanna's Town assemblage was subjected to a number of different field techniques, each of which is likely to have caused some degree of bias in the faunal assemblage itself.

Laboratory processing procedure and curation and storage technique are directly linked, particularly in the subsequent study of the Hanna's Town material. Available records did not provide details regarding the washing, sorting, and packaging of the Hanna's Town faunal material. Close inspection of the available faunal material from the site revealed a method of storage that may have been originally intended for short-term storage but was not sufficiently stable for long-term periods. While some artifact classes are less susceptible to the negative effects of improper long-term storage techniques (e.g., ceramic and glass), faunal remains are more likely to show visible signs of degradation over time.

The Hanna's Town artifact assemblage is a potential resource for significant data relating to the original settlement and growth of western Pennsylvania. The faunal analysis described in this chapter is part of the ongoing effort to interpret the substantial amount of material that has come from this site with the specific goal of addressing the subsistence practices of a community whose existence in the historical record is ephemeral but significant.

Historical Background

It was not until 1769 that the Pennsylvania Land Office began to distribute land warrants to those who claimed ownership of property or were interested in owning property west of the Alleghenies (Gresham and Wiley 1890; Hassler 1900). Prior to the opening of the Land Office, only military permits were officially issued for this geographic area, although undocumented pioneers were already beginning to settle around military forts or along the military roads, principally the Forbes and Braddock roads.

Fryman and Eddins (1985) suggest that Robert Hanna settled in the area that would soon become Hanna's Town sometime between 1769, when the Pennsylvania Land Office opened, and 1773, when Westmoreland County became an officially recognized county. At the time of its creation, Westmoreland County was much larger than what appears on maps today. It covered approximately 4,700 square miles and contained the entirety of modern-day southwestern Pennsylvania (Hassler 1900:6).

After the establishment of Westmoreland County, Hanna's Town was recognized as the most centralized settlement in the county, making it an ideal location for the county seat. Court was to be held at Robert Hanna's home, which also served as a tavern. The first court sessions took place here in April 1773, just over a month after the county was formed (Hassler 1900; Grimm 1972). For its first several years, Hanna's Town grew and thrived as the center of western Pennsylvania government, at one point competing with Pittsburgh in size and population.

With Hanna's Town at the center of political operations, Westmoreland County continued to thrive until the summer of 1782. On 13 July 1782, Hanna's Town was attacked by a group of British soldiers and Seneca Indians (Albert 1882; Gresham and Wiley 1890; Richardson 2007a, 2007b). During this attack the residents of Hanna's Town retreated to the relative safety of the Fort Reed stockade in the southern section of town, while the raiding party pillaged and set fire to the town buildings. Poorly armed and with only a small number of men capable of fighting, those who took cover within the walls of Fort Reed were able to do no more than watch as their homes burned.

While the attack itself lasted only one day, the devastation that it caused was irreparable. The entire central portion of Hanna's Town was destroyed, with the exception of Fort Reed and two other structures that Albert (1882) describes as being under cover of the fort. Exactly how close these two surviving structures were to the fort is not certain, although it is suggested that the two surviving buildings were Foreman's Tavern (Richardson and Wilson 1976) and Hanna's Tavern (Albert 1882; Gresham and Wiley 1890; Boucher 1906; Wright and Corbett 1940).

Personal accounts recorded in the years following the attack mention the rebuilding of several of the previous log homes that marked the town's lots, but Hanna's Town was never able to regain the power and notoriety it had lost. In 1787 the county seat was officially moved to Newtown (now named Greensburg), and Hanna's Town all but disappeared from the historical record (Carlisle 2005).

At the height of Hanna's Town's influence over newly founded Westmoreland County, the settlement was centrally located between Fort Pitt and Fort Ligonier on the Forbes Military Road. Originally Hanna's Town stretched across over 300 acres of land. Today the Westmoreland County Historical Society owns approximately 12 acres of what has been identified as the original settlement location.

Methodology

The objective of this research is to examine the dietary practices of the 18th-century residents of the historic Hanna's Town settlement through the analysis of faunal remains recovered during a series of excavations that spanned approximately 40 years. As noted earlier, these faunal remains are part of a larger legacy collection for which curation methods are currently being reevaluated. The research objectives applied to the Hanna's Town faunal analysis reflect a distinct lack of published research on the use of legacy collections in the study of foodways of western Pennsylvania's 18th-century frontier settlers. One study from 1994 addressed the results of excavations at the 19th-century Schaeffer Farm Site (36AR410) in Armstrong County, just to the north of Westmoreland County (Bedell et al. 1994). Despite the differences in period of occupation, the Schaeffer Farm Site currently serves as the only comparable faunal case study that is broadly representative of this temporal period and geographical region (albeit without the use of legacy collections).

The original excavators of Hanna's Town organized the historical site along a grid system that is based on a series of 50 ft. x 50 ft. squares. The X-axis of this grid runs east to west and is labeled using Roman numerals from I to XVI. The Y-axis runs south to north and is labeled using letters A to P. Each 50 ft. x 50 ft. square is divided into

16 10 ft. x 10 ft. squares labeled numerically from 1 to 16 and separated by 2-ft. balks. The 2-ft. balk is also present along the edges of each 50 ft. x 50 ft. square, providing a balk measuring 4 ft. across between all outer 10 ft. x 10 ft. squares. All 10 ft. x 10 ft. squares are broken down into four directionally labeled corners: NW, SW, NE, and SE.

The analyzed faunal assemblage consists of three sampled subassemblages: Hanna's Tavern, Foreman's Tavern, and Irish House. These assemblages included faunal material that was collected from areas immediately within and adjacent to the identified structural remains and their associated features. The subassemblage names were assigned by the original excavators, and with the exception of Foreman's Tavern have not yet been definitively linked to a specific Hanna's Town resident. Sampling strategy was consistent among the three, with specimens pulled first from feature contexts, then from surrounding nonfeature contexts, until the samples were comparable in size or no additional specimens were available for inclusion.

The discussion and interpretation of this research is largely based on the quantitative analysis of data recovered during the identification stage of research. Due to the innumerable ways of quantifying data in terms of faunal analysis (Lyman 2008), the calculations that are applied to this research were specifically chosen based on the research objectives. The quantification process of each subassemblage follows commonly accepted zooarchaeological practice, beginning with the following calculations: number of specimens (NSP), number of identified specimens (NISP), and minimum number of individuals (MNI). Both NISP and MNI are also expressed in percentages along with the dry bone weight for each identified taxon. Statistical interpretation of taxonomic diversity within each of the three subassemblages follows the Shannon-Weaver function methodology as described by Lyman (2008) and Reitz and Wing (2008).

Results

The faunal material included in this analysis consisted of 8,397 individual specimens pulled from three previously defined areas within the historic Hanna's Town site. In this section the analyzed Hanna's

Town assemblage is first described as a whole in terms of content. This description is followed by an individual discussion of each of the three subassemblages and how they statistically compare.

A large amount of the overall faunal assemblage (81.5%) was unidentifiable beyond class. This unidentified material was sorted and quantified according to class, approximate size, and subassemblage (Table 7). The percentage of unidentified bone is somewhat high but consistent across the three subassemblages, ranging from approximately 79% to 84%. A combination of specimen fragmentation and a high frequency of nondiagnostic bone such as medial rib fragments and indeterminate vertebral fragments contributed to the high percentage of specimens that were not identifiable to species. To illustrate, approximately 23% (1,592 individual fragments) of these specimens were identified as indeterminate medial rib fragments or indeterminate vertebral fragments, while approximately 29% (1,977 individual fragments) were identified as indeterminate long bone shaft fragments. The overwhelming majority of these rib, vertebral, and long bone shaft fragments are classified as mammalian and most commonly represent those of medium and large size.

The remaining 28.5% of the assemblage was identified to order or lower and includes 26 identifications to species, 4 identifications to genus, 8 identifications to family, and 5 identifications to order or suborder (Table 8). The richness (number of identified taxa) of the Hanna's Town faunal assemblage is generally high, although when broken down by subassemblage there is a sharp drop in the richness of the Irish House assemblage (16 identified taxa) when compared to the Hanna's Tavern and Foreman's Tavern assemblages (30 and 33 taxa, respectively). Additional comparison of the identified taxa in the three subassemblages reveals a clear difference in the number of wild species present in the Irish House sample versus those identified in the Hanna's Tavern and Foreman's Tavern samples. For this analysis, domestic versus wild is determined based on the basic perception that a domestic animal is one that is not native to the area and would require human assistance in order to thrive and/or is kept or bred specifically for human use. The Irish House sample contains substantially fewer wild species than are present in the Hanna's Tavern and Foreman's Tavern samples, while the number of identified domestic species is similar among the three subassemblages. This difference in the presence of wild species could be a product of sample size, or it could indicate that the occupants of Irish House focused mostly on domesticates for food.

Of the 30 taxa that were identified to genus or species, only nine are represented in all three faunal assemblages: gray squirrel, whitetailed deer, cow, pig, horse, ruffed grouse, wild turkey, chicken, and freshwater drum. The following discussion of the three individual subassemblages will show that, although these species appear in all three subassemblages, they are not representative of significant food sources for all three sample areas. Only pig and cow remains appear in substantial numbers across the three samples.

Table 7. Unidentified bone by assemblage, Hanna's Town

Taxonomic Classification	Common Name and Size	Hanna's Tavern	Foreman's Tavern	Irish House	Total NSP
Vertebrata	Vertebrate	1	2	—	3
Invertebrata	Invertebrate	1	1	—	2
Mammalia	Mammal, Unknown Size	14	155	4	173
Mammalia, M or L	Mammal ≥ 4 kg	828	726	468	2,022
Mammalia, L	Mammal > 30 kg	965	485	492	1,942
Mammalia, M	Mammal 4–30 kg	635	415	335	1,385
Mammalia, S or M	Mammal < 30 kg	64	177	37	278
Mammalia, S	Mammal < 4 kg	27	199	3	229
Mammalia or Aves	Mammal or Bird	50	39	10	99
Aves	Bird, Unknown Size	2	49	—	51
Aves, L	Large Bird	18	43	7	68
Aves, M	Medium Bird	145	331	16	492
Aves, S	Small Bird	3	14	—	17
Osteichthyes	Indeterminate Bony Fish	37	42	3	82
TOTAL		2,790	2,678	1,375	6,843

Table 8. Master species list by area, Hanna's Town

		Hanna's Tavern	Foreman's Tavern	Irish House	Total
No. of Taxa (Richness)		30	33	16	43
Total MNI		37	45	19	101
TAXONOMIC CLASSIFICATION	COMMON NAME	NISP	NISP	NISP	TOTAL NISP
Mammals					
Didelphis virginiana	Opossum	1	—	—	1
Talpidae	Moles	8	—	—	8
Leporidae	Rabbits and Hares	—	2	—	2
Sylvilagus floridanus	Eastern Cottontail	1	5	—	6
Rodentia	Indeterminate Rodent	2	12	—	14
Tamias striatus	Eastern Chipmunk	3	6	—	9
Sciuridae	Woodchucks and Squirrels	2	—	—	2
Sciurus carolinensis	Gray Squirrel	8	115	3	126
Sciurus niger	Fox Squirrel	—	6	—	6
Ondatra zibethicus	Muskrat	3	—	—	3
Rattus rattus	Black Rat	2	1	—	3
Vulpes vulpes	Red Fox	1	—	—	1
Procyon lotor	Raccoon	5	—	—	5
Mustela vison	Mink	—	5	—	5
Ungulate		25	2	7	34
Artiodactyla		8	7	—	15
Odocoileus virginianus	White-tailed Deer	56	13	31	100
Bos sp.*	Cow	153	44	125	322
*Ovis aries**	Sheep	—	1	8	9
*Sus scrofa**	Pig	140	208	81	429

*Equus caballus**	Horse	1	2	6	9

Birds

Branta canadensis	Canada Goose	10	—	—	10
Anatinae	Duck	2	1	—	3
Falconiformes	Diurnal Birds of Prey	—	—	1	1
Cathartes aura	Turkey Vulture	—	1	—	1
Galliformes	Ground-feeding Birds	5	14	3	22
Bonasa umbellus	Ruffed Grouse	5	15	3	23
Meleagris gallopavo	Wild Turkey	8	17	6	31
Colinus virginianus	Northern Bobwhite	2	14	—	16
*Gallus domesticus**	Chicken	55	123	3	181
Columba cf. *livia*	Pigeon	—	1	—	1
Cyanocitta cristata	Blue Jay	—	3	—	3

Reptiles

Chelonia	Turtle	7	1	1	9
Graptemys geographica	Common Map Turtle	3	—	1	4
Trionyx spinifera	Spiny Soft-Shelled Turtle	—	—	31	31

Amphibians

Anura	Frogs and Toads	1	4	—	5

Fish

Ictalurus punctatus	Channel Catfish	—	3	—	3
I. punctatus or *furcatus*	Channel or Blue Catfish	1	1	-	2
Catostomidae	Suckers	—	3	1	4
Perciformes	Perch-like Fish	1	1	—	2
Micropterus sp.	Smallmouth or Largemouth Bass	—	1	—	1
Pomoxis nigromaculatus	Black Crappie	—	6	—	6

Aplodinotus grunniens	Freshwater Drum	8	74	4	86
TOTAL		527	712	315	1,554

*Commonly domesticated species

Hanna's Tavern

The first archaeological excavation of Hanna's Town began in 1969 under the leadership of Jacob L. Grimm, with professional and avocational volunteers. Excavation revealed the footprint of a 20 ft. x 30 ft. structure that is believed to have been Hanna's Tavern (Grimm 1972; Carlisle 2005). Originally the home of Robert Hanna, the founder of Hanna's Town, Hanna's Tavern also served as a courthouse (Albert 1882; Grimm 1972). Prior to this study, no faunal analysis has been completed for the Hanna's Tavern area.

The Hanna's Tavern subassemblage consists of 3,319 individual specimens that were primarily collected from a pit feature and three post molds (Smith 2014:30). Approximately 14% (475 individual specimens) of the subassemblage was identified to genus or species (Table 9). The Hanna's Tavern species list contains 17 identified wild species and 4 domestic species. Initially these numbers seem to suggest a higher reliance on wild fauna at Hanna's Tavern, but a closer look at the data reveals that domestic species make up almost three quarters of the identified specimens in the sample. Contributing to the 17 identified wild species are several possibly intrusive or commensal taxa that were likely not consumed at Hanna's Tavern. These include, but are not limited to, mole, chipmunk, and black rat.

Table 9. Hanna's Tavern identified species list, Hanna's Town

Taxon	NISP		Weight		MNI	
	No.	%	g.	%	No.	%
Mammals						
Opossum	1	0.03	0.40	0.01	1	2.70
Moles	8	0.24	0.51	0.01	1	2.70

	NISP	%	Weight	%	MNI	%
Eastern Cottontail	1	0.03	0.48	0.01	1	2.70
Eastern Chipmunk	3	0.09	0.73	0.01	1	2.70
Gray Squirrel	8	0.24	4.14	0.07	1	2.70
Muskrat	3	0.09	3.23	0.06	1	2.70
Black Rat	2	0.06	1.71	0.03	1	2.70
Red Fox	1	0.03	4.45	0.08	1	2.70
Raccoon	5	0.15	8.78	0.16	1	2.70
White-tailed Deer	56	1.69	861.18	15.57	3	8.11
Cow*	153	4.61	3,771.79	68.18	4	10.81
Pig*	140	4.22	648.53	11.72	7	18.92
Horse*	1	0.03	77.89	1.41	1	2.70
Birds						
Canada Goose	10	0.30	38.89	0.70	2	5.41
Duck	2	0.06	0.98	0.02	1	2.70
Ruffed Grouse	5	0.15	1.75	0.03	1	2.70
Wild Turkey	8	0.24	35.14	0.64	1	2.70
Northern Bobwhite	2	0.06	0.53	0.01	1	2.70
Chicken*	55	1.66	58.48	1.06	5	13.51
Reptiles						
Common Map Turtle	3	0.09	10.74	0.19	1	2.70
Fish						
Freshwater Drum	8	0.24	2.18	0.04	1	2.70
TOTAL	475	14.31	5,532.51	100.00	37	100.00

*Commonly domesticated species

Several taxa are identified as occurring more frequently than others based on an analysis of NISP, MNI, and weight values. These taxa contribute the largest variety of elements to the assemblage and therefore are perhaps the most useful indicators of patterns in animal usage and consumption at Hanna's Tavern. In this subassemblage the most commonly occurring taxa are the cow, pig, white-tailed deer, and chicken. The dominant presence of these taxa suggests a heavy focus on the use of domestic taxa at Hanna's Tavern but fails to illustrate the variety of species initially identified and shown in Table 9.

Further analysis of the most frequently occurring species addresses patterns of skeletal representation. The identification of patterns or the lack thereof in skeletal representation can aid in the reliability of the faunal interpretation of a site. In the Hanna's Tavern assemblage, white-tailed deer specimens are generally representative of all areas of the skeleton, with a slightly higher number of feet, scapulae, and humeri present. It is notable that no femurs from this species are present. The absence of this element could be due to excessive fragmentation of the bones in an attempt to extract marrow or to flavor soups or stews.

Of the identified taxa, cow elements are the most common in the Hanna's Tavern sample. While at least one of most of the major elements is present, there are a noticeably larger number of skulls and feet represented than any other element. With four identified skulls and nine identified feet, these elements occur at least twice as often as any other identified element for this taxon and may represent portions of the cow that were frequently consumed at Hanna's Tavern.

The identified pig elements are almost completely devoid of long bones, with the exception of one tibia. The most frequently occurring elements for this taxon are the skull (n=7) and the scapula (n=5). The lack of identified pig long bones might be attributed to excessive fragmentation of these elements, or it may suggest that pigs were not butchered here but were instead purchased or traded piecemeal.

The identified chicken elements in the Hanna's Tavern subassemblage are generally representative of all edible parts of the bird. The elements that are not represented in this sample are those that are commonly associated with butcher's refuse: the head and the feet. The absence of these elements might suggest that chickens were not butchered on site or that butchering took place in a separate area of the Hanna's Tavern lot. The skeletal representations of the head and feet of a chicken are fairly small and fragile and are less likely to survive in archaeological deposits. Unlike Foreman's Tavern, the soil from the Hanna's Tavern excavation was never run through field or lab flotation, so it is possible that this sample is somewhat biased toward the larger and less fragile portions of the skeleton.

Foreman's Tavern

In 1970 James Richardson III of the University of Pittsburgh directed a field school at Hanna's Town. During this field season evidence of the location of a second tavern site known as Foreman's Tavern was discovered (Grimm 1972; Richardson and Wilson 1976). The owner of Foreman's Tavern was Charles Foreman, a well-known politician and businessman in the Hanna's Town community. This area was identified as Foreman's Tavern following a review of gray literature and historical documentation, including land deeds. Additional evidence for this identification was recovered during excavation in the form of a very specific spoon. The handle of the spoon is engraved with "CSF," which is believed to stand for Charles and Sarah Foreman (Richardson and Wilson 1976). Some limited faunal analysis was previously completed on the Foreman's Tavern faunal material by Sandor Bokonyi of Magyar Nemzeti Museum in Budapest while he was a visiting scholar at the University of California, Los Angeles. Bokonyi completed an analysis of 1,435 bone fragments and created a table listing the presence of domestic animals versus that of wild game. No further report discussing the analysis exists. This research expands on this information with a more complete analysis of the Foreman's Tavern bone.

The Foreman's Tavern subassemblage consists of 3,389 individual specimens that were collected from two pit features. Approximately 20% (664 individual specimens) of the subassemblage was identified to genus or species (Table 10). The Foreman's Tavern species list contains 17 identified wild species and five domestic species. Unlike the Hanna's Tavern subassemblage, this sample contains a comparable number of individual specimens in both the wild and domestic categories. Commensal species are also present in the Foreman's Tavern sample and include, but are not limited to, chipmunk and black rat.

Table 10. Foreman's Tavern identified species list, Hanna's Town

Taxon	NISP		Weight		MNI	
	No.	%	g.	%	No.	%
Mammals						
Eastern Cottontail	5	0.15	1.76	0.07	1	2.27
Eastern Chipmunk	6	0.18	1.15	0.05	1	2.27
Gray Squirrel	115	3.39	40.51	1.65	8	18.18
Fox Squirrel	6	0.18	2.60	0.11	1	2.27
Black Rat	1	0.03	1.06	0.04	1	2.27
Mink	5	0.15	1.98	0.08	1	2.27
White-tailed Deer	13	0.38	169.65	6.92	2	4.55
Cow*	44	1.30	1,222.69	49.87	1	2.27
Sheep*	1	0.03	26.47	1.08	1	2.27
Pig*	208	6.14	815.22	33.25	3	6.82
Horse*	2	0.06	40.33	1.64	1	2.27
Birds						
Duck	1	0.03	0.94	0.04	1	2.27
Turkey Vulture	1	0.03	1.40	0.06	1	2.27
Ruffed Grouse	15	0.44	5.04	0.21	2	4.55
Wild Turkey	17	0.50	22.50	0.92	1	2.27
Northern Bobwhite	14	0.41	1.80	0.07	2	4.55
Chicken*	123	3.63	85.37	3.48	10	22.73
Pigeon	1	0.03	0.55	0.02	1	2.27
Blue Jay	3	0.09	0.25	0.01	1	2.27
Fish						
Channel Catfish	3	0.09	1.85	0.08	1	2.27
Black Crappie	6	0.18	0.29	0.01	1	2.27
Freshwater Drum	74	2.18	8.44	0.34	2	4.55
TOTAL	664	19.59	2,451.85	100.00	44	100.00

*Commonly domesticated species

The Foreman's Tavern subassemblage exhibits slightly more taxonomic variation than the Hanna's Tavern subassemblage. The most frequently occurring taxa at Foreman's Tavern are cow, pig, chicken, gray squirrel, and freshwater drum. The dominant presence of these taxa suggests nearly equal use of domestic and wild taxa at Foreman's Tavern, but again fails to illustrate the variety of species initially identified and shown in Table 10. Another notable difference between the Hanna's Tavern and Foreman's Tavern fauna is based on size. At Foreman's Tavern the average size of the identified taxa is more variable than those identified at Hanna's Tavern. The identified cow elements in this sample are generally representative of all portions of the skeleton of a single cow, with the exception of the femur. These results indicate that at least one cow was butchered on site at Foreman's Tavern.

Pig elements were by far the most commonly identified in the Foreman's Tavern assemblage, appearing almost twice as frequently as any other identified taxon. The identified pig remains include a large number of feet (n=7) and skulls (n=4) and at least two of each long bone, with the exception of the tibia. Based on the appearance of most portions of the pig skeleton, it is probable that pigs were butchered and processed on site. On-site butchering and processing, while probably not always common at taverns within larger, more populated cities, would have been a matter of daily life at a tavern in a generally self-sufficient frontier town like Hanna's Town.

The identified chicken elements in the Foreman's Tavern sample are generally representative of all edible portions of the skeleton with exceptionally high numbers of axial (10 sternums and 9 furcula identified) and forelimb elements present. Elements representing the skull and the hind limbs (including the feet) were identified, but in much smaller numbers.

Perhaps the most interesting characteristic of this sample is the large number of gray squirrel elements. The forelimb and hind limb elements that are represented in this sample, with the exception of the humerus, appear more than twice as frequently as all other identified elements. It appears that the legs of these small animals were consumed at Foreman's Tavern, although it is possible that some squirrels entered the assemblage as intrusive scavengers. If all of the identified squirrel elements were representative of intrusive nesting, a more uniform pattern of elements should be present.

Although the NISP values for freshwater drum are among the highest in this sample, it should be noted that more than three quarters of the NISP for this species is made up of scales. The MNI calculation of two for this species is based on the presence of three complete and sided otoliths.

Irish House

The area referred to as Irish House is absent from the excavation reports available to the author, although according to records kept by the Westmoreland County Historical Society, this area was excavated during multiple field seasons. While the faunal material from this area was not labeled and sorted based on the season of excavation, each bag was labeled according to the block number from which it was recovered. These block numbers correspond to the color-coded excavation map that was previously used by the Westmoreland County Historical Society to identify which areas had already been excavated and by whom (Smith 2014:29–33). For the purpose of this research, Irish House serves as a representative sample of a typical Hanna's Town dwelling, as no records indicate that it was used for any other purpose. No prior faunal analysis has been completed for this area.

The Irish House subassemblage consists of 1,689 individual specimens that were primarily collected from four pit features and three other features. Additional faunal material from areas immediately surrounding the features was also included in this analysis. Approximately 18% of the subassemblage was identified to genus or species (Table 11). The Irish House species list contains seven identified wild species and five domestic species. As with the previous two subassemblages, these numbers do not illustrate the degree of contribution of each species to the sample. Here domestic taxa make up more than three quarters of the identified specimens—approximately 6.5 times that of wild species. One noticeable difference between the Irish House sample and the two previous samples is the exceedingly low number of obvious commensal species. While the identified rodent and turtle species may be commensal, it is also possible that one or more of these species were in fact consumed, particularly the spiny soft-shelled turtle, an aquatic species.

Table 11. Irish House identified species list, Hanna's Town

Taxon	NISP		Weight		MNI	
	No.	%	g.	%	No.	%
Mammals						
Gray Squirrel	3	0.18	1.36	0.02	1	5.26
White-tailed Deer	31	1.84	485.84	7.41	2	10.53
Cow*	125	7.40	5,045.24	76.90	2	10.53
Sheep*	8	0.47	81.16	1.24	1	5.26
Pig*	81	4.80	475.22	7.24	4	21.05
Horse*	6	0.36	360.23	5.49	1	5.26
Birds						
Wild Turkey	6	0.36	29.92	0.46	2	10.53
Ruffed Grouse	3	0.18	0.99	0.02	1	5.26
Chicken*	6	0.36	5.74	0.09	2	10.53
Reptiles						
Common Map Turtle	1	0.06	1.23	0.02	1	5.26
Spiny Soft-Shelled Turtle	31	1.84	73.43	1.12	1	5.26
Fish						
Freshwater Drum	4	0.24	0.18	0.003	1	5.26
TOTAL	305	18.06	6,560.54	100.00	19	100.00

*Commonly domesticated species

The most commonly identified taxa in the Irish House sub-assemblage are the white-tailed deer, the cow, the pig, and the spiny soft-shelled turtle. The identified white-tailed deer elements are generally representative of all portions of the skeleton, with at least two individuals represented. The presence of at least two skulls and three feet suggests that these animals were butchered and processed on site.

At least one of all of the major cow skeletal elements are present in this sample. The distribution of the identified elements includes between two and four of most paired elements and two of all non-paired elements. Based on these numbers and the lack of any missing elements, it appears that cows were butchered and processed on site at Irish House.

The identified pig elements in the Irish House sample include almost no long bones, with the exception of a single forelimb. Those elements that are present include the head, the feet, the scapula, and the radius. The near absence of long bones in this assemblage is likely a result of excessive fragmentation due to intensive usage of the available pig elements.

Although spiny soft-shelled turtle is a frequently occurring species within this subassemblage, according to the moderately low NISP% calculation (Table 11), it is not representative of a commonly exploited species, as nearly all of the NISP for that species is classified as neural and pleural fragments from a single, large individual. Unlike the Hanna's Tavern and Foreman's Tavern samples, very few bird elements are present in the Irish House sample. None of the bird species that were identified are representative of a substantial portion of the sample.

Diversity

This analysis follows Lyman's (2008) model of diversity applied as an umbrella term to encompass richness, heterogeneity, and evenness. Lyman defines diversity as "the structure and composition" of a faunal assemblage (173). Richness refers to the number of taxa that are represented in a given assemblage, as is addressed in Table 8.

Heterogeneity and evenness require the application of statistical concepts in order to describe the assemblage on a spectrum (Lyman 2008; Reitz and Wing 2008). Using the Shannon-Weaver function (also known as the Shannon-Wiener function or the Shannon index), the heterogeneity of each subassemblage is calculated separately (Shannon and Weaver 1949; Magurran 1988; Lyman 2008; Reitz and Wing 2008). For this analysis, heterogeneity is calculated using the following formula:

$H = -\Sigma\,(Pi)\,(logePi)$

In this formula, *Pi* is the relative abundance of each taxon (Reitz and Wing 2008), which is first found by dividing each individual MNI or NISP (*fi*) by the total MNI or NISP value (*n*).

$Pi = fi/n$

The second step is to determine the natural *loge* of *Pi*. Next, *Pi* is multiplied by the natural *loge* of *Pi* for each taxon. The sum of these products is inverted to get a positive number. Most commonly, this number will range from 1.5 to 3.5 (Magurran 1988:35; Lyman 2008:192). The closer this number is to 1, the less heterogeneity is present in the subassemblage (Lyman 2008; Reitz and Wing 2008). As illustrated in Table 12, the three subassemblages have similar rates of heterogeneity when the calculation is based on MNI values. When the calculation is completed using the NISP values, the level of heterogeneity in the Foreman's Tavern sample drops slightly but stays in the middle range, while the Hanna's Tavern and the Irish House samples drop, indicating low levels of heterogeneity.

The next calculation is evenness, also known as equitability (Reitz and Wing 2008). Evenness describes how frequently the identified taxa occur in relation to one another in a given assemblage (Lyman 2008; Reitz and Wing 2008) and is calculated using the following formula:

$e = H/logeS$

In this formula, *H* is the previously calculated level of heterogeneity, and *S* is the total MNI or NISP. Evenness values range from 0 to 1, where 1 is an even distribution, and 0 is uneven (Lyman 2008; Reitz and Wing 2008). Table 12 shows the levels of evenness as calculated by sample area. Here the level of evenness changes drastically between calculations using MNI and those using NISP. When MNI is used, all subassemblages exhibit a high degree of evenness between taxa. When the calculation is completed using NISP values, all three subassemblages exhibit rather low levels of evenness between taxa.

Table 12. Heterogeneity and evenness in the three subassemblages as calculated using the Shannon-Weaver Index, Hanna's Town

	Heterogeneity Based on MNI	Heterogeneity Based on NISP	Evenness Based on MNI	Evenness Based on NISP
Hanna's Tavern	2.785	1.8021	0.777	0.292
Foreman's Tavern	2.693	2.075	0.712	0.319
Irish House	2.368	1.673	0.804	0.292

Discussion

The Hanna's Town faunal assemblage contains three subassemblages that originated from areas defined by structural remains and their associated features. Each of the three areas was analyzed and interpreted individually in an effort to contribute valuable information regarding diet and subsistence practices on the American frontier to the current body of knowledge on the subject. Beyond the results of the faunal analysis, a review of historical resources and modern research on the topic provides insight into area identity, use patterns, and dates of occupation.

The analysis and research on the area known as Hanna's Tavern has raised questions specifically regarding the idea that this area is indeed the original location of Hanna's Tavern. Albert (1882), Boucher (1906), and Wright and Corbett (1940) state that Hanna's Tavern was one of the two structures outside of the stockade Fort Reed that were not burned during the 1782 raid on Hanna's Town. In fact, Albert (1882:140) describes the two surviving structures as being "nearest to [the fort] and covered by it." This phrasing may suggest that Hanna's Tavern was located on the same side of the Forbes Road as the fort and Foreman's Tavern (the second structure to survive the fire), or possibly adjacent to the fort on the other side of the Forbes Road. The specific meaning of Albert's phrasing is uncertain. My research suggests that the area known as Hanna's Tavern may contain evidence to indicate that it may not be the true location of the original home and tavern owned by Robert Hanna, the founder of Hanna's Town.

Some of the bone recovered from the Hanna's Tavern area was recovered from an ash layer that extended from 10 to 12 inches below the surface. This ash layer is indicative of an episode of burning, although a lack of detailed field notes from this excavation area prevents further characterization of the scale of this burning episode. The ash layer could be from an area of waste disposal that did not present itself as a pit feature during excavation. Seven pieces of burned bone were recovered from a post mold. Were these bones deposited in the post mold during a post–Hanna's Town occupation of the area, or was this deposit made during the last five years of Hanna's Town, following the reconstruction of a previously destroyed building?

The faunal analysis of the Hanna's Tavern area contained a moderately diverse faunal assemblage of both wild and domestic species. As the home and business of Robert Hanna, the town founder and arguably the wealthiest man in Hanna's Town, I expected to see a greater discrepancy in wild and domestic species than was observed, as Hanna would probably have owned a larger number of livestock than most at Hanna's Town. While the Hanna's Tavern sample is representative of a diet mostly consisting of domestic species, some wild species were included in the diet, possibly simply for the sake of variety. The relatively high number of bones from this area that are associated with the head and feet of large mammals could be representative of butcher's refuse. Conversely these parts of the animal may have been favored at Hanna's Tavern based on personal preference for popular dishes of the time like offal, tongue, pig's feet, cowheel, and calf's-foot jelly (Noël Hume 1978; Scott 2008).

Results of the research and analysis of the Foreman's Tavern area support the original identification of this area, with some interesting new information regarding the menu at this tavern. With nearly equal quantities of wild and domestic taxa, and skeletal representations suggestive of frequent on-site butchering of a moderately diverse variety of taxa, it appears that Charles and Sarah Foreman ran a well-attended tavern and were self-sufficient in providing food for themselves, their family, and the patrons of their establishment.

One unique feature of the Foreman's Tavern faunal assemblage stood out more than any other: an abundance of squirrel bones, especially the meatier forelimb and hind limb elements. There are reports of an extreme increase in the gray squirrel population in western Pennsylvania during the years of the Hanna's Town occupation. Albert (1882:164) states that squirrels "were so numerous they were a pest to the farmer, and a standing bounty was set upon their scalps to encourage their destruction." Due to the overabundance of these animals and the relative ease with which they could be trapped, it is a logical assumption that Charles and Sarah Foreman might have taken advantage of them as a relatively inexpensive food source. The apparent fact that gray squirrel played a large role in subsistence practices at Foreman's Tavern, if even for a short time, is an individual characteristic of the area that provides a bit of insight into how environmental factors contributed to dietary decisions at Hanna's Town.

The frequency with which squirrel elements appear in the Foreman's Tavern sample in comparison to the Hanna's Tavern and Irish House samples raises the discussion of field technique and recovery methods. All of the soil from the pit features at Foreman's Tavern was run through field flotation at the time of excavation. By using flotation, excavators ensured that a more comprehensive sample was recovered from the features and increased the likelihood of recovering small and fragile faunal specimens in addition to those of larger size. This process could also explain the larger variety of species identified in the Foreman's Tavern sample.

The Irish House subassemblage is distinctly different from the Hanna's Tavern and Foreman's Tavern assemblages. No additional documentation of or historic references to the original building were found over the course of this research. Based on the characteristics of the Irish House faunal assemblage, there is some speculation regarding the date of original occupation of this area. Although the assemblage contains a similar degree of taxonomic diversity compared to the previous two, the small amount of recovered faunal remains, a higher frequency of domestic taxa versus wild, and a high level of preservation of specimens with large fragment size lead me to believe that the Irish House area was occupied for only a short period of time that was somewhat later than the other areas. A 2014 preliminary study of the spatial distribution of daub and pearlware at Hanna's Town supports this interpretation (Ford 2014). Ford suggests an association between the lack of daub and the presence of pearlware as a possible distinction between areas of the site that were occupied originally and the post-raid Hanna's Town settlement. The low frequency of wild taxa may mean that by the time of the Irish House occupation, local butchering of domestic animals was the main meat procurement strategy and that hunting was a less frequent activity. Perhaps the Irish House was constructed after the burning of Hanna's Town but was soon abandoned as the settlement failed to recover. By raising questions regarding the dates of occupation for the Irish House area, I suggest a need for additional investigation into interpreting the archaeological distinction between the multiple occupations of the Hanna's Town site from its original settlement and organization, to the attempt to rebuild after the 1782 fire, and into the 19th- and 20th-century single-family farm occupation.

While this work has produced a new body of data regarding subsistence in small frontier communities, the questions and answers provided here are only a small part of the archaeological interpretation of Hanna's Town and the western Pennsylvania frontier. The Hanna's Town collection is incredibly rich in data regarding not just subsistence but all aspects of daily life during this fundamental part of Pennsylvania history. This collection serves as a compelling case study in support of pursuing the analysis and interpretation of other large, nearly forgotten legacy collections. In the five decades since the first excavations at Hanna's Town began, archaeological methods have been expanded and refined to approach artifact identification and interpretation from different angles, providing insight into aspects of life at Hanna's Town that were not previously accessible. If one collection can provide such a substantial amount of meaningful data after nearly 40 years in storage, so can others. I conclude this work with the hope that more in-depth faunal studies of Hanna's Town and similar frontier settlements, with the assistance of both old and newly recovered collections, will continue to push for answers regarding life on western Pennsylvania's frontier and beyond.

References

Albert, George Dallas (editor)

1882   *History of the County of Westmoreland Pennsylvania with Biographical Sketches of Many of Its Pioneers and Prominent Men*, Vol. 1. L. H. Everts. Philadelphia.

Bedell, John, Michael Petraglia, and Thomas Plummer

1994   Status, Technology, and Rural Tradition in Western Pennsylvania: Excavations at the Schaeffer Farm Site. *Northeast Historical Archaeology* 23:29–58.

Boucher, John N.

1906   *History of Westmoreland County, Pennsylvania*. Lewis Publishing Company. New York.

Carlisle, Ronald C.

2005   *An Overview of Prior Historical Research on Hanna's Town, the First County Seat of Westmoreland County, Pennsylvania*. Vol. 1 of 2. Narrative Report. Brown Carlisle & Associates. Submitted to the Westmoreland County Historical Society.

Ford, Benjamin L.

2014   *Preliminary Analysis of the Hanna's Town Collection and How It Can Help Present the Site to the Public*. Paper presented to the 85th Annual Meeting of the Society for Pennsylvania Archaeology, Greensburg PA.

Fryman, Robert J., and John T. Eddins

1985   1984 Archaeological Testing Project: Settlement Boundaries and Lot Placement at Old Hanna's Town. Westmoreland County Historical Society, Heritage Institute.

Gresham, John M., and Samuel T. Wiley

1890   *Biographical and Historical Cyclopedia of Westmoreland County, Pennsylvania*. Dunlap & Clarke. Philadelphia.

Grimm, Jacob L.

1972   Hanna's Town. *Carnegie Magazine* 46(6):225–235.

Hassler, Edgar W.

1900   *Old Westmoreland: A History of Western Pennsylvania during the Revolution*. J. R. Weldin. Pittsburgh PA.

Lyman, R. Lee

2008   *Quantitative Paleozoology.* Cambridge University Press. New York.

Magurran, A. E.

1988   *Ecological Diversity and Its Measurement.* Princeton University Press. Princeton NJ.

Noël Hume, Audrey

1978   *Food.* Colonial Williamsburg Archaeological Series No. 9. Colonial Williamsburg Foundation. Williamsburg VA.

Reitz, Elizabeth J., and Elizabeth S. Wing

2008   *Cambridge Manuals in Archaeology: Zooarchaeology,* 2nd ed. Cambridge University Press. New York.

Richardson, James B., III

2007a Destruction of Hanna's Town, Part I. *Westmoreland Pennsylvania History* 90(2):16–25.

2007b Who Were Those Guys? The Destruction of Hanna's Town, Part II. *Western Pennsylvania History* 90(3):26–35.

Richardson, James B., III, and Kirke C. Wilson

1976   Hannas Town and Charles Foreman: The Historical and Archaeological Record, 1770–1806. *Western Pennsylvania Historical Magazine* 59(2):153–184.

Scott, Elizabeth M.

2008   Who Ate What? Archaeological Food Remains and Cultural Diversity. In *Case Studies in Environmental Archaeology,* Elizabeth Reitz, C. Margaret Scarry, and Sylvia J. Scudder, editors, pp. 357–374. Springer, New York.

Shannon, C. E., and W. Weaver

1949   *The Mathematical Theory of Communication.* University of Illinois Press. Urbana.

Smith, Stefanie M.

2014   *Foodways in Colonial Western Pennsylvania: An Analysis of Faunal Remains from Hanna's Town (36WM203).* Master's thesis, Department of Anthropology, Indiana University of Pennsylvania. ProQuest LLC, Ann Arbor MI.

Wright, J. E., and Doris S. Corbett

1940   *Pioneer Life in Western Pennsylvania.* University of Pittsburgh Press. Pittsburgh PA.

NINE

Challenges and Opportunities with the Market Street Chinatown Collection, San Jose, California

J. RYAN KENNEDY

The faunal assemblage from the Market Street Chinatown, a 19th-century Chinese community in San Jose, California, is part of a challenging orphan collection that offers significant research opportunities. Fieldwork on the Market Street Chinatown occurred in the 1980s, and since 2002 the resulting collection has been the focus of the collaborative Market Street Chinatown Archaeology Project (MSCAP). As an affiliated researcher with the MSCAP, my work uses an old collection and intersects with the MSCAP's curation-driven research goals, which are centered on material culture analyses, food-related remains, and chemical, residue, and other specialist analyses. Although the history of the Market Street Chinatown collection is well understood, I encountered challenges in linking some of my research questions to the original archaeological field methods. Conversely my research benefited from the input of MSCAP project partners, my ability to easily control my sample, access to more expansive comparative collections than previously available, and analytical and theoretical developments in archaeology and biology since excavation. There are positive and negative aspects of working with an orphan collection, and I learned several lessons from this project.

The Market Street Chinatown

The Market Street Chinatown was founded in the 1860s in downtown San Jose, California. By the late 1880s the Market Street Chinatown's population had grown to over 1,000 permanent residents, with some estimates putting the population over 1,500 (Yu 2001:19). Beyond housing its permanent residents, the Market Street Chinatown served as a commercial and cultural "home base" to over 2,000 additional Chinese migrants living and working throughout Santa Clara County. These migrants regularly returned to the Market Street Chinatown when not working to visit the many businesses, restaurants, and cultural organizations within the community (Yu 2001:22; Voss 2008). Although the Market Street Chinatown and other Chinese communities in the United States have often been characterized as bachelor communities (Williams 2008), recent documentary research indicates that more women and children lived in the Market Street Chinatown than previously suspected (Barbara L. Voss 2016, pers. comm.). Still, upward of 95% of the Market Street Chinatown's population was male (Yu 2001:5), and daily life would have differed compared to that in southern China. The Market Street Chinatown's residents remained intimately tied to their home villages via the flow of material goods, correspondence, remittance payments, and people between the United States and southern China (Hsu 2000).

As in other Chinatown communities in the late 1800s, the Market Street Chinatown provided its residents with support and protection in the face of rising anti-Chinese sentiment in California. Chinese social organizations, such as district and family associations, took on heightened roles in the community, and the structure of Chinatown itself provided protection though the placement of "thoroughfares, work areas, and gathering places" in the interior of Chinatown, with the back walls of its buildings forming a protective wall (Voss 2008:42). But walls were not enough to keep the Market Street Chinatown safe from violence; on 4 May 1887 it was burned to the ground in an arson fire (*Daily Alta California* 1887; Yu 2001). Many of San Jose's European-descended residents supported the destruction of what they saw as a public nuisance, and they openly rejoiced, "Chinatown is dead. It is dead forever" (*San Jose Daily Herald* 1887; Yu 2001:30). Yet San Jose's Chinatown was far from dead. Many of its residents relocated to two new Chinese communities in San Jose: the

Woolen Mills Chinatown founded by Ng Fook and the Heinlenville Chinatown built on land leased from a German businessman named John Heinlen (Yu 2001; Allen et al. 2002).

Archaeology of the Market Street Chinatown

The archaeological history of the Market Street Chinatown began during an urban development project in downtown San Jose in the early 1980s (Voss et al. 2003; Voss 2005, 2008; Lum 2007; Kane 2011; Voss et al. 2013). Despite initial evaluation of the site as significant under historic preservation law and in need of protection or mitigation, this decision was ultimately reversed and construction on the site began in 1985 (Theodoratus et al. 1980:80–88; Theodoratus et al. 1981; Voss 2008:41). After archaeological monitors noted rich, historic deposits at the site, a group of archaeologists and Chinese heritage organization members, including descendants of Market Street Chinatown residents, protested the treatment of the site (Lum 2007; Voss 2008, 2012; Voss et al. 2013). Ultimately the City of San Jose Redevelopment Agency contracted a cultural resource management firm to conduct excavations at the site, and archaeological work continued periodically until 1988. These excavations were done under salvage conditions using a "rapid recovery" protocol, with archaeological technicians working alongside construction equipment and monitoring work for evidence of archaeological materials (Kane 2011:10). When construction crews encountered cultural deposits, work in that area of the site was briefly halted and archaeologists quickly removed all archaeological soils for processing and screening off-site. Unfortunately, the nature of monitoring during the project meant that the upper portions and in some cases the entirety of some archaeological features were impacted by construction equipment, and due to time constraints stratigraphic excavation was not always employed. In total, archaeologists excavated "more than 60 features—mostly wood-lined rectangular pits filled with domestic refuse" (Voss 2008:42; Kane 2011).

The collection was not analyzed immediately after excavation, and it was placed in long-term storage until 2002, when the Market

Street Chinatown Archaeology Project was formed with the goal of cataloging, analyzing, and curating the collection (Voss 2005; Lum 2007; Voss et al. 2013). The MSCAP is a collaboration of Stanford University, History San José (a historic preservation organization), Environmental Science Associates (formerly Past Forward, Inc.), the Chinese Historical and Cultural Project (a Chinese heritage organization), and the City of San Jose Redevelopment Agency. Barbara Voss of Stanford University serves as the MSCAP principal investigator. Owing to the size and complexity of the collection, what was initially envisioned as a year-long project ultimately developed into a more than decade-long examination of the Market Street Chinatown assemblage (Voss 2012; Voss et al. 2013). Since its inception, the MSCAP has cataloged over 77% of the Market Street Chinatown collection and completely analyzed several categories of material culture, including Asian stonewares, buttons, opium pipe tops, tobacco pipes, and glass medicine bottles (Voss and Kane 2014). Much of this work has been driven by undergraduate research projects, several master's theses, a doctoral dissertation, and a plethora of contracted and affiliated studies. Aiding in this work is Kane's (2011) systematic and thorough reconstruction of the field and laboratory records kept during excavation, which was critical in reconciling the many boxes of material culture from the site with their corresponding contextual information. Although Kane notes considerable variability in record keeping, her archival work provides the foundation for systematic interrogation of the archaeological material recovered from the site. Voss (2012) has argued that while the field methods employed limit the possibilities for using the Market Street Chinatown collection for fine-grained temporal comparisons within and between features, the collection still holds tremendous potential for other work, especially projects with a spatial-comparative component.

A central tenet of the MSCAP is its collaborative focus, which is most notable through the generation of research questions derived from active dialog between project partners. Voss (2005) has described the incorporation of research topics suggested by San Jose's Chinese-descendant community, including questions about the social and business relationships between the Market Street Chinatown community and others, evidence of Chinese social and kinship organizations, and examination of daily life within the community, including ritual activities, foodways, and dress. Targeted material culture studies by students and project team members have helped address some of these topics; they include spatial analysis of artifacts related to fire rituals (e.g., incense burners) (Kane 2007), stylistic and spatial study of peck-marked ceramics (Michaels 2005; Voss 2008:47), and a detailed study of nearly 300 British-produced transfer-printed wares (Chan 2013). Additionally, the collection has been the subject of faunal, floral, and other specialist studies that highlight the mix of both Chinese and North American ingredients present in the collection and the geographic and social connections required to supply the Market Street Chinatown with these goods (Henry 2012; Cummings et al. 2014; Popper 2014, 2015; Kennedy 2016a, 2017a). Recent work has focused on expanding the range of analytical techniques used on the collection, including identification of wood from the site (Seiter et al. 2015), chemical analysis of the contents of medicinal vials (Voss et al. 2015), and starch residue analysis of Chinese rice bowls (Becks 2012). The diversity of specialist analyses reflects not only the richness of the Market Street Chinatown archaeological collection but also the potential for fruitful synergy between targeted analytical methods and old collections.

Beyond traditional research questions, the MSCAP also focuses on exploring avenues for public use of the collection to raise awareness of the contributions of Chinese people to local and regional history. This was an area of particular interest for members of San José's Chinese-descendant community, and it has led to the MSCAP being heavily involved in public outreach events such as archaeology days at History San José's History Park, an art installation by Rene Yung featuring artifacts from the site, and open-house events held in Stanford University's Archaeology Center, allowing community members to discuss archaeological findings (Voss et al. 2013). Beyond illuminating San Jose's Chinese history, these events are a venue through which nonarchaeologists can contribute to the direc-

tion of the MSCAP and the research questions of its member archaeologists (Voss 2005). I have been fortunate to participate in several
of these public events, and as I discuss below, they have been critical for developing my project.

The Making of a Market Street Chinatown Faunal Study

My research with the Market Street Chinatown collection began in
2012. Although the collection promised the opportunity to explore
my theoretical interests centering on food and identities, analyzing an old collection was equally important to me. This derived
from practical concerns, particularly about the time needed to finish analysis, the risk inherent in funding a multiyear field project,
the necessity of having adequate faunal material for my project, and
an ongoing concern with addressing the field's larger curation crisis. Ultimately, working with the Market Street Chinatown archaeological collection allowed me to produce a large data set relatively
quickly and cheaply, while at the same time removing a small portion of the field's curation backlog.

As noted, I encountered positive and negative aspects of working with the Market Street Chinatown faunal assemblage. Although
not all are unique to working with old collections, there are benefits and pitfalls of conducting new research using curated materials. Despite the difficulties I encountered, the scope of my work with
the Market Street Chinatown assemblage would not have been possible through new field excavations. Perhaps more important, I aim
to show that existing collections offer tremendous research potential and opportunities to collaborate with other researchers, target
specific kinds of archaeological assemblages, and bring new theory
and methods to bear.

Collaboration and Changing Perspectives

The collaborative focus of the MSCAP contributed significantly to the
structure of my research. Throughout project planning I met with
members and leaders of the Chinese Historical and Cultural Project, staff of History San José, Rebecca Allen of Environmental Sci-

ence Associates, and Barbara Voss of Stanford University to discuss my project. I participated in MSCAP public events, where I presented zooarchaeological data and methods while talking with project partners about questions they hoped my research could answer. Many of these questions centered on the medicinal and symbolic values of food, the relationship between changes in food and ethnic identity, and the geographic origins of animals consumed at the site, and I incorporated these themes as research foci in my project. As an example, I employed an indicator group approach to fish remains to highlight the presence of subsets of fish taxa representative of multiple Chinese-operated fisheries in the San Francisco–Monterey Bay area, southern California, the San Joaquin and Sacramento river systems, the South China Sea, and freshwater sources in Asia (Kennedy 2016a, 2017a; Palmiotto 2016). This analysis promises to provide a model for interpreting complex faunal assemblages with multiple origins. Discussion with nonarchaeologist project partners was a major impetus in pursuing this analysis.

Collaborative discussions also shaped my interpretation of the Market Street Chinatown faunal data. In particular discussions with Connie Young Yu, a historian of San Jose's Chinese communities and a descendant of a Market Street Chinatown resident, offered counterpoints to archaeologists' typical exoticization of Chinese food practices by providing insight into the practical nature of 19th-century Chinese foodways as related to, for instance, incorporating new ingredients. These conversations, some of which occurred while Yu and I were attending a 2014 conference in China sponsored by the Chinese Railroad Workers in North America Project, illuminated the errors of assumption many archaeologists make about Chinese migrant cuisine and traditional Chinese cookery. These discussions and my travel in China were turning points in how I viewed the relationship between the food practices of 19th-century southern Chinese populations and residents of migrant communities such as the Market Street Chinatown. Rather than characterize pork-heavy Chinese-derived faunal assemblages in North America as continuation of tradition (McEwan 1985; Longenecker and Stapp

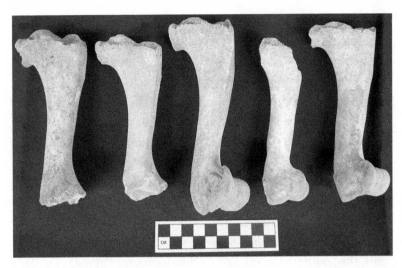

FIGURE 12. Sample of pork remains from the Market Street Chinatown.
(Photo: J. Ryan Kennedy)

1993; Diehl et al. 1998), I argue that this pattern is indicative of a shift from a vegetable-heavy diet supplemented with preserved and fresh meat in rural China (Buck 1956) to one focusing on the tremendous amounts of meat available to consumers in North America (Kennedy 2016a; Figure 12). Reframing Chinese meat consumption would not have been possible without talking to people outside of archaeology, particularly members of San Jose's Chinese-descendant community, other MSCAP project partners, and Chinese scholars living and working in southern China.

Field Documentation, Methods, and Other Challenges

I encountered several challenges while working with the Market Street Chinatown legacy collection. These problems fall into two general categories: issues with contextual control and disconnects between past field methods and modern research questions. Such problems are difficult, and sometimes impossible, to address, and because fieldwork is already complete when working with existing collections, archaeologists have limited options to mitigate them. Rather than fix problems via additional excavation, archaeologists often need to readjust their research agendas to better fit the old collections they are working with. In these cases it is more efficient for researchers to first assess the state of a legacy collection, its corresponding contextual documentation, and the kinds of materials present in the assemblage prior to developing research questions.

A major challenge of research on old (and particularly orphaned) collections stems from reconciling curated assemblages with their corresponding field and laboratory documentation. At times this may prove an impossible task due to loss or destruction of these materials. In other cases, incomplete, disorganized, and sometimes incomprehensible or illegible records can be reconstructed to a degree suitable for use in research. Fortunately, the difficult work of repiecing the fragmentary documentary record of the Market Street Chinatown collection was already completed prior to my involvement with the project (Kane 2011). This effort revealed a surprisingly full contextual record from the 1985 and 1986 excavations of the Market Street Chinatown, including field notes, plan and profile drawings of features, and archaeological interpretation of features and the material culture they contained. Kane also evaluated features for suitability for future research projects, especially in terms of modern intrusion and disturbance in features, linking individual features to the Market Street Chinatown occupation and the amounts and types of material culture present in each feature.

Kane's work made selecting a study sample significantly easier, although I still had to contend with some contextual problems. For instance, overlapping feature numbers were assigned for both the 1985 and 1986 field seasons, at times creating confusion about which specific features certain bags of faunal remains belonged to. This problem was generally not difficult to rectify, although in some cases enough information was missing or illegible on individual bags of faunal remains that I could not link them to specific contexts and ultimately had to exclude them from my study. Inconsistent use of terminology within and between individual features also made understanding the relationships between some contexts difficult to discern at times. This includes the seemingly interchangeable use of terms such as "level," "layer," and "strata," as well as designations such as "level 1" and "level a" being used for the same feature. Although many of these inconsistencies could be overcome by studying the relevant field notes and corresponding plan and profile drawings, this added an extra layer of difficulty to my project. The confusion caused by inconsistently implemented recording protocols and the necessity to remove some samples from my study should serve as a clear lesson for archaeologists planning fieldwork: that they construct, implement, and maintain consistent standards in describing their fieldwork across all field and laboratory workers.

Ultimately my major challenge was reconciling the field sampling methods used by previous archaeologists with my own research questions. Initially I intended not only to examine differences in food practices between subgroups within the site but also to explore how these practices changed over time. Unfortunately, the rapid-recovery protocol used during the Market Street Chinatown excavations made it difficult, and many times impossible, to link strata between features in efforts to begin to understand temporal variation in food practices at the site. This situation was exacerbated by the communal nature of trash disposal in the Market Street Chinatown, and it follows Voss's (2012) suggestion that this particular collection lends itself most readily to questions centered on spatial differences within the community. As a result my work focused solely on differences between spatially isolated laborer and mixed merchant-laborer households as a way to address intracommunity relationships.

I also hoped to move beyond the laundry lists of taxa typically produced by zooarchaeologists (Lyman 2015) and toward a model of food and cuisine that acknowledged the importance of flavor combinations, dishes, and meals. The faunal assemblage from the Market Street Chinatown likewise did not allow this level of resolution, as the strata within the features I was analyzing clearly represented the accumulation of waste from many meals. This is perhaps not surprising, but it did require a shift in my thinking from small-scale consumption to the large-scale patterns typically seen in much zooarchaeological work.

Most notably, I struggled to reconcile my research questions with the primarily ¼-inch mesh size used in the field. Although this was adequate for collecting the majority of the medium and large animal remains at the site, it was not appropriate for smaller fauna such as the fish taxa that were becoming central to my research. Field archaeologists collected a large number of bulk soil samples and fine-screened materials from at least two features at the site, offering the potential to address the lack of small fish remains in my samples. Unfortunately, flotation of the bulk soil samples returned comparatively few fish remains, and the fine-screened samples, although rich in fish bones, existed for only one of my 10 chosen features. I identified the remains of small fish such as herring, smelt, and silversides in three 1 liter samples of the fine-screened matrix material, but this did not yield any taxa not already represented in the ¼-inch screened material. Although the results suggested that I was not missing important taxa in the ¼-inch mesh samples, the matrix material demonstrated that I would be unable to address the relative dietary importance of small fish taxa at the site. Had I designed the excavation sampling methods, I would have used much finer-grained recovery techniques to collect more small fish bones, but in the context of working with an old collection I had to accept that the collection was missing these data.

New Theory, Methods, and Comparatives

A key advantage to working with existing collections is the ability to choose an appropriate sample before analysis (Allen et al., this volume). Prior to analysis, I assessed the Market Street Chinatown faunal assemblage to ensure that it held sufficient faunal remains from well-recorded contexts to answer my research questions. The collection had already supported two master's theses relying in part or entirely on faunal analysis (Clevenger 2004; Henry 2012), demonstrating general integrity and a high level of preservation. Examination of the faunal remains from the unanalyzed contexts, which represented the bulk of the assemblage, revealed equally good preservation and a diverse assemblage of fauna conducive to answering research questions centered on dietary patterns and the use of such ingredients as domestic fauna, wild animals, and widely traded foods such as salt fish. The problem with the Market Street Chinatown faunal assemblage was not a lack of faunal remains but a question of how best to subsample a complex assemblage of tens of thousands of faunal specimens.

Ultimately I analyzed over 16,000 total faunal remains across 10 features. The features met four primary criteria: they had suitably complete field documentation, they showed no evidence of modern disturbance, they had associated bulk soil samples that could be used for botanical analyses, and they were excavated in stratigraphic levels rather than as a single unit. These features were split between sections of the site associated with tenement housing for Chinese laborers and some families and mixed merchant-laborer households located in commercial areas of the Market Street Chinatown (Map 4). As a result I was able to address research questions centered on the similarities and differences in food practices between laborer and mixed merchant-laborer households within the community. Most previous archaeological inquiry into Chinese migrant foodways treated urban Chinatown communities as monolithic, either due to research design or a lack of data necessary to undertake truly comparative analyses, though for exceptions see Praetzellis and Praetzellis (1997) and Cummings et al. (2014).

The data from laborer and mixed merchant-laborer contexts show that both groups ate a similar base diet consisting of large amounts of pork, beef, poultry, and fish. Mixed merchant-laborer households consumed more nonmammal meats and imported Chinese salt fish (Kennedy 2016a). A notable feature near a tenement building also contained large numbers of sawn beef soup bones, likely evidence of low-cost beef-based meals such as soups and stews cooked for tenement boarders, a pattern seen at other Chinese sites in California (Praetzellis and Praetzellis 1997). Surprisingly, skeletal remains of exotic and expensive ingredients such as bear paws were found in both laborer and mixed merchant-laborer contexts. This food item in particular would have been novel to both laborers and mer-

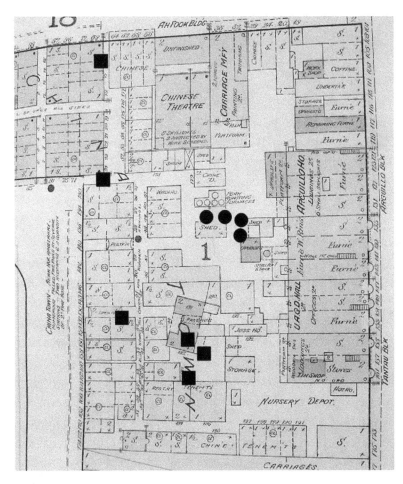

MAP 4. Archaeological features discussed in this study. Circles mark tenement contexts and squares mark merchant contexts. (1884 Sanborn Insurance Map, adapted by J. Ryan Kennedy. Base map image courtesy of History San José)

chants as it was a luxury food in China that neither group would have been able to afford prior to migration to the United States (Kennedy 2016a:191–192). The amount of meat consumed by Chinese migrants in the United States marks an extreme departure from food practices in rural southern China. Although differences exist within the faunal remains associated with laborer and mixed merchant-laborer households, the heavy meat consumption by both groups seems to have formed the basis for a shared community diet, one that ultimately contributed to emerging Chinese American identities. These interpretations were driven by broader trends in anthropology and the study of migrant food practices, but they were facilitated by analysis of the vast amount of faunal remains available in a previously excavated, old collection like that from the Market Street Chinatown.

Revisiting old collections allows researchers to bring present-day innovations in theory, method, and analytical infrastructure to bear on these projects. My work with the Market Street Chinatown collection benefited from new approaches to migration and transnationalism in anthropology and other social sciences, a growing awareness of human-animal relationships across multiple fields of study, and improvements in the comparative collections available to zooarchaeologists. Although a discussion of the full range of these examples is beyond the scope of this chapter, I provide several examples below.

Archaeologists in the 1980s and 1990s typically cast Chinese communities as insular and monolithic, and they often relied on acculturation models privileging continuity and change over hybridity and mixing (González-Tennant 2011; Ross 2013; Voss 2015). This reflects broader trends in archaeological work at the time, and it relates to archaeologists' tendency to cast Chinese migration in Americanist terms. Such approaches ignore the rural village origins of most 19th-century Chinese migrants, and they assume that the material patterns observed at Chinese migrant sites reflect traditional practices from the home country. Evidence from China suggests that rural Chinese in Guangdong Province ate fresh meat only sparingly prior to migration (Buck 1956), and thus the bounty of fresh meat available to Chinese consumers in 19th-century North America does not represent traditional foodways. Given this, the seemingly similar quality of food in Chinese migrant archaeological sites compared to high Cantonese cooking (i.e., large amounts of pork, poultry, and fish) actually represents migrants' "eating up" the social ladder rather than continuing their own village food practices.

Archaeologists studying Chinese migration have only recently turned to models emphasizing transnational migrant identities. In particular, the work of historian Madeline Hsu (2000), which emphasizes connections created by the flows of goods, money, people, and ideas between Chinese migrants and their home villages, has pushed archaeologists to consider how material culture at North American sites intersects these transnational relationships. Ross (2013), Voss (2016), and González-Tennant (2011) have all called for archaeologies of Chinese migration that embrace the multisited nature of migrant lives. Further, the role of Hong Kong–based shipping firms known as *jinshanzhuang*, or gold mountain firms, suggests that the goods supplied from China to migrant communities were not those directly used in home villages but rather products that could be mass-produced at low cost for export to migrant communities (Hsu 2006; Voss et al. 2018). The ceramics, salt fish, and other imports supplied to Chinese communities were similar but not identical to the versions used by many Chinese prior to migration; this has profound implications for archaeological notions of tradition often employed in the study of Chinese migrant communities.

In a similar vein, my work emphasizes Chinese migrants' connections to other places via the flow of preserved food items, particularly salt fish. Although much of the fish consumed by residents of the Market Street Chinatown was harvested by Chinese fishermen in North American waters, over 16% of specimens by count were imported Asian taxa, including threadfin breams and Chinese white herrings (Kennedy 2017a). Imported Asian fish were also over twice as common in mixed merchant-laborer households than in laborer contexts. This pattern suggests that relatively wealthy Chinatown merchants chose to eat imported fish that would have been familiar to them from their early lives in China. Rather than place these data into a model of continuity and change, I contextualize the consumption of imported Asian salt fish within the broader fabric of Chinese migrant foodways. Whereas salt fish would have been a potent source of flavor and protein in an otherwise vegetable-heavy diet in rural China, in North American contexts this ingredient became a familiar-tasting reminder of home in a sea of pork and beef. Thus while copious amounts of fresh meat became a marker of Chinese migrant foodways writ large, imported salt fish marked differences along lines of wealth and the ability to maintain a connection to China via imported salt fish.

My work also benefits from a growing body of literature concerning the effects of humans on the environment in anthropology, zooarchaeology, and other social and biological sciences. Although zooarchaeologists have long acknowledged a link between human action and environmental change (Chambers 1993), recent emphasis on these relationships is part of a broad research trend growing out of recognition of a shift from the Holocene into the Anthropocene, the period in which humans are the primary drivers of environmental change (Crutzen and Stoermer 2000). I have found particular inspiration in themes such as human impacts on fisheries (Braje et al. 2012; Orton 2016), the role of humans in the introduction of invasive species (West et al. 2017), and the use of zooarchaeology in conservation efforts (Lyman and Cannon 2004; Wolverton and Lyman 2012).

While reconstructing the network of Chinese-run fisheries that supplied the Market Street Chinatown with much of its fresh and salt fish, I encountered numerous records of 19th-century European American support of anti-Chinese fishing legislation. Such legislation argued that Chinese fishing methods disproportionately impacted California's fish populations relative to their Anglo counterparts (Goode 1884:617–618; Walsh 1893). Although Chinese consumers certainly bought fish from non-Chinese sources, the extensiveness of the Chinese fish trade in California (Armentrout-Ma 1981) suggests that the bulk of the Market Street Chinatown specimens likely derived from Chinese fishing operations and thus present an opportunity to evaluate the likely impact of Chinese fishing methods. The fish assemblage contained a diverse array of 50 distinct fish taxa, including rockfish, flatfish, Sacramento perch, and silversides (e.g., topsmelt), suggesting that Chinese fishermen spread their impact over a wide range of species rather than intensively targeting limited numbers of taxa, as did Anglo fishermen (e.g., in the salmon industry). This fishing strategy would likely have been less detrimental to individual taxa, suggesting that Chinese fishermen may have had less of an impact on California's 19th-century fisheries than often ascribed to them; instead they may simply have been one of many factors leading to a 19th-century decline in California's fish populations. This is a theme I continue to explore, and the Market Street Chinatown collection provides the foundation for this study due to its copious amounts of well-preserved and tightly datable fish remains.

My project also engages modern concerns about invasive species. Most notably, the Market Street Chinatown faunal assemblage contains 36 vertebrae from a member of genus *Channa*, the Asian snakeheads (Kennedy 2016b, 2017a, 2017b). These remains are the first snakehead bones identified in the Americas, and they represent the earliest known importation of this fish into the United States. Although these specimens would likely have been classed as simply another imported fish in the 1980s, recent events make them much more important in understanding the social aspects of the introduction of invasive species. In 2002 a breeding population of northern snakehead (*Channa argus*) was discovered in a pond in Crofton, Maryland, and has since become firmly entrenched throughout the Potomac River system (Fields 2005). The introduction of this species has been blamed in large part on the release of live fish into the wild by aquarium owners and the escape or intentional release of live fish imported for sale in Asian seafood markets. The latter has often been explained in terms of ignorance or mysticism, growing out of the use of snakehead for its perceived medicinal properties in Asia (Howard 2016). Archaeological evidence of snakeheads in the Market Street Chinatown collection offers an alternative interpretation of the modern introduction of this fish; rather than coming from a place of ignorance, Chinese importation of live snakehead is part of a long history of procuring this ingredient for its culinary and medicinal value (Shafri and Manan 2012; Dong et al. 2013). Although it does not change the environmental impact of the introduction of snakeheads into American waterways, understanding the role of snakeheads in Chinese cuisine and the long history of their importation into the United States can provide a more nuanced explanation for their importance as a modern-day live import that moves beyond ignorance as the primary explanation.

Finally, my research has benefited from increased access to comparative specimens over what was often available to analysts in the 1980s. For instance, Collins (1987) has stated that limited comparative specimens from Asia hampered her ability to identify fish remains from the Riverside Chinatown. I had access to a number of relevant Pacific Ocean and Asian taxa in Indiana University's William R. Adams Zooarchaeology Laboratory that were gathered from Alaska, the Pacific Northwest, and exhibits in Chicago's Shedd Aquarium. Further, I produced a personal collection of over 300 comparative fish specimens from California and China, including multiple Asian taxa ultimately identified in the Market Street Chinatown assemblage and that are currently unique to this site. These include remains of a member of both *Pseudorhombus* (a genus of flounders) and *Johnius* (a genus of drums), and the aforementioned snakehead. These fish are probably not unique to the Market Street Chinatown, but rather their identifications are the direct result of an expansive comparative collection enabling the positive identification of specimens that in the past would have typically been classified as unspecified fish remains. The data from the Market Street Chinatown suggest that other old and/or previously analyzed collections can also benefit from modern, expanded comparative collections.

Conclusion

Perhaps the most important limitation when working with old collections is that field recovery strategies have already been designed and implemented. If additional fieldwork is not possible, then, for better or worse, researchers are stuck with the collections and associated records as they stand in storage or curation. In this scenario reconstruction of field and laboratory notes is both a critical and a potentially expensive and time-consuming process. Although I was spared the bulk of this work in my project, documentary reconstruction is central to the success of the Market Street Chinatown Archaeology Project (Kane 2011). Further, even assuming that project documentation is intact or can be reasonably reconstructed, researchers are still constrained by the excavation strategies, locations of excavation, and artifact collection protocols implemented by the original field researchers. With any luck, the material recovered by past archaeologists suits new research questions, although in many cases the realities of melding old collections and new questions requires creative thinking.

As Voss (2008) notes, archaeological research questions are constrained by both the social reality of the past and the archaeological units of analysis encountered, recovered, and documented in the field, be they individual artifacts or regional settlement patterns. Field recovery and the recovery of archaeological units of analysis differ from project to project due to budget and time constraints, differing research priorities, and changing standards of practice. These realities often mean that old collections were excavated using field methods that are incompatible with some present-day research questions. In my case this occurred with the use of ¼-inch mesh screening for the bulk of recovered soils from the Market Street Chinatown, which resulted in low recovery rates of the bones of small fish, including silversides and smelts. Numerous other problems can occur, including lack of soil samples for flotation or other analyses (e.g., pollen and phytolith analysis), recovery protocols biased against the collection of particular artifact classes, sampling strategies that fail to target context types necessary to present-day research projects, and artifact-processing methods that reduce or negate the potential for certain analyses (e.g., removal of material in historic bottles that could be analyzed to determine bottle contents).

Although some of these issues may stop a project idea in its tracks (e.g., faunal analysis cannot be done if no faunal remains were collected), others simply necessitate a reorientation of one's approach to research. Rather than thinking like an excavator and implementing field methods appropriate to collecting particular kinds of data, archaeologists working with old collections must work backward and design research questions that fit already excavated material. Although seemingly simple, this approach requires a shift in thinking about project design and an acceptance of loss of some control over the process of research. Rather than intrepidly marching into the field, recovering artifacts, and using them to address a research question, archaeologists working with old collections must instead assess the collection, grapple with its strengths and weaknesses, and, only when they have clearly identified the confluences of past social realities and recovered archaeological units of analysis, finally develop appropriate research questions.

Based on this process, there emerge two diverging approaches for work with old collections. The first hinges on assessment of collections for their use with specific kinds of analyses, such as in my work on the Market Street Chinatown faunal assemblage. In these scenarios, researchers seek out collections with particular material types and recovery methods and, if appropriate, use them to answer targeted research questions. This approach is a mainstay of specialist analysts who are dependent upon specific material or sample types. Despite their predetermined focus, projects taking this approach must still maintain flexibility in relation to specificities of individual collections. The second takes a more collection-driven approach to generating research questions; the core material culture analysis efforts of the broader Market Street Chinatown Archaeology Project follow this approach (Voss 2005; Lum 2007; Voss et al. 2013). In these scenarios, archaeologists evaluate an old collection and, based on the materials present, generate collection-appropriate research questions. A researcher's own interests may become secondary to the realities of the collection; it is unsurprising that this approach favors generalist archaeologists who are not dependent on specific material types. Of course many projects centered on old collection fall between these two poles, but they offer a useful way to differentiate the approaches and goals of those doing this work.

Regardless of the approach taken toward working with old collections, if archaeologists can overcome the challenges inherent in relying on previous fieldwork and documentation, the rewards can be great. Such projects frequently offer opportunities for collaboration with archaeologists and nonarchaeologists alike, the use of new methods and theories, and greater control over the selection of a study sample. In many cases, old collections offer the perfect playground for testing new approaches and analytical techniques, particularly emerging laboratory methods such as ancient DNA and stable isotope analysis. The nature of work with old collections also lends itself to multisited projects drawing on components of multiple collections, and this in turn can encourage collaborative approaches combining data from multiple sites and/or analytical techniques, as well as dialogs with nonarchaeologist stakeholders. And as should be clear from the chapters in this volume, the flexibility required to design and implement a research project using old collections does not necessitate lower-quality research results; instead the opportunities afforded by old collections allow researchers to carry out studies that are often simply not possible through new fieldwork alone.

Acknowledgments

This research was conducted as part of the Market Street Chinatown Archaeology Project, a community-based research and education collaboration between Stanford University, Chinese Historical and Cultural Project, History San José, and Environmental Science Associates. I am indebted to the MSCAP project members for their continued support of my work. Portions of this research were generously funded by the Wenner-Gren Foundation for Anthropological Research, the Chinese Railroad Workers in North America Project at Stanford University, and the Lang Fund for Environmental Anthropology at Stanford University.

References

Allen, Rebecca, Scott B. Baxter, Anmarie Medin, Julia G. Costello, and Connie Young Yu
2002 *Excavation of the Woolen Mills Chinatown (CA-SCL-807H), San Jose.* 2 vols. Report to California Department of Transportation, District 4, Oakland, from Past Forward, Inc., Foothill Resources, Ltd., and EDAW, Inc.

Armentrout-Ma, L. Eve
1981 Chinese in California's Fishing Industry, 1850–1941. *California History* 60:142–157.

Becks, Fanya
2012 Pilot Study in Microbotanical Plant Residue Analysis, Market Street Chinatown Archaeology Project. Market Street Chinatown Archaeological Project Technical Report No. 4. Stanford University, Stanford CA.

Braje, Todd J., Torben C. Rick, and Jon M. Erlandson

2012 Rockfish in the Longview: Applied Archaeology and Conservation of Pacific Red Snapper (Genus *Sebastes*) in Southern California. In *Applied Zooarchaeology and Conservation Biology*, Steven Wolverton and R. Lee Lyman, editors, pp. 157–178. University of Arizona Press. Tucson.

Buck, John L.

1956 *Chinese Farm Economy: A Study of 2866 Farms in Seventeen Localities and Seven Provinces in China*. University of Chicago Press. Chicago.

Chambers, F. M.

1993 *Climate Change and Human Impact on the Landscape: Studies in Palaeoecology and Environmental Archaeology*. Chapman & Hall. London.

Chan, Stephanie K.

2013 Worth a Thousand Words: A Study of Transfer-Printed Wares from the Market Street Chinatown Collection. Master's thesis, Department of Anthropology, Stanford University, Stanford CA.

Clevenger, Elizabeth

2004 Reconstructing Context and Assessing Research Potential: Feature 20 from the San Jose Market Street Chinatown. Master's thesis, Department of Cultural and Social Anthropology, Stanford University, Stanford CA. Document # 7017-STR.

Collins, Donna

1987 Tradition and Network: Interpreting the Fish Remains from Riverside's Chinatown. In *Wong Ho Leun: An American Chinatown*, Vol. 2, pp. 121–132. Great Basin Foundation. San Diego CA.

Crutzen, Paul J., and Eugene T. Stoermer

2000 The "Anthropocene." *Global Change Newsletter* 41:17–18.

Cummings, Linda Scott, Barbara L. Voss, Connie Young Yu, Peter Kováčik, Kathryn Puseman, Chad Yost, J. Ryan Kennedy, and Megan S. Kane

2014 *Fan* and *Tsai*: Intracommunity Variation in Plant-Based Food Consumption at the Market Street Chinatown, San Jose, California. *Historical Archaeology* 48(2):143–172.

Daily Alta California

1887 San Jose's Chinatown Destroyed—A $6,000 Blaze in Redding. May 5. San Francisco.

Diehl, Michael, Jennifer A. Waters, and J Homer Thiel

1998 Acculturation and the Composition of the Diet of Tucson's Overseas Chinese Gardeners at the Turn of the Century. *Historical Archaeology* 32(4):19–33.

Dong, Qiufenm, Zhidong Peng, Gaoshang Mei, Song Zhang, and Yong Yang

2013 Hybrid Snakehead Fish Farming in China. *AQUA Culture Asia Pacific Magazine* November–December:32–36.

Fields, Helen

2005 Invasion of the Snakeheads. *Smithsonian Magazine* 35(11):62.

González-Tennant, E.

2011 Creating a Diasporic Archaeology of Chinese Migration: Tentative Steps across Four Continents. *International Journal of Historical Archaeology* 15:509–532.

Goode, George B.

1884 *The Fisheries and Fishery Industries of the United States.* U.S. Commission of Fish and Fisheries. Government Printing Office. Washington DC.

Henry, Shea C.

2012 Ni Chi Le Ma, Have You Eaten Yet? Analysis of Foodways from Market Street Chinatown, San Jose, California. Master's thesis, Department of Anthropology, University of Idaho, Moscow.

Howard, Brian Clark

2016 Fishermen Battle Invasive "Frankenfish" Snakeheads. *National Geographic,* 17 March. http://news.nationalgeographic.com/2016/03/160317-snakeheads -potomac-river-chesapeake-bay-invasive-species-fish/.

Hsu, Madeline Y.

2000 *Dreaming of Gold, Dreaming of Home: Transnationalism and Migration between the United States and South China, 1882–1943.* Stanford University Press. Redwood City CA.

2006 Trading with Gold Mountain: *Jinshanzhuang* and Networks of Kinship and Native Place. In *Chinese American Transnationalism: The Flow of People, Resources, and Ideas between China and America during the Exclusion Era,* S. Chan, editor, pp. 22–33. Temple University Press. Philadelphia.

Kane, Megan S.

2007 Incense and Candlesticks: Fire Ritual in Household and Small Scale Religious Practices at the Market Street Chinatown. Manuscript, Market Street Chinatown Archaeology Project, Stanford University. https://web.stanford .edu/group/marketstreet/cgi-bin/wordpress/wp-content/uploads/2007/04 /Kane.pdf.

2011 Reconstructing Historical and Archaeological Context of an Orphaned Collection: Report on Archival Research and Feature Summaries for the Market Street Chinatown Archaeology Project. Market Street Chinatown Archaeology Project Technical Report No. 1. Stanford University. Stanford CA.

Kennedy, J. Ryan

2016a Fan *and* Tsai: *Food, Identity, and Connections in the Market Street Chinatown.* Doctoral dissertation, Department of Anthropology, Indiana University, Bloomington. ProQuest, Inc., Ann Arbor MI.

2016b Snakehead: Terror from the East or a Tasty Treat? Paper presented at the 49th Annual Conference of the Society for Historical Archaeology, Washington DC.

2017a The Fresh and the Salted: Chinese Migrant Fisheries Engagement and Trade in Nineteenth-Century North America. *Journal of Ethnobiology* 37(3):421–439.

2017b Invasive Species, Yellow Peril, and the Myth of Purity. Paper presented at the 116th Annual Meeting of the American Anthropological Association, Washington DC.

Longenecker, Julia G., and Darby C. Stapp

1993 The Study of Faunal Remains from an Overseas Chinese Mining Camp in Northern Idaho. In *Hidden Heritage: Historical Archaeology of the Overseas Chinese*, Priscilla Wegars, editor, pp. 97–122. Baywood. Amityville NY.

Lum, Rodney M.

2007 Finding Home Again: The Story of the Chinese Historical Cultural Project and Its Efforts to Reclaim the Forgotten Historic Chinatowns of San Jose, California. *Chinese America: History and Perspectives* 21:125–128.

Lyman, R. Lee

2015 The History of "Laundry Lists" in North American Zooarchaeology. *Journal of Anthropological Archaeology* 39:42–50.

Lyman, R. Lee, and Kenneth P. Cannon (editors)

2004 *Zooarchaeology and Conservation Biology.* University of Utah Press. Salt Lake City.

McEwan, Bonnie G.

1985 Appendix B: Faunal Analysis. In *Beneath the Border City, Vol. 2: The Overseas Chinese in El Paso*, Edward Staski, editor, pp. 262–283. University Museum Occasional Papers No. 13. New Mexico State University, Las Cruces.

Michaels, Gina

2005 Peck-Marked Vessels from the San José Market Street Chinatown: A Study of Distribution and Significance. *International Journal of Historical Archaeology* 9:123–134.

Orton, David C.

2016 Archaeology as a Tool for Understanding Past Marine Resource Use and Its Impact. In *Perspectives on Oceans Past: A Handbook of Marine Environmental History*, Kathleen Schwerdtner Máñez and Bo Poulsen, editors, pp. 47–70. Springer. New York.

Palmiotto, Andrea

2016 Indicator Groups and Effective Seasons on the Coast: Zooarchaeology of Fish in the Lower Suwannee Region of Florida. *Journal of Archaeological Science: Reports* 7:330–343.

Popper, Virginia S.

2014   The Overseas Chinese Experience as Seen through Plants: Macrobotanical Analysis from the Market Street Chinatown, San Jose, California. Market Street Chinatown Archaeology Project Technical Report No. 9. Stanford University, Stanford CA.

2015   The Analysis of Flotation Samples from Market Street Chinatown, San Jose, California. Report to R. Kennedy, Department of Anthropology, Indiana University, Bloomington.

Praetzellis, Mary, and Adrian Praetzellis

1997   Historical Archaeology of an Overseas Chinese Community in Sacramento, California. Report to U.S. General Services Administration, from Anthropological Studies Center, Sonoma State University, Rohnert Park CA.

Ross, Douglas E.

2013   An Archaeology of Asian Transnationalism. University Press of Florida. Gainesville.

San Jose Daily Herald

1887   Among the Ruins: Chinese and Whites Digging for Valuables in the Ashes; Chinatown Swept from the Map of San Jose." 5 May. San Jose CA.

Seiter, Jane, Michael J. Worthington, Barbara L. Voss, and Megan S. Kane

2015   Carving Chopsticks, Building Home: Wood Artifacts from the Market Street Chinatown in San Jose, California. International Journal of Historical Archaeology 19(3):664–685.

Shafri, Mohd, and Abdul Manan

2012   Therapeutic Potential of the Haruan (Channa striatus): From Food to Medicinal Uses. Malaysian Journal of Nutrition 18(1):125–136.

Theodoratus, Dorothea J., Albert L. Hurtado, Robert Docken, and Marley Brown III

1980   Historical Resources Overview for the San Antonio Plaza Redevelopment Area. Report to the Redevelopment Agency, City of San Jose CA from Theodoratus Cultural Research, Fair Oaks CA.

Theodoratus, Dorothea J., Ann Hagerman Johnson, Tom Trimbur, Teri Paul-Dawson, and Clifford Hersted

1981   The Location of Cultural Resources on Block 1, San Antonio Plaza Project, San Jose California: Verification and Clarification of the Location of Cultural Resources on Block 1 According to the Documentary Historical Record. Theodoratus Cultural Research, Fair Oaks CA.

Voss, Barbara L.

2005   The Archaeology of Overseas Chinese Communities. World Archaeology 37(3):424–439.

2008   Between the Household and the World System: Social Collectivity and Commu-
        nity Agency in Overseas Chinese Archaeology. *Historical Archaeology* 43(2):37–52.

2012   Curation as Research: A Case Study in Orphaned and Underreported Archae-
        ological Collections. *Archaeological Dialogues* 19(2):145–169.

2015   Towards a Transpacific Archaeology of the Modern World. *International
        Journal of Historical Archaeology* 20(1):146–174.

2016   What's New? Rethinking Ethnogenesis in the Archaeology of Colonialism.
        American Antiquity 80(4):655–670.

Voss, Barbara L., Rebecca Allen, R. Scott Baxter, R. Ezra Erb, Lynsie Ishimaru,
        Gina Michaels, Stephanie Selover, and Bryn Williams

2003   2002–2003 Progress Report: Market Street Chinatown Archaeological Proj-
        ect. Document # 7006-STR. Stanford Archaeology Center and Cultural and
        Social Anthropology, Stanford University, Stanford CA.

Voss, Barbara L. and Megan S. Kane

2014   2013–2014 Progress Report: Market Street Chinatown Archaeological Proj-
        ect. Stanford Archaeology Center, Stanford University, Stanford CA.

Voss, Barbara L., J. Ryan Kennedy, Jinhua (Selia) Tan, and Laura W. Ng

2018   The Archaeology of Home: *Qiaoxiang* and Nonstate Actors in the Archae-
        ology of the Chinese Diaspora. *American Antiquity* 83(3).

Voss, Barbara L., Anita Wong Kwock, Connie Young Yu, Lillian Gong-Guy, Alida
        Bray, Megan S. Kane, and Rebecca Allen

2013   Market Street Chinatown Archaeology Project: Ten Years of Community-
        Based, Collaborative Research on San Jose's Historic Chinese Community.
        *History & Perspectives: The Journal of the Chinese Historical Society of Amer-
        ica* 63–75.

Voss, Barbara L., Ray Von Wandruszka, Alicia Fink, Tara Summer, Elizabeth S.
        Harman, Anton Shapovalov, Megan S. Kane, Marguerite De Loney, and
        Nathan Acebo

2015   Stone Drugs and Calamine Lotion: Chemical Analysis of Residue in
        Nineteenth-Century Glass Bottles, Market Street Chinatown, San Jose,
        California. *California Archaeology* 7(1):93–118.

Walsh, Robert F.

1893   Chinese and the Fisheries. *Californian Illustrated Magazine* 4:833–840.

West, Catherine F., Samantha M. Dunning, Steve Ebbert, Courtney A. Hofman,
        Patrick G. Saltonstall, and Jack Withrow

2017   Archaeology and Invasive Species Management: The Chirikof Island Proj-
        ect. *Journal of Island and Coastal Archaeology* 12:133–137.

Williams, Bryn

2008   Chinese Masculinities and Material Culture. *Historical Archaeology*
        42(3):53–67.

Wolverton, Steve, and R. Lee Lyman (editors)

2012 *Conservation Biology and Applied Zooarchaeology.* University of Arizona Press. Tucson.

Yu, Connie Young

2001 *Chinatown, San Jose, USA.* San Jose Historical Museum Association. San Jose CA.

[TEN]

Pictures Speak for Themselves

*Case Studies Proving the Significance and Affordability
of X Ray for Archaeological Collections*

KERRY S. GONZÁLEZ AND MICHELLE SALVATO

In nearly every collection, old and new, there are metal artifacts entered into a database simply as "indeterminate." Typically, and unfortunately, information on the artifacts will never be expanded upon as iron corrosion masks their true form, rendering them a mystery. Even when the basic form of the object is identifiable, the diagnostic features are hidden beneath layers of corrosion. What are catalogers to do in situations when many of the metal objects from a site are unidentifiable and so highly corroded that in just a short time they will turn to a bag of rusty bits? A solution in many cases is x-radiography.

X-ray technology is not new to the scientific community. In fact x-ray technology has been in use since its discovery in the late 19th century. Its application by archaeologists to aid in determining artifact details, to inform cull-and-discard procedures, or to help make conservation priorities is not a widespread endeavor. In this chapter we highlight the affordability and accessibility of x-radiography and its usefulness for old and new collections. To highlight our personal experiences, histories of the three sites used as our case studies are addressed after a brief history of X ray. This background information is presented as a necessary component to the understanding of why X rays were a crucial factor in site analysis and interpretation. Additionally, within the three case studies the results and limitations for each collection are highlighted, as x-radiography was conducted on material from each site for different reasons. Following the case studies, the methodology used by Dovetail Cultural Resource Group is outlined to provide guidance for those interested in x-raying their own collections. Methods implemented on older collections are also proposed. These guidelines are based on discussions with other collections managers who have experience dealing with assemblages recovered more than a decade ago. There are limitations and challenges encountered when dealing with both old and new collections. X rays can alter or confirm interpretations on new collections as well as bring life to older collections.

X Ray History

The physicist Wilhelm Conrad Röntgen first discovered X rays in the winter of 1895 while attempting to determine whether cathode rays were ethereal or particulate (Assmus 1995). He observed crystals fluorescing in his laboratory while experimenting and spent the next six weeks working to explain the fluorescence. Just before Christmas in 1895, Röntgen brought his wife, Anna, into his laboratory and x-rayed her hand, producing an image of her bones and finger ring.

Within a month of Röntgen's initial announcement in 1895, the whole global scientific community was aware of the discovery. Due to its photographic nature, this new x-ray technology was easily showcased; newspaper and scientific journal articles featuring images of x-rayed objects, including Anna's hand, rapidly spread the news of the discovery. On 16 January 1896, the *New York Times* published an article announcing X ray as "a new form of photography, which revealed hidden solids, penetrated wood, paper, and flesh, and exposed bones of the human frame" (Assmus 1995:11).

The use of x-ray technology remained almost exclusively in the medical and dental fields. Industrial use was restricted due to the lack of available equipment at the time. The invention of high-vacuum x-ray tubes by William D. Coolidge in 1913 and the 1,000,000-volt x-ray generator by the General Electric Company in 1931 provided the necessary advancements for widespread industrial use of radiography (Collaboration for NDT Education 2012). Technological advancements in photography throughout the 20th century allowed for more widespread applications of X rays in a variety of industries. Within the field of archaeology, X rays can be used to identify corroded and indeterminate metals to aid in the identification of artifacts. This information can bolster the analysis of a site and assist in making important cull-and-discard decisions.

Over the past few years, Dovetail has been using X rays on collections with a high density of corroded or indeterminate metals. This process was first introduced to Dovetail by the Maryland Archaeological Conservation Lab (MAC Lab). The MAC Lab was assisting Dovetail with making strategic conservation choices for two large assemblages collected during excavation efforts for the Federal Highway Administration and Delaware Department of Transportation. MAC Lab staff, knowing the utility of x-radiography, suggested that Dovetail use this technology prior to choosing artifacts for conservation. This proved to be the best first step in this process for three reasons: (1) X rays could help identify diagnostic or interpretive objects masked by years of corrosion; (2) the x-ray image would reveal how much metal was left in an object, thus possibly negating the need for conservation if only a mass of corrosion existed; and (3) X ray can help to identify the material composition.

Case Studies

For the purpose of this chapter, three sites are presented as case studies to emphasize the usefulness and importance of X rays when examining and interpreting archaeological collections, large and small. The first two sites consist of archaeological data recoveries that produced sizable assemblages. Dovetail was also responsible for processing and analyzing the artifacts from previous excavations from both these sites in order to fully evaluate the collections as a whole. For these assemblages, the artifacts were x-rayed after cataloging, and the challenges that come with x-raying materials that have already been entered into a database were immediately recognized. The third site was part of an archaeological salvage operation. This particular site was unique in that Dovetail's use of x-radiography was not to identify a large collection of corroded metal objects but rather to examine the interior of a mass of artifacts fused together by iron, copper, and organic materials. Unlike the two other projects, these X rays were taken prior to cataloging, and the resulting data were essential to creating an accurate database for the site.

Case Study 1: The Houston-LeCompt Site (7NC-F-139)

In 2012 Dovetail conducted Phase III excavations at the Houston-LeCompt site in New Castle County, Delaware, at the request of the Federal Highway Administration and Delaware Department of Transportation as part of the Route 301 Improvement Project. The site, a late 18th- through early 20th-century farmstead, was examined over the course of three months and consisted of plow zone sampling, stripping of plow zone to expose features, and feature excavation. Fifty-nine of the 304 identified features were excavated and included a brick-lined cellar, three wells, several outbuildings, a work pad or outdoor kitchen, and a possible box privy (Barile et al. 2016). Nearly 60,000 artifacts were recovered from the site as a whole, with the postdiscard count (artifact count after brick, coal, oyster shell, and slag were weighed and discarded) for the site being 52,867. The results of the fieldwork and ensuing artifact analysis highlighted the changing use of the property from a late 18th-century, owner-occupied farmstead to a late 19th- and early 20th-century tenant farm (Barile et al. 2016).

During excavations at the Houston-LeCompt site a substantial number of personal adornment artifacts were recovered, spurring discussion between Dovetail and the client (Federal Highway Administration and Delaware Department of Transportation) on the need for specialized studies and conservation measures for the entire collection. Prior to deciding what to conserve, Dovetail, in consultation with the MAC Lab, elected to x-ray a large portion of the metals that were unidentifiable due to corrosion. This method helped to create a more accurate catalog and aided in the ensuing specialized study on the personal adornment artifacts recovered from the site.

A total of 936 artifacts from the Houston-LeCompt site were x-rayed. Prior to x-raying, the majority of these materials were initially cataloged as indeterminate due to the amount of corrosion. Of the 936 artifacts, identifications were made on 807 artifacts (86.2%) using x-radiography. Of the 807 identified artifacts, 623 of them were nails; X ray allowed 549 to be identified by manufacturing technique. These data alone highlight the utility of x-radiography and why it should be used more frequently when cataloging or assessing collections (González and Salvato 2016).

Identifying a nail as wrought, cut, wire, clinched, and so on can greatly add to the interpretive value of collections. These data can be crucial in narrowing construction dates and aid in the analysis of site evolution, particularly showing how landscapes have changed over time. There is also the benefit of being able to make informed cull-and-discard decisions on nails once they have been x-rayed and identified, as well as making decisions on artifacts that remained listed as indeterminate use, even after x-raying. This can greatly aid in space saving at collection facilities and save money for those submitting collections to federal and state facilities.

Personal items, hardware, and other artifacts were instrumental in crafting our analysis, especially the adornment study completed by Sara Rivers Cofield (2015). Approximately 60 personal items were identified from the assemblage and consisted of whole buckles, buckle chapes and frames, hooks and eyes, corset fragments, folding knives, forks, and a percussion lock (González and Salvato 2016; Figure 13). Many of these items were completely unidentifiable before X ray, while others had a basic, partially identifiable form. After X ray, conclusive identifications were made that, in most cases, allowed us to date the object. Additionally, it is possible to take accurate measurements of the concreted objects as the original surface can be revealed in the X ray, and the image is a 1:1 scale representation.

All data obtained from the X rays were thoroughly documented in the artifact catalog, noting which artifacts were subjected to X ray. Information from X rays taken of the Houston-LeCompt artifacts were integrated into the documentation of the site and were submitted with the collection to the Delaware State Historic Preservation Office.

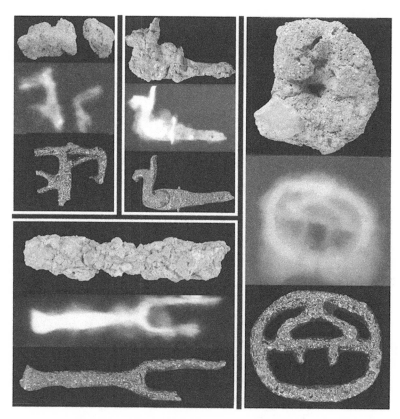

FIGURE 13. Selected artifacts from the Houston-LeCompt site examined through x-radiography. *From top left, clockwise*: shoe buckle chape, percussion lock, shoe buckle, and fork. Image shows artifact prior to conservation, x-ray image, and artifact after conservation. Image not to scale. (Photos: Kerry S. González)

Case Study 2: The Armstrong-Rogers Site (7NC-F-135)

Data recovery was also conducted at the Armstrong-Rogers site as part of the Route 301 Improvement Project for the Federal Highway Administration and Delaware Department of Transportation, also in New Castle County, Delaware. Excavations focused on the side yard of the main house, as it was this portion of the site that was in the right-of-way for the Route 301 Improvement Project.

Archaeological excavations revealed two buildings (a smokehouse and a dairy), two wells, and landscape features representing a work yard. The 6,545 recovered artifacts were consistent with an occupation beginning in the late 18th century and extending into the first half of the 19th century. These dates correspond best with the occupation of the site by Cornelius Armstrong, the tenants of the Armstrong family, and James Roger, spanning from 1767 to 1849 (Hatch et al. 2016).

Of the two identified wells on the property, the first most likely served to provide water to the main house as well as the work yard. Dendrochronological analysis of its structural wood marked the felling of the timber sometime after the winter of 1767 to 1768, or shortly after Cornelius Armstrong settled the site. The artifacts within the fill of the well suggest it was capped after 1820, around the time James Rogers purchased the land. The second well served the dairy. Its fill revealed artifacts with a timeline consistent with that of the dairy: a construction around 1767 and falling out of use around 1824, again when Rogers purchased the property (Hatch et al. 2016).

The identification of artifacts from the Armstrong-Rogers site differs slightly from the Houston-LeCompt site in that the x-radiography focused primarily on the large amount of corroded, unidentified nails, with barely any emphasis on personal items due to their paucity at the site. Like the Houston-LeCompt site, nails were x-rayed in an effort to determine the construction period for various buildings on the property, as the majority of the nails in the assemblage were so corroded that their manufacturing techniques were completely unidentifiable. Of the nearly 900 nails recovered from the site, 454 were x-rayed. X rays allowed the identification of 142 nails, the majority of which were cut with wrought heads.

As we learned from the resulting images, a large portion of the nails were so corroded that the X rays were unable to pick up enough remaining metal to clearly outline the artifact, or the fragments were too small to offer a defined shape in the resulting image. In these cases, the objects remained in the catalog as "indeterminate." While it was unfortunate that such a large number of nails could not be identified during the x-ray process, it provided valuable information regarding the collections' condition and integrity. In this case, x-radiography helped to confirm the suspected date range of the site's buildings and offered a glimpse into the collections' condition, supporting a future cull and discard of corroded iron alloy artifacts that serve no research purpose. Cull and discard was eventually implemented for this collection prior to curation and reduced the size of the collection from 25 flats to 22 flats by discarding 70 percent of the highly corroded nails. Assuming a curation fee of $350 for the State of Delaware, this reduced the curation fee by $1,050. Factoring in the cost of the X rays, which was $271, that is still a savings of $779, a testament to the cost effectiveness of X ray.

A small number of indeterminate metal objects from the Armstrong-Rogers site were also x-rayed in hopes of obtaining information regarding its inhabitants. These included two utensil fragments (one fork tine and one knife blade), one iron alloy chain, one bolt, one spike, one hook, and two shank-back buttons, one with extant fabric (Figure 14). As with the Houston-LeCompt site, all data obtained from the X rays were thoroughly documented, noting which objects were subjected to X ray. X rays taken of the Armstrong-Rogers artifacts were incorporated into the associated documents.

Case Study 3: Riverfront Park Site (44SP0069-001)

In 2015 Dovetail conducted a salvage operation at the request of the City of Fredericksburg at the Riverfront Park site, located on what were historically known as Lots 1 and 2 in Fredericksburg, Virginia. At the outbreak of the Civil War, Lots 1 and 2 were under the ownership of A. P. Rowe, containing his main house and a secondary dwelling. When Fredericksburg became a battleground and subsequent encampment for thousands of soldiers during the winter of 1862 to 1863, several of the houses on Sophia Street, including those on Lots 1 and 2, were at times situated behind Union lines. The 14th Connecticut Regiment, among others, used the Rowe House and secondary dwelling on Lots 1 and 2 as a divisional hospital for their wounded soldiers.

During Dovetail's excavation a number of features were explored as part of the salvage operation, one of which contained an abundance of Civil War–specific materials, including human remains.

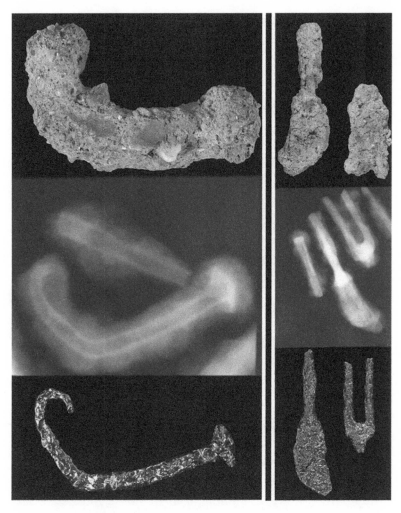

FIGURE 14. Selected artifacts from the Armstrong-Rogers site examined through x-radiography. *On left:* wrought nail; *on right:* knife and fork. Image shows artifact prior to conservation, x-ray image, and artifact after conservation. Image not to scale. (Photos: Kerry S. González)

Within this assemblage was a mass of textiles, most of which were in a bundle measuring 5 in. x 4 in. (González and Salvato 2016).

In an effort to retain the original shape of the cluster of materials, Dovetail performed a lift and removed the mass of artifacts as one piece to be later deconstructed in the hopes of better understand-

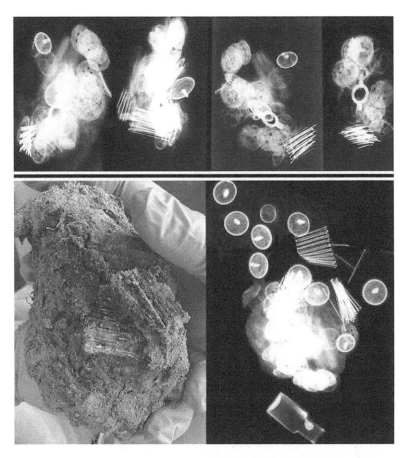

FIGURE 15. Mass of artifacts examined through x-radiography. *Top row*: phased X ray taken during deconstruction of the mass of materials. *Bottom row*: original mass (left) and identifiable artifacts and leftover mass after deconstruction (right). (Photo: Kerry S. González).

ing its original deposition. Looking at this object with the naked eye revealed a mass of materials surrounded by fabric, with a few buttons, a pack of straight pins, and a lead round ball. It seemed likely that many more artifacts were within the cluster of materials. Archaeologists wanted to examine their original context prior to peeling the layers back. X-radiography was the most cost-effective way to view the interior of the collection of materials and also potentially provide information on the types of materials within the assemblage.

The X ray revealed a total of 113 artifacts, not including textiles, within the small mass (Figure 15). Some of these materials included eagle buttons, a small patent medicine bottle, straight pins, a pocket watch key, a small horsehair brush, and a cuff-size Connecticut button. The identification of the Connecticut button was especially significant because the 14th Connecticut was the only Connecticut unit in the 3rd Division, providing additional information as to the potential troops camped at the site. This button was completely corroded. Researchers never would have known which state it represented without the X ray. An additional interesting piece of information was gleaned from the small patent medicine bottle included in the mass of materials. The X ray showed trace amounts of a liquid, visible on the X ray (Figure 15). The contents of the bottle were analyzed by Mishka Repaska and Ruth Ann Armitage (2016) from Eastern Michigan University; they found the substance contained turpentine, mercury, and possibly animal fat, likely ingredients used in topical medicines. The mercury was visible on the X ray because of its high molecular weight.

The x-ray images produced during the site's analysis provided a prime example of how an X ray can highlight the metal composition of an artifact. Material such as copper has a much sharper outline than iron or lead. As seen in Figure 15, the straight pins and shank-back buttons, all copper alloy, have very distinct outlines. Iron, on the other hand, tends to have a more diffused boundary, visible on the X ray of the fork and knife from the Armstrong-Rogers site (see Figure 14). Lead will appear diffused like iron but is much brighter. Knowing what metals are in a collection can help with the interpretation of the site, and, if conservation is an option, the composition of the materials is extremely important information for conservationists to determine their approach to treating the object.

As so much data were obtained from the first X ray of the mass of materials and because some of the iron objects were masking other artifacts, the wad of artifacts was dissected and a progression of x-ray images was taken (see Figure 15). The MAC Lab staff produced a single x-ray sheet containing multiple phased images of the mass of artifacts as it was deconstructed. From this process, researchers were able to obtain a clear picture of a pocket watch key, as well as several metal buttons, which allowed for an exact count of the iron buttons. This would not have been possible without X ray, and having this count helped to determine a potential minimum number of garments represented in the artifact mass. Unlike the previous two sites discussed, X ray of this collection was done prior to cataloging, which made the process for both situations more apparent.

Methodology

Through a number of trips to the MAC Lab, as well as trial and error, a process was created by which artifacts could be efficiently pulled from an existing collection and x-rayed allowing information to be integrated into the final catalog. X-raying new collections proves to be much easier than x-raying old collections because decisions can be made during the initial laboratory process. This is not always possible, especially with older collections whose report and catalog have been finalized. If a need for x-radiography is foreseen, a project's budget can be adjusted to allow for the x-raying of certain materials, as done with the materials recovered during excavations at the Riverfront Park site. As was true in the first two case studies, previously cataloged collections can be more difficult. This section follows the x-ray processes for these cases, highlighting the challenges of adding x-ray information from recently excavated materials, as well as reintegrating new information into an old collection.

The initial step when x-raying older collections is to determine which artifacts, if any, are suitable for x-radiography. If possible, catalogs can be sorted to show any metal artifacts labeled "indeterminate" and decisions can be made based upon the artifact's frequency in the collection, research potential, and the context in which it was recovered. After entries are flagged in the catalog as potential artifacts to x-ray, those items are pulled from the collection for further investigation. These decisions should be project-specific and primarily driven by the site's research questions. For example, during analysis of the Armstrong-Rogers site, Dovetail chose to x-ray the vast

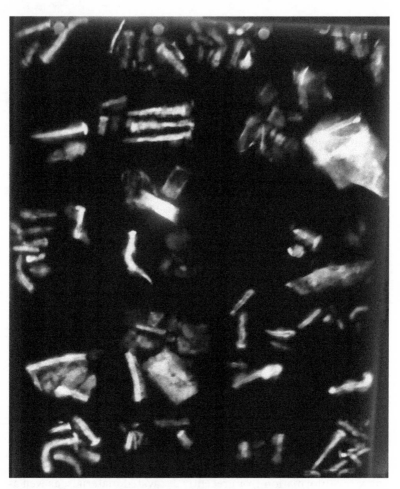

FIGURE 16. X ray showing the potential number of artifacts that can fit on one film. (Photo: Kerry S. González).

number of corroded nails to establish construction periods for the site's buildings. Analysis of the Houston-LeCompt site did not solely depend on the x-raying of nails, but instead focused on the personal items and other large indeterminate iron fragments to help establish a timeline surrounding the inhabitance of the site. Once decisions to x-ray an artifact were made, each artifact was pulled from the collection in preparation.

When x-raying a large number of artifacts from several proveniences, it is important to properly organize the bags to maximize the quantity of artifacts per film. For some perspective, through careful orchestration, 157 artifacts fit on one 14 x 17-in. film depicted in Figure 16 (note: only 10 artifacts remained indeterminate after X ray).

The next step involves the photo documentation of the bag placement on the film, which aids in later comparison with the x-ray image. A sketch of the bags on the tray with provenience information, or an x-ray "map," is also created prior to x-raying. This map depicts bag numbers to each provenience; the number was written on the exterior of each bag large enough to be visible in the photograph. The exact placement and rough size of each bag should also be transcribed on the map to ensure an accurate transfer of data after X ray.

Upon the completion of the X rays, the new data were transferred to the existing catalog. It is important when transferring data to record that the identification was based on the X rays. Catalogs were altered to include a column headed "X ray" in which to mark the artifacts that were taken to the MAC Lab for analysis. At this point in the process it was simply a matter of filtering the catalog by the artifacts flagged as being x-rayed and then filling in the diagnostic information gleaned from the X ray. Again, older collections can be much more challenging because often the catalogs and site reports have been finalized. In this situation, the best-case scenario is to thoroughly document the x-ray process and create a brief addendum report to go with the collection and site report for future researchers.

Limitations and Challenges of X-ray Analysis

X-ray technology provided invaluable information in all three case studies, but the process also has some limitations. Cost and availability can be deterring factors when considering the use of X rays in the analytical process; many firms and agencies operate on tight project-based budgets that do not allow for in-depth scientific analysis. Table 13 provides a brief list of institutions that perform x-ray for archaeological collections.

Table 13. Examples of facilities that may x-ray archaeological collections

Institution	State	Contact information
Mashantucket Pequot Museum and Research Center	Connecticut	860–396–6936 www.pequotmuseum.org
Maryland Archaeological Conservation Lab	Maryland	410–586–8577 http://www.jefpat.org/mac_lab.html
Cowell Health Center at University of California, Santa Cruz	California	831–459–2780 https://healthcenter.ucsc.edu/
Queen Anne's Revenge Conservation Lab, East Carolina University	North Carolina	252–744–6721 http://www.qaronline.org/conservation/queen-annes-revenge-lab
North Carolina Museum of Art	North Carolina	919–839–6262 http://ncartmuseum.org/
Archaeology Conservation Lab, University of West Florida	Florida	850–474–2706 http://uwf.edu/cassh/departments/anthropology-and-archaeology/about-us/facilities/
Conservation Research Laboratory, Nautical Archaeology Program, Texas A&M	Texas	979–862–7791 http://nautarch.tamu.edu/CRL/
Virginia Department of Historic Resources	Virginia	904–482–6442 http://www.dhr.virginia.gov/arch_DHR/collect_info2.htm

Cost is typically a driving factor in the cultural resource industry, and affordability is often one of the largest concerns with x-ray analysis. Because the number of artifacts that can be x-rayed at once does vary based on the size of the artifact, the following calculation serves to merely indicate one possible cost analysis. During the examination of the Houston-LeCompt site, 1,000 artifacts were x-rayed across 10 films. While some films contained more artifacts than others, the average was 100 artifacts per film. For these 10 films, the cost averaged approximately $0.35 per artifact. Obviously the numbers will vary, especially when only a few items need to be x-rayed, although this certainly serves as an example to highlight how easy and affordable it is to x-ray collections of indeterminate iron and other metals, including nails.

X-ray analysis is reasonably priced considering the information it can yield. If the x-ray images allow for discard of multiple bags of heavily corroded indeterminate metal objects or nails, less space is needed for the collection in its final repository, reducing future curation costs. In a large collection it is possible to reduce the size by one or more boxes through cull and discard, especially when implementing the discard of x-rayed iron objects. Using a standard curation fee for the mid-Atlantic region of $350/box as a base, approximately two to three X rays could be purchased by reducing the collection by just one box. While it may not always seem feasible due to budgetary restraints, there are other options available to make x-ray analysis a possibility. Contact a local dentist, chiropractor, university, or large animal vet. Often they are willing to help for free or at a greatly reduced cost.

As learned from the x-ray analysis of the Armstrong-Rogers site, if metal objects are too corroded, the image produced may not yield useful information. More important, X rays can illustrate the extent to which an artifact is corroded and allow for informed conservation and cull-and-discard decisions. If an x-ray image shows an ample amount of metal left in an object, an archaeologist may choose to conserve the artifact. But what happens when there is little to no metal left underneath the mass of corrosion? In some cases, casting may be an appropriate next step. In the casting process the hollow shell, or cast, of the object at hand is filled with an epoxy resin which takes the shape of the nonextant artifact before the corroded shell is removed from its surface (Rash 2010). Often used in maritime archaeological endeavors, casting may be another route an archaeologist chooses in order to preserve some of the research and educational value of a heavily corroded collection. Most often highly corroded objects have very limited long-term research value, and once they have been identified and recorded, there is no need for them to be curated in perpetuity.

Many facilities already allow for the cull and discard of excess brick and oyster shell, but nails and iron objects are often in such a state of corrosion that they will continue to disintegrate even in the best of storage conditions. If there are accurate identifications on severely corroded iron objects, update the catalog accordingly or provide documentation in the collection and with the report. There is no need to continue curating every highly corroded nail or iron object. Many of these artifacts are so degraded that the original iron has corroded away and all that is left is a cast of the original object, with very little research potential unless a casting process is to be undertaken. Some repositories, such as the New Jersey State Museum, will not accept iron unless it has been conserved. Other facilities, such as the Pennsylvania Historical and Museum Commission, also have stringent policies on accepting iron, a testament to this discard policy already taking shape. Following the proper procedures for documentation, nails and other highly corroded iron artifacts can be discarded.

As X ray is not widely used, especially in an archaeological setting, there are limited resources on best practices for this kind of analysis and documentation. Due to this lack of information, many people are hesitant to approach clients and state historic preservation offices about discard of these types of objects. This chapter clearly outlines the many benefits of this process, and we strongly encourage utilization of this alternative methodology. We hope this information can be used by archaeological collections managers as guidelines for their own x-ray endeavors. We are optimistic that the data provided here will aid in making the case for X ray as a standard operating procedure on most collections, especially those with a high density of corroded irons.

Acknowledgments

First, our gratitude goes to Ben Ford and Rebecca Allen for organizing this volume. This paper is a manifestation of our work at

Dovetail over the past few years using x-radiology on our collections; as such we would like to thank the company owners, Kerri Barile and Mike Carmody, for allowing us to explore new and creative lab techniques. We would also like to thank Emily Anderson, Emily Calhoun, Brad Hatch, and Danae Peckler, who authored the data recovery reports used for our case studies. The histories and ensuing analysis played a significant role in making this paper a cohesive document. Last but not least, thank you to the staff at the MAC Lab, namely Sara Rivers Cofield, Nichole Doub, and Francis Lukezic, for introducing us to the power of x-radiology on collections. Without your encouragement and insistence, we would not be part of this volume. As with any undertaking of this nature, we, the authors, bear responsibility for the accuracy of interpretations presented in this work.

References

Assmus, Alexi

1995   Early History of X Rays. *Beam Line* Summer:10-24.

Barile, Kerri, Emily Calhoun, Mike Klein, Danae Peckler, Kerry S. González, D. Brad Hatch, and Michelle Salvato

2016   Archaeological Data Recovery at the Houston-Lecompt Site (7NC-F-139; N-14517), New Castle County, Delaware. Report to Delaware Department of Transportation from Dovetail Cultural Resource Group, Fredericksburg VA.

Collaboration for NDT Education

2012   History of Radiography. https://www.nde-ed.org/EducationResources /CommunityCollege/Radiography/Introduction/history.htm. Accessed March 2016.

González, Kerry, and Michelle Salvato

2016   *Inexpensive X-rays, Invaluable Information: A Case Study from Two Data Recoveries.* Paper presented at the 49th annual conference of the Society for Historical Archaeology, Washington DC.

Hatch, D. Brad, Danae Peckler, Joseph R. Blondino, Kerry S. González, Emily Calhoun, and Kerri S. Barile

2016   Archaeological Data Recovery at the Armstrong-Rogers Site (7NC-F-135; N-14517), New Castle County, Delaware. Report to Delaware Department of Transportation from Dovetail Cultural Resource Group, Fredericksburg VA.

Markel, Howard

2012 "I Have Seen My Death": How the World Discovered the X-ray. *The Rundown, PBS News Hour,* 20 December. http://www.pbs.org/newshour/rundown/i-have-seen-my-death-how-the-world-discovered-the-x-ray/.

Rash, Kimberly

2010 Casting the Assemblage of Iron Artifacts from Kızılburun. *Center for Maritime Archaeology and Conservation News and Reports* 2(2):31–32.

Repaska, Mishka, and Ruth Ann Armitage

2016 *Chemical Characterization of a Civil War Bottle Residue.* Poster. Department of Chemistry, Eastern Michigan University, Ypsilanti.

Rivers-Cofield, Sara

2015 Houston-LeCompt Personal Adornment. Appendix I, Archaeological Data Recovery at the Houston-LeCompt Site (7NC-F-139; N-14517), New Castle County, Delaware. Report to Delaware Department of Transportation from Dovetail Cultural Resource Group, Fredericksburg VA.

ELEVEN

From Ship to Kindling to Ship

The Digital Reconstruction of the Royal Savage *Timber Assemblage*

JONATHAN CRISE, BEN FORD, AND GEORGE SCHWARZ

Royal Savage is an important physical link to one of the seminal events of early U.S. Revolutionary War history (Figure 17). This importance drew the attention of an interested public long before archaeological science and ethics were advanced enough to provide for the long-term preservation of the hull and its artifacts. The result was a collection of disassociated timbers and artifacts that several institutions wanted to own, but which never received the interpretation they deserved. Now, using state-of-the-art three-dimensional imaging technology, it is possible to regain some of the information that was lost. In addition to contributing to the generation of a timber catalog, 3D documentation of the *Royal Savage* timbers via laser scanning and photogrammetry provides a visually appealing, permanent, and versatile record of the physical characteristics of the ship's remains. The resulting digital models are permanent in that, as visual reproductions, and if stored and managed appropriately, they will remain impervious to the physical decay to which the actual remains of the ship have and will continue to be subjected. As such, they will also remain available to continued and varied analyses to which the physical remains cannot be subjected, both as individual timbers and, when digitally reconstructed, as a partially intact hull. Similar methods have been applied to a wide variety of collections (Virtual Curation Laboratory 2017). From a technological perspective, the models produced are demonstrative of an alternative methodology for terrestrial 3D laser scanning of individual objects

FIGURE 17. *Royal Savage.* (Courtesy of and with permission from Naval History and Heritage Command, Washington DC)

and their subsequent integration as a whole. The redundant nature of the digital format ensures the perpetual preservation of what is left of *Royal Savage* independent of its physical state.

From Ship to Timbers: The History of *Royal Savage*

Royal Savage is part of a larger narrative of how the American colonists won their Revolution. Its significance lies in its association with the Battle of Valcour Island and as an example of British naval construction designed to operate on North America's inland waters. The story of the vessel and its role in U.S. history begin in 1775. In May of that year Benedict Arnold and Ethan Allen seized the British forts of Crown Point and Ticonderoga on the southern shores of Lake Champlain. Connected to the St. Lawrence River in the north through the Richelieu River and to the Hudson River through Lake George to the south, Lake Champlain is part of a natural north-south thoroughfare that historically allowed whoever controlled it to control much of New England. By under-garrisoning their forts on the lake, the British allowed the rebels to gain a strategic foothold in the region. Pressing this advantage, and seizing or destroying vessels as he went, Arnold sailed down the lake to St. Johns (St. Jean) on the Richelieu River, capturing the post and a sloop, before destroying the remaining British vessels and retreating back up the lake. (Lake Champlain flows from south to north, so that "up lake" is south.) When a superior British force arrived overland at St. Johns the next day, Arnold was gone; with no vessels and no roads south, they were unable to pursue him (Mahan 1969:7–9; Malcomson 2004:26). These actions gave the rebels control of Lake Champlain and provided the Continental Congress time to send Gen. Richard Montgomery to officially take command of forces in the region. Meanwhile the British fortified St. Johns and quickly built a schooner they called *Brave* or *Royal Savage* to augment their forces on the lake (Lyon 1993:298; Malcomson 2004:27).

Montgomery arrived at Crown Point on 4 September 1775 and moved down Lake Champlain to attack St. Johns. After an extended siege, the rebels captured St. Johns on 3 November (Mahan 1969:9). During the attack, red-hot shot from rebel cannon burned and sank *Royal Savage* near shore. After the vessel's surrender, American forces raised it and renamed the resurrected vessel *Yankee*, although the name did not stick and the schooner continued to be referred to as *Royal Savage* in both British and Colonial accounts (Bredenberg 1966:136–137; Bellico 1992:124; Lyon 1993:298). From St. Johns, Montgomery continued down the Richelieu River to take Montreal on 13 November 1775. He and Arnold, who had led a second force along the Kennebec River, rendezvoused at Québec and attacked the city on 31 December. Montgomery was killed, Arnold wounded, and the Americans were beaten back in the course of the battle. The rebels then blockaded the city and went into winter quarters, retreating back to Crown Point the next summer (Mahan 1969:9–12; Gardiner 1996).

Despite the unsuccessful invasion of Canada, there were still no British ships on Lake Champlain and no roads south of St. Johns, so that the colonists retained control of the lake and could temporarily prevent the British from advancing south. The ability to stymie the British took on renewed importance during the summer of 1776. Just as the rebels had attempted a two-pronged attack on Canada, the British were invading New England on more than one front. Sir Guy Carleton, governor and commander in chief of Canada, was leading a force up the Richelieu River while a larger force under Gen. William Howe was planning to invade New York City and the mouth of the Hudson River. If the British were successful in connecting along the Richelieu-Champlain-Hudson corridor they would be able to cleave the northern colonies from southern support and likely bring the rebellion to a speedy close. Arnold, who took command of the rebel squadron on Lake Champlain from Jacobus Wynkoop on 17 August 1776, was aware of Washington's defeat at Long Island on 27 August, as he prepared his vessels for a British advance (Nelson 2006:xv, 259–261).

Royal Savage became Arnold's flagship, as it had been for Wynkoop before him, and the nucleus of the American squadron. Maj. Henry Livingston described the approximately 70-ton schooner as "very long and something flat bottom'd—elegantly built and finish'd off mounts 14 brass 6 pounders besides a number of swivels . . . a very handsome and elegant vessel" (Bellico 1992:124). The ship was an estimated 50 ft. (15.2 m) in length, with a 15-ft. (4.6-m) beam and a complement of 40 to 50 sailors (Dictionary of American Naval Fighting Ships 2005). Under the rebels, *Royal Savage* was armed with 4- and 6-pound cannon as well as 12 1-pound swivel guns (Barbieri 2014). The squadron included the schooners *Revenge* and *Liberty* as well as the sloop *Enterprise*, all of which had been captured from the British in 1775. The Continental Army also built the cutter *Lee* using frames seized when they captured St. Johns (Bellico 1992:132, 141; Nelson 2006:244). To complete the squadron during the summer of 1776, the rebels built three approximately 75-ft. (22.9-m) row galleys (*Congress*, *Trumbull*, and *Washington*) and eight flat-bottomed, 53-ft. (16.2-m) gondolas (*Boston*, *Connecticut*, *New Haven*, *Jersey*, *New York*, *Philadelphia*, *Providence*, and *Spitfire*) at Skenesborough (Whitehall), New York (Bellico 1992:128, 140, 191; Gardiner 1996).

Reports from Arnold's chief spy, Ben Whitcomb, conveyed that the British were building only bateaus and not large vessels at St.

Johns. This intelligence gave Arnold confidence that the rebels maintained a superior fleet, an impression that lasted until the encounter at Valcour Island (Bredenberg 1966:141). On the contrary, the British were amassing a force to retake Lake Champlain. They disassembled two schooners, *Maria* and *Carleton*, and brought them up the Richelieu River from the St. Lawrence. Similarly the ship *Inflexible*, three times the tonnage of *Royal Savage*, was partially complete at Québec but was disassembled and brought to St. Johns to be rebuilt. *Loyal Convert*, a large gondola that was captured from the Americans during the invasion of Canada, was dragged over the rapids of the Richelieu to join the force. The British built 28 gunboats using timbers that were likely cut elsewhere and imported to St. Johns. And they built a type of floating battery called a radeau at St. Johns and named it *Thunderer* (Bredenberg 1966:141; Bellico 1992:145; Malcomson 2004:27–29). The estimates vary, but in all accounts, the British force was significantly stronger than the rebels', with more and larger guns and more and better trained sailors (Skerrett 1935:1648; Mahan 1969:17; Bellico 1992:152), though neither squadron was particularly large. The most substantial ship in either squadron, *Inflexible*, was dwarfed by its saltwater cousins. As Alfred Mahan (1969:18) wrote, this truly was "a strife of pigmies for the prize of a continent."

As soon as their flagship *Inflexible* was completed in early October the British began to advance up the lake with Thomas Pringle commanding the squadron and Sir Guy Carleton traveling with them. The rebel squadron, minus the schooner *Liberty*, had been cruising the lake, but had by this time fallen back to Valcour Island, approximately halfway up the west shore of Lake Champlain (Mahan 1969:15–17). There Arnold described his position as "in a small bay on the west side of the island, as near together as possible, and in such a form that few vessels can attack us at the same time, and those will be exposed to the fire of the whole fleet" (Mahan 1969:20). Based on other accounts, he arranged his vessels in a crescent between the island and the shore to make it difficult for the British to engage all of their ships at one time. The topography and position of Valcour also hid the rebels from the British as they sailed south up the lake. Arnold took the final precaution in the hours before the battle to shift his flag from the roomy *Royal Savage* to the more heavily armed and maneuverable galley *Congress* (Skerrett 1935:1647; Bellico 1992:152; Nelson 2006:xv).

Due to faulty intelligence, the British expected the rebels in the vicinity of Grand Island, so with their attention focused on that shore and with a fair northeast wind, much of the squadron was south of Valcour Island before they realized the Americans were between Valcour and the western shore. Apparently to ensure that the British saw them, Arnold sailed *Royal Savage* and the row galleys toward the south end of Valcour Island. Seeing the rebel vessels, the British squadron turned up wind to engage them (Mahan 1969:19; Nelson 2006:xiv, 295). The battle began at approximately 10:00 a.m. on 11 October 1776 (Malcomson 2004:33).

As Arnold had expected, the British had difficulty sailing against the wind to attack his vessels. This was easiest for the approximately 20 gunboats, which could be rowed up wind, and they quickly formed a line from the southwest tip of the Island to the New York shore. *Inflexible* was also able to maneuver into position, joining the gunboats early in the battle. *Loyal Convert* and *Thunderer* were never able to work their way up wind and were effectively removed from the fray. Meanwhile the rebel row galleys had returned to their line, but *Royal Savage* struggled. Never an agile vessel, *Royal Savage* failed several times to turn its bow through the wind while tacking. As the British gunboats and *Inflexible* came into line they mauled the schooner. Damage to *Royal Savage*'s masts and rigging made it even more unmanageable, and it was taking heavy damage to its hull from the British 12- and 24-pound cannon balls. As a result of all of these factors, Capt. David Hawley ran *Royal Savage* aground on the southwestern tip of Valcour Island and abandoned it (Mahan 1969:17, 21; Bellico 1992:152; Nelson 2006:296–297). With *Royal Savage* out of the fight, *Inflexible*, *Carleton*, and the gunboats moved farther into the bay to engage the main rebel force. Meanwhile Lt. Edward Longcroft, the commander of *Thunderer*, and a boat crew rowed to *Royal Savage*, captured the few crew remaining on board as well as Arnold's papers, and turned *Royal Savage*'s guns on the rebel vessels. The rebels responded by firing on *Royal Savage* until half of Longcroft's crew was killed and he was forced to return to *Thunderer* (Bellico 1992:152; Nelson 2006:308).

Late in the day the British commander Pringle withdrew the British squadron several hundred yards toward the tip of Valcour Island, out of range of the rebel grapeshot but within range of the larger British long guns. He also sent a boarding party to burn *Royal Savage*. Eventually the fire reached the powder magazine and the schooner exploded, but it continued to burn for much of the night (Skerrett 1935:1649; Bellico 1992:154). By the end of 11 October the rebels had also lost the gondola *Philadelphia* and the British had lost two of their smaller vessels (Skerrett 1935:1649; Mahan 1969:22; Bellico 1992:154).

As night fell, Pringle extended his vessels from the New York shore to the tip of Valcour Island in an attempt to hem in the rebels and allow him to finish the victory in the morning. Arnold's squadron slipped through his line during the night and began a retreat southward toward their fortifications at Ticonderoga and Crown Point. Pringle blamed the escape on a heavy fog, although no one else mentioned poor visibility. The burning *Royal Savage* may have been a distraction on an otherwise moonless night, but the real culprit was likely a large gap between the British line and the New York shore (Mahan 1969:23; Bellico 1992:155; Nelson 2006:308–309). The next morning the British found their cannon aimed at an empty bay and the rebels approximately 7.5 miles south at Schuyler Island, where they had stopped to repair their damaged vessels. Due to poor winds during 12 October, the chase began in earnest the next morning, 13 October. *Inflexible*, *Carleton*, and *Maria* sailed considerably faster than the damaged rebel vessels and were able to overtake the galleys *Congress* and *Washington* that were protecting the rear of the squadron. A 9-mile running battle with the rebels receiving the worst of it carried the vessels to a small bay, now called Arnolds Bay, approximately 10 miles north of Crown Point, where Arnold ran ashore four of the gondolas and his galley *Congress* and ignited them. He and his men managed to escape overland to Ticonderoga, where he rejoined *Enterprise, Revenge, Trumbull*, and *New York*, his only vessels to survive the battle (Mahan 1969:24–25; Bellico 1992:155–160).

The British defeated the rebels in the Battle of Valcour Island. *Philadelphia* and *Royal Savage* were lost during the battle. *Lee, Washington*, and *Jersey* were captured by the British and one of the gondolas was scuttled during the escape. Arnold destroyed *Congress* and four other gondolas at Arnolds Bay (Malcomson 2004:34). The British also quickly retook Crown Point as the small rebel force there withdrew. Despite these significant losses, Benedict Arnold and the Lake Champlain squadron may have won the Revolution. After a brief attack on Ticonderoga, Carleton decided it was too late in the year to continue the campaign and withdrew to winter quarters. The next summer Gen. John Burgoyne led the British forces up Lake Champlain, taking Ticonderoga and proceeding to Saratoga, where he was forced to surrender on 17 October 1777. The rebels were successful at Saratoga because Washington had time to organize his troops during the winter of 1776–1777, a direct consequence of Arnold's efforts to stymie the British attempt to split the colonies. The rebel victory at Saratoga helped convince France to enter the war, and with the arrival of their fleet the naval war shifted to the Atlantic and the metaphorical tide of war shifted to the rebels (Mahan 1969:25–28; Gardiner 1996).

Salvage of *Royal Savage* began three years after it sank, when, in November 1779, the British removed most of its guns. Into the late 19th century the site was a tourist attraction. Resting in shallow water, the hull was visible from the surface, and it was a popular attraction for lake guides. Visitors regularly removed artifacts and pieces of hull as mementos or to make souvenirs. In 1860 the bow was pulled out of the water during an attempt to raise the hull, but the rest of the vessel broke free and slipped into deeper water. In 1868 Capt. George Conn anchored above the shipwreck and used a grapnel to pull off oak timbers that were used to make souvenirs (Skerrett 1935:1650; Bellico 1992:192). In preparation for the 1909 Champlain Tercentenary, a hard-hat diver from Boston was hired to raise the hull. He removed a frame and musket ball and noted, "About forty five feet of hull is in a fair state of preservation and can be raised practically as it is," but left the hull where it lay (Bellico 1992:192).

The location of *Royal Savage* was likely fading from the collective memory when Lorenzo Hagglund was in military training at Plattsburg, New York, in 1917, but the story of the schooner was still alive enough to spark his interest. By the time he returned in 1932, having retired from the army and become a successful marine salvage engineer, the location of the wreck had been totally lost and the remains were nearly impossible to see from the surface. Hagglund dedicated his vacation that year to locating *Royal Savage* and spent most of his time on an orderly, but unsuccessful, underwater search expanding from the shore. On the last day of his vacation, which happened to be sunny and calm, he rowed out in a small boat to search from the surface. After several hours he spotted the remains and had to be satisfied with recording bearings to the site without actually exploring the shipwreck (Skerrett 1935:1650; Bellico 1992:193).

Hagglund spent the next two years attempting to find state and federal support to salvage the vessel, but when he learned that its location had been leaked he determined to use his own resources to recover *Royal Savage* (Skerrett 1935:1651; Beil 2015). Earlier that year U.S. Navy Lt. Horace Mazet explored the wreck using a hard-hat diving suit and described it as "14 ribs still standing," "Whitened musket balls of lead gleamed dully against dark oak timbers, and we were soon finding groups of rust-welded grape-shot oxidized to planks . . . [and] cannon balls coated with thick encrustations of rust" (Bellico 1992:192). Hagglund arrived a few weeks later to begin salvage.

The wreck was 34 ft. (10.4 m) long and 15 ft. (4.6 m) wide and consisted of a keel, keelson, stern assembly, bow components, frames, and some bottom planking. It lay in 16 ft. (4.9 m) of water at the bow and 24 ft. (7.3 m) of water at the stern, with the stern buried beneath 4 ft. (1.2 m) of mud. Believing that any remaining artifacts that could identify the shipwreck would be buried in the stern or in the surrounding sediment, Hagglund and his team of locals and professional diving friends used a bucket to excavate the stern and surrounding area. Each bucketful was washed at the surface to recover artifacts. They recovered regimental buttons from troops stationed at Crown Point and Ticonderoga in 1775 and 1776, a pewter spoon engraved "1776" by its owner, a canteen, a frying pan, a drumstick, and other items. They also found fragments of an iron pot both inside and outside of the hull, evidence of the explosion that ended the vessel (Skerrett 1935:1651; Bellico 1992:192; Barbieri 2014; Beil 2015). Neither these artifacts nor the hull was mapped in situ. Hagglund seems to have gifted some artifacts to the crew and influential colleagues (Barbieri 2014). After freeing the hull from the mud, Hagglund lashed 22 road-tar drums to the frames and proceeded to systematically fill them with air, moving from the bow toward the stern. This was a slow process because the team had only one pump. A diver had to secure the air hose to a drum, and then return to the surface so that his air supply hose could be exchanged for the one attached to the drum. The men would then work the pump until bubbles were seen at the surface. The diver reconnected his hose, returned to the wreck, sealed the drum, moved the air hose to the next drum, and the process was repeated. After the 20th drum was filled, *Royal Savage* broke free of the bottom and floated to the surface. Then all the salvors had to do was winch it ashore (Skerrett 1935:1562).

Once ashore the timbers were numbered and the hull disassembled before it was loaded into a boxcar and moved to storage near New York City. The timbers eventually made their way back to Lake Champlain, where many of them were stored on Long Island. A 6-ft. (1.8-m) section of the stern, including gudgeons, was displayed at the David M. Stewart Museum in Montreal before being loaned to the National Canadian War Museum in Ottawa. Other artifacts and timbers were displayed at Hotel Champlain in Plattsburgh. In the 1950s and 1960s other divers removed additional timbers and artifacts from the site (Skerrett 1935:1652; Bellico 1992:193).

In 1995 Lorenzo Hagglund's son, Hudson, sold the *Royal Savage* collection to the City of Harrisburg, Pennsylvania, for a planned museum exhibit. The museum plans changed and *Royal Savage* was never displayed (Barbieri 2014; Beil 2015). The artifacts and timbers were retained by the city until an agreement was made to return

FIGURE 18. *Royal Savage* timbers with the Leica C10 scanner in the background. (Photo: Heather Brown)

Royal Savage and associated materials to the U.S. Naval History and Heritage Command (NHHC) for preservation, documentation, and eventual exhibit. In July 2015 Mayor Eric Papenfuse of Harrisburg formally returned the artifacts to NHHC director Sam Cox during a press event at City Hall. The disassembled hull amounts to 67 timbers, including sections of floor timbers, futtocks, keel, keelson, stem, and planking (Figure 18). In April 2014 NHHC received the stern assembly, including parts of the aft keel, keelson, and sternpost, directly from Hudson Hagglund. The Harrisburg materials were inventoried, packed in cushioned containers, and transported to an NHHC curatorial facility at the Washington Navy Yard for assessment, cleaning, documentation, and conservation.

Because the science of waterlogged wood conservation was underdeveloped when Lorenzo Hagglund recovered the schooner from Lake Champlain, the hull was unsystematically dried and stored in less than ideal conditions during the past three-quarters of a century. Not surprisingly, the integrity of the hull suffered and the remaining timbers exhibit shrinking, warping, cracking, flaking, and general degradation. Despite the general neglect, however, many of the hull members retain enough detail to render valuable information regarding ship design and construction, and thorough documentation is planned in an attempt to reconstruct the schooner and record as many features as possible for study and exhibit. Over 2,000 artifacts originally recovered by Hagglund accompanied the hull to NHHC; these range from eating utensils and hand tools to ordnance. Material types include glass, ceramic, wood, iron, pewter, and textile. Akin to the hull remains, the artifacts were not all properly conserved and will undergo full assessment by NHHC conservators and be treated as necessary.

As an aside, *Royal Savage* is not the only archaeological remains of the Lake Champlain squadron. Hagglund returned to Valcour Island in 1935 and salvaged the gondola *Philadelphia*. The Smithsonian acquired this nearly intact vessel in 1961 and it is now on display in the National Museum of American History (Bellico 1992:193). *Philadelphia*'s sister-ship *Spitfire* was found by the Lake Champlain Maritime Museum in 1997 and still rests nearly intact on the lake floor as a National Historic Landmark (Sabick et al. 2000). The British salvaged the cannon and other useful items from *Congress* and the gondolas scuttled in Arnolds Bay. The vessels themselves were hauled out of the water and broken up for souvenirs. Fragments of *Congress* still exist in a private collection and on the bay floor in much deteriorated conditions (Bellico 1992:199–200). All of the extant remains of these vessels are government property. While they were not protected by historic preservation laws at the time of their salvage, they are now protected from unauthorized disturbance under the Sunken Military Craft Act of 2004 and other applicable submerged cultural resources laws.

From Timbers to Ship: The Digital Recording and Reconstruction of the *Royal Savage* Assemblage

Maritime researchers have made use of recent technologies—light detection and ranging (LiDAR, also called laser scanning) and digital photogrammetry—to record a variety of shipwrecks (Hunter et al. 2016; Yumafune et al. 2016). In the case of *Royal Savage* this was not possible. The shipwreck is no longer a ship, wrecked or otherwise. It is instead an assemblage of disarticulated timbers with little written indication of their original configuration. Digital recording and reconstruction offers an efficient way to recapture and reinterpret data that have been lost. Through a combination of digital 3D reconstruction techniques and traditional recording methods, the chapter's authors were able to reconstruct elements of *Royal Savage*. This creates a tangible link to an important episode in U.S. history and helps to reclaim the ship's place in the history of European American ship construction.

The focus of the current study and digital documentation efforts is on the hull remains, as they afford an opportunity to learn more about late 18th-century ship design. This ongoing digital documentation project has four primary objectives: (1) production of individual scale models of the timbers for documentation and analysis, (2) reconstruction of the vessel, (3) public display of the remains of *Royal Savage*, and (4) technical comparison and feasibility of digital documentation techniques. This digital study is giving this neglected collection new research life.

Virtually every shipwreck documentation project involves the production of a systematic catalog of the diagnostic features of individual timbers, including structural dimensions, scale drawings, surface characteristics, carpenter's marks, wood type, fastener details, signs of charring, general state of preservation, and other relevant details. The first objective of this study, producing high-quality 3D, or tridimensional, scale models of each timber, contributes significantly to the generation of the timber catalog, preserving in perpetuity the surviving features of the hull for further analysis.

This objective lends itself to the second goal, which is the virtual reconstruction of *Royal Savage* based on hull analysis. Production of scale models and drawings permits manipulation of the timbers digitally before having to handle large and fragile timbers. Tridimensional models will help researchers determine the original position of the timbers based on form, design characteristics, and construction features. This can also be done with printed scale models from the 3D renderings.

The third goal is sharing the gathered information with the public, the academic community, and the modern-day sailor to highlight this era of naval history and maritime heritage. Generation of tridimensional models creates opportunities to present the data in virtual exhibits, printed 3D models, and physical reconstruction of the actual hull timbers. In this way the history of the earliest American navy, the Battle of Valcour Island, and the challenges of preserving and interpreting neglected material culture remains can be brought to public attention.

The final objective of this project is to contribute to the studies of digital archaeology by comparing methods of recording *Royal Savage*'s remains. Digital documentation methods for cultural heritage have been used for decades with the application and development of various digital recording systems, from computers and tablets to digitally rendered photogrammetry (Boehler and Marbs 2004; Remondino and Campana 2014; Averett et al. 2016). Tridimensional scanning of cultural heritage objects and archaeological sites has been used and improved upon for at least 10 years, but relatively new technologies have advanced the practicality and affordability of such documentation efforts and have been expanded to underwater archaeological sites. Unlike some recent studies in tridimensional documentation of in situ wreck sites (Drap 2012; Demesticha et al. 2014; Yamafune et al. 2016), *Royal Savage* was raised and disassembled with minimal documentation, and hull timbers were periodically lent out over the course of 83 years, making this a somewhat unique experiment in 3D modeling and reconstruction of an old collection.

The use of digital scanning methods in archaeological documentation has increased as more accurate, innovative, and user-friendly tools continue to develop. Practitioners have asserted that increased speed, accuracy, and reproducibility of digital methods can result in standardized and multidimensional archaeological data in support of more sophisticated studies. Rather than altering accepted archaeological practices, digital archaeology provides enhanced toolsets for such analyses as volumetric measurement and geographic information system (GIS) modeling (Roosevelt et al. 2015:326, 339; Gordon et al. 2016:6).

Not everyone agrees that cyber archaeology should completely supplant traditional recording methods. Rabinowitz (2015) argues that digital renderings lack the interpretive framework of line drawings and sketches. Manual documentation strategies, posits Rabinowitz, impose a level of engagement and interpretation for the archaeologist that digital recording does not necessarily invoke (Rabinowitz 2015:34; Olson 2016:240). This may arguably be a relevant case for the study of hull timbers, which often benefits from a preliminary interpretation of the original artifact to gain a full understanding of the data at hand. There are certainly a wide range of considerations in using digital tools to record and interpret archaeological data, many of which are influenced by environmental circumstances, time constraints, funding availability, research goals, knowledge of digital methods, ethical concerns, availability of tools, and the condition of the specific material culture or archaeological site under investigation.

Views on the topic have been discussed in recent publications on digital archaeology (Remondino and Campana 2014; Averett et al. 2016), and some have drawn a distinction between virtual archaeology and cyber archaeology. Forte (2014:118) describes the process of virtual archaeology, as it was developed throughout the 1990s, as capturing data in analog form (using traditional methods), converting these to a digital format, and producing a tridimensional static or preregistered rendering. The cyber archaeology workflow involves collecting and processing the data in digital form, with the outcome consisting of virtual reality and interactive environments. An argument is made that, with some constraints, a virtual reconstruction has the ability to stimulate new and advanced discussions by pushing researchers to move beyond a textual description (Forte 2014:118). In his analysis of collecting and interpreting digital archaeological data, however, Caraher (2016: 421–437) advises that, although new digital tools can enhance efficiency, consistency, and accuracy, these reasons alone should not be used to justify the rapid collection of digital data. He notes that the pressures of development and the efficient management of heritage have promoted the adoption of digital tools and practices, but that a "slow archaeology" approach should be applied, which takes into account the process of collection, interaction with the environment, and the adaptations that need to be made for the processing and interpretation of these data sets. In short, with the advent and use of these advanced tools, a deliberate approach to fieldwork and to the adoption of digital technologies that recognize the influence of speed on archaeological practice should be encouraged (Caraher 2016: 421–437). For this project, the use of digital tools was deemed worthwhile as these efforts complement the traditional documentation methods used by nautical archaeologists. Furthermore, as the compromised hull remains will naturally continue to degrade, tridimensional documentation will preserve the current existing data to a high level of accuracy and with texture and color details unattainable through drawings alone. It is hoped that the combination of methods used throughout the recording and reconstruction of the hull will further the discussion of the use of digital tools alongside traditional techniques.

The two digitization techniques used during this project were 3D laser scanning and multi-image photogrammetry. Three-dimensional laser scanning is a terrestrial light detection and ranging (LiDAR) tool used to create accurate, detailed drawings and models of the physical environment (Tyler et al. 2009:212). A typical 3D laser scanning instrument emits a single laser beam while rotating on horizontal and vertical axes, allowing for near-complete coverage of the physical environment. The laser beam is reflected by surrounding physical objects and registered by the scanner, which records the 3D location of a single point. The 3D laser scanner used in this study, a Leica Geosystems C10 ScanStation, has a horizontal scanning radius of 360° and a vertical scanning radius of 270° and is capable of recording billions of points for a single project. The scanning unit can be relocated to multiple "stations" surrounding an object or structure for complete coverage. Special software applications are then used to manipulate the resulting collection of individual 3D point data, or "point cloud," creating fully textured digital 3D models or 2D measured drawings of the scanned environment (Leica Geosystems 2015). Stationary terrestrial 3D scanners like the Leica C10 cannot be relocated while actively scanning and are ideal for large, immovable objects and structures that can be fully captured from multiple discrete vantage points. Occupying a large area when arranged for scanning, the disarticulated timbers of *Royal Savage* presented some challenge to standard terrestrial 3D scanning methodology due to their size and physical condition.

Prior to scanning, each of the 67 individual timbers of *Royal Savage* were laid flat on a level, indoor floor surface approximately 4 ft. (1.25 m) below the level of the C10 scanning unit. The timbers were arranged in a generally rectangular space, with several inches to several feet between each timber. This setup resulted in a relatively acute, downward scanning angle between the scanner itself and the visible surface of the timbers, in contrast to ideal conditions under which the object(s) to be scanned would be level with or above the scanner. Given the physical requirements for scanning and due to time constraints, researchers determined that attempting to maneuver, stage, support, and scan each timber individually to produce a more desirable scanning angle would have been both difficult and inefficient. It was also determined that scanning at such an acute angle would not preclude the production of accurate scan data if done properly. To achieve full visual coverage of the entire project space, the timbers were scanned as a group from seven separate locations within and around the perimeter of the space. Once this series of scans were completed, all timbers were inverted and repositioned in their original placements and rescanned from the same seven scanner locations. The stern assembly, which stands upright supported by wooden bracing, was scanned separately from four locations around its perimeter. All of the timbers were scanned over the course of two days.

Data processing involves the merging, or "registration," of separate point clouds and their subsequent editing and visual cleanup. Leica Cyclone, a proprietary 3D data editing software package, was used to complete initial registration of *Royal Savage* scan data. Registration is the process by which individual point clouds within each data set are aligned and merged into a single, unified point cloud. Accurate and valid registration requires sufficient visual overlap between consecutive scans such that at least three common points can be identified between scans. Manual registration of scans was performed using a "cloud to cloud" technique whereby common points between scans are used to tie them together spatially. Artificial targets are often used during the scanning process to provide easily identifiable common points among scans; however, these were deemed unnecessary and were not used as the discrete edges and hardware features on the timbers provided natural visual targets suitable for common identification.

Scanning resulted in three sets of point clouds: the top sides of all timbers, the bottom sides of all timbers, and the stern assembly, each registered and edited separately. The estimated average point position accuracy for each point cloud is approximately 5 to 7 mm. Once initial registration of the two sets of timber scans was completed separately, individual timbers were digitally isolated so each top side and bottom side could be registered to produce complete 3D representations of individual timbers (Figure 19). The four scans of the stern assembly were also registered successfully.

In the future the 3D models of each timber and the stern assembly will be migrated to AutoDesk ReCap, a user-friendly 3D data editing and visualization program. Through ReCap the models will be digitally cleaned to remove unwanted data points and to apply true-color visual textures to each model. The intended result will be visually accurate, digital scale models of each piece of *Royal Savage* that can be fully manipulated, integrated, analyzed, and reproduced in various media. Overall, and partially due to limitations of the computing hardware being used, 3D data processing time from start to finish for each individual timber is approximately three to four hours.

As an alternative method for digitization and means for comparison, NHHC is using multi-image photogrammetry techniques to acquire dense point cloud data for each timber. Agisoft PhotoScan is a software program that has recently been used to achieve this goal

FIGURE 19. Agisoft PhotoScan (*left*) and Leica Cyclone (*right*) renderings of
Royal Savage timber number 31. (Images: Jonathan Crise and George Schwarz)

and has been applied successfully to tridimensionally record wreck
sites both underwater and on land with a high degree of accuracy.
Recent examples include the 19th-century Shelburne Bay shipwrecks
in Lake Champlain (Bishop and Yumafune 2016), the 19th-century
Lagoa do Peixe shipwreck in Rio Grande do Sul, Brazil (Yumafune
et al. 2016), the 16th-century Gnalic shipwreck in Croatia (Yumafune
et al. 2016), and the 18th-century Alexandria shipwreck in Alexandria, Virginia (NHHC 2016).

The process of capturing the images and manipulating them in
Agisoft is somewhat different for each project based on the environment and site characteristics and has been described in detail in
some of the above-mentioned studies. The basic photogrammetry
process used for the *Royal Savage* timbers, however, is discussed here
as these hull remains are individually recorded instead of assembled in situ. First, the selected timber was elevated and positioned
upright to the extent possible. It was carefully cleaned with a HEPA
filter vacuum to reveal surface features such as construction marks
and fastener holes. To aid in postprocessing, the timber was placed
against a mottled or variegated background, such as the concrete slab
floor or a newspaper. This assisted PhotoScan in matching reference
points in each photo. Lighting was important because Agisoft allows
for textures and colors to be incorporated into the rendering, and
well-placed and appropriate lighting will provide the truest colors,
reveal diagnostic features by eliminating shadows, and aid in masking the object during processing. We used InterFit SXT 3200 tung-
sten studio lights positioned above and to the sides of the timbers to
illuminate the surfaces in a way that would minimize stark contrast.

Choice of camera and settings will naturally affect the final product, but Agisoft does not discriminate based on focal length or distance from the object being photographed (within reason). We used a Nikon D-90 single lens reflex to photograph the timbers, and captured imagery at the highest resolution saving both the JPEG and RAW files. This is advisable in case images need to be manipulated in another program, as it provides the greatest flexibility with digital darkroom software. On large objects with hundreds or thousands of photographs, it is often advisable to batch-reduce the size of the photos before importing them into PhotoScan to reduce processing time.

Once the timber was positioned and illuminated according to preference, the photography began in a circular pattern around the artifact, beginning at the lowest point of the timber and spiraling up and around the frame at a distance of approximately two to three feet from the structure. The pattern is somewhat object-dependent, but the principal objective is to cover the length of the timber in a systematic way and to make sure there is a clear transition point from one side of the artifact to the other. Overhead photographs of the structure were required to complete the collection of data, and in some cases the timber needed to be moved and lighting readjusted to capture the bottom surfaces. Large frames were placed on the floor and photographed one side at a time. Caution was taken to ensure that each photograph was in focus, as the software has difficulties meshing surfaces if some of the images are out of focus. The photographs were taken in a way that ensured sufficient overlap of data so that the software could detect common reference points when aligning photos. On larger hull remains or intact shipwrecks, it is often advantageous to use coded tiles placed strategically over the site so the software can more accurately align the images. Small and medium-size *Royal Savage* timbers took approximately 25 minutes each to photograph. For larger elements, such as frames, 40 to 50 minutes were required to gather images.

After the photographs were collected, they were uploaded into Agisoft and the models were processed according to the software workflow. The basic procedure is to align photos, build dense cloud, build mesh, and build texture. There are several options within each of these steps, and while some studies have published successful settings specific to the site in question (Yamafune et al. 2016), due to varying features and ambient settings of each project, the user must usually experiment with the settings to obtain the best results. Depending on the density of data, software settings, and computer performance, processing can take under an hour to several weeks. The average processing time for each *Royal Savage* timber was two hours for small and medium-size timbers and up to several hours for large frames. The latter time frame was required because each side of the timber needed to be masked and then combined to ensure full and seamless coverage. The finished model could then be manipulated in Agisoft or exported to another program as a 3D PDF, GeoTiff, or other file type for interpretation. The accuracy level of outputs depends on several factors, such as resolution of photos and software settings, but for areas less than 25 m^2, sub-centimeter precision is attainable (Olson 2016: 239). Such replication also allows for direct measurements within Agisoft or other programs such as AutoCAD and RHINO. These levels of accuracy coupled with the incorporation of textured surface details allow for the production of highly detailed orthophotos of the models, which can then be printed to produce scale drawings of plan and profile views of the timbers. Because the software generates point cloud data, the digital models can also be printed on a 3D printer to be used for display or analysis.

Having now used both LiDAR and digital photogrammetry to record the *Royal Savage* timbers, it is possible to compare the techniques for recording disarticulated ship timbers. In this instance 3D photogrammetry using Agisoft appears to be preferable to 3D scanning using Leica Cyclone, using the methods described here, for several reasons. Operation of the Leica C10 or a similar laser scanning instrument requires an understanding of the particular system user interface to successfully collect, store, and manage data. The scanning unit itself is rather cumbersome and, although not prohibitively so, requires some level of physical ability for its transport and setup. The physical demands of operation may be alleviated or exacerbated depending on the project. For this project they were fortunately minimized due to its indoor location for documentation. Conversely, data collection for use with PhotoScan requires only that the user be able to successfully operate a digital camera. On the data processing side, the same ease of use differential is evident. Leica Cyclone is a robust program with correspondingly steep learning curves and processing times. The same can be said of PhotoScan, although successful operation of PhotoScan is much more intuitive and streamlined than for Cyclone, decreasing total processing time significantly. Both software packages are computationally demanding. For basic modeling and visualization purposes, PhotoScan achieves such goals with surprising quality given its relative ease and, as noted, can also achieve a high level of accuracy. The Leica scanning process achieves a greater level of accuracy, but at the cost of greater processing times. The "batch approach" taken to 3D scanning the *Royal Savage* timbers, as opposed to the individual timber approach used in 3D photogrammetry, was necessitated in part by time and physical constraints. Had the same technique of individually 3D scanning each timber been utilized, the significant increase in required recording and processing times, as well as physical demand, would have almost certainly outweighed any increase in achieved accuracy and visual quality of the resulting digital 3D models.

Applying the two 3D documentation techniques to *Royal Savage* as described has made clear a few considerations relevant to other archaeological objects. Size and maneuverability of the object(s) in question are two determining factors in choosing the most appropriate method of documentation for any project. Maneuverability is tied directly to the size of an object, as well as to its physical condition. Photogrammetry was applied successfully to *Royal Savage* in part because the size and condition of each timber allowed them to be placed and held in ideal positions under controlled lighting without an unreasonable amount of work. The photographing process proceeds simply once an object is positioned as desired, as the photographer can work around the object without needing to move it again. As stated, the same approach could not have been attempted with 3D laser scanning without significantly and unreasonably multiplying the number of scans necessary to capture each timber. Generally speaking, when it comes to size, the larger an object is and the less it needs to be maneuvered to be able to capture its relevant physical aspects, the more suitable 3D laser scanning becomes.

Data collection that requires the repositioning of the scanned object(s) in addition to the relocation of the 3D scanner itself creates issues that require additional and significant processing times. Because we are attempting to align several versions of a scanned reality in the form of point clouds, changes to this reality, that is, rotating or flipping each *Royal Savage* timber, make this impossible without first eliminating a majority of the collected data down to the individual object of study. It is precisely these eliminated data that, under normal circumstances (not requiring repositioning of objects), provide overlap between subsequent scans and allow separate point clouds to be quickly and easily registered to one another. Though it was a necessity in this case, by repositioning the timbers we ensured that no other data or LiDAR points other than those that represent a timber itself were of any use. If the timbers of *Royal Savage* could have been arranged in such a way as to allow them to be scanned as a group from a series of locations without having to reposition them at all (which their size and condition dictated was not feasible), they would have more closely resembled the type of large, stationary object (e.g., a building) for which terrestrial 3D laser scanning is better suited.

Looking toward Interpretation

In addition to using the laser scanning and digital photogrammetry models for reconstructing the hull remains, these data serve to preserve the archaeological record and provide future researchers with the opportunity to study and even handle physical scale models of timbers from one of the earliest examples of an American naval vessel lost during the Revolutionary War.

The NHHC's Underwater Archaeology Branch is also documenting the hull remains using traditional archaeological recording methods and preparing scale drawings of the timbers. In this case, both digital and traditional methods will be employed for a number of the timbers, and a comparison of the data sets can be made. Approaches to reconstruction of the timbers for exhibit purposes can be examined based on the results of the documentation efforts.

While the process to fully clean, document, preserve, and exhibit the remains of the *Royal Savage* hull and associated artifacts will likely span a few years, one long-term objective is to reconstruct the schooner to the extent possible and design an NHHC museum exhibit to bring this interpretation to the eyes of the public and U.S. sailors. A traveling exhibit to display conserved artifacts and digital reconstruction has also been discussed as a way to further share the story of *Royal Savage*. The digital data collected during this project will contribute significantly to the reconstruction by complementing traditional documentation strategies, particularly by allowing for hypothetical configurations of the tridimensional hull timber models. These data sets will also allow for studies into the schooner's design characteristics, such as the use of floating frames, type and distribution of fasteners, and methods of connecting larger timber elements such as keel and keelson, stem and sternpost.

Acknowledgments

We thank the Naval History and Heritage Command for access to hull remains and repository, and Indiana University of Pennsylvania for use of the Leica C-10 ScanStation terrestrial LiDAR.

References

Averett, E. W., J. M. Gordon, and D. B. Counts (editors)

2016 *Mobilizing the Past for a Digital Future: The Potential of Digital Archaeology*. Digital Press, University of North Dakota. Grand Forks.

Barbieri, Michael

2014 The Fate of the *Royal Savage*. *Journal of the American Revolution*. allthingsliberty.com/2014/05/the-fate-of-the-royal-savage/. Accessed 1 December 2016.

Beil, Eloise

2015 A Well-Travelled Lake Champlain Shipwreck. *Burlington Free Press*, 25 September. Burlington VT.

Bellico, Russel

1992 *Sails and Steam in the Mountains: A Maritime and Military History of Lake George and Lake Champlain.* Purple Mountain Press. Fleischmanns NY.

Bishop, Daniel, and Kotaro Yumafune

2016 Photogrammetric Recording of 19th-Century Lake Champlain Steamboats. Paper presented at the 49th annual meeting of the Society for Historical and Underwater Archaeology, Washington DC.

Boehler, W., and A. Marbs

2004 3D Scanning and Photogrammetry for Heritage Recording: A Comparison. In *Proceedings on the 12th International Conference on Geoinformatics,* 291–298. University of Gävle, Sweden.

Bredenberg, O.

1966 The *Royal Savage. Bulletin of the Fort Ticonderoga Museum* 12:128–149.

Caraher, William

2016 Slow Archaeology: Technology, Efficiency, and Archaeological Work. In *Mobilizing the Past for a Digital Future: The Potential of Digital Archaeology.* E. W. Averett, J. M. Gordon, and D. B. Counts, editors, pp. 421–441. Digital Press, University of North Dakota. Grand Forks.

Demesticha, Stella, Dimitrios Skarlatos, and Andonis Neophytou

2014 The 4th-Century B.C. Shipwreck at Mazotos, Cyprus: New Techniques and Methodologies in the 3D Mapping of Shipwreck Excavations. *Journal of Field Archaeology* 39(2):134–150.

Dictionary of American Naval Fighting Ships Online

2005 Royal Savage. https://www.history.navy.mil/research/histories/ship-histories /danfs/r/royal-savage.html. Accessed 1 November 2016.

Drap, Pierre

2012 Underwater Photogrammetry for Archaeology. In *Special Applications of Photogrammetry,* D. C. de Silva, editor, pp. 111–136. InTech. Rijeka, Croatia.

Forte, Maurizio

2014 Virtual Reality, Cyberarchaeology, Teleimmersive Archaeology. In *3D Recording and Modelling in Archaeology and Cultural Heritage: Theory and Best Practices,* F. Remondino and S. Campana, editors, pp. 115–129. British Archaeological Reports, International Series 2598. Oxford.

Gardiner, Robert

1996 The Battle of Valcour Island, 11 October 1776. In *Navies and the American Revolution, 1775–1783,* Robert Gardiner, editor, pp. 3–36. Naval Institute Press. Annapolis MD.

Gordon, J. M., E. W. Averett, and D. B. Counts

2016 Mobile Computing in Archaeology: Exploring and Interpreting Current Practices. In *Mobilizing the Past for a Digital Future,* E. W. Averett, J. M.

Gordon, and D. B. Counts, editors, pp. 1 E.W.32. Digital Press, University of North Dakota. Grand Forks.

Hunter, J. W, E. A. Jateff, N. Herath, and A. Van den Hengel

2016   *Protector* Revealed: An Initiative to Archaeologically Document, Interpret and Showcase an Historic Australian Warship with Laser Scanning Technology. *Journal of Cultural Property Conservation* (China) 37(September):27–42.

Leica Geosystems

2015   HDS Laser Scanners and sw. http://hds.leica-geosystems.com/en/HDS-Laser-Scanners-SW_5570.htm. Accessed 25 October 2016.

Lyon, David

1993   *The Sailing Navy List: All the Ships of the Royal Navy, Built, Purchased and Captured, 1688–1860.* Conway Maritime Press. London.

Mahan, Alfred T.

1969   *The Major Operations of the Navies in the War of Independence.* Greenwood Press. New York.

Malcomson, Robert

2004   *Warships of the Great Lakes, 1754–1834.* Knickerbocker Press. Edison NJ.

Naval History and Heritage Command (NHHC)

2016   Field Notes and Digital Files for Documentation of Shipwreck Site 44AX229, 220 South Union Street, Alexandria VA. Manuscript, Naval History and Heritage Command Underwater Archaeology Branch, Washington Navy Yard DC.

Nelson, James

2006   *Benedict Arnold's Navy.* McGraw Hill. New York.

Olson, B.

2016   The Things We Can Do with Pictures: Image-Based Modeling and Archaeology. In *Mobilizing the Past for a Digital Future*, E. W. Averett, J. M. Gordon, and D. B. Counts, editors, pp. 237–249. Digital Press, University of North Dakota. Grand Forks.

Rabinowitz, A.

2015   The Work of Archaeology in the Age of Digital Surrogacy. In *Visions of Substance: 3D Imaging in Mediterranean Archaeology*, B. R. Olson and W. R. Caraher, editors, pp. 27–42. Digital Press, University of North Dakota. Grand Forks.

Remondino, Fabio, and Stefano Campana (editors)

2014   *3D Recording and Modelling in Archaeology and Cultural Heritage: Theory and Best Practices.* British Archaeological Reports, International Series 2598. Oxford.

Roosevelt, C., P. Cobb, E. Moss, B. Olson, and S. Ünlüsoy

2015   Excavation Is Digitization: Advances in Archaeological Practice. *Journal of Field Archaeology* 40:325–346.

Sabick, Christopher, A. Lessman, and S. McLaughlin

2000 *Lake Champlain Underwater Cultural Resources Survey, vol. 2: 1997 Results and vol. 3: 1998 Results.* Lake Champlain Maritime Museum. Vergennes VT.

Skerrett, Robert G.

1935 Wreck of the *Royal Savage* Recovered. *United States Naval Institute Proceedings* 61(383–94):1646–1655.

Tyler, Norman, Ted J. Ligibel, and Ilene R. Tyler

2009 *Historic Preservation: An Introduction to Its History, Principles, and Practice.* Norton. New York.

Virtual Curation Laboratory

2017 Virtual Curation Laboratory, Virginia Commonwealth University. https://vcuarchaeology3d.wordpress.com/. Accessed 9 February 2017.

Yamafune, K., R. Torres, and Filipe Castro

2016 Multi-Image Photogrammetry to Record and Reconstruct Underwater Shipwreck Sites. *Journal of Archaeological Method and Theory* 24(3):703–725. https://link.springer.com/article/10.1007/s10816-016-9283-1. Accessed 4 June 2018.

TWELVE

Reconstructing Site Provenience at Ouiatenon, Indiana

KELSEY NOACK MYERS

In 1717 the government of French Canada established a trading post across the Wabash River from a large Miami village near present-day Lafayette, Indiana. After passing from French to English control, and finally to the Americans, this site experienced a new life in the early 20th century as it became a focus of local avocational historians and preservation groups. The Tippecanoe County Historical Association contacted James Kellar, an archaeologist at Indiana University, Bloomington, in 1968 to propose that the site, known as the "Old Poste" or "Post Ouiatanon," be used as the subject of an archaeological field school. An additional year of excavation in 1969 led to a successful nomination of the site for listing on the National Register of Historic Places. Following this listing, the Tippecanoe County Historical Association purchased the land and allowed both professional and avocational archaeologists to actively excavate the site for the next nine years.

This long-term fieldwork resulted in a large archaeological data set, with little standardization among research designs, collection methodology, or spatial controls on the site from one project to the next. While much of the later work in the 1980s resulted in multiple doctoral dissertations by students at Michigan State University (MSU), Kellar was never able to summarize or publish the earliest work at Ouiatenon, leaving a large portion of the data produced from the site unusable and the individual projects at the site disconnected. This chapter highlights the steps taken and sources of information used to revitalize the 1968–1969 field school data, allowing it to become a part of the larger data set available from the site. For my own research on the legacy collection from the site, I found it necessary to first address spatial metadata issues. I originally intended my research to focus on the faunal analysis of the 1968–1969 Kellar materials as the zooarchaeological remains from these contexts had never before been analyzed. I soon learned that this was impossible due to context recording errors for the entire assemblage, which had been created during excavation and persisted through several decades of curation. As my preliminary research continued over a period of months and then years, the majority of my work became associated with finding the root of this issue and taking steps to translate the spatial data into a usable format, as detailed within this chapter. The resulting synthesis allows materials and documentary records, which were collected and created nearly half a century ago, to contribute to the study of this often overlooked period of culture contact and colonialism in the midwestern United States. By linking the data across field seasons and research institutions, this information is now more accessible for future research and can inform preservation planning for the site following the 300th anniversary of its colonial settlement.

Archival Excavation and Site Reconstruction

It is sometimes said that an archaeological assemblage is created twice: once when objects are deposited at a site, and again when they are collected and interpreted by the archaeologist. In the case of the curated collections discussed within this volume, they are created a third time. With each re-creation, the data available become increasingly selective as the inherent assumptions made influence the characteristics of the resulting data set. For this reason, it is not only fascinating but also extremely helpful to consider those on the other end of the shovel: the archaeologists who conducted the original field research that created these collections. As an important part of the natural and cultural processes that impact the formation of an assemblage, the excavation and subsequent curation of a collection over several years or decades sets the stage for research that can be conducted in the future. Whether recognized or not, archaeologists are active participants in the creation of archaeological knowledge. The knowledge we produce is derived only from the material remains on which we choose to focus and is limited by the ways in which we view and discuss them.

In the case of Ouiatenon, the earliest archaeological research conducted at the site was never exactly forgotten, but due to extenuating circumstances it was not completed to the level originally planned. Like many other archaeological projects, the quantity of material available exceeded the capacity for research, and arguably the level of professional interest, during the early 1970s. Even for those who completed dissertations and other research focusing on Ouiatenon in later years (Tordoff 1983; Noble 1983; Jones 1984; Martin 1986; Noble 1991; Bush 2010), the data resulting from excavations conducted in 1968 and 1969 remained inaccessible. After their excavation by James and Jane Kellar and their field school students, the materials collected were curated in the collections of the Glenn A. Black Laboratory of Archaeology at Indiana University, Bloomington. The current Glenn A. Black Laboratory facility had just been opened in the fall of 1969, and the Ouiatenon collection was one of the first to be housed there.

The complicated logistics of moving into a new laboratory facility took up a great deal of James Kellar's duties, and he requested additional time from those seeking updates on his excavations to produce the information. In addition to directing this institutional rehousing, Kellar assumed the responsibility of completing his late research partner and predecessor's magnum opus around this time: Glenn Black's (1967) two-volume summary of the archaeological research at Angel Mounds. Last but not least, the unexpected passing of his wife and research partner, Jane Kellar, in the following year likely contributed to deprioritization of the project. Jane Kellar is featured in both the student journals and a few of the photographs that remain in the archived materials from that year as an important figure who guided the direction of research and reportedly recorded most of the daily notes from the site. Her loss was therefore not only a deeply personal one for James Kellar but also a professional one regarding continuing research at the site as her presence would throughout the resulting data.

As years went by, the Ouiatenon collection became more obscure, known by only a few as a well-preserved but disjointed assemblage. Often utilized piecemeal for conference papers and class projects, different material types were removed from the general assemblage and rehoused at various times over the 44-year period before I began my research with the collection. Terrance Martin (1986) had sampled and analyzed faunal remains from features identified within the footprint of Post Ouiatenon, and Judith Tordoff (1983) and Vergil Noble (1983) had each spent several years at the site as Michigan State University graduate students directing excavations for their dissertation research. None of the materials from the Kellars' excavations had ever been analyzed or utilized in other analyses as a whole. Primarily this was due to issues with the spatial data attached to these materials and the incomplete state of field notes, as well as a lack of any final report. James Kellar wrote an article that was first created as an internal lab report and later published by the Indiana Historical Society under the title "The Search for Ouiatanon." This was only a short, topical piece confirming the discovery of the site and meant to coincide with the addition of the site to the National Register.

My original interaction with the collection consisted simply of the identification of a few faunal remains for a temporary exhibit in the display area of the Glenn A. Black Laboratory for an upcoming regional conference on historical archaeology. As a zooarchaeologist, I was appreciative of the level of preservation and completeness of the faunal remains from this collection. Many of the other materials, I found, were in a similar state of preservation, and the assemblage from Kellar's 1968 and 1969 field schools even included the remains of textiles and small metal trade ornaments. In order to find more information about this collection, I reviewed internal reports and archived documents at the Glenn A. Black Laboratory. The paucity of published information on the archaeology, as well as the academic setting of the research conducted, are both described in Vergil Noble's chapter in John Walthall's (1991) edited volume,

French Colonial Archaeology: The Illinois Country and the Western Great Lakes. I had long been aware of Ouiatenon from reading Noble's (1991) chapter during my undergraduate study but had never realized the research potential that remained for the original excavation data.

Creating a Master Map and Reconstructing Field Notes

Noble's (1991) chapter provided a starting point for my own work. Following the thread of research as it led through various academic departments, archives, and local communities, I found additional details describing the creation of the complete Ouiatenon assemblage that exists today. I assembled metadata related to the various field crews and research objectives bit by bit through many emails to former researchers and visits with Del and Colby Bartlett, father and son avocational historians who have been active members and officers of the Tippecanoe County Historical Association for several decades spanning back to the Kellars' research. The recollections of the Bartletts, as well as accounts written in the field school students' journals, allowed me to create a more comprehensive record of research conducted at the site. Although this information was generally delineated in previous work (Noble 1991), it had only been superficially discussed. It became obvious that I needed to create a master database of excavation projects (Table 14) and, more important, a map of all excavations at the site (Map 5) in order to conduct the additional analyses required.

Table 14. Summary of excavation projects at the Ouiatenon site

Year	Primary Investigator	Institution and Project	Contexts
1968–1969	James Kellar	Indiana University, Bloomington, archaeological field school	Central excavation block along northern palisade wall
1971	Larry Chowning	Tippecanoe County Historical Association, avocational excavation in plow zone	Northeast interior of the post, adjacent to southwest corner of 1969 Kellar excavation block

1972	Claude White	Tippecanoe County Historical Association, avocational excavation in plow zone	Unknown
1973	Larry Chowning	Tippecanoe County Historical Association, avocational excavation	Southwest corner of post, including portions of palisade wall and bisection of large pit feature
1974–1976	Judith Tordoff	Michigan State University investigation, dissertation research	Sampling of entire site; focused excavation on structures located during early field seasons
1977–1979	Vergil Noble	Michigan State University investigation, dissertation research	Sampling of northern portion of site; revisited some contexts excavated by Kellar
2013	Michael Strezewski	University of Southern Indiana archaeological field school	Magnetic anomalies outside of western palisade wall; complete excavation of burned, round native-built structure

Note: Spatial representations of each project are included within the composite plan map shown in Map 5.

The primary issue preventing coherent spatial references to this point had been the lack of standardization. Each of the projects conducted at the Ouiatenon site (12T9) had used different data points, surveying equipment, personnel, units of measurement, grid orientation, and map production methods. Only recently, during geophysical survey and excavation conducted by Michael Strezewski under an American Battlefield Protection grant in 2012–2013, was a computerized theodolite (or total station) used to collect spatial data at

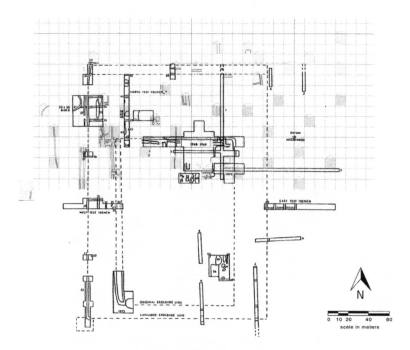

MAP 5. Composite map of excavations, Ouiatenon, Indiana.
(Map: Kelsey Noack Myers)

the site to allow for geographic information system (GIS) analysis. Because the older excavations predated this technology, no georeferenced points within the previous excavation areas existed. It was possible to translate the grid coordinates and overlay the 1968–1969 and 1974–1979 excavation plan maps with Strezewski's remote sensing and GIS data. This method did not provide exact coordinates for the older excavation areas, but allowed for the approximation of corner coordinates for each, including the excavation block from Kellar's field school as represented by Tordoff.

An outstanding question that initially made this process difficult was a discrepancy between that the documented location of Kellar's 1969 excavation units and their actual location. During her 1970s research effort, Tordoff spent a field season and a half searching for Kellar's elusive research area and excavating nine backhoe trenches around the site. Her field crew eventually located back-filled areas matching the 1968–1969 descriptions, but they were not where they expected to find them. The reason this area was not where Tordoff expected was something I did not discover until much later, while reading and synthesizing several of the 1969 field school students' journals.

The four field school student journals that survive in the Glenn Black Archive include approximately 300 pages of notes, running accounts of daily activities, personal impressions, and sketches of the units in which each of the students worked throughout their eight weeks at the site. From these I synthesized a complete field journal approximately 40 pages long, which, accompanied by a few short letters written by James Kellar, could provide feature and artifact descriptions, allowing the features represented on the plan map to be matched to their written descriptions. While the synthesized field journal was meant to provide impressions of the overall research design and implementation at the site, as well as the biases and events that shaped the progress and results of the excavation, it also provided an overview of the site based on a summary of the students' observations and Kellar's single archival source describing the features.

I read the first few days' entries, discussing the creation of the excavation grid. Within these descriptions the students recounted that they were the ones to set the markers identifying the grid (under Kellar's supervision) and that two data points were used as controls for the 1969 field season. Their explanation of the process provided the missing details.

Following the 1968 field season, the area had been plowed during regular agricultural activity, leaving only one datum marker in place near the road leading to the site. In addition, one of the students included a statement referring to the displacement of the original 1968 datum by the backhoe on the first day of excavation of the 1969 field season. Because of this the students were required to switch from using the first (1968) datum to the second (1969) datum as the primary reference, but they did not recalculate the arbitrary coordinates for their grid. The difference between the two data points was approximately 36 ft. latitudinally and 5 ft. longitudinally. This coincides with the difference between where Tordoff expected to find Kellar's excavation area and where it was actually found. While this did not greatly affect the context information for the 1969 excavation as the grid was already set before the first datum was displaced, it re-created approximately the same error from this point forward as each subsequent project set its grids using the second datum.

Using this information, I could then translate the coordinates recorded by James Kellar and his students to a newer grid based on the 1974 Michigan State University datum point. I used this datum as a control to create the complete plan map of all excavations. The 1970s excavations by MSU researchers used a grid set from what was assumed to be the (only) previous datum point near the center of the known archaeological site; they had not known that two separate data points had been used by Kellar. The MSU team marked their datum point using a piece of rebar embedded in concrete buried just below the ground surface. Because this marker was easily found and georeferenced through magnetometry survey by Strezewski and McCullough in 2012, the MSU-marked datum point serves as the primary datum for the site today.

This updated spatial information was used to ground-truth the hand-mapped MSU datum point in reference to the 1974–1979 excavation areas. In addition, in 2013 Strezewski led a field school using this same datum, with excavations taking place just outside of the proposed western stockade wall of the trading post. Therefore, the most recently established grid (2013) uses the same datum point as the 1974–1979 excavation grids, creating a degree of continuity in spatial definition that had previously not existed between the earlier excavations at the site. In addition, in early 2015 the Indiana Geological Survey made remote sensing data for the entire state publicly available. These data were also used to confirm the site's locale. A rectangular outline of what is assumed to be the mid-18th-century expanded palisade wall is visible in a shaded relief digital elevation model with adequate hillshading and can be georeferenced to further validate the site location.

One final step to complete the map entailed standardizing grids for the 1977–1979 excavations. When all plan maps of the MSU excavations led by Noble were placed on a standardized grid map using Adobe Photoshop and Illustrator software, it became clear that there was likely an error or series of small errors in the creation of the grids or of the plan maps used in 1977–1979 based on the ways associated features failed to align. This is likely due to the exclusive use of noncomputerized surveying equipment and hand-drawn maps to represent archaeological excavations at the site prior to 2012, and is to be expected. Additional distortions of the maps may have occurred during photocopying or printing steps taken to complete the final reports from which my base maps were created. At the end of each excavation project in the 1970s all datum or unit corner stakes and any traces of archaeological field research were removed to allow the site to be used for agricultural purposes when excavations were not taking place. The grid was reestablished for each field season, creating slight variations in the measurements and markers used each time. Without having reliable georeferenced points for each of the excavations that occurred prior to 2014, it was not possible to create a useful GIS for the site using the old maps. Although each of the old maps had intended to show a perfectly square grid, this was not always the case. The errors encountered in each map were corrected simply by minor scaling of each grid to fit a standard square 10 x 10-ft. digital grid map. In places where the combined maps suggested that a feature had been encountered and sampled multiple times, feature notes were reviewed to confirm that each researcher had likely been excavating the same area.

With a complete map in hand showing the approximate location of all of the previous excavations (including the rough location of Kellar's excavations), my focus then turned to the box in the center of the map representing Kellar's field school units (Map 5), with the intent of determining the location of particular features. Identifying the location of features required returning to the synthesis of the student's field notes. For the purposes of clarity, I altered a few of the students' terms to create the synthesis. Because these accounts were written by undergraduate students working on their first, and in most cases only, field projects in archaeology, conflicting terms were often used or common terms were misused. In the same way that two witnesses to the same incident likely never report their observations to law enforcement in exactly the same way, the students often contradicted one another or mentioned details that the other left out. While it is sometimes enlightening to have the input of multiple voices, it can be confusing when trying to create a cohesive narrative detailing the daily actions of the crew during fieldwork. The resulting work is a diplomatic attempt at approximating an accurate account of the project from several perspectives at once, and is not unlike many other summary site reports in that regard.

As the field school progressed, the students demonstrated a fixation on visually describing the artifacts themselves in their journal entries, similarly measuring the success or failure of work each day by the volume and uniqueness of the material recovered. This antiquarian approach resulted in less description of the features and fill excavated and, combined with a lack of systematic photography of each unit, prevented a clear reconstruction of every level of excavation. It was possible, however, to verify the levels excavated in each contiguous unit and the order in which each was reached.

While the students were not as meticulous as a professional might have been about terminology and the specification of features or materials, an important additional piece of information that they documented was the plan view of the field school excavation area. (The student who likely drew the final composite map, Michael Whalen, was the only field school student who appears to have gone on in the field professionally, completing a Ph.D. in anthropology and becoming a professor in the Department of Anthropology at the University of Tulsa.) To my knowledge, this composite map was the only plan map representing the features identified in 1968. The individual unit plan maps from the 1968 excavation have not been discovered. Tordoff had never seen the plan map produced for Keller's excavations and had therefore left the interior of this box blank on her own plan map.

At some point prior to my work with the site, an unknown individual digitized the composite map for unknown purposes and saved it in digital archives at the Glenn A. Black Laboratory. This digitized version was used as a template on which I overlaid scans of the original plan maps from each year's excavations to create a digitized overview. I used only Adobe Illustrator and Photoshop software to adjust and complete the translation of each grid to correspond to the qualitative descriptions of each excavation in their related reports and field notes. Ultimately I was able to create a site plan view map that combined the spatial information from the 1968 and 1969 field seasons with the plan maps from all other excavation projects at the site, conducted from 1971 to 2013.

With the master map created, the last step was to identify descriptions of each feature depicted by Kellar's students and to reference these by the corrected data points used to name each square. The only description of the 1968 and 1969 field school features that could initially be located within the scope of this project were the short summaries included in James Kellar's archived correspondence, which summarized all of the features assigned numbers throughout both field seasons. This summary is approximately two pages long. In the first field season, during 1968, four features and a wall trench were identified during excavation. During the 1969 field season, excavations identified an additional 11 features and two sections of "stockade trench." Kellar also provided spatial coordinates for these features, all of which were based on the 1968 datum point, as discussed earlier. I translated the coordinates listed by Kellar using the known error, translated the field school students' coordinates using the same error, and combined descriptions of each context from both sources. It was at this stage that I discovered the 1968 grid was also offset from the 1969 grid by five feet, north to south. This was not due to a recording error but rather Kellar's decision to offset the excavation units for the second year by five feet north-south to better fit the proposed length of the stockade or palisade wall feature.

Selecting Samples for Analysis

With translated coordinates, a map contextualizing the features identified by the 1969 field school within the larger site, and feature numbers and descriptions matched to those represented on the plan map, I then selected sample features for my dissertation analysis. This comprehensive view of all work at the site illustrates the density of previous excavation areas and the relatively small percentage of the potential footprint of the post that has been archaeologically documented. James Kellar's work at the site alone demonstrates the vast amount of information available in relatively small excavation areas at Ouiatenon.

In the interest of creating a comprehensive data set for Ouiatenon, my preliminary research synthesized Kellar's 1968–1969 excavation data. When combined with the dissertation projects conducted by Tordoff (1974–1976) and Noble (1977–1979) through MSU and the University of Southern Indiana field school taught by Strezewski in 2013, similarities in various excavated features become visible. Linking the individual excavations to one another, along with the researchers who designed and conducted them, allows for the artificial boundaries between years and methodological choices to be blurred or nearly erased. I chose to focus on two features described by the student journal synthesis that match in description several other features of a similar type excavated during later field research.

The first is one of many house basins or subfloor storage features that represented larger residential structures. This feature was in the southeast corner of Kellar's 1969 excavation basin and was only partially excavated due to time constraints. The house basin, known as Feature 69-9, was of particular interest to my analysis for its potential association of the structure with known persons who inhabited the post in its early years, as well as the unique artifact and faunal assemblages recovered from the area. It is perhaps fortunate that the feature was not completely excavated in 1969 as it may be possible to revisit the area with new excavation one day and to employ updated methodologies. This could potentially produce comparative data that would add further value to the existing data set derived from the legacy collections from the site.

The second feature is a large, circular pit filled with refuse and large amounts of animal bone, associated with adjacent residential structures. From both of these features students recorded recovering Woodland ceramic sherds, a late Mississippian projectile point, a key, salt-glazed ceramics, "T-rim" ceramic sherds, brass buttons, a piece of canvas, carved bone, catlinite, French gun flints, and a spigot. According to student journals, artifacts found in this feature also included multiple pieces of copper presumed to have been used for personal ornamentation, a fork with a bone handle, a section of saber blade seven inches in length, and a dozen gunflints. This assemblage presents an interesting combination of artifacts manufactured by both European and Native sources and can help to adjust our view of the site as one where the exchange of goods and social interaction between cultural groups occurred not only on an official and bureaucratic basis but also on a more personal, household level (Lightfoot et al. 1997; Silliman 2001; Voss 2008). Generally characteristic of the features excavated that summer, these contexts provide only two examples of the many, many wall trench and large refuse pit features identified in 1969.

With the master map and features descriptions now available, it is possible to pursue several questions that previous researchers were unable to answer. One of the primary questions asked by archaeologists, historians, and the local community alike has been what the post itself looked like as a whole at the various stages of its colonial occupation. Although the entire footprint of the enclosure has not been excavated, and several features remain somewhat ambiguous, it is now possible to view an archaeological map of a large portion of the post's northern half. Should the Tippecanoe County Historical Association or another entity wish to create a reconstruction of the post for interpretive purposes, this can now be more easily accomplished. Lingering questions addressed by Tordoff's (1983) dissertation research comparing Ouiatenon with other French fortifications in the region can be answered, regarding the type and number of structures included within the post walls. Questions regarding change in the layout and size of the post over time can also be considered, as further analyses of specific material types from the legacy collections can be used to assign dates for features. Additional issues related to household types and the comparison of private versus public use of space within the fort might also be investigated. The work I completed to rectify spatial metadata issues represents only the first steps in bringing new life to the old collections excavated at Ouiatenon and will hopefully enable other researchers to broaden the analyses of this and other legacy sites.

Conclusion

As Noble (1991) mentions in his chapter on Ouiatenon, none of the personnel who excavated at this site had much experience working with historic archaeological contexts. This was not unusual at the time, as Fort Michilimackinac in Michigan was the only large-scale historical archaeology site under excavation in the region. Those who worked at Ouiatenon generally came from an academic tradition that focused on methods designed for precolonial contexts. None of those who worked on Ouiatenon in their early careers continued their research with materials from the site except for Martin, who is currently conducting faunal analysis of the Kellar materials in conjunction with my own research and meta-analysis of legacy collections from the site.

This well-known site is today the center of attention of an annual historical reenactment known as The Feast of the Hunter's Moon. This event tells a story meant to bring to life the daily experiences of individuals who inhabited the trading post at Ouiatenon in the 18th century, who may have identified varyingly with Native American or European American cultural groups. With this enthusiastic expression of interest in the history of the site and the proposed interpretive installations that will soon occupy the planned archaeological and prairie preserve nearby, this review of legacy data may help to encourage a revitalization of archaeological research at Ouiatenon. While we await future efforts that will add further value to the existing collections and continued georeferencing of the legacy data associated with Kellar's excavations of the 1960s, Ouiatenon stands as one of the richest and most valuable legacy collections available in the Midwest.

References

Black, Glenn A

1967   *Angel Site: An Archaeological, Historical, and Ethnological Study.* Indiana Historical Society. Indianapolis.

Bush, Leslie

2010   *Plant Remains from Fort Ouiatenon (12T9), an 18th Century French Trading Post on the Wabash River.* Report of Investigation. Glenn A. Black Laboratory of Archaeology, Bloomington IN.

Jones, James R., III

1984   An Archaeological Survey of an 18th Century Wea Village Neat Fort Ouiatenon, in Tippecanoe County, Indiana. Department of Anthropology, Indiana University, Bloomington.

Kellar, James H.

1970   The Search for Ouiatenon. *Indiana Historical Bulletin* 47:123–133.

Lightfoot, Kent G., Ann M. Schiff, Antoinette Martinez, Thomas A. Wake, Stephen Silliman, Peter R. Mills, and Lisa Holm

1997   Culture Change and Persistence in the Daily Lifeways of Interethnic Households. In *The Native Alaskan Neighborhood: A Multiethnic Community at Colony Ross. The Archaeology and Ethnohistory of Fort Ross, California,* Vol. 2, Kent G. Lightfoot, Ann M. Schiff, and Thomas A. Wake, editors, pp. 355–419. Contributions of the University of California Archaeological Research Facility No. 55, Berkeley.

Martin, Terrance J.

1986   *A Faunal Analysis of Fort Ouiatenon, an Eighteenth Century Trading Post in the Wabash Valley of Indiana.* Doctoral dissertation, Department of Anthropology, Michigan State University. University Microfilms International, Ann Arbor MI.

Noble, Vergil E.

1983   *Functional Classification and Intra-Site Analysis in Historical Archaeology: A Case Study from Fort Ouiatenon.* Doctoral dissertation, Department of Anthropology, Michigan State University. University Microfilms International, Ann Arbor MI.

1991   Ouiatenon on the Ouabache: Archaeological Investigations at a Fur Trading Post on the Wabash River. In *French Colonial Archaeology: The Illinois Country and the Western Great Lakes,* John A. Walthall, editor, pp. 65–77. University of Illinois Press. Champaign.

Silliman, Stephen W.

2001   Agency, Practical Politics and the Archaeology of Culture Contact. *Journal of Social Archaeology* 1(2):190–209.

Tordoff, Judith Dunn

1983　*An Archaeological Perspective on the Organization of the Fur Trade in Eighteenth Century New France.* Doctoral dissertation, Department of Anthropology, Michigan State University. University Microfilms International, Ann Arbor MI.

Voss, Barbara L.

2008　Gender, Race, and Labor in the Archaeology of the Spanish Colonial Americas. *Current Anthropology* 49(5):861–893.

Walthall, John A. (editor)

1991　*French Colonial Archaeology: The Illinois Country and the Western Great Lakes.* University of Illinois Press. Champaign.

PART 3

New Futures for Archaeological Collections

[THIRTEEN]

Integrating New Archaeology and Outreach into Existing Collections and Exhibits from the Cooper-Molera Adobe Complex, Monterey, California

CANDACE EHRINGER AND REBECCA ALLEN

The Cooper-Molera Adobe site is a complex of 19th-century residential and commercial buildings that are an element of the Monterey Old Town National Historic District in California, designated as a National Historic Landmark in 1970. Construction of this set of adobe and frame buildings began in the 1820s and evolved as part of the civilian community that grew up around the Monterey Presidio following the Mexican War of Independence (Figure 20). Historic buildings constructed between 1829 and 1902 now occupy the site, including the Corner Store, Diaz Adobe, Cooper Adobe, Skylight Room, Cooper Cookhouse, Red House, Spear Warehouse, North Barn, Shed Addition, and South Barn. The site covers approximately 2.4 acres, with large areas of open space and gardens, and is filled with layers of archaeological history of this residential and commercial site. The National Trust for Historic Preservation owns the site, although the California Department of Parks and Recreation (State Parks) managed the site for decades.

To make the site more suitable for historic interpretation to the general public, State Parks undertook major restoration work at the Cooper-Molera complex and in the process generated one of the most extensive historical archaeological collections in California, part of which was on display at the adobe, with more artifacts in storage at the State Parks' facility in Sacramento. During a decade of archaeology (1973–1983), almost 100 archaeological and architectural features were encountered. Most of these features can be broadly cat-

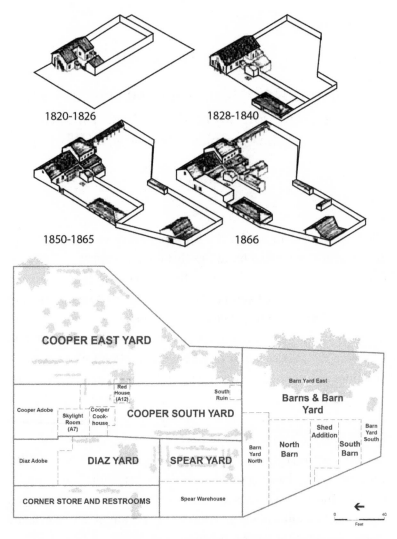

FIGURE 20. Cooper-Molera Adobe complex, as it developed from 1820 to 1866, and current site layout. (Drawing: Adrianna Allen, adapted from Architectural Resources Group 2015)

egorized into two groups, structural (built) features and intrusive residential-related features (pits, ditches, etc.), although the categories are not always mutually exclusive. Artifact assemblages represent the Mexican Republic era (late 1820s–1846) and early American era (1846–1860s). For reasons discussed at greater length below, these assemblages contain important artifacts exemplifying their type and age in California.

In anticipation of the site lease reverting back in 2016, the National Trust created a new operating model, working with a local development partner and input from a variety of local stakeholders. The National Trust strives to balance compelling historic interpretation and education programs with appropriate and complementary commercial uses. The site's revitalization includes maintenance and updating of the on-site museum and adding a restaurant and event center. These proposals created ground disturbance within areas known to contain archaeological features, as well as some disturbance of previously undisturbed soils. The National Trust coordinated with Architectural Resources Group, Inc. ([ARG] 2015) to plan for historic preservation of the standing structures and emphasized that the archaeological resources still present at the Cooper-Molera Adobe site merited continued study and protection as site use changes. ARG coordinated with Environmental Science Associates (ESA), and the authors' review of the archaeological field notes and published reports indicated that proposed construction areas were highly sensitive for the presence of historical archaeological resources. We recommended a program of archaeological testing, data recovery, and intermittent monitoring prior to and during construction activities. When all construction and archaeological work is finished, the National Trust envisions commercial activities that will balance interpretation and education, and new exhibits and public programming that will take advantage of a wider-range audience attracted by the new venues (Figure 21).

Working with a site that has been the subject of many archaeological excavations, each of which created its own archaeological collection that has been on display or in storage for years, presents challenges as well as opportunity. Primarily it caused the authors to consider how best to approach a well-known historic site, extract useful information from old files and artifact collections, and meaningfully integrate new findings. While collections research generally focuses on the artifacts, the authors' challenge was also to consider

FIGURE 21. The National Trust's vision for a new commercial and interpretive space at the Cooper-Molera Adobe will highlight the site's history and historic buildings, including exhibits of old and new archaeological findings. (Drawing courtesy of the National Trust. Photo: C. Ehringer)

the documentation that accompanies the artifacts. Review of reports, field notes, photographs, and oral history with the previous archaeologist made us consider how to approach a previously investigated site, what we leave behind for the next generations of researchers to find, and what to present to an interested public when an old site is dug and interpreted anew.

Historical Overview

California has long been known for attracting immigrants from many countries. Its native and immigrant population can be described as multicultural; trade and migration are an integral part of California's history. In many ways the Cooper-Molera Adobe embodies this cosmopolitan past.

John Rogers Cooper was a sea captain and merchant born in England in 1791 and raised in Massachusetts. He arrived in Monterey in June 1823 at the helm of *Rover*, his trading vessel, and quickly established himself as a leading merchant. In 1827 he was baptized as a Catholic, changed his name to Juan Bautista Cooper, and married Encarnacion Vallejo, a member of one of Alta California's most prominent families. Among several of his landholdings, Cooper purchased what is now known as the Cooper-Molera Adobe property in 1832, which included an existing adobe structure believed to date to the late 1820s. He and his family lived in Monterey until 1864, when they moved to San Francisco. After Cooper died in 1872, his widow inherited the adobe, and upon her death in 1902 deeded it to her daughter Ana Cooper Wohler, who had married a German immigrant. The Coopers' other daughter, Amelia, married Eusebio Molera, a native of Spain.

The western half of the property changed hands several times over the years but is most closely associated with Manuel Diaz, who was born in Tepic, Mexico, in 1812. Diaz came to California sometime in the late 1830s or early 1840s. In 1843 he married Maria Luisa Merced Estrada, a Native Californian, at Mission San Carlos Borromeo. The Diaz family lived in the adobe from about 1843 until Luisa's death in 1900; Diaz passed away in 1868. Ana Cooper Wohler purchased the Diaz adobe after Luisa's death and bequeathed the entire property to her niece, Frances Molera, in 1912. In turn Frances Molera deeded the property to the National Trust in 1968. At the time, the site suffered from deferred maintenance and was in need of substantial repair work. Other caretakers for the site were sought, and in 1972 State Parks signed a lease agreement to restore and operate the property as part of Monterey State Historic Park.

State Parks Archaeological Studies

In 1971 State Parks approved a major restoration project for the Cooper-Molera Adobe complex. A series of historical, architectural, and archaeological investigations was initiated to provide information required to plan an accurate restoration and guide preservation of the resources present. These investigations also identified and evaluated resources likely to be impacted by restoration efforts and related new construction at the site.

In 1973 William J. Wallace and Edith Wallace began the first archaeological investigations at the site. Their work included historical research and architectural investigations, as well as traditional archaeological excavations. The crew removed floors inside the building and excavated the fill below, stripped plaster from walls to investigate and document architectural modifications, and uncovered the foundations of a number of outbuildings and courtyard walls in the surrounding yard areas. The Wallaces' work was documented in a series of reports on historical research (Wallace 1975a), the buildings (Wallace 1975b), and grounds (Wallace 1975c). Several additional historical studies were undertaken as part of the restoration and interpretive planning efforts and provided additional information on the residents of the property, real estate transactions, and building history (Reese 1972; Kirker and Bry 1975; Dittmer 1977; Napoli 1977). The detailed archival history available for the site was helpful for the archaeological studies and architectural renovations.

State Parks also contracted with Robert F. Heizer (1977) at the University of California, Berkeley, to perform additional archaeological work. This consisted of small-scale excavations to address questions posed by the consulting architect, Kenneth Cardwell, and which had not been resolved by the Wallaces' earlier work. The contribution of the archaeological investigation to the architectural study was limited by the small scale of the excavations, but exploration continued to demonstrate the presence of significant archaeological resources throughout the residential site and adobe complex.

In August 1979 State Parks archaeologist Lee Motz directed additional investigations on the property. The purpose of this work was to survey the grounds, conduct test excavations in areas explicitly scheduled to be impacted by restoration and site work, and recommend mitigation measures to ensure the preservation of the resources present during upcoming demolition and construction phases (Felton and Motz 1997). Archaeology also contributed to a better understanding of the building's history and architectural changes over time (Felton and Motz 1993). This work included excavation of 16 scattered units placed to test proposed utility corridors, areas to be graded, and more. Although of modest size, these excavations exposed 12 new archaeological features, representing building and courtyard walls, as well as five pits containing rich assemblages of mid-19th-century artifacts.

Demolition and construction work began in late 1979 and continued until 1983. During this period, archaeologists worked closely with crews from the Office of the State Architect. Unlike the earlier test excavations, ongoing demolition and construction activities dictated the scope and scheduling of work. The primary construction-phase archaeological strategy was that archaeologists direct and monitor virtually all ground-disturbing work. The project archaeologist was authorized to halt or redirect demolition and construction activities when potentially significant archaeological resources were found to be present. This allowed archaeologists time to expose and evaluate the significance of finds and to execute appropriate treatments for any significant resources encountered. In most cases it was not necessary to halt development work entirely but instead to redirect it away from sensitive areas and resume once appropriate archaeological treatment was completed. Treatment plans for significant resources typically consisted of data recovery excavations and documentation, using traditional archaeological methods. In some instances agreed-upon modifications of development plans permitted minimizing further damage. This monitor-evaluate-treatment strategy was successful and resulted in the further discovery and documentation of an array of significant archaeological features and artifact assemblages. Successful use of this approach was dependent on close coordination and communication between the construction and archaeological crews.

In 1983 State Parks published *The Diaz Collection: Material Culture and Social Change in Mid-Nineteenth-Century Monterey* (Felton and Schulz 1983). This publication highlighted one of the archaeological features at the Cooper-Molera site (the Diaz privy, site feature 23), demonstrating the potential of the site for providing opportunities to integrate the study of archaeological features with social, architectural, and landscape history. The privy deposit contained at least 118 ceramic vessels, 146 glass and stoneware bottles, 39 glassware vessels, faunal material, and a variety of other artifacts. The report was groundbreaking at the time of its publication, as the review of the volume in *Historical Archaeology* attests:

> Interpretations focus on the economic scaling of the ceramics and vessel form distribution. . . . Rather than seeking to explain the artifact pattern in terms of ethnicity alone, Felton and Schulz have redressed a frequent imbalance in Mexican-American site studies by reconsidering the causes and effects of imputed ethnic behaviors in the light of stratification within the California community. They adduce census data and a variety of historic information to place the Diaz family in perspective against the economic, political, and social climates of the period so soon after the American conquest of California. . . . They emphasize the importance of class structure and class culture as primary causal factors. . . . Felton and Schulz have pointed out the need to broaden research objectives to define a historic community, and not concentrate solely upon the occupants of a given site. (Greenwood 1987:110)

Artifact Assemblages and Significance

Barker et al. (1995:18) reported that while there are other archaeological collections from California sites that contain early 19th-century materials, the Cooper-Molera collection is one of largest and most comprehensive recovered. This is still true today. Ceramic artifacts recovered from the Cooper-Molera site were prominently featured in on-site exhibits and have recently been featured in a publication by the Society for Historical Archaeology (Allen et al. 2013; Farris 2013). Overall this collection provides a baseline of material culture for archaeologists studying the Californio period (also called the Mexican period, 1822–1848) in California.

These assemblages include a wide array of items, including large quantities of British earthenware and Chinese Export porcelain, glass bottles, small personal items, household goods, and tremendous quantities of animal remains, especially cattle bones. The richness of the deposits probably reflects the wealth of the residents, who were predominantly affluent merchants and their families. Archaeologists have also speculated that the large volume of ceramics and glass represents mass breakage, possibly as the result of earthquakes such as those that occurred in 1838 and 1858. There is an historic account citing William Warren, believed to be a resident of the Spear Warehouse, which describes the effects of the June 1838 earthquake:

> The earthquake had occurred just before my arrival at Monterey. Major Warren told me that it was the severest one he had ever experienced, and it seemed to him as if the town would be destroyed during the vibration. The inhabitants were frightened out of their wits. *Crockery and glassware were broken, and some of the walls of the adobe dwellings were cracked* [emphasis added]. It was a shake up of no ordinary severity and the town of Monterey was pretty well shaken up. (Davis 1967:14–15)

These artifact assemblages were frequently disposed of over short periods of time, typically after the feature in question had been abandoned for its original purpose (often as borrow pits for the soil needed to make adobe bricks). As such, these features and their contents constitute veritable "time capsules," the ages of which can often be tightly dated, based on the artifacts present (e.g., ceramic makers' marks, bottles, coins, etc.). This tight chronological control, coupled with the detailed historic record of the site's occupants and their activities, imbue these features and related artifact assemblages with significance that cannot usually be ascribed to individual or scattered artifacts. In addition, the site also produced the atypical: mid-1860s locally made pottery by a Frenchman, Honoré Escolle, who operated a shop in the Corner Store, has been recovered on site (Barter 2003). The archaeological features and artifact collections closely correlate with the history of the standing structures at the site, and part of the existing archaeological display shows exposed foundations, fragments of original wallpaper, and other elements of the building's history.

New Excavation and Findings

In 2015 the National Trust site revitalization plans prompted new archaeological investigations. We reviewed State Parks notes on the Cooper-Molera site to better understand the extent and intent of previous excavations. We also contacted the State Archaeological Collections Research Facility, where all previously excavated materials, as well as field notes and photographs, are curated. We were fortunate that this is an accessible and organized facility (Farris, this volume). Materials that we were looking for were readily available. Not all curation facilities are so well organized. Any researcher beginning work on a legacy collection should consider the status of the facility before making schedules, budgets, and assumptions about accessibility.

Previous researchers are always an important source of information. In our case, David L. (Larry) Felton was very accessible, and we were able to hire him as a consultant to help us navigate the collections, reports, and field notes. We were also fortunate that several formal archaeological reports had been written on the site. Before the new program of archaeological testing, data recovery, and monitoring began, we could anticipate the kinds of features and artifacts we were likely to encounter. A review of reports resulted in good insights into the site's chronology and land use. Collecting, digitizing, and compiling map information was critical to the identification stage. This is generally true when multiple excavations have occurred. Most archaeological collections have at least one map that shows features and deposits, but frequently not everything from field note maps is transferred to a central map. We quickly learned that digitizing all hand-drawn, interim, and final maps is a critical part of the identification process (Myers, this volume).

Felton scanned in field notes from some of the earlier State Parks excavations, and made them available as Adobe Acrobat (pdf) documents. This was essential for our understanding of the site. As most archaeologists know, not all information about the site is included in the formal reports. Having digitized field notes meant that we could rapidly search for keywords and features and made the notes accessible to us during fieldwork. Reading notes in the office is a different experience from reading them while in the field, with the site and features immediately available for reference. We did not digitize the photographs taken during initial phases of fieldwork; for future work on legacy sites and collections, we would take the time to do so.

Once our "archaeology on the archaeology" was performed, Ehringer and Felton reviewed existing and proposed site improvement descriptions and drawings at an on-site meeting with project developers. On the basis of this meeting, new excavations were planned and completed. Over the course of two years we encountered two significant trash pits dating to the mid-1830s that were more extensive than previously thought, previously unknown mudstone foundations, and features that helped us better understand site layout and use over time. Monitoring and data recovery during utility installation found more old and new deposits and features, including a well. Despite having previous collections, field notes, maintenance staff, and one of the principal investigators available to us, interpretation of the site findings was sometimes still a challenge.

During the course of our excavations at the Cooper-Molera site, we were also reminded that at many historic sites, maintenance and museum staff have often worked at a particular site for a long time. They may recall changes to the site subsequent to archaeological investigations that are not formally documented, and can influence archaeological interpretation and findings. They also often have an-depth understanding of the site condition. As an example, in the midst of wet-screening operations, it became apparent that areas of the Cooper-Molera site do not drain well. State Parks Archaeologist Glenn Farris (now retired) pointed out that during the 19th century the area immediately east of the Cooper-Molera complex was a slough. It has since been filled in and is now a paved parking lot, limiting the efficiency of drainage. Discussions with maintenance staff confirmed that drainage is and has always been a concern, and the staff were able to help us identify and interpret two concentrations of mudstone that at first did not seem to have an obvious purpose (they were neither foundations nor walls). Walking over the site with maintenance staff, we realized that these concentrations directly related to drainage, current site topography, and topography of the site during various historic periods, as it has changed over time.

We also learned that previously reported depths of features may no longer be accurate due to soil accumulation, erosion, or other factors. At the Cooper-Molera site, in the area between the North Barn and Spear Warehouse, previous excavators had documented a large, artifact-rich pit and noted that it was likely not entirely excavated. The remaining portion of the feature was described as being approximately 6 in. below the surface. Ehringer and crew placed a 3-ft. x 3-ft. unit over the documented location of the trash pit. Hand excavation proceeded downward to 12 in. and did not encounter the feature. We assumed that the remaining extent of the feature had either been destroyed by more recent nonarchaeological excavations to control drainage (we encountered a French drain), or that the feature did not in fact extend beyond the previous limits of investigation. During subsequent monitoring of controlled mechanical excavation in the area, the feature was encountered 20 in. below the present ground surface. Longtime maintenance staff confirmed that fill had been brought in several times over the intervening decades to assist with erosion caused by tourist foot traffic and weather conditions. This had not come up during on-site discussions prior to excavation, but staff remembered filling events as archaeology encountered features at a much greater depth than anticipated.

Sites also change in ways not documented or remembered. While some agencies or individuals may retain paperwork, plans, and drawings for what is considered routine maintenance work, most do not. Circa 1980 the archaeologist who excavated a mudstone wall in the Shed Addition indicated that the wall may turn to the south and east. Stabilization work since the 1970s–1980s investigations had precluded resolving or testing the hypothesis made in the previous field notes. Our recent excavation found a scatter of mudstone in the east that gave some indication that the wall might have had more to it, but it had been impacted by pouring cement (likely sometime between 1990 and 2000) to stabilize the adobe wall. With that realization, further archaeological excavation in that area was halted.

Drawings on field notes sometimes suggested shapes of features that did not match reality. This is perhaps to be expected; field drawings are an interpretation and represent the archaeologist's best guess. Still, there can be surprises. While previous excavators did their best to capture features in photographs, not all photographs are equally useful. From the drawing and notes, we expected another trash pit in the area between the North Barn and Spear Warehouse to be "ovoid" in shape. We also expected that we would encounter only small portions of it based on the previous mapping. It turned out to be a much more amorphous feature and extended well beyond the anticipated horizontal extent, significantly increasing our artifact sample. There is more archaeology to come, and we are looking forward to integrating new artifact collections with old collections from this important Californio site.

Preparing for New Interpretations

Based on our archaeological journey into the records of the Cooper-Molera complex, we offer suggestions for those working with legacy sites and collections (both artifact and documentation records) to conduct new archaeological investigations. One of the more challenging aspects of digging a legacy site is reconciling multiple interpretations of features and deposits, both new interpretations as well as conjectures of the past. Archaeology is about interpretation. This holds true for interpretation of the archaeology as it unfolds and of the documentation of previous archaeological investigations. This experience caused us to consider what we would ideally like to leave behind for future researchers:

- Establish permanent vertical and horizontal datum points that can be easily relocated.

- Create a comprehensive map (or set of maps) that compiles data from all previous maps (hand-drawn in field notes, interim interpretive maps, and final maps). This is going to be a detailed map; its purpose is to show the relationships of the features to one another, stressing interpretation.

- Create a field map layered over an aerial depiction. The purpose of this map is to help establish the relationships of the features to the site surroundings. It can be an indispensable map should later archaeologists need to relocate elements and features of the site.

- Talk to the maintenance staff. When possible, convince them to create a site drawing (or set of drawings) that depict all irrigation, drainage, stabilization work, and so on, all on one map on an aerial background. The base map is likely going to be something that you provide; make sure that it is big enough to accommodate handwriting. Document what you have already learned, and be sure to include that in the curatorial record.

- Talk to and gather information and photographs from excavation crew members. Often it is not only the principal investigator who has important information. Staff archaeologists often have memories of the excavation and sometimes field notes and photographs that are not stored with the "official" documentation of a site. When additional sources are found, carefully consider the need to curate these materials as well. Not all photographs and field notes are equal.

- When digitizing old field notes, use common, readily accessible software, and include a statement on the internal organization of the field notes. Assuming that the intent is to curate these digital files, discuss the format with the curation repository.

- Document how the new field notes (and their digital versions) correspond to older notes.

- Do the same for old and new photographs. As these are digitized, link the photographs to field notes whenever possible.

- After lab work is complete, revisit old and new field notes. If specific or groups of artifacts are highlighted or mentioned in the field notes, reference the catalog number.

- Consider the long-term curation needs of the artifacts as well as the field documentation (Brady et al. 2006).

- Whenever possible, articulate the links between the paperwork, digital documentation, and artifacts.

Study of the artifacts and the documentation that accompanied them, as well as oral histories with previous archaeologists and maintenance staff, helped us to better understand the Cooper-Molera site and to recognize what features and artifacts were significant to the site history. It also helped us to recognize features and artifacts that were not considered important, and why. This, in turn, helped us to make critical decisions about what to add to the previously curated artifacts, and what to discard, although sampling methodologies and discard policies are large topics that merit much more attention than this chapter can give! Suffice it to say that earlier in this volume, Farris stated that while curation space for California State Parks collections has increased, it is still finite.

Long-term curation is vital to archaeological investigations and later public interpretation. Revisiting a legacy site and its artifact collections reminds us to carefully consider the act of curation for new archaeological investigations. It is also making us consider anew how the site features and artifacts have been interpreted within the museum and what the potential is for future interpretive efforts planned by the National Trust, which intends to present site history throughout all of the grounds, including the new commercial areas and museum spaces. As the site may yet change again, if other archaeologists revisit the legacy site and its collections, what do they need to know? All new collections become legacy or old collections sooner than any of us expect. Will your collections be ready for future researchers and public interpretation efforts?

Acknowledgments

We are grateful to the National Trust for Historic Preservation and Architectural Resources Group for giving us the opportunity to work at this important heritage site. Reviewing past notes made us appreciate the contribution of State Parks archaeologists, in particular our *compadre* Larry Felton. Many thanks also to Ben Ford, Glenn Farris, and Sara Rivers Cofield, whose review and insights made for a better article.

References

Allen, Rebecca, David L. Felton, and Christopher Corey
2013   Ceramic Trends and Timeline from a California Perspective. In *Ceramic Identification in Historical Archaeology: The View from California, 1822–1940*, Rebecca Allen, Julia E. Huddleson, Kimberly J. Wooten, and Glenn J. Farris, editors, pp. 25–51. Society for Historical Archaeology, Special Publication Series No. 11. Germantown md.

Architectural Resources Group, Inc. (arg)
2015   Cooper Molera Adobe Historic Preservation Report, Monterey, California. Report to City of Monterey from arg, Inc., San Francisco.

Barker, Leo, Julia G. Costello, and Rebecca Allen
1995   The Archaeology of Spanish and Mexican Alta California. In *The Archaeology of Spanish and Mexican Colonialism in the American Southwest*, James E. Ayres, editor, pp. 3–51. Guides to the Archaeological Literature of the Immigrant Experience in America, No. 3. Society for Historical Archaeology. Ann Arbor mi.

Barter, Eloise Richards
2003   The French Potter of Monterey: Archaeological Investigations of a 1860s Kiln in Monterey, ca. California State Parks, Cultural Resource Division, Sacramento.

Brady, Colleen, Molly Gleeson, Melba Myers, Claire Peachey, Betty Seifert, Howard Wellman, Emily Williams, and Lisa Young
2006   Conservation faqs and Facts. Online module hosted by Society for Historical Archaeology, May. https://sha.org/conservation-facts/.

Davis, William Heath

1967 *Seventy-Five Years in California: Recollections and Remarks by One Who Visited These Shores in 1831, and Again in 1833, and Except When Absent on Business Was a Resident from 1838 until the End of a Long Life in 1909.* Harold A. Small, editor. John Howell Books. San Francisco.

Dittmer, Hazel Barrien

1977 John Rogers Cooper, Final Report. Interpretive Planning Unit. California Department of Parks and Recreation, Sacramento.

Farris, Glenn J.

2013 Mexican-Period Ceramics in California. In *Ceramic Identification in Historical Archaeology: The View from California, 1822–1940*, Rebecca Allen, Julia E. Huddleson, Kimberly J. Wooten, and Glenn J. Farris, editors, pp. 105–123. Society for Historical Archaeology, Special Publication Series No. 11. Germantown md.

Felton, David L., and Lee Motz

1993 Historic Changes to Doors and Windows in the Diaz House, Cooper-Molera Adobe Complex, Monterey shp. Manuscript, Cultural Resource Management Unit, Resource Management Unit, California Department of Parks and Recreation, Sacramento.

1997 A Summary of Archeological Features Encountered during the Restoration of the Cooper-Molera Adobe Complex, Monterey, California. Incomplete draft manuscript, California Department of Parks and Recreation, The Resources Agency, Resources Protection Division, Cultural Heritage Section, Sacramento.

Felton, David L., and Peter D. Schulz

1983 *The Diaz Collection: Material Culture and Social Change in Mid-Nineteenth Century Monterey.* California Archeological Reports No. 23. California Department of Parks and Recreation, Sacramento. http://www.parks.ca .gov/?page_Id=28329.

Greenwood, Roberta

1987 Review, The Diaz Collection: Material Culture and Social Change in Mid-Nineteenth-Century Monterey, by David L. Felton and Peter D. Schulz. Historical Archaeology 21(1):110–111.

Heizer, Robert F.

1977 Report on Archaeological Examination of Sub-floor Soils and Features in the Cooper-Molera Adobe, Monterey, Carried Out from August 7–15, 1977. Cultural Resource Management Unit, Sacramento.

Kirker, Harold, and Stanleigh Bry

1975 John Rogers Cooper: New England Merchant in Mexican California. California Department of Parks and Recreation, Sacramento.

Napoli, Donald

1977   Cooper-Molera Adobe, Monterey State Historic Park. Cultural Resource Man-
       agement Unit, California Department of Parks and Recreation, Sacramento.

Reese, Robert W.

1972   A Preliminary Historical Study of John Rogers Cooper. Cultural Resource
       Management Unit, California Department of Parks and Recreation,
       Sacramento.

Schulz, Jeanette K.

1981   Salvaging the Salvage: Stratigraphic Reconstruction and Assemblage Assess-
       ment at the Hotel de France Site, Old Sacramento. Master's thesis, Depart-
       ment of Anthropology, University of California, Davis.

Wallace, William

1975a Captain Cooper's House: An Historical Study of an Early Nineteenth Cen-
       tury Monterey Adobe. Cultural Resource Management Unit, California
       Department of Parks and Recreation, Sacramento.

1975b Captain Cooper's House: Archaeological Explorations in 1974. Part I: Archi-
       tectural Elements. Cultural Resource Management Unit, California Depart-
       ment of Parks and Recreation, Sacramento.

1975c Captain Cooper's House: Archaeological Explorations in 1974. Part II: The
       Grounds. California Department of Parks and Recreation, Sacramento.

FOURTEEN

Thinking outside the Hollinger Box

Getting National Park Service Archaeological Collections out of the Box and into the Public Eye

ALICIA PARESI, JESSICA COSTELLO, NICOLE WALSH, AND JENNIFER MCCANN

When the general public thinks of the National Park Service (NPS), they envision the natural wonders of Yellowstone and the Grand Canyon. In reality, National Park sites preserve as many cultural resources as they do natural: over 200 of the 417 National Park units were designated primarily for their historical significance, according to their enabling legislation. These National Parks preserve not only historic sites, structures, and battlefields but also a wide array of material culture, represented in a collection that makes the NPS one of the largest museums in the world. Often these cultural objects are not visible to the public, despite their significance in the history of our country. The Northeast Museum Services Center (NMSC) is actively working to change this. NMSC staff have developed methods and strategies to get National Park Service collections out of their boxes and into the public eye.

The mission of the National Park Service is to "conserve the scenery and the natural and historic objects and the wild life therein and to provide for the enjoyment of the same in such manner and by such means as will leave them unimpaired for the enjoyment of future generations" (https://www.nps.gov/grba/learn/management /organic-act-of-1916.htm). Federal historic preservation laws, including the National Historic Preservation Act of 1966 and the Historic Sites Act of 1935, further dictate that the NPS has a responsibility to preserve cultural resources for the benefit and education of the people of the United States. These guiding documents clearly prioritize public visibility of NPS property; however, this is not always feasible with a constant reduction in cultural resources staff and funding. As a regional center where cultural resource expertise is concentrated, the Northeast Museum Services Center is well-positioned to acquaint the public and other cultural resources professionals with park collections through social media, traditional public outreach, and other means. The NMSC's goal is ultimately that park museum collections will be better preserved and studied. We believe that greater awareness of the resources held by NPS sites will increase public interest in and visitation to these sites, which in turn will raise the profile of the collections and help culturally focused parks better compete for the limited funding available for collections care.

The Northeast Region of the NPS recognized that its archaeological collections were in need of attention over 30 years ago. In the early 1980s the Regional Office developed the Archaeological Collections Management Project (ACMP) to process, catalog, analyze, and prepare the uncataloged artifacts for storage. They sought to address a lack of accountability and to establish curatorial standards for the NPS archaeology collections. The ACMP team tracked down missing artifacts and associated documentation at universities, cultural resource management firms, and private homes. They determined that many collections were stored in substandard conditions in basements, attics, and outbuildings and housed in nonarchival enclosures like acidic cardboard boxes, liquor flats, and disintegrating brown paper bags. The ACMP was successful in locating, organizing, and documenting NPS archaeology collections that might otherwise have continued to deteriorate. Artifacts once stored in abysmal conditions were now housed in archival-quality Hollinger boxes, which had become the standard for long-term curation of archaeological collections. At some point after the ACMP team disbanded, an unknown curator came up with the idea of sealing the boxes of archaeology with tamper-proof evidence tape. The tape was supposed to save staff time: if the tape remained unbroken, the box could be considered intact, with no need for staff to reopen and reexamine it. Once returned to park shelves, the archaeology collections at many parks received little attention, and as staff turned over, the ACMP reports became buried in libraries and their valuable suggestions for exhibits and interpretation were soon forgotten. This was the status quo at many parks until the creation of the Archaeology Program at the NMSC in 2003.

The primary function of the Archaeology Program at NMSC is improving accountability and preservation of archaeology collections from National Parks in the Northeast Region. Most of these collections were excavated prior to 1987, during Section 106 compliance projects, but for various reasons remain uncataloged. NMSC archaeologists clean, identify, and catalog these collections and rehouse them in archival enclosures in preparation for long-term storage. Since 2003 NMSC staff has cataloged and rehoused over 1.2 million artifacts, averaging 50,000 artifacts per year (McCann 2016).

In recent years NPS sites have experienced significant employee reductions, especially in cultural resources departments. Remaining staff frequently have no background in archaeology, so they appreciate any assistance with this aspect of their museum collection. Funding for a multiyear cataloging or rehousing project is awarded by the NPS through a competitive process. These projects allow the time for NMSC staff, interns, and volunteers to survey, document, photograph, and analyze artifacts. This time and focus allows NMSC to closely examine a large part—sometimes all—of a park's archaeological holdings. Reviewing the archaeological assemblages from many field seasons and compiling the data afford us the opportunity to solve the inevitable mysteries that arise. Making new discoveries within a park's archaeological collection is always exciting, such as the day we discovered scratch-blue creamware sherds from Petersburg National Battlefield (discussed below). Finding creative ways to deliver such information has proven complex but not impossible.

Curating an exhibit at the NMSC office space is not possible for multiple reasons. NMSC is located in a regional office space with restricted access and limited parking, which creates difficulties for visitors. Also, collections are brought to NMSC for cataloging or rehousing and eventually returned, traveling as far as 500 miles away.

Finally, NMSC staff is funded only to catalog; there is no funding for staff time for public education and interpretation. While we continue to pursue traditional outreach, such as exhibits and lectures, we have found that social media platforms such as WordPress, Facebook, and Instagram have provided an efficient outlet for the Northeast Region's archaeological collections to be enjoyed by the public and studied by researchers and scholars.

Traditional Public Archaeology at the National Parks

Parks regularly ask us to provide a list of ready-to-go research and ideas that enable them to put together exhibits and publications. To accomplish this, NMSC archaeologists identify artifacts with exhibit potential in the catalog records and completion reports, which serve as guides to the collections for park staff. Publication-quality photographs are always included for exhibit-worthy pieces. Accurate, detailed catalog records are also essential since at some point they may become the basis for museum labels. A recent example of this is when park curator Christine Valosin cited one of NMSC's completion reports in her 2016 article about artifacts from Saratoga National Historical Park. In this article, Valosin highlights artifacts from the park's collection that "tell the stories of soldiers and civilians at Saratoga." She concludes with a call for further research on the park's collection, pointing out that "many more [artifacts] await further research and all have the potential to bring greater understanding to the conflict and the characters that shaped the nation's future at Saratoga" (Valosin 2016:225).

NMSC archaeologists have also assisted with the development of exhibits that highlight parks' archaeology collections. If an exhibit is in the planning stages and the park has not considered archaeology pieces or topics, we are always available to consult. For example, in 2012 NMSC's curator of archaeology, Alicia Paresi, helped Minute Man National Historical Park in Concord, Massachusetts, select archaeological artifacts to incorporate into an exhibit for the North Bridge Visitor Center. The exhibit tells the story of "the shot heard 'round the world" and helps to bring the Minute Men to life by featuring personal artifacts that they would have worn and used on a daily basis; these include a hand-painted pearlware tea bowl, spur, buckles, pewter buttons, and a stone button mold. The artifacts were excavated in the 1960s and spent two decades in boxes sealed with evidence tape, but due to NMSC efforts, they now help visitors better understand the life and times of the people commemorated by the park (Figures 22 and 23).

In 2015 NMSC worked with park staff to select artifacts from the archaeology collection at Salem Maritime National Historic Site in Massachusetts for a temporary exhibit at the Narbonne House. The exhibit, called *A House at Play*, featured historic and archaeological artifacts related to children and playing. Toys included a wooden die, clay marbles, a metal whistle, and a toy porcelain tea set that were all excavated at the park during 1973–1975 and that had remained in boxes until this exhibit. This exhibit illuminated a charming part of the Narbonne House's history that is not visible during a typical tour. Having these artifacts out of their boxes and on display allowed visitors a glimpse into the innocence of childhood in 19th-century Salem.

While artifact exhibits are important, nothing can replace the visitor's experience of meeting an actual archaeologist and asking questions. Since 2009 NMSC has been participating in the Battle Road Open House program every fall at Minute Man National Historical Park. This program features a wide variety of events and activities at the park, including presentations, house tours, and living history programs. NMSC's archaeologists present a casual and engaging show-and-tell-style exhibit featuring highlights from the park's archaeological collection. Visitors are invited to view and ask questions about refined English teawares, local pharmaceutical bottles, pewter spoons, bone toothbrushes, brass coat buttons, and wooden dominoes, among many other artifacts. Each year this program is a great success, drawing hundreds of visitors who express interest and excitement at the opportunity to see this collection. For NMSC staff, getting these artifacts out of storage and into a space where visitors can safely engage with them is incredibly rewarding. This event and others like it also serve a function that is even less obvious and far

Sword

Known as a "small sword," a common design carried by officers on both sides, this was more a badge of rank than a fighting weapon. However, it is very light, very fast, and tapers to a strong, thrusting point.

LOAN, COURTESY OF R. W. ROSE

Shoe Buckle
ca. 1770s
HISTORY COLLECTION,
MINUTE MAN NHP

Metal Breeches Knee Buckle
ca. 1770–1790
ARCHAEOLOGY COLLECTION,
MINUTE MAN NHP

Stone Button Mold
18th century
ARCHAEOLOGY COLLECTION,
MINUTE MAN NHP

Pewter Buttons
18th century
With embossed floral decoration
ARCHAEOLOGY COLLECTION,
MINUTE MAN NHP

FIGURE 22. Archaeological artifacts on exhibit at Minute Man National Historical Park. (Photo: Northeast Museum Services Center).

more significant: facilitating important and even difficult conversations with children who are uninhibited enough to say things to us like "I did not realize girls could be archaeologists" or "You are way younger than I thought you would be."

NMSC archaeologists regularly participate in Massachusetts

FIGURE 23. Northeast Museum Services Center archaeologists display artifacts during "Battle Road" at Minute Man National Historical Park. (Photo: Norm Eggert for Northeast Museum Services Center).

Archaeology Month. We have worked primarily with Minute Man National Historical Park because it is nearby, we are well-acquainted with their collection, and the park recognizes the benefit of having us research a new aspect of their collection each year. New topics and approaches have been introduced to highlight the endless research possibilities of the artifacts within a single collection and how they relate to other NPS archaeology collections. One popular topic was "Message in a Bottle: Identifying and Dating Old Bottles." For this presentation, we took 18th-century freeblown wine bottles, 19th-century molded pharmaceutical bottles, and 20th-century machine-made condiment bottles out of storage and displayed them. The event was specifically targeted at bottle collectors, and we encouraged people to bring their own collections to learn how to date them. Inviting visitors to bring their own collections for identification and to share stories brought a better response than the traditional lecture format. Most of the visitors were local and had not been to the park before or in many years. It was inspiring to know that the archaeology brought about the new visitation. For the program "Setting the Table in 18th-Century Massachusetts," collections from both Salem Maritime National Historical Park and Minute Man National Historical Park were highlighted to demonstrate some of the differences between rural and urban table settings. In addition to the lecture, staff brought out many examples of tableware, cutlery, and glassware. Whenever possible, examples from other museums' archaeology collections were illustrated in the presentation so that visitors could understand just how common these wares were and recognize them as they visited other museums and National Parks.

To explore another area of Minute Man's holdings, NMSC hosted a lecture and temporary exhibit that focused on the park's prehistoric artifacts. NMSC archaeologists talked to visitors about the ancient residents of the area and showed them examples of projectile points and stone tools that these people made and used. For a park whose period of interpretation spans just three days in 1775, this event provided a rare opportunity to showcase the artifacts from the previous 6,000 years of habitation at the site. Native American culture is frequently sidelined at parks that have such narrow focus on one historic event, but archaeology allowed us to broaden the story to be more inclusive, more interesting, and more accurate.

Another event included a lecture and public display at Minute Man that highlighted the archaeological artifacts excavated at the Wayside. The artifacts represented the literary families that occupied the Wayside during the 19th and 20th centuries: the Alcotts, the Hawthornes, and the Lothrops. Items selected for display included transfer-printed ceramics, a 19th-century baby's boot, and a wood burnisher (which, as pointed out by one visitor, is a perfect material representation of a busy author). This event was timed to coincide with the reopening of the house after renovations and a major historic housekeeping project that NMSC curators undertook. Using archaeology collections to support such publicity opportunities reinforces their significance and pertinence as integral cultural resources.

Gratifying as it is to have personal interaction with visitors, only a tiny percentage of the public attend lectures or events at parks, and NMSC is beholden to understaffed parks to provide event and exhibit space, access to collections, and staff time. To maximize our limited resources, we began to turn to social media to reach the most people with the least amount of staff time. NMSC began using social media to reach the general public and other museum professionals in 2010. In 2011 a social media policy was written for NMSC by a consultant and has been only slightly altered since. The policy provides guidance on posting policies and best practices for the use of social media. Though the social media policy has remained the same, the way that NMSC has developed and presented content, and the platforms it uses, has evolved with the changing technology and needs of our audiences. Since 2010 many more archaeological and museum institutions have joined social media, and we are able to adjust our content based on what other institutions are discussing or what is trending. Many institutions find it difficult to get posts up on social media quickly due to perfectionism and concern over maintaining the reputation of the institution. Obviously some planning and thought needs to go into creating posts, but we have found that oftentimes spontaneous posts (especially those based on what is "trending" on a particular day or platform) perform better than overly prepared posts. This does not mean that posts are not edited and reviewed before posting, but we have begun to match the editing process with the nature of the platform. Editing and management review is most thorough for blog posts, as this is our most formal and academic platform. Facebook posts will frequently be reviewed by only one or two staff members, and Instagram posts are rarely reviewed at all before posting. Managers do monitor all three platforms and will make suggestions to staff members who they feel are straying too far off topic or using language considered too casual or flippant. The nature of NMSC's works means that our staff are frequently on the road, on site at parks, or just not in the office together, so a strict review process would unnecessarily impede the use of social media. While all NMSC staff are invited to contribute content, some choose not to, and only three staff members are able to post content. These responsibilities were granted based on the individual staff member's interest and experience rather than being position-specific duties. Successful social media engagement relies heavily on enthusiasm from the participants, and making participation voluntary rather than compulsory maintains a consistent level of engagement.

Though our goal of better preserving and studying archaeology collections has remained the same, our methods of achieving that goal have expanded over the years to include greater public awareness, specifically reaching out to students and scholars about potential research topics, and working with specific NPS sites to inform park staff about the resources in their collections. While the general guidelines provided by our 2011 Social Media Policy were a helpful place to start, the nature of social media requires flexibility and relatively free rein over content in order to successfully engage any audience.

Blog

Since publication of its first post in 2010, NMSC has been using its blog to educate the public about NPS museum collections (https:// nmscarcheologylab.wordpress.com). The NMSC Archaeology & Museum Blog has published about 100 posts, has been viewed over 60,000 times, and has elicited numerous positive comments, many of which contain the words "thank you." Readers are eager to learn about NPS cultural resources and are grateful for the opportunity to do so. For NMSC staff, it is a duty and a privilege to share NPS museum collections with the public, and such gracious responses to NMSC's efforts make the work even more rewarding.

NMSC has written about a variety of artifact types from archaeology collections across the Northeast Region of the NPS. Examples include tobacco pipes from Petersburg National Battlefield; 18th-century wine bottles from Longfellow House, Washington's Headquarters National Historic Site; gravestones from Minute Man National Historical Park; redware flower pots from Salem Maritime National Historic Site; a carrier pigeon message from Saratoga National Historical Park; personal artifacts from Lowell National Historical Park; and stoneware bottles from Gateway National Recreation Area. NMSC's goal is to keep the tone of the blog educational but also friendly and casual, so that it will appeal to a wide audience and engage readers at multiple levels.

As stated on the NMSC Archaeology & Museum Blog home page, part of NMSC's mission is making NPS museum collections accessible for "research, education, and public enjoyment." NMSC recognizes the importance of each of these three elements. One goal is that the blog will inspire scholarly research by illuminating the great potential of NPS archaeology collections. Another is that the blog will allow the public to simply see and enjoy NPS archaeology collections that would otherwise remain invisible in collections storage.

NMSC has published a series of posts dedicated to a curious and exciting handful of scratch-blue creamware sherds from the archaeology collection at Petersburg National Battlefield in Virginia (Figure 24). The sherds were excavated during a survey of the City Point Unit of the battlefield in 1983 and were cataloged by NMSC in 2012. NMSC archaeologists often conduct research on archaeological artifacts in order to accurately identify and describe them for cataloging purposes. In this case, the unusual scratch-blue decoration on what appeared to be creamware (instead of the expected white salt-glazed stoneware) demanded research beyond that typically required for cataloging. NMSC archaeologists approached this demand with enthusiasm, using comparative research and innovative technology to bring new light to this old but amazing archaeology collection.

The title of the first post in this series, "Are You Sure That's Not White Salt-Glazed Stoneware?" (Walsh 2012), reflects a common response to NMSC's initial inquiries about this surprising ceramic type. Many archaeologists and curators wondered whether the sherds were actually stoneware, never having heard of scratch-blue decoration on creamware. NMSC staff spent countless hours researching

FIGURE 24. Scratch-blue creamware from Petersburg National Battlefield.
(Photo: J. Costello)

documentary sources and consulting with material culture experts in the United States and abroad and found that, although surviving examples are rare, scratch-blue creamware does exist. The second post about these artifacts, "Scratch-Blue at Petersburg: Redefining Creamware on American Archaeological Sites" (Costello 2012) details NMSC's research into various potteries that may or may not have produced the ware and shares the early date range (pre-1763) of the archaeological context in which the City Point creamware sherds were found.

NMSC then used an XRF scanner to determine the chemical makeup of the glaze and definitively concluded that it is chemically characteristic of creamware and not white salt-glazed stoneware. After more extensive historical research, aided by the staff at Petersburg National Battlefield, as well as an in-depth analysis of the City Point archaeology collection, NMSC published its third blog post on this subject: "Scratch-Blue at Petersburg, Part 2: The Scottish Connection" (Costello 2015). In January 2016 NMSC presented this research at the Society for Historical Archaeology conference in Washington DC.

NMSC's blog posts about scratch-blue creamware have been some of its most popular and engaging posts. Collectively the three posts have been viewed over 2,500 times and have elicited comments by and conversations with archaeologists and material culture specialists. For NMSC staff, these statistics are encouraging and confirm that our blog is an effective means of sharing and inviting new research into NPS archaeology collections. According to NMSC archaeologist Jessica Costello (2016c), "The 8 small sherds of scratch-blue creamware from City Point sparked the most comprehensive and exciting research we have yet to conduct in our lab." This ongoing research, begun in 2012, revolutionized the way NMSC archaeologists and others in the field think about creamware on American archaeological sites. The collection of artifacts containing these sherds was untouched and its research potential unrealized for almost 30 years following excavation until NMSC began cataloging it in 2012. The City Point example illustrates the wealth of information waiting to be discovered within old archaeology collections. With new technologies, comparative research, and fresh insights, the new research potential in these old collections is limitless.

In addition to sharing and encouraging new research, NMSC also uses its blog to foster a sense of personal connection with NPS archaeology collections. One of the most popular posts is entitled "Little House in the Archaeology Lab: How Laura Ingalls Wilder Made Me a Historical Archaeologist" (Costello 2016b). In this post, one of NMSC's archaeologists writes about how reading Wilder's *Little House* books as a child instilled in her a lifelong love of history and material culture. She states that many of the types of objects lovingly referenced in Wilder's writing are present in NPS archaeology collections and represent other individuals' and families' hardships, hopes, and triumphs. This post has been viewed over 1,500 times and elicited more readers' comments than any other post to date. Readers connected personally with this article and, through comments, shared their own experiences with Wilder's writing. Comments included "Thank you for an interesting post"; "What a lovely post"; and "Bravo!" The extent to which this post reached and engaged its readers is an example of how NMSC shows the public that every archaeological artifact has a story of its own.

Facebook

The Northeast Museum Services Center's Facebook page (https://www.facebook.com/NPS.NMSC/) has attracted over 3,600 followers since its creation in 2010. NMSC started the page as an inexpensive tool to educate the public about the work they do and increase accessibility to NPS museum collections. The NMSC WordPress blog typically features articles about collections management and specific archaeological or archival collections. NMSC staff use Facebook as a quicker and less formal way of sharing photographs and information with an audience that includes other museum professionals and resource managers as well as students and the general public. Although NMSC aims to keep posts informative and relevant, we also try to maintain a light and friendly Facebook presence that is appealing to a wide audience.

Facebook connects NMSC with the Society for Historical Archaeology, Ceramics in America, Boston City Archaeology Lab, hundreds of National Park Sites and other federal organizations, and many other institutions who share our work and provide content for NMSC to share. These connections have strengthened NMSC's Facebook presence and have generated hundreds of followers. Although NMSC does share content from other parks and museums, statistically our own original posts have been the most popular. Original posts typically adhere to a few themes: current projects, current travel to parks, and collection or artifact highlights. NMSC staff travel frequently to Northeast Region parks to conduct technical assistance projects, help parks with planning needs, and pick up and return collections. Facebook has been an effective way of spreading the word about the work conducted on site at parks and helping people to realize all of the effort that goes into preserving our historic and cultural resources. In addition to work at parks, NMSC also posts regularly about the work going on in the office. Followers see photographs of NMSC archaeologists washing, mending, and cavity-packing artifacts, and NMSC archivists surveying and cataloging rare books and oversized maps and drawings. Facebook is also a tool for sharing important or interesting articles related to National Parks or the wider museum field.

In 2016 NMSC began a series of posts called "Meet NMSC," which feature photographs and introductory biographies of staff members. These posts have been well-received by NMSC's audience, prompting many "likes" and friendly comments. Other posts that have been particularly well-received include "Mystery Artifact," where we invite followers to identify an unusual artifact, and "National Day," when we post a photograph and brief description of an artifact, site, or project related to a national day. Examples include a collage of buttons from various Northeast Region parks posted for National Button Day, ceramic pitchers from Saratoga National Historical Park posted for National Coffee Day, and a tooth powder pot from Gateway National Recreation Area posted for National Smile Power Day.

Taking advantage of national days is one example of the way NMSC uses Facebook and trending social media culture to bring NPS archaeology collections into public view. We also post regularly about interesting artifacts we come across from whatever collection we are working on. These posts are often shared by the parks who own the collections, increasing awareness of and exposure to these amazing resources. NMSC has used Facebook to highlight a double-sided "trick" coin from Gateway National Recreation Area in Staten Island, New York; a pearlware muffin plate from Saratoga National Historical Park in Saratoga, New York; hand tools and fossils from Delaware Water Gap National Recreation Area in Bushkill, Pennsylvania; teawares from Salem Maritime National Historic Site, and a commemorative medallion from Women's Rights National Historical Park in Seneca Falls, New York. Archaeological artifacts, once unseen in collection storage, are brought out of their boxes onto NMSC's Facebook page, where they can be seen and appreciated by potential researchers.

NMSC performed a social media audit in October 2015 to determine what types of posts are most effective at connecting with our audience. Poring through years of posts, it was clear that certain types of posts performed better than others. NMSC judged whether a post was successful based on the number of "likes," shares, and comments it received. Original posts, especially those with a high-quality, eye-catching photo, were the most popular. The popularity of the topics within each original post varied slightly, but it was clear that our audience was most interested in original research and artifact spotlights, especially ones that involved some sort of audience participation. The least successful type of post on the NMSC Facebook page was shares, or redistributing of information from other Facebook pages. Though this is convenient, especially when NMSC staff are short on time or material to post, our audience does not respond as well to these. After conducting this social media audit, NMSC staff concluded that the new focus would be on original posts, which is one of the ways the March Madness campaign was developed a year later.

Museum Madness

One of NMSC's most successful Facebook campaigns began in March 2016, with something less conventional. NMSC created a friendly "Museum Madness" competition in which parks from the Northeast Region were pitted against one another in hopes of winning the grand prize: an NMSC blog post about the winning park's museum collections. NMSC staff created a randomly ordered elimination bracket in the style of the NCAA "March Madness" basketball tournament and posted several "face-offs" each day throughout the month. Each face-off pictured representative scenes from two Northeast Region parks and invited the audience to vote for their favorite park between the two.

The competition started off slow, as parks and the audience gradually became aware of the new social media campaign. NMSC was soon reaching new audiences, as park staff and fans alike drew in their social networks to boost the ranking of their favorite park. Some parks started creating memes advocating for themselves, and there was even some friendly "smack talk" that appeared in the comments. At the conclusion of the competition, Fort Stanwix National Monument in Rome, New York, emerged the victor, and NMSC archaeologists made a visit to work with their staff on the blog post that was the grand prize. The competition and the visit were featured in the local newspaper, the *Rome Sentinel* (2016), and the local community (already well-populated with supporters of their National Park) seemed even more invigorated.

NMSC and Fort Stanwix staff decided on a blog post format that emphasized the variety and historical importance of the Fort Stanwix National Monument museum collection. The post, entitled "The History of Fort Stanwix in 10 Objects" (Costello 2016a), features ten diverse artifacts from the park's collection of 700,000 items that staff members felt best represented the rich history of the site. Included are a Brewerton projectile point from the Archaic period, an exploded mortar from the 1777 siege at Fort Stanwix, and a Two Row Wampum Belt that was gifted to Fort Stanwix National Monument by the Oneida Nation in 2005. As the park's superintendent, Frank Barrows, said, "The blog post by the Northeast Museum Services Center really helps to elevate the visibility of the park's cultural resources and highlights the value of Fort Stanwix as an archaeological site" (*Rome Sentinel* 2016).

NMSC's Museum Madness competition allowed one of the Northeast Region's smaller parks a great opportunity to spread the word about its museum collection. One of the artifacts highlighted in the blog post about Fort Stanwix is a brass grenadier's match case, which was designed to hold a slow match used for igniting incendiaries. According to Keith Routley, museum curator and chief of cultural resources at Fort Stanwix National Monument, it was "originally identified as a hose nozzle and was later determined to be an exceptionally rare item from an archaeological context. This underscores the potential for further discoveries and the untapped research potential of the museum collection at Fort Stanwix National Monument" (Costello 2016a). Independent scholar Joan M. Zenaen (2008:141) echoed this sentiment in her 2008 book about Fort Stanwix: "The breadth and scope of this collection provides numerous potential research avenues." Similar untapped research potential exists in archaeology collections throughout the Northeast Region of the National Park Service. We hope that by increasing awareness of these collections through various means of public outreach, including innovative methods like the Museum Madness Facebook campaign, students and scholars will know where to look for new and exciting research topics.

Though it might seem that there would be little crossover between college sports and museum collections, the model is simple, easily understood, and effective. NCAA basketball brackets are wildly popular (even President Obama shared his bracket that year) and engage a wide cross-section of the general public, including people who may not think of museums or archaeology as being among their interests. By plugging National Parks into this model, even in this somewhat peripheral way, NMSC reached new audiences. Elevating the content of the competition to the parks themselves engaged a broader audience and gave them the opportunity to access information about collections.

The Museum Madness campaign came with many lessons regarding the way NMSC and other institutions can use social media. First, it is important to plan such long-term campaigns well in advance. NMSC staff thought of the campaign the morning of March 1 and implemented it the same day. This was problematic for many reasons. One of the biggest problems was a lack of time to produce high-quality graphics that will grab the audience's attention. Because NMSC implemented the campaign in less than a day, there was no time to publicize this competition to the parks, and some did not know about it until their park had already been eliminated. Despite our best efforts, voting methods were unclear at first, and initially few people voted. As people caught on, more votes were cast and parks began actively campaigning. In March 2017 we ran the same campaign again and there was a major increase in participation by park staff. The parks that knew about it from the previous year were ready with memes. All parks were sent emails alerting them to the competition so that cultural resources and interpretation staff had the opportunity to work together to produce memes and rally votes from their local communities. At the end of the competition, Weir Farm National Historic Site in Wilton, Connecticut, posted the following comment on the Northeast Regional Office website: "A big thank you to NMSC for putting this competition together. What a fun way to learn about all the different parks in the Northeast Region; and it's a great opportunity to use memes to show our historic photographs and collections in a new way" (Weir Farm: Northeast Regional Office, Monday Mashup April 1, 2017).

Perhaps the best lesson learned, however, was that stepping outside the comfort zone of the traditional academic approach should be encouraged. If archaeologists and museum professionals want to engage a diverse audience, we have to think differently, take risks, and provide diverse content. Looking just to other cultural institutions for social media models and ideas is insufficient; we have to look to other industries that capture the public's attention. NMSC's social media and park collections will always hold an interest for cultural resource staff and academics, who certainly make up the bulk of NMSC's audience. Bringing in the general public requires that NMSC not cater exclusively to colleagues but instead elevate the content to a more generally accessible level. Campaigns like Museum Madness and "Meet NMSC" have proven successful, and staff are constantly looking for new ways to get followers involved with the page.

Instagram

In March 2016, inspired by the success of the Museum Madness campaign, NMSC decided to branch out from Facebook and the WordPress blog and join Instagram to specifically target younger audiences. Instagram, a photo-sharing social media platform, was founded in 2010 (Lagorio-Chafikin 2012), right around the time Facebook was losing the interest of younger millennials (Lang 2015). As with other social media platforms, the National Park Service was slow to accept Instagram but eventually realized its potential for connection with the next generation of stewards. Since Instagram caters to a primarily younger, millennial audience, there was a steep learning curve for some at NMSC who had never heard of the platform and were confused by hashtags, one of the most important parts of Instagram. NMSC staff who were well-versed in Instagram took charge and held a meeting to educate the rest of the staff about the app and its capabilities, how useful hashtags could be, and how successful it had already been for NPS's "Find Your Park" campaign. During the National Park Service's 2016 centennial year, parks and centers encouraged people to get out and #FindYourPark, a hashtag that, as of this publication, was linked to nearly 1 million photos.

Although Instagram is NMSC's newest form of outreach, it is the fastest growing and has helped NMSC target younger audiences that are not using Facebook. Instagram has also proved to be a great communication and networking tool within the National Park Service by connecting parks and centers that normally may not interact through the use of high-quality photos and witty captions. The most successful part of Instagram has been the overwhelming enthusiasm the audience has for seeing previously unseen collections. Some of these collections include prehistoric artifacts from Delaware Water Gap National Recreation Area; historic ceramics, glass, and other objects from Hampton National Historic Site in Towson, Maryland; and artifacts excavated from the Schuyler House at Saratoga National Battlefield. By adding Instagram to an already successful social media presence, NMSC diversified our audience and increased our reach and ability to bring hidden collections into the public eye.

A major difference between Facebook and Instagram is the amount of text we can use to describe a photo or video. On the NMSC Facebook page, staff are able to explain artifacts and objects in a larger context. On Instagram, staff does their best to limit the text and focus on providing the followers with a photo that will capture their attention. Although it can be a challenge to keep captions concise, during audits of NMSC's Instagram account, it became clear that our audience is looking for a high-quality photo with some explanation and will ask questions if they want more information. Though users can employ hashtags on Facebook, they do not connect photos and stories as well as Instagram does. Along with selecting a photo and writing a short explanatory caption, NMSC staff also research trending hashtags and develop hashtags that will amuse or connect their audiences. Common hashtags have included #funartifactfriday, #artifactoftheday, #triviatuesday, and #museummonday.

The audit of Instagram made clear that photo quality is the single most important indicator of a successful post. Luckily NMSC benefits from the generous efforts and advice of its volunteer professional photographer, Norm Eggert. Clear, well-composed photos of artifacts with proper lighting and background are absolutely necessary to get someone interested enough to take a closer look or to read the caption. In addition to artifact photos, NMSC has found that outdoor scenery, again photographed and edited with at least a semiprofessional eye, gets more "likes" and comments. After some trial and error, NMSC has found that photos of people do not perform very well, likely due to the fact that they are not as attention-grabbing as other photos in the Instagram timeline. This is not to say that all photos of people should be excluded from Instagram. NMSC has found that high-quality professional photos of people, especially with a fun prop or expression, such as in the "Meet NMSC" campaign, are successful. Additionally, well-composed "selfies" are also popular. Though the audience does not connect to lower quality photos of people, professional photos and "selfies" that humanize staff are successful.

The addition of Instagram has generated more work for NMSC staff, but the account has gained over 800 followers in a one-year time period. Many of these followers include youth, our original target audience, and National Park sites throughout the country, an additional audience that, although unexpected, has been the most interactive. These connections between NMSC and other National Park sites have been particularly beneficial since many of the sites are outside of the Northeast Region and are not parks with whom we normally work. Another benefit of connection to other National Park sites through Instagram is that many of the pages are run by interpretation staff with whom NMSC does not usually get to interact but who are very interested in the material culture and other information shared on the NMSC Instagram page.

One of NMSC's most popular campaigns on Instagram involves asking the public to help identify an object. As NMSC archaeologists are processing backlog collections, sometimes there are "mystery objects" or objects of interest that the audience may have never seen before. When we find these artifacts, they are saved for "What is it?" Instagram posts. These posts often generate 30 to 50 "likes" per photo, as well as numerous comments and guesses. For instance, on 10 June 2016 NMSC posted a photo of a copper projectile point rediscovered in a collection from Delaware Water Gap National Recreation Area. While sorting the collection, NMSC came across a report that included a photo of a copper projectile point but noted its status as "missing." NMSC staff had read about metal projectile points but had never seen one in person, and we were heartbroken that such a unique and interesting artifact had gone missing. After some intense searching, the copper point was found in a mislabeled bag. A photo of the point was posted on Facebook and Instagram, and our audience joined us in celebrating the rediscovery of this important artifact. When the NMSC archaeology curator called to share the good news, the park's museum technician replied, "Oh, I already saw it on Instagram!" (Lori Rohrer 2016, pers. comm.) That is certainly what we consider a measurable result.

Using Instagram in addition to Facebook and our blog has increased NMSC's overall number of followers and has greatly diversified the audience. Being on the lookout for possible photo opportunities has also changed our way of looking at artifacts and landscapes and has taught staff to focus on quality over quantity. Social media has proved to be an excellent way to get artifacts out of their boxes and into public view.

The Future of Collections-Based Public Archaeology in the National Parks

Archaeological collections provide opportunities to connect with visitors on a personal level and invite new discussions. As mentioned earlier, children often speak their minds, and such candid comments are critical to having difficult but necessary discussions. These conversations bring us to a new awareness and hopefully to actions that have the potential to shape the future of archaeology as a profession. One of the most truthful and appreciated comments that has been presented to NMSC archaeologists was "Archaeology is a white person's job." That comment resulted in several in-depth discussions that have left a long-standing impression and a new life for an old collection.

During the summer of 2016 NSMC took the initiative to work on a project for two National Park Service partners: the Museum of African American History in Boston and the Boston City Archaeology Program. The Museum of African American History owns the African Meeting House, which was built in 1806 in what was once the cultural center of Boston's black community. Adjacent to the Meeting House is the Abiel Smith School, which was built in 1834 as the first school to educate black students. The Abiel Smith School and African Meeting House make up the Boston African American National Historical Site, which is administered by the National Park Service. The Smith School backlot and associated privy were excavated by the National Park Service Regional Archaeology Program in 1991, 1996, and 1997 (Mead and Pendleton 1998). These excavations yielded many artifacts tied to the building's time as a school for African American children and later as an integrated school and community center in the still largely African American community on Beacon Hill in Boston. Though some reports have been written about the site and artifacts, only minimal research has been done to truly understand the material culture within its larger context of place and time. NMSC is working as part of the Cultural Resources Civil Rights Initiative to catalog, rehouse, and research this site and its associated artifacts. This old collection is ideal as a training opportunity in archaeology collections management but is also perfect for demonstrating to minority students that archaeology can be local and relevant to issues still facing their own lives, such as inequitable education.

During public archaeology presentations, middle and high school students observed that there was not a diverse representation of archaeologists. NMSC took note and sought out Dania Jordan, an archaeology student at the University of Massachusetts, Boston, to work with them on the Abiel Smith School project. As a female African American archaeologist, Jordan has a unique voice and can provide much-needed perspective to the interpretation of the archaeological assemblage. She keenly observed that despite the story of African Americans at the school and what their lives were like in the early 19th century, the neighborhood of Beacon Hill is now a predominantly white neighborhood that is very expensive and out of reach of the majority of Boston residents (Dania Jordan 2016, pers. comm.). Though the ranger-led tour through the neighborhood points out many sites related to African Americans and abolitionism, it is hard to truly picture the neighborhood as it was since it has changed so dramatically. Jordan went on to say, "If I'm going to tell the story [of African Americans in the Beacon Hill neighborhood] I'm going to tell the whole story of the community and how they resisted racism." The National Park Service is responsible for engaging minority groups as part of its audience, especially since many of these minorities may have unique personal perspectives on historic sites and artifacts.

Archaeologists in the 1990s linked beads and cowry shells to African American site use (Mead and Pendleton 1998); NMSC and its interns are working to use a more intersectional lens to think about all of the artifacts in a larger context of resistance and empowerment. Women and children (of all races) remain largely missing from the documentary record at this time, and yet the artifacts provide clues about what life was like during the school day. Inkwells, slate pencils, and writing slates are testament to the actual learning that took place in the school. Other objects show us an even more personal and human side to the interactions and activities of the school day. Teachers may have supplied products for personal hygiene, such as combs for removing lice, bone toothbrushes for dental care, and medicines to treat common ailments so children could remain in class even while they were feeling unwell. The children who attended the school gain a voice through the personal objects they brought to school and sadly lost to the privy, such as toys, paste gems, and beads. These artifacts show us that even though life in segregated Boston was far from fair, it was not all work and no play. While the blue beads and cowry shells do speak to the African diaspora, the other household items acquired at local shops are just as revealing in telling the story of the lives of African Americans in 19th-century Beacon Hill.

As we continue to develop ideas for programming and the future of public outreach at NMSC, our goals are to further expand the audience and reach out to the local community as much as possible. With an eye to where the fields of public archaeology and museum studies are headed, NMSC is working toward putting the artifacts from Boston African American National Historic Site's Smith School in both historical and modern-day context, touching upon issues like career opportunities for minority youth. The Smith School collection facilitates discussions about school segregation in Boston, civil rights, and why nearly 200 years after the Abiel Smith School was built a student may still consider archaeology to be a career path available only to white people. It is important that the NPS continue to hire an increasingly diverse work force. Doing so demonstrates that we are listening and responding to the keen observations of our audience and enables us to recognize the ways that race, class, and gender influence archeological interpretation.

Conclusion

The National Park Service has made great strides in the past few decades in documenting, cataloging, and preserving its archaeology collections. Continuing and building on these efforts requires public interest and investment. It is time to "think outside the Hollinger box" and get these collections out into public view where people can engage with them, learn from them, appreciate them, and offer new interpretations about the sites at which they were deposited. The Northeast Museum Services Center's ongoing work with scratch-blue creamware is just one example of 21st-century archaeologists using innovative technology and original research to challenge existing theories about North American historical archaeology and material culture. Increasing visibility and access to existing archaeology collections will encourage more of this type of research and, as in the case of the Abiel Smith School collection, will also facilitate important discussions of social justice issues like inequitable education. To help reach its goal of increasing access to and promoting research on National Park Service archaeology collections, the Northeast Museum Services Center has developed a successful outreach and education program that includes working with staff at National Parks and fostering public interest and engagement through lectures, presentations, and various social media platforms. NMSC's efforts can serve as an example to other institutions who lack formal exhibit space and who work with limited funding and staff. The renowned historical archaeologist James Deetz (1977:259) wrote, "We must use them [artifacts] in new and imaginative ways so that a different appreciation for what life is today, and was in the past, can be achieved. The written document has its proper and important place, but there is also a time when we should set aside our perusal of diaries, court records, and inventories and listen to another voice." For National Park Service archaeology collections, that time has come. By opening the old boxes and starting new conversations, NPS archaeologists can facilitate important, innovative research that will tell the stories of *all* Americans.

Disclaimer: The views and conclusions contained in this article are those of the authors and should not be interpreted as representing the opinions or policies of the U.S. government. Mention of trade names or commercial products does not constitute their endorsement by the U.S. government.

References

Costello, Jessica

2012   Scratch-Blue at Petersburg: Redefining Creamware on American Archeological Sites. NMSC Archaeology & Museum Blog. 28 June. https://nmscarcheologylab

.wordpress.com/2012/06/28/scratch-blue-at-petersburg-redefining-creamware
-on-american-archeological-sites/.

2015   Scratch-Blue at Petersburg, Part 2: The Scottish Connection. NMSC Archae-
        ology & Museum Blog. 9 January. https://nmscarcheologylab.wordpress.com
        /2016/01/09/scratch-blue-at-petersburg-part-2-the-scottish-connection/.

2016a   The History of Fort Stanwix in 10 Objects. NMSC Archaeology & Museum
        Blog. 27 May. https://nmscarcheologylab.wordpress.com/2016/05/27/the
        -history-of-fort-stanwix-in-10-objects/.

2016b   Little House in the Archaeology Lab: How Laura Ingalls Wilder Made Me
        a Historical Archaeologist. NMSC Archaeology & Museum Blog. 5 Feb-
        ruary. https://nmscarcheologylab.wordpress.com/2016/02/05/little-house
        -in-the-archeology-lab-how-laura-ingalls-wilder-made-me-a-historical
        -archeologist/.

2016c   Scratching the Surface: New Discoveries within Old Archaeological Col-
        lections. Paper presented at the 49th annual meeting of the Society for His-
        torical Archaeology, Washington DC.

Deetz, James

1977   In Small Things Forgotten: An Archaeology of Early American Life. Anchor/
        Doubleday. New York.

Lagorio-Chafkin, Christine

2012   30 under 30: Kevin Systrom and Mike Krieger, Founders of Instagram. Inc.
        9 April. https://www.inc.com/30under30/2011/profile-kevin-systrom-mike
        -krieger-founders-instagram.html. Accessed April 2017.

Lang, Nico

2015   Why Teens Are Leaving Facebook: It's "Meaningless." Washington Post. 21
        February. https://www.washingtonpost.com/news/the-intersect/wp/2015/02/21
        /why-teens-are-leaving-facebook-its-meaningless/?utm_term=.233d3a97a70d.

McCann, Jennifer

2016   A Horrible Quantity of Stuff: The Untapped Potential of Northeast Region
        NPS Collections. Paper presented at the 49th annual meeting of the Soci-
        ety for Historical Archaeology Conference, Washington DC.

Mead, Leslie A., and Nancy Pendleton

1998   "The Old School Houses Which Have Been Abandoned Were Palaces in
        Comparison with This": The Abiel Smith School House in the Second Half
        of the 19th Century. Paper presented at the 31st annual meeting of the Soci-
        ety for Historical Archaeology. Atlanta GA.

Paresi, Alicia

2016   Thinking outside the Hollinger Box: Bringing Northeast Region Archaeo-
        logical Collections to the Public. Paper presented at the 49th annual meet-
        ing of the Society for Historical Archaeology, Washington DC.

Rome Sentinel

2016   Fort Stanwix Honored Online. *Rome Sentinel,* 28 May. http://romesen
-tinel.com/rome/fort-stanwix-honored-online/QBqpeA!EfH2WDMNSN4
-ytW4FF0VNfA/. Rome NY.

Valosin, Christine

2016   The Saratoga Battles in Fifty Artifacts. In *The Saratoga Campaign: Uncovering an Embattled Landscape,* William Griswold and Donald W. Linebaugh, editors. University Press of New England. Lebanon NH.

Walsh, Nicole

2012   Are You Sure That's Not White Salt-Glazed Stoneware? NMSC Archaeology & Museum Blog. 14 June. https://nmscarcheologylab.wordpress.com/2012/06/14/are-you-sure-thats-not-white-salt-glazed-stoneware/.

Zenzen, Joan M.

2008   *Fort Stanwix National Monument: Reconstructing the Past and Partnering for the Future.* State University of New York Press. Albany.

FIFTEEN

Artifacts of Outlander

Using Popular Culture to Promote Maryland's Archaeological Collections

SARA RIVERS COFIELD AND CAITLIN SHAFFER

The Maryland Archaeological Conservation Laboratory (MAC Lab) at Jefferson Patterson Park and Museum (JPPM) is the repository of Maryland's State Historic Preservation Office, the Maryland Historical Trust. Collections recovered throughout the state are curated at the MAC Lab, where holdings include an estimated 8.5 million objects from more than 6,000 sites. One of the primary missions of the MAC Lab is to make these collections accessible for research, exhibit, and education (Morehouse, this volume), so finding new ways to raise awareness of the collections and attract users is always a priority. Niche audiences such as archaeological researchers and school groups regularly access artifacts at the MAC Lab, but attracting the interest of the general public is more of a challenge. While the MAC Lab holds collections in the public trust and for the public benefit, it is designed as a research, curation, and conservation facility, not a facility that the general public can simply wander into and explore without a scheduled guided tour. As a result, staff are always looking for alternative ways to get the word out about collections through the JPPM website (www.jefpat.org), loans, and other forms of outreach.

In the early spring of 2015, one of the MAC Lab's conservators, Caitlin Shaffer, had the brilliant idea of making an exhibit that uses the popular novel and television series *Outlander* to promote and interpret Maryland's collections. This chapter is about how that idea became the most successful outreach program for the general public that the MAC Lab and JPPM have ever undertaken. What started as a plan to fill one case in the local library for two months turned into an ongoing multiyear project to keep up with the public's interest in the resulting exhibit, titled *Artifacts of Outlander.*

The Allure of *Outlander*

The *Outlander* book series by Diana Gabaldon (1991, 1992, 1994, 1997, 2001, 2005, 2009, 2014) is difficult to define, as it crosses all kinds of genres; it has romance, war, time travel, and royal intrigue. The series opens in the 1940s with a focus on a young couple, Claire and Frank Randall, who are taking an extended visit to Scotland. The couple had married just before the outbreak of World War II, but when war broke out, they lived apart so that Claire could serve as a nurse in France while Frank served as a British intelligence officer. In an attempt to rekindle their marriage after years of forced separation, they travel to Scotland, where Frank pursues his hobbies in history and genealogy and Claire spends her time studying botany and visiting tourist attractions, such as a circle of standing stones known as Craigh Na Dun.

While in pursuit of a particular floral specimen at Craigh Na Dun, Claire accidentally discovers that the circle of stones represents a sort of rift in time, and she falls through the stones to find herself in 1740s Scotland. The locals there find her quite suspicious since she shows up alone in the woods wearing a dress that looks like a woman's shift (18th-century underwear), but she speaks with the accent and vocabulary of the English gentility. She is suspected of being a spy. Thanks to her lack of identity and credibility, Claire finds herself caught up in political conflicts between the local Scots and the occupying English forces, and for her own protection she is forced into marriage with a young Scottish outlaw named Jamie Fraser. While initially Claire is torn between attempting to get back to her first husband and trying to survive in the 18th century, as she adjusts to her new circumstances, it becomes clear that the real love story of the *Outlander* series is between Claire and Jamie rather than the husband Claire left behind in the 1940s.

Now consisting of eight (and counting) very lengthy novels, the *Outlander* saga spans decades, following the characters through war, more accidental and intentional time travel, generations of family, new continents, and all of the family's big and small dramas. The books have an incredibly devoted fan base, and Starz network wisely picked up the story to make into a television series, the first season of which debuted in August 2014. It was this adaptation of books to television that inspired the MAC Lab to use *Outlander* as the inspiration for an exhibit.

The Exhibit Idea

Anyone who works in archaeology knows that many parts of the job are slow, repetitive, and mindless. Cleaning, labeling, counting, data entry, and other repetitive tasks that commonly take place in a curation and conservation facility such as the MAC Lab do not always require the full and complete attention of the human brain. Staff often rely on podcasts and audiobooks to keep up motivation when the work itself is not engaging the imagination. Over the past few years, several members of the MAC Lab staff have been immersed in the novel *Outlander* and its sequels, leading to impromptu book-club-like conversations at tea breaks and lunch time. (Unless otherwise specified, all references to *Outlander* refer to both the book and the television series.) Among other things, these conversations delved into how well the historical accuracy of the series holds up, at least where material culture is concerned. The MAC Lab's curators and conservators spend their days surrounded by the actual objects of everyday life from centuries past, making it difficult to tolerate blatant anachronisms in historical fiction, but these seem to be minimal in the *Outlander* novels. On the contrary, listening to the *Outlander* books while working with 18th-century artifacts is an immersive experience, where the fictional story helps put the objects in the context of people's daily lives and dramas.

The attention to detail with regard to material culture is also evident in the Starz television series. While the show is clearly not a 100% accurate depiction of 18th-century life, most of the props and costumes do reflect the period well, and there are clear parallels between the objects depicted in the show and the real artifacts that are recovered from Maryland's colonial sites and curated at the MAC Lab. Although *Outlander* is set in 1740s Scotland, both Scotland and Maryland were under English political and economic control at the time, and both represented markets for similar English trade goods.

Shaffer was the first to recognize that using these collections to create an *Outlander*-themed exhibit not only would be incredibly fun for the *Outlander* fans on staff, but it also represented an opportunity to ride on the coattails of *Outlander*'s popularity to showcase Maryland's colonial archaeological collections. Shaffer took the idea to the federal curator, Sara Rivers Cofield, whose combined knowledge of the MAC Lab's 18th-century collections and the *Outlander* book and television series would be necessary to create such an exhibit, and the MAC Lab's director, Patricia Samford, another *Outlander* fan. All agreed that this was an idea worth pursuing even though exhibit design and fabrication is not typically something the MAC Lab takes on.

While JPPM has exhibit fabrication equipment, such as large-scale printers and a wood shop, the staff position devoted to exhibit fabrication has been vacant since 2013. The JPPM maintenance chief, Jim House, has ensured that the shop remains functional and able to keep up with park signage, but there is no full-time exhibit support. At the MAC Lab, conservators are focused on treating objects to ensure their long-term survival, while the curators oversee collections management, providing collections access to visiting researchers and promoting the collections through various web-based research tools. In short, the *Outlander* exhibit would constitute a special project that would take some time away from other staff duties, but the idea was not entirely without precedent.

In recent years Samford has worked with JPPM's Education Department to develop a relationship with the local library, Calvert Library in Prince Frederick, Maryland, to periodically use the built-in showcases there as a venue to feature small exhibits on the MAC Lab's collections that are designed by the local high school's Archaeology

Club (Samford and Green, this volume). This relationship became a model for pursuing the *Outlander*-themed exhibit. Samford called the library to gauge their interest, which was more than enthusiastic, so she booked the library case for May–June 2015 and gave Shaffer and Rivers Cofield the green light. As originally envisioned, the exhibit would be designed and fabricated in about a month, and it would enjoy a two-month show at the Calvert Library.

Artifacts of Outlander: First Generation

Shaffer and Rivers Cofield started work on the exhibit by selecting themes and images from the show that would best complement the MAC Lab's collections. This was perhaps the most exciting part of the process from a curatorial perspective. Having *Outlander* as the theme—as opposed to a particular site or region—allowed the exhibit team to choose from any collection that fit the time period, making it possible to include exemplary artifacts from throughout the state.

The artifacts had to be matched with thematic images from the television show. While excellent examples of stills from the series are widely available from fan sites on the internet, the exhibit required crisp, high-resolution photos. Additionally, JPPM wanted to be sure that there would be no issues with copyright infringement, which meant going the official route and getting permission from Starz. As the first season had just started to air, Starz was actively promoting the show and working to connect with fans. The network promptly responded to the request. Given that JPPM and the MAC Lab were strictly engaging in noncommercial, not-for-profit educational outreach, Starz gave the project their blessing and offered a password to access their online press kit so that high-resolution images were available.

By the end of April 2015, Rivers Cofield and Shaffer, with fabrication support from Jim House, completed the exhibit, titled *Artifacts of Outlander*, which comprises seven thematic panels:

- **Bonny Wee Baubles** depicts the main character, Claire Fraser, in her wedding dress and showcases artifacts of personal adornment such as shoe parts, silver threads, earring fragments, and sleeve links (Figure 25, *top left*).

- **Buttons, Buckles, and Blades** shows Jamie Fraser in a coat, waistcoat, and kilt, along with artifacts that reflect 18th-century examples of the blade weapons, buttons, buckles, and personal items he might have carried in his sporran (Figure 25, *top right*).

- **Sassenach Soldiers** shows a shaving scene from a British Army garrison. Artifacts were chosen either because similar items appear in the scene (e.g., window leads, a candlestick, a pitcher and basin) or because they might depict some aspect of daily life for soldiers in the 18th century (e.g., dice, tobacco, wig curlers, and gold-thread buttons).

- **Going Armed** combines images of *Outlander* characters from the television series wielding flintlock weapons with fragments of firearms such as gun barrels, ammunition, gunflints, and flintlock fragments (Figure 25, *bottom*).

- **Jamie's Mount** shows Jamie Fraser on horseback next to elements of horse furniture from the MAC Lab's collections, such as stirrups, a bridle bit, a saddle pommel, buckles, and leather ornaments.

- **Claire's Surgery** features a scene where Claire Fraser is processing herbs as a healer, along with artifacts such as a pestle, apothecary weights, glass vials, assorted dishes, and seeds.

- **Slàinte!** depicts a feasting scene from the show, complemented by artifacts from the table such as dishes, utensils, stemware, and a wine bottle.

A title banner ties these panels together, along with an introductory sign about the exhibit and a backdrop depicting a Scottish landscape. Additionally, the exhibit team decided to make a companion catalog offering details about the artifacts such as site name and number information, as well as brief archaeological site summaries so that visitors could read more about archaeological sites that might be in their area. In total, the exhibit features about 200 artifacts from 30 different archaeological sites. Creating a separate catalog allowed the team to highlight the different collections rep-

FIGURE 25. Examples of panels featured in the *Artifacts of Outlander* exhibit.
(Graphics and photos: Sara Rivers Cofield and Caitlin Shaffer)

resented while keeping the panel labels brief and aesthetically unob-
trusive. Finally, thanks to exhibit team member House, a full-size
cut-out of Jamie Fraser accompanies the exhibit, which has proven
to be a crucial element for drawing fans and engaging visitors.

Expanding the Vision to Meet Demand

Even before the display was completed for the Prince Frederick library
venue, the exhibit team started to think about how to get more expo-

sure. Organizers of JPPM's annual lecture series asked Rivers Cofield to give a talk at the Calvert Library to go with the opening of the exhibit. An additional opportunity that seemed worth pursuing was to complete the panels about a week before they were due to appear in the library in May 2015. The Southern Maryland Celtic Festival is held annually at JPPM and was scheduled for April 25. Knowing that the Celtic Festival draws thousands of visitors each year, and suspecting that the attendees would include *Outlander* fans, the exhibit team decided to debut *Artifacts of Outlander* in the JPPM Visitor's Center during the event. In order to do so the team adapted some old exhibit cases and stands to hold the new artifact panels. The setup used for this effort did not fully enclose the panels, however, leaving fragile artifacts exposed to the public's touch. Staff supervision was needed. This proved to be a benefit because it ensured that staff were present to observe the public response to the temporary display, which informed future efforts.

Thanks to some strategic signage and unseasonably cold, damp weather, over 200 people ventured away from the Southern Maryland Celtic Festival's popular outdoor activities to see the *Artifacts of Outlander* exhibit on its opening day in the JPPM Visitor's Center (Figure 26, *top left*). Many stayed to see JPPM's permanent exhibit, *FAQ Archaeology*, as well. The enthusiasm for the new exhibit was palpable. The life-size Jamie Fraser cut-out was especially popular and in great demand for selfie photographs among the festival attendees, some of whom were delighted to show off their own kilts and *Outlander*-themed T-shirts. Rivers Cofield manned the exhibit, helping with "Flat Jamie" photography, answering questions, making sure the artifacts did not suffer any harmful handling, and promoting the upcoming display and companion lecture at the Calvert Library. The Celtic Festival debut provided the exhibit team with some experience in adapting the exhibit into something that could stand alone—experience that would prove useful as the popularity of the exhibit spread.

In May 2015, as planned, the exhibit team installed *Artifacts of Outlander* at the Calvert Library, where visitors were so interested in

FIGURE 26. The *Artifacts of Outlander* exhibit at four different venues: *top left*, the exhibit's Southern Maryland Celtic Festival debut in the JPPM Visitor's Center; *top right*, the Prince Frederick, Maryland, branch of the Calvert Library; *bottom left*, Historic London Town and Gardens; *bottom right*, the C. Burr Artz Public Library in Frederick. (Photos: Sara Rivers Cofield and Caitlin Shaffer)

the new exhibit that they slowed the installation process with their questions (Figure 26, *top right*). Over the next two months the librarians reported that some visitors spent up to 30 minutes in front of the exhibit case. Since Flat Jamie selfies were popular, library staff put up a sign asking folks to post their Jamie selfies on social media with the hashtag #libraryJamie.

The exhibit was already considered a success, having connected with the library's visitors and raised awareness of JPPM and the MAC Lab's collections, but on the day of the 7 May JPPM Lecture Series talk at the Prince Frederick library, *Outlander* fans' enthusiasm forced JPPM and the MAC Lab to rethink the original small-scale, short-term plan for the exhibit. The presentation by Rivers Cofield, originally titled "Outfitting *Outlander*: So Much More Than Kilts Ya Ken!," discussed the making of the exhibit, highlighted artifacts from the collections, celebrated the material culture that the show gets right with regard to accuracy, and covered some of the historical inaccuracies in the show, particularly with regard to costumes. Before giving the talk Rivers Cofield went to eat at a nearby restaurant where she was approached by *Outlander* fans who recognized her from the flyer, announced excitedly that they were looking forward to the lecture, and then pointed out that they had worn their *Outlander*-themed jewelry for the occasion. This was the first big indication that the *Artifacts of Outlander* effort had tapped into a fan base that would prove to be much more enthusiastic than the audiences that JPPM and the MAC Lab were used to expecting for their programs.

The lecture itself had about 60 attendees, including many devoted *Outlander* fans, and in the traditional question-and-answer session following the talk, one audience member raised her hand to announce that she had Tweeted about the exhibit to the author of the books, Diana Gabaldon, the producer of the show, Ron Moore, and the show's costume designer, Terry Dresbach. In fact Dresbach had already Tweeted back wanting to know more. The helpful lecture attendee then took a picture of Rivers Cofield's business card, Tweeted it to Dresbach, and the following day Dresbach emailed a request to write about the exhibit on her blog.

At that point it became necessary for the exhibit team to meet with other JPPM staff to form a response and engage with the *Outlander* fan base through social media. Having rushed to complete the exhibit in time for the Celtic Festival, adapted the panels for two different venues with a quick turn-around time, and developed a 60-minute talk to accompany the exhibit within a week of its opening, all of the exhibit team's time had gone into meeting deadlines and coming up with finished products. No time whatsoever had been devoted to preparing for the consequences of having an overwhelmingly positive response to the effort. Frankly, it had not occurred to anyone that a small archaeology exhibit for a local library would get so much buzz, and when it did, it became clear that the exhibit team's work had just begun.

JPPM had no presence on Twitter, nor did anyone involved in organizing the exhibit or the lecture series, meaning that no one on JPPM's staff knew how to follow or take part in the conversation about the exhibit that was happening between fans and the creators of the book and television series. Furthermore, there was nothing clean and polished that JPPM could immediately send to Dresbach to write about on her blog. Addressing these issues became the immediate priority.

The exhibit team and JPPM administrative staff quickly formulated a plan. Rivers Cofield wrote up some information to create a new page for the JPPM website, which at that point had no mention of the *Artifacts of Outlander* effort. She then worked to combine all of the elements of the exhibit catalog—a bound and laminated book combining several separate files with artifact details and site summaries—into one integrated PDF that could be distributed and linked to the JPPM website. At the same time, Shaffer concentrated on using Adobe Photoshop to populate each exhibit panel image with its requisite artifacts, so that clean images of each artifact panel could be sent in digital form.

By the end of the week following the lecture, Rivers Cofield sent Dresbach a link to these finished products: the new web link, the exhibit catalog, and images of each artifact panel. By then Dresbach's blog was on hold as she worked on costumes for Season 2 of the series, and Dresbach never responded. This was perhaps a mixed blessing, since the exhibit as originally envisioned was intended to be a local short-term effort rather than something that would be presented to an international audience. While JPPM wanted to capitalize on the popularity of the exhibit, this had to be done in ways that would be manageable given the limited staff time and resources available for exhibit projects.

After the successful launch at Calvert Library, the exhibit team consulted with other JPPM staff and decided to keep the momentum going in two ways. When additional local libraries requested the exhibit, JPPM agreed to keep it traveling if the requesting library had a secure, enclosed case, but adapting the panels to existing cases at different library branches proved to be inefficient and time-consuming. The Maryland Historical Trust's Board of Trustees (MHT Board) awarded JPPM funding in order to create traveling Plexiglas cases to enclose the artifact panels. This allowed *Artifacts of Outlander* to travel as a stand-alone exhibit using the same recycled exhibit cases and stands that had been used for the debut at the Celtic Festival (Figure 26, *bottom right and left*). A comment book was also added at this time, since the only feedback gathered so far had been anecdotal. The result of this conversion was a much more versatile and compact traveling exhibit that can be arranged as an island or along a wall, making it suitable for many different kinds of venues.

The second plan adopted to capitalize on the popularity of *Artifacts of Outlander* was to develop an online version of the exhibit. While JPPM has created a lot of web content for archaeologists, such as the websites *Diagnostic Artifacts in Maryland* and *Maryland Archeobotany* and the collections finding aid *Archaeological Collections in Maryland*, these represent research tools that draw from the collections and expertise of MAC Lab staff. An online *exhibit* aimed primarily at nonarchaeologists is a different kind of project, representing a challenge and learning curve for JPPM staff. Rivers Cofield spent about a year adapting the original exhibit panels to a web-friendly format, writing content to flesh out the stories behind each artifact, and making graphics to illustrate how artifacts were used or what they looked like when they were new (Rivers Cofield et al. 2016). The MAC Lab's administrative assistant and JPPM webmaster Sharon Raftery converted the resulting content to HTML, and *Artifacts of Outlander* launched online in December 2016, getting over 20,000 page views from 56 countries in its first week.

Both the traveling exhibit and online exhibit remain active at the time of this writing, a full 43 months after the initial opening, getting the artifacts out to additional libraries and venues beyond Calvert County, and reaching audiences internationally through the website. The *Artifacts of Outlander* project has expanded from the initial investment in a two-month display into an ongoing multiyear effort with no end in sight, and the expanded vision for the exhibit has had significant consequences for both JPPM's budget and community outreach.

Financial Considerations

JPPM maintains a modest budget for the production and upkeep of exhibits and signs, and the initial costs for exhibit supplies came out of this budget. As the exhibit shop at JPPM has fabrication equipment, the initial costs for extra paper, foam board, printer ink, and adhesives were relatively low. Those costs rose as the exhibit was adapted for different venues, and outside funding from the MHT Board was necessary to adapt the exhibit to stand alone, even though all of the cases and stands used were recycled from old exhibits. The initial investment in creating the exhibit, and the injection of funds for cases to keep it traveling, had the intended consequence of raising visibility, but ultimately these costs proved minimal compared to the continued need for staff time and travel to keep the exhibit going.

The flexibility afforded by the new exhibit configuration means that more venues qualify to host, and bookings continue. Consequently, the costs for setup and travel add up with each new destination scheduled. In its first year the exhibit went to six venues, representing 930 roundtrip miles traveled. On top of travel costs, at least two staff members must be present for each delivery and takedown. While the exhibit generates excellent exposure for JPPM and the MAC Lab, the costs for such a prolonged effort have a significant impact on the overall JPPM budget.

Given the permission agreement with Starz, JPPM has to stick with its original educational mission and avoid charging fees for the exhibit. All of the hosting institutions either have no admission charges or place the exhibit in an area that visitors can access without paying admission fees. JPPM also rejects any requests to raffle off the "Flat Jamie" that travels with the exhibit, since this would exploit a Starz image for financial gain. This strict adherence to the noncommercial, nonprofit use of images from the *Outlander* television series is paramount, and it prevents JPPM from making any money on the exhibit.

After moving the exhibit to different venues free of charge for a year, the JPPM administration had to consider whether to try to recoup some of the costs or stop offering the exhibit to new hosting institutions. JPPM made the difficult decision to require reimbursement from hosting institutions for delivery and take-down, even if that meant reducing the number of audiences reached. In 2016 the momentum slowed, and the exhibit spent most of the year in the JPPM Visitor's Center. This was the inevitable result of requiring reimbursement for delivery, as potential venues need time to plan ahead for funding. The costs did not quash all interest, however, and as of December 2018, the exhibit was still traveling. Each destination pays customized travel and setup costs based on the distance of the venue from JPPM.

Collections and Community Outreach

The *Artifacts of Outlander* may have started as a "just for fun" idea on the part of the MAC Lab's *Outlander* fans who wanted to feature collections in an archaeology/pop-culture mash-up, but the community engagement sparked by this effort is proving to be seriously valuable for JPPM and the MAC Lab. In its first year the exhibit traveled to four local library branches, the visitor's center at Historic London Town and Gardens, the headquarters of the Maryland Historical Trust in Crownsville, Maryland, and two events: the Southern Maryland Celtic Festival at JPPM and the 2015 Council for Northeast Historical Archaeology Conference in Fredericksburg, Virginia. Total visitor figures from the months *Artifacts of Outlander* spent at these libraries and venues indicate that the exhibit was available to an audience of over 100,000 people—far surpassing visitation at the MAC Lab, which totaled about 1,000 people in 2015–2016, and the JPPM Visitor's Center, with just over 7,500 visitors in 2015–2016. Bookings for 2017–2018 included three libraries and five small museums in different regions, further increasing exposure to new audiences (Map 6).

MARYLAND

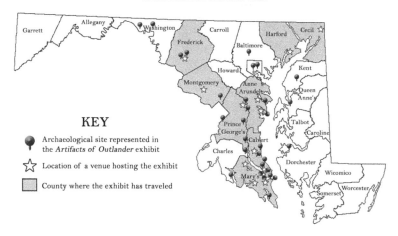

KEY

🔴 Archaeological site represented in
the *Artifacts of Outlander* exhibit

☆ Location of a venue hosting the exhibit

▢ County where the exhibit has traveled

MAP 6. The approximate locations of archaeological sites with collections represented in the *Artifacts of Outlander* exhibit, the approximate locations of host sites for the exhibit, and the counties represented by these host sites. (Graphic: Sara Rivers Cofield)

The "Outfitting *Outlander*" lecture continues to be popular as well, reaching about 270 people either as an accompaniment to the exhibit as it travels or as a stand-alone talk connecting Maryland's artifacts to the popular show. At each lecture Rivers Cofield sets up a table featuring artifacts from the MAC Lab's collections so that individuals can get a closer look at the kinds of 18th-century objects featured in the exhibit. The postlecture artifact table has proved to be an ideal opportunity for one-on-one interaction between Rivers Cofield and interested audience members. With each lecture visitors learn more about 18th-century material culture and costume, and Rivers Cofield is educated about the fan base for the exhibit and the network they use to get the word out about *Outlander*-themed events.

Devoted fans have posted about their visits to the exhibit and lectures on social media like Twitter and Facebook, which act as discussion boards when the series is on and serve as a platform to schedule fan activities during the periods between seasons, known to fans as "Droughtlander." The JPPM exhibit team continues to learn how to reach new interested audiences through social media such as the various *Outlander* fan Facebook pages, and these serve as a platform to make announcements such as destinations for the traveling exhibit and the launch of the online exhibit.

As a result of the connections made on social media and word-of-mouth publicity, requests for the exhibit and lecture have continued without any organized advertising efforts on JPPM's part. Reliance on word-of-mouth publicity has been a practical way to keep the exhibit traveling without overbooking and completely overwhelming the museum's resources. When the exhibit is not fully booked, there is time for maintenance and repairs or for having the display at home base in the JPPM Visitor's Center.

When the exhibit is out traveling, it fulfills one of the primary missions of the MAC Lab at JPPM: to ensure that the Maryland collections held in the public trust are accessible. While the MAC Lab provides collections access to visiting researchers and public tour groups, it is in a relatively isolated location. Sending artifacts back out to the regions where they were originally excavated through loans and exhibits has been an ongoing priority since the MAC Lab opened in 1998 (Morehouse, this volume). Whether viewed by Maryland's *Outlander* fans or walk-in library patrons, the exhibit exposes new audiences to a diverse assemblage of artifacts, including finds from the very regions that have hosted the exhibit (Map 6).

Audiences Reached

In terms of audience, the goal was simply to reach members of the public who might not otherwise have ever heard of JPPM or the MAC Lab or who were not familiar with Maryland's archaeological resources. While JPPM has not conducted any formal visitor studies or surveys to measure the demographics reached, in practice it seems that the members of JPPM's staff who were fans of *Outlander* at the beginning of the project, namely five women between the ages of 30 and 60, proved to be a predictor of the most enthusiastic demographic attracted to the exhibit and lecture. Observation of the *Outlander* fan groups on social media and enthusiastic attendees at the Southern Maryland Celtic Festival and "Outfitting *Out-lander*" lectures suggest that the fan base skews heavily toward white women ages 30 and up. Although the series includes representations of 18th-century soldiering and warfare during the Jacobite rebellion, a period that has not been neglected by male-dominated reenacting groups, and the exhibit includes panels on firearms, male dress, blade weapons, and soldiers, it is still primarily women who go out of their way to see the exhibit, attend lectures, and share comments on social media. Coincidentally this demographic seems to include a lot of librarians who control programming at local public libraries, which has helped keep up demand for the exhibit.

This seems to have little to do with the artifacts or themes presented in the exhibit and much to do with *Outlander*'s Jamie Fraser/Sam Heughan factor, whereby the strong, kilted, romantic warrior of the novels (Fraser), is played on television by a fit, young, attractive actor (Heughan), much to the delight of the female audience. Well aware of this phenomenon, those who designed the exhibit opted to have it travel with a full-size cut-out of Jamie rather than a full-size Claire, a decision that proved wise given the enthusiasm for Jamie selfies that followed. At the Celtic Festival opening, for example, several women were observed relegating their husbands to photographic duty so they could get a picture with the fictional Jamie.

It is also notable that *Outlander* fans seem to have time and money to spend on merchandise and travel. Group Facebook pages feature organized trips to see cast members in person, to tour Scotland, and to gather with fellow fans, and the fans share their finds when they stumble upon T-shirts and other *Outlander*-themed goods. While these observations are primarily anecdotal, it seems that demand for *Outlander* experiences and merchandise currently outweighs the products offered, which may be a factor in the success of the *Artifacts of Outlander* exhibit.

Having an exhibit that appeals to a fan group composed primarily of adults represents a departure from most JPPM exhibit efforts, since younger, school-age audiences have traditionally been a major target of public outreach (Samford and Green, this volume). The

Outlander book series contains violence and sexual content that makes it unsuitable for younger audiences, and this is reflected in the TV-MA rating of the television series. The exhibit itself does not contain adults-only content, though, and children find the imagery attractive even if they are not familiar with the show. At one library the exhibit team overheard a little girl exclaiming excitedly about the "princess" when looking at the panel with Claire in her wedding dress, and children on school groups leave positive remarks in the comment book. It may not always be the *Outlander* angle that draws people to the exhibit; it may simply be high-quality graphics of attractive people in historic costume.

In a similar manner, the artifacts themselves are the draw for history and archaeology fans. On several occasions Rivers Cofield has spoken about the *Artifacts of Outlander* project to archaeological groups, such as the Archaeological Society of Maryland and the Council for Maryland Archaeology, and at these meetings individuals who had never heard of *Outlander* expressed an interest in reading the books or watching the show. Similar reactions came from talks Rivers Cofield gave as part of the JPPM summer lecture series, the Historic London Town and Gardens winter lecture series, and at meetings of local chapters of the Daughters of the American Revolution, as these organizations have audiences who attend lectures regularly regardless of topic, ensuring that attendees were not limited to *Outlander* fans. The project has helped to promote the show and book series even while riding the coattails of *Outlander*'s preexisting popularity in order to reach a wider audience.

Discussion

After 43 months (and counting) of keeping up with popular demand for the *Artifacts of Outlander* exhibit, it is possible to better understand just how JPPM ended up with a breakout success as opposed to the short-term local outreach exhibit that was originally envisioned. It is clear that the popularity of the exhibit is, in large part, thanks to the fame of the Starz television series, with its attractive actors, props, and costumes. The pop-culture representation of a historical fiction series turned out to be a much more effective hook to lure new audiences than more traditional archaeological exhibit themes such as stories of local history, or a concentration on aspects of domestic life such as cooking, entertaining, and consumption of goods. This, in itself, is not surprising, since the reason the idea for the exhibit was attractive to MAC Lab staff in the first place is that *Outlander* offers the reader (or television viewer) immersion in a tale that is a fantasy, but a fantasy whose plot is interwoven with actual historical events. *Outlander's* storyline connects its audience to fictional characters set in a real time and place. Through Maryland's colonial collections, visitors to the *Artifacts of Outlander* exhibit can extend their connection with the series to the sites, artifacts, and stories of 1740s Maryland. The traveling exhibit's comparison of 18th-century artifact collections to still images from a television show may not be a deep exploration of Maryland's colonial history and culture, but it does increase awareness of the collections held in the public trust, and it prompts viewers to make mental connections between history as portrayed in the fictional *Outlander* television and book series and the very real lives of those who lived closer to home.

Because JPPM and the exhibit team adapted to capitalize on the exhibit's popularity, the products that eventually resulted—the standalone traveling exhibit and the online version of the exhibit—continue to increase the visibility of JPPM and the collections held at the MAC Lab. In addition to continued bookings and website hits, *Artifacts of Outlander* has helped JPPM and the MAC Lab have an unprecedented year for winning national awards. In 2016 the MAC Lab received the Society for Historical Archaeology's Daniel G. Roberts Award for Excellence in Public Historical Archaeology in recognition of all of its public outreach projects, including the *Artifacts of Outlander* exhibit (King 2016). Additionally, JPPM was awarded its first Leadership in History Award from the American Association for State and Local History (2016), which recognized *Artifacts of Outlander* as a superior and innovative approach to the interpretation of state and local history that makes the past more meaningful to all Americans. On top of the positive public response to the exhibit, these accolades help to affirm JPPM's commitment to effective collections-based community outreach.

JPPM does not currently plan to pursue additional exhibits with a similar pop-culture focus, but that has less to do with a lack of interest in doing so than with the ongoing momentum of *Artifacts of Outlander* and its demands on the limited staffing and resources available to support exhibits. Starz has committed to at least six seasons of the *Outlander* television series, so interest may continue, especially if the exhibit team occasionally updates *Artifacts of Outlander* with new panels to keep the exhibit current with the progress of the show. Should enthusiasm die down, or should JPPM decide to retire the exhibit for other reasons, such as wear and tear and concern for the condition of the artifacts, the project may well serve as a model and inspiration for a new outreach program with a popular culture theme, one that JPPM will be much better prepared to promote and manage thanks to the experience gained through the *Artifacts of Outlander* effort.

Acknowledgments

The authors thank everyone who has helped with the *Artifacts of Outlander* effort. Special thanks go to Jim House, JPPM's maintenance chief, stand-in exhibit fabrication specialist, and integral *Artifacts of Outlander* exhibit team member, who not only orchestrates every move of the exhibit but who also made the life-size cut-out of Jamie Fraser without being asked, greatly enhancing the draw of the exhibit to *Outlander*'s fans. Thanks also to the rest of the JPPM maintenance staff for helping as needed with fabrication, setup, loading, and unloading. Additionally the authors thank the following staff members for their contributions to the exhibit: MAC Lab director Patricia Samford, who handles venue scheduling and reimbursement charges for the traveling exhibit; Sharon Raftery, administrative assistant and webmaster, for converting the online exhibit to HTML and maintaining all of the *Artifacts of Outlander*'s online components; Special Events and Marketing Coordinator Sherwana Knox, who serves as the contact for Starz on JPPM's behalf; Collections Assistant Erin Wingfield, for administering all of the exhibit loan agreements and helping with moves; State Curator Rebecca Morehouse, for helping with artifact selection and exhibit moves; conservators Nichole Doub and Francis Lukezic, who helped with mounting artifacts; and Ed Chaney, MAC Lab deputy director and copy editor for *Artifacts of Outlander* online. Finally, the authors are grateful to all of the librarians, hosting institutions, *Outlander* fans, and other members of the public who keep the exhibit on the move, helping JPPM and the MAC Lab fulfill the mission of making collections accessible.

References

American Association for State and Local History

2016   Leadership in History Award Winners. http://about.aaslh.org/2016-leadership -in-history-award-winners/. Accessed 13 February 2017.

Gabaldon, Diana

1991   *Outlander.* Bantam Dell. New York.

1992   *Dragonfly in Amber.* Dell. New York.

1994   *Voyager.* Dell. New York.

1997   *Drums of Autumn.* Dell. New York.

2001   *The Fiery Cross.* Bantam Dell. New York.

2005   *A Breath of Snow and Ashes.* Bantam Dell. New York.

2009   *An Echo in the Bone.* Dell. New York.

2014   *Written in My Owns Heart's Blood.* Dell. New York.

King, Julia

2016   Daniel G. Roberts Award for Excellence in Public Historical Archaeology: The Maryland Archaeological Conservation Laboratory. *Historical Archaeology* 50(2):11–13.

Rivers Cofield, Sara, Caitlin Shaffer, Patricia Samford, Alex Glass, and Sharon Raftery

2016   *Artifacts of Outlander.* Online exhibit. http://www.jefpat.org/Outlander /index.html. Accessed 13 February 2017.

[SIXTEEN]

Raising Interest with Archaeological Currency

Student Engagement with the Federal Reserve Bank Site Collection in Baltimore, Maryland

PATRICIA SAMFORD AND RACHELLE M. GREEN

As the national K–12 public education system grapples with how to balance authentic learning experience with the academic culture of standardized testing, students participating in Huntingtown High School's Archaeology Club are challenged to think, quite literally, outside the box. Each year archaeologists from the Maryland Archaeological Conservation Laboratory (MAC Lab) arrive at Huntingtown High School with archival Coraplast boxes containing artifacts from a mid-19th-century site in Baltimore. Since their initial recovery in 1980, the artifacts have been largely untouched and unstudied. The students become budding archaeologists, exploring Baltimore's history through analysis of these pieces of the past. As the archaeologists and students collaborate throughout the year, numerous positive academic and professional benefits surface. Academically students develop research and composition skills through primary source analysis, as well as exhibit design and label writing skills. Professionally, students engage in networking through conference attendance and community meetings. The MAC Lab staff also benefits professionally as more data are uncovered about this underreported Baltimore site. Last, the community partnerships formed between Huntingtown High School, the MAC Lab, the site's Baltimore neighborhood, and the state's avocational archaeological organization have created a rich environment for archaeological discovery.

Archaeological Site Background

Jefferson Patterson Park and Museum's collaboration with Calvert County Public Schools' Huntingtown High School began in 2009, when the museum's former education director Kim Popetz began to work with teachers and students in the social studies curriculum to produce thematic cell phone tours of the park. After the successful completion of three audio tours, the museum and the school were ready to take the collaboration in a different direction. The school wanted a project that would "allow students to work with professionals and gain proficiency in skills such as collaboration, critical thinking, and communication" (Popetz 2015:301). Kim turned to the MAC Lab, the state's curation and conservation facility, conveniently located at the museum, to see what opportunities might be available.

It happened that just such an opportunity existed. Archaeological collections from the Federal Reserve Site (18BC27) had recently become part of the lab's permanent collections. The site had been excavated through a salvage project conducted in early 1980 by Mid-Atlantic Archaeological Research during the construction of the Federal Reserve Bank in downtown Baltimore (McCarthy and Basalik 1980). Initially settled in the late 18th century, economic and population growth in this part of south Baltimore adjacent to the city's harbor was slow during the early 19th century. By midcentury both residential and business development in the Otterbein neighborhood had dramatically increased (Basalik 1994:315). Many of the lots along Sharpe Street, north of Welcome Alley, were residences of slaveholding property owners, suggesting this area may have been more upscale than farther south along the block. At the end of the century, homes for individuals who worked in the neighborhood were interspersed with saloons, general stores, stables, a sash weight factory, and a pickle plant. Development south of Welcome Alley was all industrial by the early 20th century and included a lime and cement plant, a cooper, and a blacksmith shop (Basalik 1994:321). By the late 1920s standing row houses were demolished for the expansion of the Baltimore and Ohio Railroad's Camden Yard terminal (McCarthy and Basalik 1980:1-1).

Archaeology, unfortunately, was an afterthought in the bank project; it was only after below-ground traces of the neighborhood began to appear during construction that cultural resource management came into play. With large-scale earthmoving and archaeology taking place concurrently, excavations were conducted in a hurried fashion. The project's goal was to recover as much archaeological data as possible before construction forced the archaeologists to discontinue work. Most of the excavation occurred in the backyards of the former residential properties, and large-scale stripping of soil allowed the archaeologists to map where features—primarily wells and privies—cut through subsoil.

A summary report of the project was prepared later that year (McCarthy and Basalik 1980; Basalik 1994), but lack of funding meant the artifacts remained uncataloged and no full technical report was ever completed. Since the salvage excavations had revealed numerous discrete archaeological features with manageable-size artifact assemblages, this collection seemed ripe for use as an educational tool.

High School Students Performing Archaeological Tasks

Each year the high school students work on the artifacts from one feature, usually a mid-19th-century privy with an assemblage that fits into three or four standard banker's boxes. Over the course of the school year students are exposed to the fundamentals of archaeological lab work and analysis. They catalog artifacts under the supervision of a professional archaeologist and enter information into a database, cross-mend ceramics and glass, and calculate minimum vessel counts (Figure 27). Students also conduct supervised research into the occupants of the property, perform in-depth research on artifacts, explore patterns within the overall data, examine changing technology and style, and date artifacts. Results of their analysis and research are disseminated in several ways. The students work singly or in pairs to write a detailed study of an artifact of their choosing for JPPM's Curator's Choice series (http://www.jefpat.org/curatorschoice

.html). These photographic essays are put on the museum website, as well as being made into posters that line the halls of the school (Figure 28). The culminating project of the year is the creation of an exhibit for the local branch of the county library. This collaborative effort involves brainstorming ideas for the exhibit theme and title, choosing artifacts, designing the layout, and writing and editing exhibit labels. The exhibit goes up at the library at the end of the school year and then, in September, moves to an exhibit case at the high school, where it remains until the end of the school year. In effect, these students are treated like young professionals, undertaking activities that would be typical of a college undergraduate lab methods course.

While museum staff worked with structured elective social studies classes for the first two years of this collaboration, the archaeology-based project generated such interest among the students that they decided, in the fall of 2014, to form a school Archaeology Club. At this time the decision was made to base the collections project around the newly formed Archaeology Club. Entering its third year in the fall of 2016, the club has a membership of around 30, with a strong core group of around a dozen students. The club has recently expanded its activities beyond the weekly work sessions on the Baltimore project. It has been officially "adopted" by the Archeological Society of Maryland, the state's avocational organization, and with its assistance, club members have attended two regional professional conferences and are working to start a new county chapter of the group. They were also able to bring Becca Peixotta, one of the Rising Star Cave expedition members who excavated the newest hominid fossil species, *Homo naledi*, for a wildly popular school-wide lecture in 2015.

Working with a previously excavated assemblage naturally led the students to ask questions about the fieldwork that generates artifacts. Jefferson Patterson Park and Museum is located on a 560-acre park that contains approximately 70 known archaeological sites. So it was a relatively simple matter to provide the students with field experiences. In 2014 the students assisted with shovel testing on a mid-17th-century site to help establish site boundaries. The next spring,

FIGURE 27. Archaeology Club member mending a printed dish from a mid-19th-century privy. (Photo: Patricia Samford)

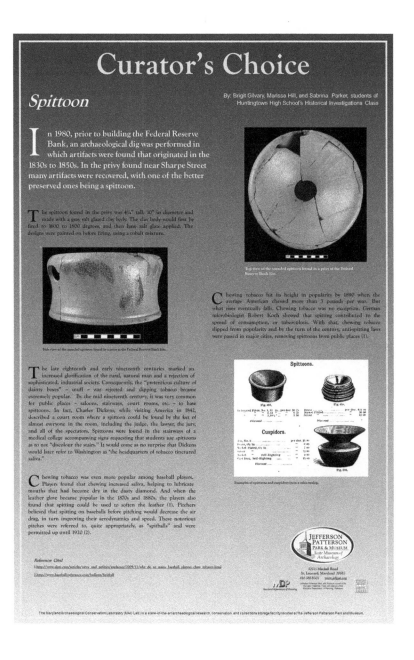

FIGURE 28. Curator's Choice poster focusing on a stoneware spittoon mended by students. Students worked singly or in pairs to write detailed studies of an artifact. (Photo courtesy of Jefferson Patterson Park and Museum)

FIGURE 29. A JPPM staff member and a Huntingtown student recover a surface find from a postbellum tenant house. (Photo: Patricia Samford)

a staff member hiking in a wooded area on the museum grounds discovered the stone foundation of a late 19th-century tenant house and brick kiln. The club has adopted this site as their own, and with guidance from the museum's archaeologists and educators, they have mapped the foundation, piece-plotted and washed about 75 surface finds, and are completing a state site form (Figure 29). In upcoming months, museum staff plan to perform systematic shovel testing and excavate test units in order to learn more about postbellum tenant life in southern Maryland.

Results and Outcomes

Interest in archaeological fieldwork and research has surged at Huntingtown High School with the offering by social studies instructors of two elective courses, Introduction to Historical Investigation and Introduction to Archaeology. Students enrolled in these courses often joined and participated in Archaeology Club activities throughout the year. The basic tenets of the two courses exposed students to the field of archaeology through analysis of primary and secondary sources, including oral histories, legal documents, and physical artifacts. Students also learn about archaeological methods of excavation and anthropological theories of human development that enhance their study of archaeology. Coupled with the hands-on approach to examining a collection of artifacts during club meetings, students gain an in-depth understanding of the field of archaeology, as well as have authentic experiences working with professional archaeologists, historians, and community members (Calvert County Public Schools [CCPS] 2016).

The development of such courses at the high school level serve to augment the Calvert County Public Schools' middle school social studies curriculum, which incorporates the study of archaeology in the 6th grade World History course. Students examine themes, patterns, and events in world history, tracing the development of societies and technological change over time (CCPS 2016). Additionally, every 6th grader in the county participates in a field trip to Jefferson Patterson Park and Museum for the Discovering Archaeology component of the Chespax program, an environmental education program supported by the Calvert County Public Schools for hands-on environmental learning experiences. Students use the replica Woodland Indian Village as well as archaeological artifacts to uncover the history of people who inhabited the landscape along the Patuxent

River. With this cursory introduction to artifact analysis and historical methods in the 6th grade, Calvert County students are exposed at an early age to the field of archaeology.

In terms of both the middle school and high school coursework with focuses on archaeology, historical investigation, and anthropology, students are meeting curriculum standards in nontraditional forms through the Chespax fieldtrip as well as the Huntingtown High School Archaeology Club. Recently the Maryland State Department of Education initiated a plan, entitled c3 Framework for Social Studies Standards, to incorporate an instructional program developed by the National Council for Social Studies ([NCSS] 2013). The College, Career, and Civic Life (c3) Framework primarily aims to provide guidelines and instructional support for concepts and skills related to student preparation in those three areas: college, career, and civic life. The standards identify four dimensions within the framework that focus on informed inquiry in the field of social studies. The four dimensions are (1) develop questions and plan inquiries, (2) apply disciplinary concepts and tools, (3) evaluate sources and use evidence, and (4) communicate conclusions and take informed actions. Throughout the academic year the informal curriculum of the Archaeology Club embodies the essence of the c3 Framework, promoting collaboration between students as well as using evidence to support and present content findings (NCSS 2013).

Of the four dimensions of the c3 Framework, applying disciplinary concepts, evaluating sources and using evidence are incorporated most frequently and are directly relevant to the study of anthropology and archaeology as part of the social studies curriculum. Under the broader categories of "Human-Environmental Interaction" and "Spatial Patterns," students examine the Otterbein neighborhood by "evaluating how political and economic decisions throughout time have influenced cultural and environmental characteristics of various places and regions" (NCSS 2013:42). Students also research imported ceramics and the possibility of a free black community by "analyzing the reciprocal nature of how historical events and the spatial diffusion of ideas, technologies and cultural practices have influenced migration patterns and distribution of human population" (NCSS 2013:43). As students begin evaluating sources and using evidence provided by the archaeological artifacts, they fully engage with the content and fulfill dimension 3 of the C3 Framework. Through oral histories, maps, city directories, and professional diagnostic websites students "gather relevant information from a multitude of sources and evaluate the credibility by examining how experts value the source" (NCSS 2013:54).

Under anthropology, methods of ethics and inquiry are highlighted as anthropologists and archaeologists use a more scientific approach to data collection, including conducting and reporting research. According to the C3 Framework, college-, career-, and civic life–ready students should be able to "develop an understanding of the methods by which anthropologists collect data on cultural patterns and processes and of ways of interpreting and presenting these data in writing and other media" (NCSS 2013:78). Another goal realized by the Huntingtown High School Archaeology Cub is that students, guided by a teacher, undertake a research project, study local culture, and visit an archaeological site.

As a result of the hard work, dedication, and professional-level research demonstrated by senior students of the Archaeology Club, the Jefferson Patterson Park and Museum Education Department created an internship program for college students interested in pursuing archaeology or social studies education as a career. Through this internship, students gain professional teaching experience, develop and implement a weekend family program, participate in park-wide events, and create a résumé as a professional development exercise. The first recipient of the internship was Lydia Gamber, a Huntingtown High School graduate and former member of the Archaeology Club. Gamber, a first-year student at St. Mary's College of Maryland, joined the Jefferson Patterson Park and Museum Education department as a lead educator for the 4th grade field trip program, "Is Your Share Fair?" This program focuses on using archaeological artifacts and oral history to teach about the life of African American sharecroppers on the property in post–Civil War–era Maryland. Students actively participate in artifact analysis, chores, games, and storytelling.

Another student, Christiana Nisbet, completed a summer internship working with the lab director to analyze an assemblage from an early 20th-century Chinese laundry in downtown Baltimore (Nisbet et al. 2013). That analysis resulted in the publication of a coauthored article in the state archaeology journal, providing the student with a publication citation to put on her college applications.

Does this project require a lot of time and effort on the part of Jefferson Patterson Park and Museum? Of course. But museum staff know that the benefits of this collaboration far outweigh the time it takes to accomplish it. This project provides the museum with a good working relationship with a local school and with a future generation of potential archaeologists and historians. With the current climate of deregulation and cutting science and humanities funding, it is critical that archaeologists educate a larger number of people about the importance of our discipline. Getting students interested at an early age leads to an awareness and appreciation of archaeology and what it can reveal about the past. Inroads are being made into working on a neglected collection that might not otherwise ever receive any attention. The high school coordinator and the museum staff have learned over the years to scale the project so annual goals get accomplished. For example, lab staff now label the artifacts in advance of taking them to the school; this not only saves time but ensures that professionals with legible labeling skills are doing that part of the work. We have also learned to focus on the exhibit and the Curator's Choice essays rather than a final feature report, since time constraints make it impossible to successfully complete a report. Both the school and the museum are very much invested in having the students succeed, so this goal is made a priority.

Given a receptive school system, this project should be relatively easy for other archaeologists to replicate. Most archaeological museums or repositories have stray, neglected collections that await an opportunity for some love. Most archaeological professionals want the chance to shape a generation of future preservationists.

Creating Your Own Program with High School Students

As the partnership with Jefferson Patterson Park and Museum, the Federal Reserve Bank, and the surrounding neighborhoods of Otterbein and Sharp-Leadenhall continue to strengthen, new opportunities for student involvement in archaeology are becoming a reality. In an attempt to replicate the experience at Huntingtown High School, a local Baltimore high school expressed interest in creating a combination of coursework and archaeology club. From our experiences with Huntingtown High School, we offer this three-year approach to creating a successful course or club. Navigating school schedules and professional schedules in addition to gaining momentum and student interest is quite a large undertaking. Student interest is imperative to beginning a course and club model undertaking. During year 1, promote thematic or project-based units around community history within the existing social studies curriculum. Incorporating community history connects students' everyday lives and creates a platform for discussing national history within a local context. Field trips might include exploring a local neighborhood during a walking tour or visiting a local community center to speak with elders or longtime residents of the neighborhood. Building relationships with community members, who could gather at a school assembly to present on their experiences with the Archaeology Club or class, is imperative to the continued success of a program. From an administrative standpoint, the first year should provide qualitative and quantitative data on student interest to petition for approval of the creation of an Archaeology Club the following school year.

After approval to create an Archaeology Club, identifying a local archaeologist willing to help facilitate the club with the instructor will provide the professional guidance required when examining a collection. Presenting the new club at a student activity fair with students from the previous class will entice new members to join and increase interest among the student body. There is a need to identify a central meeting location—be it at the school or a local historical site—for the archaeologist who might be coming from a distance. During year 2 the newly formed Archaeology Club should take a field trip to an archaeological site or lab to meet with archaeologists and explore artifact collections. The club faculty sponsor and club archaeologist should also contact local libraries during year 2 to advocate for an exhibit display created by the students showcasing their research and work throughout the year. In addition, the faculty sponsor should promote and gain approval for a new elective course in archaeology, anthropology, or historical investigations.

With a newly created student interest group from the Archaeology Club, the faculty advisor should be able to fill at least one course section in year 3 with relative ease. Depending on the school course schedule, offer either a semester or yearlong course using local and regional case studies to explain process and methodology. To be clear, the course does not replace the Archaeology Club but provides yet another opportunity for students interested in archaeology to pursue the field academically as well as through an extracurricular activity such as a club. Students in the course should be invited and encouraged to participate in club activities, including the yearly field trips or other neighborhood outings.

Conclusion

Huntingtown High School is producing graduates who excel in required standardized tests and have a solid understanding of research, collaboration, and project completion. These students have a firm grasp on 21st-century research skills, as well as on history, and they know why both are important. They will become the adults responsible for the preservation of Maryland's historic treasures and will be able to look at an old building or an archaeological site and understand why preserving it is important to our shared history. Because of the work accomplished through this ongoing project, Huntingtown High School won a Maryland Preservation Award for Excellence in Education in 2014. It was exciting to work with students on a project that provided them with real-world experience in a supportive setting, conducting the type of analysis normally done by professional archaeologists. Even better was watching the thrill of the students as they opened each new artifact bag and began to glean the information it holds.

Acknowledgments

The authors would like to acknowledge assistance and support from the following individuals and organizations: the students of Huntingtown High School's Historical Investigations class, Archaeology class, and Archaeology Club; teacher Jeff Cunningham and principal Rick Weber of Huntingtown High School; Claude Bowen and the Archeological Society of Maryland; Rebecca Morehouse, Erin Wingfield, Sharon Raftery, and Jim House of Jefferson Patterson Park and Museum; Sarah Avant and the Calvert County Public Library; and Margaret Burns and the Federal Reserve Bank of Richmond, Baltimore Branch.

References

Basalik, Kenneth

1994   *Urban Development in the Eastern United States: An Archaeological View from Baltimore, Maryland.* Doctoral dissertation, Department of Anthropology, Temple University. University Microfilms, Ann Arbor MI.

Calvert County Public Schools (CCPS)

2016   Social Studies Program: High School Course Offerings. Prince Frederick MD.

McCarthy, John P., and Kenneth J. Basalik

1980   Summary Report of Archaeological Investigations Federal Reserve Bank Site, Baltimore, Maryland. Report to Maryland Historical Trust from Mid-Atlantic Archaeological Research, Inc., Newark DE.

National Council for the Social Studies (NCSS)

2013   The College, Career, and Civic Life (C3) Framework for Social Studies State Standards: Guidance for Enhancing the Rigor of K–12 Civics, Economics, Geography, and History. Silver Spring MD.

Nisbet, Christiana, Makenli Essert, and Patricia Samford

2013   "We Wash Everything but the Baby": Archeological Investigations at the Wysing Lung Laundry, Baltimore, Maryland. *Maryland Archeology* 49(1):1–9.

Popetz, Kimberley

2015   Turning Privies into Class Projects. *Advances in Archaeological Practice* 3(3): 301–312.

[SEVENTEEN]

Beyond the Shelf

Anthropological Collections at the University of Montana

C. RILEY AUGÉ, MICHAEL BLACK WOLF, EMERSON BULL CHIEF,

KELLY J. DIXON, VIRGIL EDWARDS, GERALD GRAY, CONRAD FISHER,

TEANNA LIMPY, KATIE MCDONALD, IRA MATT, JOHN MURRAY,

RAYMOND "ABBY" OGLE, SADIE PEONE, ALVIN WINDY BOY,

AND DARRELL "CURLEY" YOUPEE

PREAMBLE TO PROGRAMMATIC AGREEMENT,
DEVELOPED AT THE 2015 THPO SUMMIT

In the spirit of acknowledging past, present, and future relationships with Montana tribes; in the name of mutual respect, repatriation, and reconciliation; and in aim of upholding the elements of integrity, the University of Montana commits to repatriating culturally sensitive objects, including materials representing objects associated with the cultural life force of descendant communities that sustain the cultural livelihood of people who made and used these items. The parties will, in good faith, include all concerned participants in consultations and outcomes.

Nash et al. (2011) argued that museum anthropology should engage in the concept of beneficence, especially when dealing with descendent communities. This resonated with those of us working collaboratively to ensure that the University of Montana's Anthropological Curation Facility's (UMACF) policies and procedures for handling objects aligned with the region's indigenous ways of treating, storing, and using those objects. We wanted to ensure that UMACF practices did not cause harm to the objects or their handlers because of cultural misunderstandings and sought to bridge the divide between anthropologists and museum staff with the tribal communities whose heritage we all sought to protect and understand (Edwards et al. 2006; Sleeper-Smith 2009; Wilcox 2010; Atalay 2012).

We argue that it is essential to incorporate descendant community concerns about the interpretation and representation of cultural heritage collections to ensure that collaborations between these—and other—descendant communities and museums serve as agents of social change and to better understand the nuances of culturally sensitive museum practices (Edwards et al. 2006). It is vital for museum curators and collections managers to understand that there are cases where objects are seen as having life; in such cases, the objects may be in dire need of human contact instead of sitting idle and untouched in boxes and cabinets for decades. While not all cultures share such beliefs about objects in museum collections, museum staff need to be sensitive to descendant communities' cultural comprehension of objects and be prepared to establish respectful handling protocols that align with descendant cultures' worldviews. Cultural collections may include sentient objects that have not been properly nurtured due to conventional collections management protocols. While wearing nitrile gloves to protect certain objects from the oils on human hands—or to protect handlers from toxic chemicals that were once considered suitable for conservation—is standard protocol, it is also necessary to ensure that certain objects are appropriately handled. This is among the post–Native American Graves Protection and Repatriation Act (NAGPRA) legislation paradigm shifts that museum professionals need to be prepared to handle.

NAGPRA was enacted to restore Indigenous Americans' sovereignty over their dead and important cultural artifacts, despite the fact that some museum specialists might find the results unsettling (Daehnke and Lonetree 2011). On the one hand, museums are faced with the prospect of returning collections to tribal nations without requirements for those entities to demonstrate intentions to preserve collections as part of repatriation. On the other hand, one of the goals of NAGPRA—to put sacred objects back in use—means that museum pieces have the potential to be used until they are worn out and discarded, which can be a disheartening prospect for curators who have dedicated their professional lives to the conservation of such objects (Brown 2004; Harms 2012:605). In Clavir's (2002:xiii) words, "Preserving the *physical* integrity of an object and preserving its *conceptual* integrity [are] very much in conflict" (emphasis added). Indeed this represents the epitome of new life for old collections, wherein the "new life" actually refers to intended *use* life, including more organic and culturally informed handling. This requires museum professionals to be open to alternative approaches to collections management and also requires tribal communities to be open to the requirements of collections management. We have found that integrating multiple, multivocal worldviews—and meeting in a caucus-style format—affords a platform for momentum.

Over the past few years the UMACF has hosted meetings and tribal historic preservation officer (THPO) summits to gather cultural heritage representatives of tribal governments in Montana to collaborate on the design of long-range plans for the University of Montana's cultural collections. Among the poignant outcomes of these summits was that Western scientific ways of handling and storing artifacts may go against certain cultural protocols that ensure the livelihood of those artifacts and the health of their handlers. For example, some objects are intended to be touched only by men, while others are intended to be handled only by women. In another instance, during the first summit, attendees discussed UMACF's goal of hiring a conservator to assist with the preservation of certain objects, such as quillwork on moccasins. Summit participants conveyed to UMACF staff that the best conservators for those types of artifacts were elders from their communities, because those individuals not only had knowledge of the traditional ways of repairing those objects, but they also were aware of the cultural handling protocols.

In addition, while museum specialists follow the protocol of wearing nitrile gloves when touching artifacts, we learned that such protocols can be perceived by indigenous stakeholders as potentially harmful to many objects since those items are considered living entities in dire need of human contact and some are intended to be used. However, the UMACF has evidence via x-ray fluorescence (XRF) research (Berger 2014) of these objects being treated with pesticides, and some of them are actually too toxic to handle. This is another issue that needs to be worked out between the UMACF and tribal partners as we move forward with artifact handling protocols. We have yet to draft guidelines for handling those items or raise funds to address possible reversal of the pesticide treatment processes (Ogden 2004).

UMACF staff, as well as museum professionals in the region, are learning from and adapting to these museum protocol paradigm shifts. Future plans of the UMACF are evolving in partnership with the region's tribal cultural heritage leaders, with documents such as a cross-cultural Procedural Policies Manual and a Programmatic Agreement guiding UMACF staff and tribal colleagues. These documents are currently being drafted and are co-authored by Summit participants to guide decision making for the next several years. Such documents are intended for long-term relevance, care, conservation, and, in some cases, repatriation of UM's cultural collections, and represent the products of the UMACF's collaborative, community-based approach to collections management.

History of UMACF

The UMACF includes upward of 1 million items representing the traditional and transformative cultural heritage of the American West, including materials such as clothing, ornate horse tack from Northern Plains and Rocky Mountain Front horse cultures, an extremely rare rock art paintbrush, an extensive moccasin collection, artifacts from Montana Chinatowns, and materials from the region's early colonial outposts. The collections include archaeological and cultural (i.e., ethnographic) objects representing the vast prehistory and history of the region. Given its history as a repository for regional cultural heritage, particularly heritage representing early and mid-20th-century archaeology and ethnology on the Northern Plains and along the Rocky Mountain Front, the UMACF collections have been and will continue to be tremendous resources for research, education, and public outreach.

During the mid-20th-century the state of Montana's art and cultural collections were assigned to various stewards and storage locations, and the UM Department of Anthropology accepted materials recovered by eminent archaeologists and anthropologists, including William Mulloy, who wrote the first chronology of Northwestern Plains, and Carling Malouf, who was one of the chief practitioners of cultural heritage collections-based research in the region. Besides those collections, the UM acquired collections via gifts from key donors and as a consequence of the Smithsonian's River Basin Survey, which involved both collections and antiquities records. The UM Department of Anthropology housed both anthropological museum collections and the Montana Site Records Office. The University of Montana's Department of Anthropology's department's Self-Study (Douglas 2011) addressed the anthropological and historical significance of the collections for research, education, and lifelong learning and the subsequent importance of long-term, sustainable planning for the storage facility. This was accompanied by a master's thesis (Campbell 2011) that presented a condition assessment of the UMACF and was pivotal in helping the facility continue its ongoing NAGPRA process.

For the past several years the UMACF has asked for help from the region's THPOS and cultural heritage leaders to uphold the human rights intentions of NAGPRA (Harms 2012) and to open up discussions about cultural patrimony and the cultural collections at the UMACF. Here we focus on cultural rather than archaeological materials since those items represent the starting point of the events described herein. Among the discussions that took place at the summits were those that addressed the power of words; attention was drawn to problematic associations with terms such as "ethnographic," which connotes indigenous material culture being the subject of Western scientific study; thus the term "cultural" is used here rather than "ethnographic."

As noted, the meetings stimulated collaborations with tribal stake-holders and descendant communities to ensure that the UMACF's object handling protocols are culturally appropriate and aligned with the region's indigenous considerations of conservation and handling. In doing so, the UMACF has set a precedent in the region for underscoring how community engagement cultivates respect and reconciliation, as well as institutional resilience and sustainability. "Resilience" is defined here as the UMACF's capacity to continue its existence by remaining stable and being highly adaptive in the face of risk, vulnerability, or unanticipated hazards to ensure that adequate resources are available for future generations. "Sustainability" is defined as the UMACF's ability to serve the region's cultural heritage needs and meet the conservation and "modernizing" requirements of the present without sacrificing the ability of future generations to continue to use and apply lessons learned from cultural heritage collections and related programs, workshops, and narratives.

Teamwork: THPOS, Culture Committees, and the UMACF

The request for assistance from THPOS with sustainable anthropological collections management brought opportunities for more frequent and enlightening contact and ensured that cultural heritage branches of tribal governments were involved with UMACF planning and decision making. In spring 2015 and spring 2016, the UMACF hosted summits that included Tribal Culture Committees, curators, anthropologists, archaeologists, historians, and Montana THPOS from the Blackfeet Nation, Chippewa-Cree Tribe of the Rocky Boy's (Stone Child) Reservation, Confederated Salish and Kootenai Tribes of the Flathead Reservation, Crow Nation, Fort Belknap Indian Community of the Fort Belknap Reservation of Montana, Little Shell Chippewa Tribe, and Northern Cheyenne Nation.

These summits were inspired by the fact that it is challenging for THPOS, culture committees, and NAGPRA coordinators to find time and funds to assist with developing policy and procedures for handling, interpreting, and using cultural objects for ceremonies. As a result, the summits hosted by the UMACF provided a foundation for forming respectful, cooperative relationships with the region's tribal cultural heritage representatives. The gathering established a platform for dialogue at the regional level and provided springboards for meetings with individual tribes and culture committees.

The relationship-building process sparked at these summits has evolved, fostering genuine trust and respect between the tribal government offices and UM and providing a united foundation for formal documents such as a Programmatic Agreement, a Scope of Collections, and a Procedural Policies Manual, which will be the step-by-step handbook governing all aspects of the care, management, access, use, and possible repatriation of the items contained in the UMACF cultural collections. While the 2015 summit yielded the outlines and initial ingredients of those documents, the majority of the 2016 summit's two days was spent considering the legal and authoritative force behind these documents. To ensure the documents are going to have the legal and long-term power to govern and guide decisions about and interactions with the cultural collections, some THPOs asserted that they must take these documents to their respective tribal councils and other ruling bodies for consideration and discussion. Similarly, UMACF staff need to have all the documents reviewed by entities such as UM's legal counsel and the dean of UM's College of Humanities and Sciences.

As a group we went through each of the two documents item by item and discussed and noted areas for clarification and revision. As revealed through discussions at the first summit, the importance of clear, culturally respectful and appropriate terminology is key in writing cross-cultural documents intended for long-term relevance and implementation. This issue surfaced again as we considered each section and item in both the Programmatic Agreement and the Scope of Collections, with the most worrisome words (e.g., "sensitive," "ceremonial," "purification," "tradition") expressing relative concepts or practices related to ritual and belief. It was left to the UMACF curator, C. Riley Augé, to revise the drafts, choosing more universally appropriate words while expressly explaining that each tribe will be accommodated as is suitable and proper according to its protocols and traditions. After this editing, the documents were shared with tribal councils and committees for further review, though concern over specific terminology continues to be a critical component of these discussions. Even so, the preamble to one of the documents, co-authored at the 2015 Summit, encapsulates the spirit of these collective documents:

> Preamble to Programmatic Agreement, Developed at the 2015 THPO Summit

> In the spirit of acknowledging past, present, and future relationships with Montana tribes; in the name of mutual respect, repatriation, and reconciliation; and in aim of upholding the elements of integrity, the University of Montana commits to repatriating culturally sensitive objects, including materials representing objects associated with the cultural life force of descendant communities that sustain the cultural livelihood of people who made and used these items. The parties will, in good faith, include all concerned participants in consultations and outcomes.

Curley Youpee, THPO for the Assiniboine and Sioux Tribes of the Fort Peck Reservation, stressed that these documents cannot be rushed; they will require a great deal more time before they are finalized, signed, and implemented. It became apparent that the process of crafting agreements and policies concerning the UMACF's cultural collections with the tribes is a more complex and multifaceted undertaking than originally conceived, especially in regard to each respective tribe's structure and hierarchy of authority. To clarify and streamline this process, it was agreed that each tribe would create a flowchart delineating the people and their positions to whom the documents must pass for review and approval.

The flowcharts not only prevent a "pan-Indian" approach to cultural heritage collections management (Bench 2014) but will allow us to understand the structure of authority within each tribe so that the appropriate people are involved in the document review process. These flowcharts will be incorporated into the Programmatic Agreement and Procedural Policies Manual to facilitate ongoing interactions with the tribes concerning the collections. The flowcharts will also help distinguish who needs to be the contact person for NAGPRA-related items and issues—a constantly recurring theme throughout the summit discussions, even though it has been reiterated that the cultural collections do not fall under NAGPRA and that current UM NAGPRA repatriation consultations are distinct from these summit gatherings that concern only the cultural collections.

Virtually all discussions concerned access to and handling of objects, including emphasis on the educational uses of the collections, especially for Native American students. This led to a tangential conversation about future collaborative projects between the region's tribal nations and UM to create statewide educational opportunities and materials. Additionally, these gatherings fueled ongoing conversations that resulted in the Museums Association of Montana inviting our curator to present a workshop at an Association conference to share the forward-looking outcomes of the summits with other museum professionals in the region. Throughout the summits and subsequent forums, our goal has been to ensure meaningful integration and involvement of tribal communities in the future of UM's cultural collections.

Rehousing, Sustainability, and Resilience

At this point the UMACF needs to plan for appropriate rehousing to ensure the sustainability and resilience of the cultural heritage collections in perpetuity. Implementation procedures for rehousing will be initiated in consultation with tribal cultural heritage experts to ensure that collections are stored in ways that are sensitive to people and objects and guided by the principles and strategies for sustainable preservation in artifact care as defined by 36CFR79 *Curation of Federally-Owned and Administered Archeological Collections* and the American Alliance of Museums Code of Ethics and Standards (National Park Service n.d.; American Alliance of Museums n.d.). Additional plans include purchasing and installing an energy-efficient heating and cooling system to control environmental conditions of the UMACF and to improve the facility's security system. UM's Office of Sustainability worked closely with UM's Facilities Services and UMACF Collections Committee to discuss various options for upgrading the UMACF space. As a result, several UM programs have provided the cooperation necessary to generate the proposed project and are aware of the relevance of the UMACF's humanities' resources.

The anthropological collections housed in the UMACF are among the UM's most powerful means of creating knowledge about Montana's past and present peoples and culture and are instrumental in education and community building. The collections enable professors to use hands-on examples of artifact typologies; give undergraduates the opportunity to directly employ the methodologies they learn in class in a lab setting; enable graduate students to have research material without the extreme expense and limited time frame of fieldwork; and support UM as a regional learning center having strong relationships with the region's tribal colleges, creating a platform for helping to disseminate curation methods to descendant communities throughout the region. Ongoing NAGPRA compliance has provided opportunities for additional dissemination, dialogue, and socially responsible decision making that uphold the human rights–oriented spirit of NAGPRA (Harms 2012). It has also sparked a broader wave of scholarship emphasizing decolonization and the post-NAGPRA impact of conducting indigenous and community archaeologies (Watkins 2000, 2003; Colwell and Ferguson 2008; Teeman 2008; Wilcox 2010; Nash et al. 2011; Atalay 2012; Weik 2012; Conaty 2015; Borck and Sanger 2017).

The most significant part of the rehousing process is that it will be undertaken in tandem with tribal stakeholders and partners, as well as the Collections Committee. The UMACF staff and Collections Committee members regularly visit with elders, cultural counsels or committees, and museum professionals to gain insight into how each community and culture handles specific types of items and also to discuss curatorial issues in general. The UMACF's curator consults with in-house specialists, descendant communities, and regional specialists to address the specific needs of each of the pieces within the

UMACF's care. This allows the ethnographic collection to be divided into general categories and prioritized for rehousing purposes.

Among the categories are the following: items that are culturally sensitive and those that are not; items at high risk of curation damage and those that are relatively stable; and items that require little or simple rehousing and items that require elaborate mounts to be built. Those items identified as culturally sensitive or needing special handling will be addressed first and in conjunction with the tribal representatives from the region to ensure that the most appropriate and sustainable archival care is given each object, and also to ensure that the tribe's cultural needs are addressed. ("Culturally sensitive" refers to items needing specific care, such as those that are to be touched only by men, items that should face east, and those that are not to be housed with other objects.) This process has the potential to take the longest amount of time and will be the first task attended to in order meet all benchmarks throughout the project. Tribal representatives will be consulted throughout the entire rehousing process, whether or not objects are deemed culturally sensitive, in order to help reestablish the link between objects and the cultures from which they originated. Clearly the UMACF's organizational sustainability and resilience represent more of a process and an ethic as opposed to an outcome (Moldavanova 2014). In order for the UMACF to fulfill its purpose via intergenerational sustainability and institutional survival, we are seeking support from granting agencies like the National Endowment for the Humanities and Humanities Montana to support this collective commitment to build relationships and develop multivocal plans, training, and outreach that will sustain UM's cultural heritage collections.

While we have the momentum and have established trust with our indigenous partners, the UMACF is, like many other museums, the victim of reduced budgets due to the larger organization dealing with ongoing funding cuts. Many museums are developing new business models and visions to cope with diminishing funds; the UMACF too has a plan for institutional resilience. Our resilience plan is grounded in a commitment to developing sustainable strategies for UMACF collections by working collaboratively with tribal cultural heritage colleagues via THPO summits. The summits inadvertently established a precedent in the region for incorporating participatory community engagement as a management strategy for sustainable stewardship, conservation, and care of museum collections that secures the rights of future generations. This is a collaborative and culturally respectful model that few institutions employ. The one major exception is the Glenbow Museum under the visionary guidance of Gerald Conaty. In the prologue to Conaty's (2015) *We Are Coming Home: Repatriation and the Restoration of Blackfoot Cultural Confidence*, Robert Janes (2015:4) captures the intent of the Glenbow's approach and, as it turns out, our own at the UMACF, when he says, "[It] is about relinquishing power and authority and learning to listen."

Revitalization and Reconciliation

While it may seem an admirable plan to reconnect cultural heritage collections with the communities from which they originated and to which they remain vital and meaningful aspects of cultural identity, serious obstacles inhibit the reintegration and traditional use of these objects. Some objects have deteriorated from poor environmental storage conditions; some may be considered contaminated by inappropriate handling or storage; still others may be toxic as a result of pesticide treatments. Those suffering from deterioration may be resurrected through conservation efforts, especially in collaboration with tribal experts who best know the construction techniques, material properties, and culturally appropriate handling protocols necessary to revive the particular object (Ogden 2004). For items too fragile or degraded to repair, options like replication or 3D scanning offer preservation alternatives. Such options must be approved by and undertaken with the guidance of tribal authorities.

Replication has two divergent intentions: replications for museum display or handling and replications for tribal use while the fragile original remains "protected" in museum storage. The first is usually antithetical to museum and repository missions that are dedicated to preserving the authentic past for future generations. The second is problematic to tribal communities who believe new replications lack the accumulated history and power from association with numerous events and ceremonies through their life histories that give them agency (Conaty 2015:110). In addition to working in caucus formats like the summits, the UMACF also works individually with tribal representatives to determine the best approach to the conservation, preservation, and use of particular objects. As an example of this process, we are temporarily housing a tribal-owned archaeological collection until they can arrange a 3D scanning of the entire collection through the UM's Social Science Research Lab's Digital Scanning Laboratory. After the 3D scanning is complete, the original artifacts will be returned to the site from which they were excavated, making the digitally scanned images and data available to researchers rather than the artifacts themselves. The second issue confronting the handling, use, or return of cultural items to tribal communities concerns the contamination or desacralization as a result of inappropriate handling or storage of particular items. This issue may be more readily resolved than objects in poor condition. By providing tribal spiritual authorities access to and accommodations for conducting purifying and healing ceremonies, including smudging, prayers, and songs, they can reestablish proper relationships and balances between the objects, human communities, and spiritual forces. By incorporating tribal expertise and cultural protocols into our storage and handling procedures, we are conscientiously avoiding any future contamination issues associated with potentially harmful gender, material, or object interactions.

The final obstacle to repatriation or reintegration of cultural items concerns their potential treatment with pesticides to protect such objects from insects, rodents, and mold. These chemical substances protect various materials from these potentially harmful agents. While use of chemicals has been a common and acceptable museum and curatorial procedure for over a century, these toxic treatments permeate cultural objects, leaving residues harmful to those who would handle and use them in traditional ways (Ogden 2004:69).

The processes for determining the presence and type of contamination vary in effectiveness and expense. No one test is comprehensive in identifying all potential contaminants and their levels. Using XRF technology, we have spot-tested our entire cultural collection to determine the presence and levels of arsenic, mercury, lead, zinc, and chromium (Berger 2014). Among our current solutions are investing in having pesticides removed from certain objects, though that could cause more harm to the objects. Pesticide removal is difficult and uncertain. According to Ogden (2004:75), "Currently available methods are still in early stages of testing, and all have disadvantages." An alternative is to use 3D scanning and printing to create replicas of the objects, but as already noted, these methods also have their objections. In the meantime, we have a poster (Figure 30) in the UMACF with information about handling procedures, with color codes drawing attention to objects with contaminants. Tribal visitors to the UMACF have been appreciative of our efforts to identify potentially harmful treatments to their cultural heritage items and have willingly followed the suggested protective protocols delineated on the poster, including the wearing of nitrile gloves. Everyone, including the UMACF, would prefer these precautions were not necessary. We will continue to collaborate to find feasible solutions to this problem that are sensitive and acceptable to all parties.

In addition to directly serving and impacting the region's indigenous descendent communities, the UMACF as part of a state university must also utilize its collections for continuing education of students and the public. Our mission is to accomplish this directive with the collaboration and cooperation of the region's tribal cultural heritage leaders and communities. To this end, the UMACF includes a teaching collection that can be used for curricula that emphasizes Montana's multicultural and transnational heritage, as well as Indian Education For All (IEFA). IEFA is a Montana State Law passed in 1999 (Montana Code Annotated 1999) to implement the following state constitutional requirement: "The state of Montana recognizes the distinct and unique cultural heritage of American Indians and

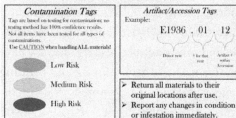

ATTENTION!

Follow these rules for handling ethnographic collections:

Materials may be contaminated with pesticides, heavy metals, or other poisons –
ALWAYS handle with care.

✓ Wear Nitrile gloves
✓ Wear an apron or lab coat
✓ Wipe down the counter/table with disinfectant after use
✓ Keep "contaminated" supplies (pens, pencils, etc.) separate and clearly marked from "clean" supplies
✓ Wash hands and arms after working with collections
✓ Launder clothing separately

Collection Identification

Contamination Tags

Tags are based on testing for contamination; no testing method has 100% confidence results. Not all items have been tested for all types of contaminations.
Use CAUTION when handling ALL materials!

⬤ Low Risk

⬤ Medium Risk

⬤ High Risk

Artifact/Accession Tags

Example:

E1936 . 01 . 12

Does not   The that   Artifact #
test   year   within
                       Accession

➤ Return all materials to their original locations after use.
➤ Report any changes in condition or infestation immediately.

Culturally Appropriate Handling

Materials in the ethnographic collection are from a wide variety of cultures. When a specific piece has particular handling requirements, these will be noted in its file and, whenever possible, at its storage location. If you are unsure of an item's restrictions, err on the side of the strictest handling restrictions. Don't be afraid to ask for help in identifying handling procedures.

ALWAYS handle materials carefully and with RESPECT.

FIGURE 30. This poster is displayed in the UMACF to provide information about handling procedures, with color codes drawing attention to objects with contaminants. (Poster prepared by Bethany [Campbell] Hauer, courtesy of the UMACF)

is committed in its educational goals to the preservation of their cultural integrity" (Montana Constitution 1972:Article X, Section 1).

Additionally, the new Common Core standards and requirements for increased analytical and experiential learning are met through the inclusion of archaeological lessons facilitated by the UMACF's collections and outreach programs. The UMACF's ongoing collaborations with local and regional museums means that our audiences also include patrons of institutions such as children's museums, as well as individuals and groups who go to Montana State Parks' visitor centers linked with archaeological and cultural sites—including National Historic Landmarks—associated with the collections. UM graduate and undergraduate students, as well as scholars, produce theses, dissertations, and publications that highlight the collections. Descendant populations, American Indian individuals, families, and communities continue to demonstrate the significance of the cultural collections for their personal and collective cultural heritage. The collections are intended to be used by tribal communities and for ongoing outreach programs, including books, documentaries, and education, but mostly as elements of cultural revival and resilience.

Concluding Thoughts

Thomas (2004) argues that cultural heritage experts need to work with local communities to preserve cultural heritage in a way that makes sense for people, particularly as people become more interested in deciphering and engaging with their own past(s) on their own terms. This case study from Montana can be applied to others seeking to involve all descendant communities in collections management. While this example can be applied to non-Indian collections, the concept of giving new life to old collections is especially relevant and poignant when engaging indigenous communities with their traditional material culture. In fact, "giving new life," otherwise referred to as "revitalization," has been an important aspect of cultural recovery for tribes across the United States for many years and includes the revival of traditional languages as well as customs, beliefs, and material culture. A vital culture requires that all these aspects be practiced and transmitted to future generations, and must also include a lineage, a dynamic connection to a shared past. We have witnessed the objects held in the UMACF's collections actively trigger individual and shared memories during tribal delegation visits to review objects under consideration for conservation, preservation, or possible repatriation.

The human-object interactions occurring during these visits reveal that revitalization operates on multiple levels. First, the objects (believed by many indigenous people to possess an inherent life force) themselves are awakened through human contact and nurturing. Second, rediscovering the objects generates a renewed sense of pride and ancestral connection for the elder community members. The reconnection also provides an opportunity for teaching the younger generations about the past and how to embrace and continue traditional practices into the future. Through this process of re-membering (rejoining the disarticulated pieces of tradition), tribal communities regain a sense of personal and cultural worth. This can be applied to nontribal collections associated with other descendant communities as well, fostering settings for dialog that crosses cultural, social, intergenerational, and ideological barriers and for social interactions that bring together multigenerational participants to reconnect to their heritage (Janes 2009). Such a reconnection promotes social change by healing historical wounds through the recovery of and renewed engagement with lost objects of personal and cultural significance, revitalizing multigenerational cultural pride and respect.

Acknowledgments

We are especially grateful to the eight tribal nations in Montana for their support of the region's cultural heritage and THPOS and culture committees: Assiniboine and Sioux Tribes of the Fort Peck Reservation, Blackfeet Nation, Chippewa-Cree Tribe of the Rocky Boy's (Stone Child) Reservation, Confederated Salish and Kootenai Tribes of the Flathead Reservation, Crow Nation, Fort Belknap Indian Community of the Fort Belknap Reservation of Montana, Little Shell Chippewa Tribe, and Northern Cheyenne Nation. We also laud and recognize the following organizations for providing institutional and/or financial support for the summits, where the dialogue and processes presented here were forged: National Endowment for the Humanities (Sustaining Cultural Heritage Collections); Humanities Montana, the University of Montana's College of Humanities and Sciences, UM's Department of Anthropology, UM's Office of the Provost, UM's Office of Research and Sponsored Programs, the UM Foundation, and an anonymous donor.

We also acknowledge our colleagues who have provided input along the way, representing organizations such as the Bureau of Land Management and the BLM's Billings Curation Center, the MacFarland Center, the Museums Association of Montana, the Montana Historical Society, the Montana Museum of Arts and Culture, the Montana State Historic Preservation Office, Montana State Parks, Montana State University, UM's Native American Studies Department, the U.S. Forest Service, and the Yellowstone Heritage and Research Center. We send special thanks to Rebecca Allen and Ben Ford for their foresight, time, and effort on this volume. We are sincerely appreciative of the feedback of Glenn Farris, Sara Rivers Cofield, and anonymous reviewers.

References

American Alliance of Museums

n.d. American Alliance of Museums Code of Ethics and Standards. https://www .aam-us.org/programs/ethics-standards-and-professional-practices/code-of -ethics-for-museums/. Accessed 22 May 2018.

Atalay, Sonya

2012 *Community Based Archaeology: Research with, by, and for Indigenous and Local Communities.* Left Coast Press. Walnut Creek CA.

Bench, Raney (editor)

2014 *Interpreting Native American History and Culture at Museums and Historic Sites.* Rowman and Littlefield. Lanham MD.

Berger, Alexis

2014 Pesticide Contamination of Ethnographic Collections and the Implications for Repatriation and Research. Master's thesis, University of Montana, Department of Anthropology, Missoula.

Borck, Lewis, and Matthew C. Sanger

2017 An Introduction to Anarchism in Archaeology. *SAA Archaeological Record* 17(1):9–16.

Brown, Michael F.

2004 *Who Owns Native Culture.* Harvard University Press. Cambridge MA.

Campbell, Bethany H.

2011 Our Collective History: The Curation Crisis and the Excavation of an Archaeological Repository. Master's thesis, Department of Anthropology, University of Montana, Missoula.

Clavir, Miriam

2002 *Preserving What Is Valued: Museums, Conservation, and First Nations.* University of British Columbia Press. Vancouver.

Colwell, Chip (John Stephen), and Thomas J. Ferguson

2008 *Collaboration in Archaeological Practice: Engaging Descendant Communities.* AltaMira Press. Lanham MD.

Conaty, Gerald T. (editor)

2015 *We Are Coming Home: Repatriation and the Restoration of Blackfoot Cultural Confidence.* Athabasca University Press. Edmonton, Alberta.

Daehnke, Jon, and Amy Lonetree

2011   Repatriation in the United States: The Current State of the Native American Graves Protection and Repatriation Act. *American Indian Culture and Research Journal* 35(1):87–98.

Douglas, John

2011   Anthropology Department Self-Study, 2010–2011 Program Review. Manuscript, University of Montana, Department of Anthropology, Missoula.

Edwards, Elizabeth, Chris Gosden, and Ruth Phillips Bliss

2006   *Sensible Objects: Colonialism, Museums, and Material Culture.* Berg. New York.

Harms, Cecily

2012   NAGPRA in Colorado: A Success Story. *Colorado Law Review* 83:593–632.

Janes, Robert

2009   *Museums in a Troubled World: Renewal, Irrelevance or Collapse?* Routledge. London.

2015   Prologue. In *We Are Coming Home: Repatriation and the Restoration of Blackfoot Cultural Confidence,* Gerald Contay, editor, pp. 3–20. Athabasca University Press. Edmonton, Alberta.

Moldavanova, Alisa

2014   Two Narratives of Intergenerational Sustainability: A Framework for Sustainable Thinking. *American Review of Public Administration* 46(5):526–545.

Montana Code Annotated

1999   Indian Education for All (IEFA). MCA 20-1-501. http://leg.mt.gov/bills/mca /title_0200/chapter_0010/part_0050/sections_index.html. Accessed 10 February 2017.

Montana Constitution

1972   Montana Constitution Article X, Section 1(2). http://leg.mt.gov/bills/mca /CONSTITUTION/x/1.htm. Accessed 4 June 2018.

Nash, Stephen E., Chip Colwell-Chanthaphonh, and Steven Holen

2011   Civic Engagements in Museum Anthropology: A Prolegomenon for the Denver Museum of Nature and Science. *Historical Archaeology* 45(1):135–151.

National Park Service

n.d.   *36CFR79 Curation of Federally-Owned and Administered Archeological Collections.* https://www.nps.gov/archaeology/TOOLS/36cfr79.htm. Accessed 22 May 2018.

Ogden, Sherelyn (editor)

2004   *Caring for American Indian Objects: A Practical and Cultural Guide.* Minnesota Historical Society Press. St. Paul.

Sleeper-Smith, Susan (editor)

2009   *Contesting Knowledge: Museums and Indigenous Perspectives.* University of Nebraska Press. Lincoln.

Teeman, Diane

2008 Cultural Resource Management and the Protection of Valued Tribal Spaces: A View from the Western United States. In *Handbook of Landscape Archaeology*, Bruno David and Julian Thomas (editors), pp. 626–637. Left Coast Press. Walnut Creek CA.

Thomas, Roger

2004 Archaeology and Authority in the Twenty-first Century. In *Heritage Reader*, G. Fairclough, R. Harrison, John H. Jameson, Jr., and J. Schofield, editors, pp. 139–148. Routledge. London.

Watkins, Joseph E.

2000 *Indigenous Archaeology: American Indian Values and Scientific Practice.* AltaMira Press. Walnut Creek CA.

2003 Beyond the Margin: American Indians, First Nationals, and Archaeology in North America. *American Antiquity* 68:273–285.

Weik, Terrance

2012 Race and the Struggle for a Cosmopolitan Archaeology: Ongoing Controversies over the Representation and the Exhibition of Osceola. *Historical Archaeology* 46(1):123–141.

Wilcox, Michael V.

2010 Saving Indigenous People from Ourselves: Separate but Equal Archaeology Is Not Scientific Archaeology. *American Antiquity* 75(2):221–227.

[CONTRIBUTORS]

Rebecca Allen is director of the Tribal Historic Preservation Department at the United Auburn Indian Community. She loves material culture and archaeological collections and publishes on those topics as often as she can. She also serves as associate editor for *Historical Archaeology*; series editor for joint publications with the Society for Historical Archaeology and University of Nebraska Press; a community partner for the Market Street Chinatown Archaeological Project and Chinese Railroad Workers in North America Project at Stanford University; and a research associate of the Archaeology Research Lab at the University of California, Berkeley.

The contributors to chapter 17 include members of the University of Montana's Anthropological Collections Committee (C. **Riley Augé** and **Kelly Dixon**) and Tribal cultural heritage leaders from Montana. The tribes represented by the authors include the following: Assiniboine and Sioux Tribes of the Fort Peck Reservation (**Raymond "Abby" Ogle** and **Darrell "Curly" Youpee**); Blackfeet Nation (**Virgil Edwards** and **John Murray**); Chippewa-Cree Tribe of the Rocky Boy's (Stone Child) Reservation (**Alvin Windy Boy**); Confederated Salish and Kootenai Tribes of the Flathead Reservation (**Ira Matt, Katie McDonald, Sadie Peone**); Crow Nation (**Emerson Bull Chief**); Fort Belknap Indian Community of the Fort Belknap Reservation of Montana (**Michael Black Wolf**); Little Shell Chippewa Tribe (**Gerald Gray**); and Northern Cheyenne Nation (**Conrad Fisher** and **Teanna Limpy**). The information they present is based on the results of summits where the authors gathered to develop sustainable plans that will guide the future of the region's cultural heritage collections.

Elizabeth Bollwerk is a senior archaeological analyst with the Digital Archaeological Archive of Comparative Slavery. She received her doctorate in 2012 from the University of Virginia. Her research examines tobacco pipe and colonoware production and exchange networks in the mid-Atlantic region of the United States. Her other research interests include digital archaeological data management and analysis and digital public archaeology.

Jessica Costello is a museum specialist in the Archaeology Program at the Northeast Museum Services Center in Boston. She holds a B.A. in history and an M.A. in historical archaeology.

Jonathan Crise is a graduate student in the Applied Archaeology Program at Indiana University of Pennsylvania. He has worked as a field archaeologist for several cultural resource management firms in the Mid-Atlantic and Midwest and is currently employed as a mapping specialist for a technology start-up in Pittsburgh.

Candace Ehringer, M.A., RPA is a senior archaeologist at ESA. She has more than 18 years of experience in cultural resources management and works throughout California's desert and coastal environments. Her strengths include managing field surveys and excavations, lab analysis, coordinating with Native American representatives, and engaging members of the public with their past.

Glenn J. Farris is an historical archaeologist, now retired from a career as an archaeologist with California State Parks. His special interests are in mission-era sites in California, including the site of the Russian American Company outpost, Fort Ross. His last eight years in state service were spent as supervisor of the State Archaeological Collections Research Facility in West Sacramento.

Ben Ford is a professor and chair of the Anthropology Department at Indiana University of Pennsylvania. He loves all archaeology—wet and dry, in a box and in the ground—but tends to gravitate to questions about how people organize themselves in spaces big and small. He is the former editor of *Technical Briefs in Historical Archaeology* and the author of *The Shore Is a Bridge: The Maritime Cultural Landscape of Lake Ontario*.

Mark A. Freeman is a lecturer at the University of Tennessee, Knoxville, where he recently completed his M.Sc. in information science. His research interests are in the presentation and preservation of museum and archaeological data.

Jillian E. Galle has directed the Digital Archaeological Archive of Comparative Slavery since its inception in 2000. She specializes in early modern Atlantic World material culture and studies how women and men used material culture to navigate slavery and freedom throughout the Caribbean and Southeast U.S. in the 18th and 19th centuries.

Kerry S. González manages the laboratory at Dovetail Cultural Resource Group in Fredericksburg, Virginia, where she oversees the processing of all collections and ensuing artifact analysis. Her interests lie in late 18th- through mid-19th-century domestic occupations, but she is passionate about material cultural from all archaeological sites.

Rachelle M. Green is currently the assistant director at Jefferson Patterson Park and Museum. Prior to her tenure at JPPM, she spent time as a preservation planner at the Delaware County Planning Department before entering the field of education as a high school social studies instructor. She earned a B.A. in history from the University of Delaware, an M.A. in historic preservation from the University of Kentucky, and an M.S. in secondary education from Saint Joseph's University.

D. Brad Hatch is the archaeological division manager at Dovetail Cultural Resource Group, Inc. in Fredericksburg, Virginia. He earned his M.A. from the College of William and Mary and his Ph.D. from the University of Tennessee, Knoxville. His research interests include gender, politics, community, and rural lifeways, focusing on the early colonial Chesapeake region.

Barbara J. Heath is a professor of anthropology at the University of Tennessee, Knoxville. She is an historical archaeologist who specializes in the archaeology of the African diaspora, colonialism, and materiality.

J. Ryan Kennedy is a zooarchaeologist who has worked with old collections from archaeological sites in California, Wyoming, New York, Georgia, and Louisiana. His research interests include the role of food in identity formation and the impact of human food practices on the environment. He is currently an adjunct professor at the University of New Orleans.

Jennifer McCann is a museum specialist at the Northeast Museum Services Center. She holds a B.A. in archaeology and an M.A. in museum studies.

Lauren K. McMillan is an assistant professor in the Department of Historic Preservation at the University of Mary Washington, where she teaches archaeology, introduction to historic preservation, architectural history, and material culture theory. Her research focuses on the production and trade of tobacco pipes in the Chesapeake region.

Rebecca J. Morehouse is the curator of state collections at the Maryland Archaeological Conservation Laboratory. She received her B.A. in anthropology and English from the State University of New York, College at Geneseo, in 1995 and her M.A. in anthropology with a concentration in museum studies from George Washington University in 1997. She has over 20 years of experience in archaeological collections curation.

Fraser D. Neiman is the director of archaeology at Monticello, where he and his colleagues study the landscape and household dynamics that unfolded at Monticello Plantation from initial settlement by Europeans and enslaved Africans in the early 18th century to the present.

Kelsey Noack Myers is currently a project partner and the tribal liaison for the Digital Index of North American Archaeology. She holds a B.A. from Southern Illinois University Carbondale, an M.A. from the College of William & Mary, and an M.A. and Ph.D. from Indiana University, Bloomington. Her recent research has focused on cultural contact, incorporating indigenous perspectives in the reuse of legacy collections, anthrozoology, and multiscalar spatial analyses related to contexts stretching from the East Coast to the Great Plains.

Alicia Paresi is the curator of Archaeology Collections for the Northeast Region of the National Park Service. She holds a B.A. in anthropology/archaeology, and a M.A. in historical archaeology.

Katherine Ridgway received her master's degree in conservation of historic objects from Durham University in 2001. She is currently the conservator for the Virginia Department of Historic Resources, specializing in archaeological materials.

Sara Rivers Cofield is the curator of federal collections at the Maryland Archaeological Conservation Laboratory at Jefferson Patterson Park and Museum. She holds a master's degree in applied anthropology from the University of Maryland and a B.A. in history from Murray State University. She specializes in archaeological collections management and material culture research with a focus on small finds and metal artifacts.

Michelle Salvato is the archaeological lab assistant for Dovetail Cultural Resource Group. She also serves as the GIS technician, allowing her to marry her archaeological interests with digital analysis.

Patricia Samford is the director of the Maryland Archaeological Conservation Laboratory at Jefferson Patterson Park and Museum. She received her doctorate from the University of North Carolina at Chapel Hill. Her research interests include the archaeology of the African American diaspora, English ceramics, and urban archaeology.

George Schwarz is an archaeologist for the Naval History and Heritage Command and part of a team that manages, preserves, and studies the U.S. Navy's sunken military craft. He is also involved in studies of early modern Iberian shipwrecks and 19th-century American steamboat wrecks.

Eric Schweickart is a Ph.D. candidate in the Anthropology Department at the University of Tennessee, Knoxville. His work focuses on kinship, commodification, materiality, and inequality as represented in the archaeology of the Atlantic world.

Caitlin Shaffer is an objects conservator at the Smithsonian National Museum of African American History and Culture, previously at the

Maryland Archaeological Conservation Laboratory. She earned an M.A. in conservation studies from West Dean College in England and a B.A. in art and visual culture from Bates College. Her areas of interest include ceramics and preventive conservation.

Stefanie M. Smith is a zooarchaeologist with New South Associates, Inc., in Stone Mountain, Georgia. She received her undergraduate degree in historic preservation from Savannah College of Art and Design and her graduate degree in applied archaeology from Indiana University of Pennsylvania. She has spent the entirety of her professional career working in cultural resource management and specializes in the zooarchaeology of historic sites in the Southeast and Mid-Atlantic.

Nicole Walsh is a museum specialist in the Archaeology Program at the Northeast Museum Services Center. She holds a B.A. in geological sciences and history and an M.A. in historical archaeology.

Emily Williams is an associate professor and director of the M.A. in conservation of archaeological and museum objects at Durham University in England. Between 1995 and 2018, she was the archaeological conservator for the Colonial Williamsburg Foundation, where she enjoyed working with its collections, both old and new. She has a Ph.D. in archaeology from the University of Leicester.

[INDEX]

Page numbers in italic indicate illustrations.

legacy, xiv–xv, xxiv–xxix, xxxiv, 35, 41–42, 45, 49, 74, 79, 100, 174, 177, 273, 284, 285–286, 300, 301, 305–306; management, 6, 22, 60, 202–203, 322, 331, 340, 373–375, 377, 378–379, 387; orphan, xiv–xv, xxiv–xxv, xxvii, xxviii, xxx, xxxii, xxxiv, xxxvi, 257; research, xiii, xvi, xvii, xxii–xxvii, xxviii, xxxi, 3, 5–6, 8–11, 15–17, 20–23, 291–306, 319–321, 340, 386; study (with students), xxix, xxxvi–xxxvi, 3–4, 6, 358–371; teaching, 376, 385

Colonial Encounters, 92, 100–101, 106

Colonial Williamsburg, xxxi, 55, 62, 64, 121, 123–126, 130, 132, 135–136, 138

community: archaeological, 70; community of users, 74, 325; historical, 60, 145–167

community outreach. *See* outreach

comparative analysis (research), xiv–xv, xxiii, xxx–xxxii, 56, 76, 80, 319, 321

completion report, 312

condition survey, 123

Conner's Midden, 126–128

conservation (artifact), xiv, xvi, xviii–xxi, 3, 5–6, 9–11, 115–140, 231, 234, 255, 337, 339, 374, 383–384; education, 126–130; preventive, 135

conservators, 130, 135, 138–140, 256, 337, 339–340, 357, 374, 383

context (archaeological), 58, 64–65, 73

contextual control, 206

Continental Army, 248

Coolidge, William D., 227

Cooper, John Rogers, 295

Cooper-Molera Adobe, xxxiv, 291–306, 292, 294

correspondence analysis, 64

costume, 340, 346–47, 351, 354

Council for Maryland Archaeology, 354

Council for Northeast Historical Archaeology, 350

court, 36–38

cowry shells, 332–333

Creative Common licenses, 108

cultural heritage collections, 373, 375–376

culturally appropriate protocols, 373–374, 382–384

culturally sensitive objects, 382, 384

cultural resource management, xv, xxix, 35

Cultural Resources Civil Rights Initiative, 331

curation, xiii–xvi, xvii, xx, xxii–xxv, xxvii, xxix, xxxi, xxxiii, xxxiv, 3, 5–6, 9–11, 18, 23, 35, 41, 63, 79, 93, 109, 174, 175, 177, 204, 216, 233, 241, 273, 304, 305, 310, 311, 337, 380, 381, 382; crisis, xiv, xxiii, xxvi, 151, 204; ethics, xvii–xxiii; facility (facilities), xv, xxix, 3, 18, 300, 339, 359, 288; plan, 109; research, xxiii, 23, 199; standards, xv, xxii, 6, 11, 96, 97

Curator's Choice (Curator's Choice Archive, Jefferson Patterson Park and Museum), 7, 360, 363, 368

Curles Neck site (Virginia), 91–110; database, 98–99, 101–103

curricula, social studies, 359, 361, 365–367, 369

cutter (vessel), 248

cyber archaeology, 259

DAACS (Digital Archaeological Archive of Comparative Slavery), xxx, 54–80, 65, 71, 92, 100; database, 61–62, 68–72, 74, 76, 79; Research Consortium, 68, 70, 72, 83

data (archaeological), xiv, xvii, xxix, xxx–xxxii, xxxiv, xxxvii, 91–110; analytical, 94; citation, 107, 108; comparative (comparable), 92, 100, 101; conversion, 102; crowdsourced, 92; curation of, 63, 79; digital, 93; dissemination, 72–75; diversity (model), 191–193; evenness, 191, 192, 193; heterogeneity, 191, 192, 193; interoperability, 100; legacy, 93, 96, 98, 110, 286; linked, 43; literacy (literate), 72, 74–75; normalization, 102; Open Data concept, 109; presentation, 106; preservation, 75–76; provenance, 107; relational, 105; richness, 179, 181, 191; sets, 92, 93, 100, 107; Shannon-Weaver function, 178, 191, 192, 193; sharing, 54, 71, 78–79, 94, 107; standardization, 43–44, 56, 62; structures, 54, 60, 61, 70, 101, 173, 176, 193; synthesis, 273; usability, 56

photo(s), photograph(s): (documentation), xv, xxix, 5, 7, 20, 62, 94, 95, 105, 155, 239, 263–264, 274, 294, 300, 301, 303, 304–305, 312, 322–324, 327–330, 344, 361; digitization, 62, 301, 305

photo archive, photo collection, 15, 105

photogrammetry, 33, 245, 256, 258, 260, 262, 263, 265–267

photograph (verb, taking photographs, photographed, photography), xxviii, 97, 104, 227, 264–266, 282, 311, 329, 344, 353

pipe(s), (ceramic, clay, tobacco), 60, 62, 77, 99, 147, 148–150, 154, 155, 157, 162–165, *164*, *165*, 167, 202, 318; opium, 202

pit(s), refuse or trash, 40, 201, 284–285, 297, 301, 302, 303

Pittsburgh PA, 37, 176

plantation, 57, 66, 67, 77

Plattsburg NY, 253, 254

plow zone, 40, 46, 47, 103, 104, 153, 155, 229, 276–277

point cloud, 260–262, 265, 267

polyethylene glycol, 125

Potomac River, 145, 147, 152, 154, 161–162, 165

Potomac River Valley, 146–147, 149, 151–152, 163, 166–167

preservation, xiv, xvi–xvii, xix–xxiii, xxiv–xxv, xxviii, xxx–xxxi, 115, 116, 135, 136, 139, 174, 196, 245, 246, 253, 255, 257, 374, 383–384

Pringle, Thomas, 249, 251

protocols: cataloging, 61–62, 64, 69, 71; classification and measurement, 54, 56, 60, 63–64, 70, 73, 76–77; object handling, 374–375, 385–386, *386*

provenience system, 41, 43, 46

Public Works Employment Act of 1976 (Title Two), 14

publish (studies, based on artifacts or collections), xxiii, 24, 67, 70, 72, 92, 156, 275, 293, 298

quarantine, 119–120

Québec, 247, 249

query (queries), xiv, 43, 61, 63, 71, 73, 74, 131

radeau (vessel), 249

reanalysis (of data, site, or collections), 45, 110, 145, 148, 151, 153, 154–155, 157, 158–159, 162, 166

reassess, reassessment(s), 79, 91, 92, 95, 96, 98, 102, 105, 107, 108, 112, 122, 127, 138

reburial, 136–140, *139*

recataloged (recataloging), 92, 97, 147, 148

record(s), archaeological and laboratory, including paper and digital, xiii, xvii–xx, xxiv–xxv, xxviii, 5–6, 21–23, 41–45, 55, 61–62, 65, 93, 95, 96, 97–98, 102, 104–105, 106, 109, 135, 138, 146, 148, 155, 175, 189, 202, 207, 216, 245, 267, 273, 276, 299, 303, 304, 312, 376. *See also* archive; digital: recording; documentation; field notes; photo(s)

regional variation, 55–56, 59, 61

Register of Professional Archaeologists, xviii

rehoused (rehousing, artifacts and/or collections), xiv, xxix, xxx, xxxv, 5–6, 13, 42, 66, 120, 131, 135, 137, 148, 274–275, 311, 331, 380–383

Repaska, Mishka, 236

repatriation, 373–374, 375, 379, 384, 387

repository (repositories), xxix, 17, 19, 74, 115, 117, 119, 241, 268, 304, 337, 375, 383. *See also* archive; curation

research design, 209–210, 216–218, 272, 279. *See also* comparative analysis

research question(s), xxiv–xv, xxix, 34, 35, 41, 49, 60, 74–75, 92, 100, 116, 140, 149, 151, 199, 202–204, 206–210, 217–218, 237

revitalization, 374, 384, 386–388

Richardson, James, 40, 186

Richelieu River, 246–249

Riddell, Francis, 13

Riker mounts, 120

Riverfront Park site (Virginia), 233–237

Rivers Cofield, Sara, 230, 337, 340–41, 343–48, 351, 354, 357

Rocky Mountains (region), 375–376

Röntgen, Wilhelm Conrad, 227

Route 301 Improvement Project (Delaware), 229, 231

row galley (vessel), 248, 250, 251

Russians, 19

Sacramento CA (including Old Sacramento), 13, 15, 18, 291

Salem Maritime National Historic Site, 313, 316, 319

salvage archaeology (salvage excavations), xv, 201, 252, 256

sample selection, xxiv, 178, 207–209, 218, 275, 281, 283–286

San Luis Reservoir, 14

Santa Cruz Mission Adobe, 18

Saratoga National Historic Park, 312, 319, 323, 328

Saratoga NY, 252, 312, 319, 323, 328

Save America's Treasures (SAT), 66, 75

Sayenqueraght (Seneca), 38

Schaeffer Farm Site (Pennsylvania), 177

schooner (vessel), 247–251, 253, 255, 256, 268

Schupp, Katherine, 132

Schuyler, Robert, 18

Schwarz, Ken, 132, 134

screen recovery, 175

Seneca, 36, 38, 176

sentient objects, 373, 397

Shawnee, 37

ship, 245, 247–249, 256, 257

ship construction, 256, 257

skeletal representation, 185, 194

slavery (slave societies), xxx, 54–55, 57, 65–66, 68–69, 80. *See also* Africans (African Americans), enslaved; Native Americans, enslaved

sloop (vessel), 247, 248

slow archaeology, 260

snakehead, 215–216

social media, 317–330; blog, xxiii, 317, 318–322, 324–325, 327, 330, 346–347; Facebook, xxxv, 312, 317, 322–330, 351–353; Instagram, xxxv, 312, 317, 327–330; Twitter, 347, 351

Society for American Archaeology (SAA), xvii, xxiii, 41

Society for California Archaeology, xxvii

Society for Historical Archaeology (SHA), xvii, xxii–xxiii, 41, 108, 299, 320, 355

software: Adobe Illustrator, 281, 283; Adobe Photoshop, 281, 283, 347; Agisoft Photo-Scan software, 262–266, 263; ARGUS, 22; AutoDesk ReCap Software, 262; collections management, 60–61; Cyclone Software, 261, 263, 265, 266; GeoTiff, 265; Ruby-on-Rails, 61–70; WordPress, xxxv, 312, 318, 322

Southern Maryland Celtic Festival, 344–346, 348, 350, 353

species list, 181–184, 186–187, 189–190, 208

Speke, Thomas, 152, 156, 157, 160, 163, 165

squirrel, gray, 46, 180, 188, 195

Stanford University (Stanford Archaeology Center), xxiv, xxvi, xxxii, 202–203, 205

Starr Carr site (England), 136

Starz, 339, 341, 349, 354, 356

State Archaeological Collections Research Facility (California), 15–16, *16*, 19, 23, 300

State Indian Museum (California), 13

Steel family, 39

stewardship (archaeological, collections), xx, 41, 383

St. Johns, Quebec, 247–249

St. Lawrence River, 246, 249

St. Mary's City, Maryland, 55, 151, 152, 162, *164*

Strezewski, Michael, 277–278, 280, 284

student engagement, 358–371

subsistence, 59, 175, 195, 196

summits, 374, 377–378

sustainability, 74, 135, 139, 376, 378

terminology, 56, 99, 102, 107, 207, 282, 378

thesis (theses), xxix, xxx, 18, 20, 21, 23, 24, 34–35, 41, 45, 46, 48, 49–50, 76–77, 92, 202, 209, 376, 386

3D, 94, 129, 257, 258, 260–262, 265–267; documentation, 245, 260, 263; model(s), 257–259, 262, 265–268; printer, 129, 265; scan (scanning), 94, 129–130, 245, 265–267, 383–385

tinned iron, 132–135

Tippecanoe County Historical Association, 272, 276–277

tobacco pipes, 60, 62, 77, 99, 147, 148–149, 155, 162, 202, 318

Tordoff, Judith, 275, 277, 278–279, 280, 282, 284

tourism, 252

tribal experts, 383

Tribal Historic Preservation Officer (THPO), 374, 376, 377–379

turtle, spiny soft-shelled, 189–190, 191

uncataloged, 310, 311, 360

undergraduate research (with artifacts, collections), xxiii, xxix, 8, 19, 34, 35, 44, 45, 46, 48, 74, 78, 202, 281, 361, 381, 386

CPSIA information can be obtained
at www.ICGtesting.com
Printed in the USA
LVHW090421180319
610813LV00004BA/70/P